Virgil

# THE AENEID

Translated by
C. H. SISSON

*Edited by*
DENIS FEENEY
*New College, Oxford*

*Consultant Editor for this volume*
RICHARD STONEMAN

EVERYMAN
J. M. DENT · LONDON
CHARLES E. TUTTLE
VERMONT

This translation of *The Aeneid* first published
by Carcanet Press in 1986

Translation © C. H. Sisson 1986

This edition first published by Everyman in 1998

Introduction, notes and other critical apparatus
© J. M. Dent & Sons Ltd, 1998

J. M. Dent
Orion Publishing Group
Orion House, 5 Upper St Martin's Lane
London WC2H 9EA
and
Charles E. Tuttle Co. Inc.
28 South Main Street
Rutland, Vermont 05701, USA

Typeset by SetSystems Ltd, Saffron Walden, Essex

Printed by the Guernsey Press Co. Ltd, Guernsey, Channel Islands

British Cataloguing-in-Publication Data
is available on request

ISBN 0 46087 754 2

£2·50

*Everyman, I will go with thee,*
*and be thy guide*

# CONTENTS

# NOTE ON THE AUTHOR AND EDITOR

PUBLIUS VERGILIUS MARO was born near Mantua on 15 October 70 BC. Despite the great fame he enjoyed during his lifetime, the evidence for his life and career is poor, with much of it probably constructed from quasi-allegorical interpretation of his early poetry. The ancient biographical tradition says, for example, that he was well built and rustic in appearance, and inclined to pederasty, all of which may be the product of the rural and occasionally homosexual subject-matter of his early verse. Nothing definite is known about his family background, although tradition later said his parents were poor and obscure. After initial education in Northern Italy he came to Rome, and was soon settled permanently in the Naples area, studying and composing; he never married. He probably suffered loss in the land-confiscations of 42 BC, but before long was in the circles of Maecenas, the close friend of Octavian (the future Augustus); he certainly died a very wealthy man. His first work, the *Eclogues*, consisted of a single book of ten short pastoral poems, and was probably published in 38 BC. He then turned to the *Georgics*, a longer work in four books on farming, which occupied him for the next seven or eight years: he recited the finished version to Octavian when he returned in triumph from the East in 29 BC. By this time Virgil was famous: he was mobbed on his rare visits to Rome, his *Eclogues* were adapted to music for the public stage, and his poetry was the object of scholarly attention. From now until his death he was engaged on the *Aeneid*, an epic in twelve books which was not yet finally complete when he died on 21 September 19 BC. According to tradition, his dying wish that the poem should be burnt was thwarted by the emperor, who entrusted its posthumous publication to Varius and Tucca.

DENIS FEENEY is Fellow and Tutor of New College, Oxford, and the author of *The Gods in Epic: Poets and Critics of the*

*Classical Tradition* (Oxford, 1991), and *Literature and Religion at Rome: Cultures, Contexts, and Beliefs* (Cambridge, 1998). He is co-editor with Stephen Hinds of the Cambridge University Press Series, *Roman Literature and its Contexts*.

# CHRONOLOGY OF VIRGIL'S LIFE

Many of the dates, especially in Virgil's *Life* and in
*Artistic Events*, are approximate and controversial

| Year | Age | Life |
| --- | --- | --- |
| 70 BC | | Born Andes, near Mantua, 15 October |
| 38 | 31 | *Eclogues*; joins the circle of Maecenas, Augustus' subordinate |

# CHRONOLOGY OF HIS TIMES

| Year | Artistic Events | Historical Events |
|------|-----------------|-------------------|
| 70 BC | Cicero, *Verrines* | First consulate of Pompey and Crassus |
| 63 | | Conspiracy of Catiline |
| 55–54 | Catullus and Lucretius published | Caesar's invasions of Britain |
| 49 | | Outbreak of Civil War between Caesar and Pompey |
| 48 | | Battle of Pharsalus; death of Pompey in Egypt |
| 46 | Cicero, *Brutus* and *Orator* | Battle of Thapsus; suicide of Cato |
| 45–44 | Cicero, philosophical writing | Dictatorship of Caesar, and his assassination (15 March, 44 BC) |
| 43 | | Coalition of Antony, Lepidus and Octavian; proscriptions; murder of Cicero |
| 42 | Sallust, *Catiline* | Deaths of Brutus and Cassius at Philippi; land-confiscations; turmoil in Italy |
| 40 | Sallust, *Jugurtha* | Marriage of Antony and Octavia; Empire divided between Antony (East) and Octavian (West) |
| 35 | Horace, *Satires* 1 | |
| 32 | | Antony divorces Octavia, is linked with Cleopatra |
| 31 | | Battle of Actium (2 September); Antony and Cleopatra defeated by Octavian and Agrippa |
| 30 | Horace, *Epodes* and *Satires* 2 | |

| Year | Age | Life |
|------|-----|------|
| 29 | 40 | *Georgics* |
| 23 | 46 | Recitation to Augustus and Octavia of portions of *Aeneid* (Books 2, 4, 6?) |
| 19 | 50 | Falls ill on a journey to Greece; accompanies Augustus back to Brindisium; dies (21 September); *Aeneid* 'edited' and published by Varius and Tucca |

| Year | Artistic Events | Historical Events |
| --- | --- | --- |
| 29 | | Octavian's return to Rome and triple triumph |
| 28 | Propertius 1 | |
| 27 | | Octavian Princeps and Augustus |
| 25 | Livy 1–5, Tibullus 1 | |
| 23 | Horace, *Odes* 1–3 | Death of Marcellus |
| 22 | Propertius 2–3 | |
| 20 | Horace, *Epistles* 1 | |

# INTRODUCTION BY DENIS FEENEY

Even before Virgil died with his *Aeneid* still unfinished, the poem was a classic, hailed as a rival to Homer's *Iliad* by the poet Propertius and eagerly awaited by the first Roman emperor, Augustus, as the masterpiece that would guarantee immortality for himself and his new Rome. As Rome's most famous living poet, writing in the most prestigious literary form of all, the epic, Virgil felt at times crushed by the massive burden of expectation, responding to the emperor's requests for a glimpse of some portions before completion with the remark that the task was so enormous that he felt as if he must have been momentarily out of his mind to embark upon it (Macrobius, *Saturnalia* 1.24.11). He worked slowly, taking some ten years to produce the almost 10,000 lines of our extant text, with another three years supposedly still to come for revision. The poem he left is indeed a fitting monument to the Rome of his day, but it is far more than that, providing readers ever since with resources for exploring the experience of history, the construction of poetic and national traditions, the dynamics of imperialism, and the conflict between the public and the private life, between duty and happiness.

Virgil wrote at a time when twenty years of civil war had apparently been terminated by Antony and Cleopatra's defeat at the hands of Octavian and Agrippa in the Battle of Actium (described on Aeneas' shield at the end of Book VIII). The Roman Republic had lasted 450 years (a record for republican government that is rivalled only by the Swiss); now it was gone, and although no one could know at the time what the future held, it was clear to Virgil and his contemporaries that Octavian (renamed Augustus in 27 BC) would be the supreme figure in any conceivable order. The years of the composition of the *Aeneid* (30–19 BC) were years of ongoing political experimentation, as Augustus and the new governing class felt their way towards a symbiosis that would prevent recurrence of anarchy while avoiding the appearance of outright monarchy, and which would respect the Romans' veneration of inherited tradition while allowing for the creation of unprecedented political and social patterns.

Virgil chose not to narrate this most recent transition in Roman life directly, as might have been expected. Instead, he took the drama of Roman history back to its ultimate origins and narrated the foundational act of imperial transition, with Aeneas' journey from Troy to Italy. The outline of the story is comparatively simple. One of the greatest Homeric heroes on the Trojan side, Aeneas, the son of Venus, survives the sack of Troy and leads the remnants of the Trojan people to Italy, where he fights a war to establish his right to settle. The poem ends here, but the poem's scenes of prophecy have already informed the reader that, although Aeneas does not actually found the city of Rome, the Trojans will mingle with the native Latins and form a new race, from whom in time will spring Romulus and Remus, the founders of the city of Rome itself.

Even this bald summary shows how successfully the poem transplants contemporary Augustan preoccupations with transition, continuity and change into the remote time of the poem's action. In the course of the poem we move from the East to the West, from Troy to Italy, as Aeneas moves from being a Trojan towards being something else, a Roman in embryo. Even in such minor matters as sacrificing with his head covered, Aeneas is starting to behave in distinctively Roman ways; above all, in advocating the amalgamation of national groups into larger units with a new identity he anticipates the political genius of the historical Romans. The poem's migratory movement, together with its wholesale assimilation of Homer, acts out another great transition, the transition of Greek culture to Italy: just as the people of ancient Italy become the inheritors of Troy, so the people of Virgil's Italy become the inheritors of Greece. The very location of the poem in time is transitional, at the pivot between myth and history: the poem's characters, whom we first encounter at the site of the city of Carthage, are moving out of the era of Homer into the era of what Virgil would have considered non-fabulous history.

The timeframe of the poem's action begins at Troy, whose fall was not only the most celebrated event in Greek myth, but the starting point for ancient scientific chronology, corresponding to 1184 BC in our modern enumeration. The fall of Priam's kingdom was not actually narrated by Homer (he does give an abbreviated report of another singer's version in *Odyssey* VIII); but the fall of Troy is the inevitable result of the *Iliad*, and the everpresent backdrop to the *Odyssey*. Other early Greek epics, now lost, told of the sack and its consequences, while the poets of Athenian tragedy returned to the theme again and again. Although Homer already knows that Aeneas will be a survivor, he does not tell of a migration. By Virgil's time, as a result of centuries of 'invention of tradition', the wanderings of Aeneas and the migration of the Trojans to found a new race in Italy were accepted elements of inherited knowledge. These connections between Troy and Rome were not regarded as poetic fairy-story, but were an integral part of Mediterranean propaganda and ideology, and had been for over 200 years before Virgil's birth. The Greeks were the instigators, using the Trojan migration as a way of fitting the parvenu Romans into their own genealogical and historical frameworks. This Greek story was eventually combined with the Romans' own folktale of the foundation by the twins Romulus and Remus. The resulting blend, as we see it in Virgil, tells of Aeneas' son, Iulus, founding a city called Alba Longa, which is ruled by a succession of kings to fill the more than 400-year gap between Aeneas' arrival and the foundation of Rome; it is to a princess of Alba Longa that the twins are born, sons of the war-god, Mars.

This story, an amalgam of Greek antiquarianism and Roman folklore, had acquired a powerful extra resonance in Virgil's lifetime. In line with the common Greek and Roman aristocratic fashion of claiming descent from famous heroes or demigods, the patrician clan of the Julii had long cultivated associations with Alba Longa, saying that their family name (*Iulius*) was derived from the name of Aeneas' son Iulus. When Virgil was only two or three years old, the up-and-coming young Julius Caesar stood up in the forum and delivered a funeral speech in praise of his aunt, in the course of which he bragged about the fact that his family was descended from the goddess Venus, mother of Aeneas, and grandmother of Iulus. When this same Julius Caesar destroyed the Roman Republic to become supreme ruler of the Roman state, and was in time succeeded by his adopted son, Augustus, the family myth of the Julii must have appeared eerily prophetic. Any other of the top hundred families could have emerged victorious from the civil wars, after all: the fact that it was the family who claimed descent from the son of Venus is to us a fantastic fluke, an outrageous statistical improbability, yet Virgil constructs the pattern of history in such a way that the link between the first founder and the current ruler appears to be the inevitable end of the entire progression of Roman history.

The beginning and end of the poem's vast timescales are linked, then, by the family connection between Aeneas and Augustus – fortuitous to us, no doubt providential to many people at the time. Virgil strengthens these links throughout the poem, binding together the moment of origin and the contemporary end result. In this way, the poem participates in both of the dominant ways of constructing history, the aetiological (from Greek *aition*, 'cause', 'beginning'), and the teleological (from Greek *telos*, 'end', 'purpose', 'goal', 'accomplishment'). The poem explains the present state of affairs not only by referring it to its origins (everything in the world is the way it is because of the 'beginning', the *aition*, which is narrated in the poem), but also by describing the present as the outcome, the fulfilment, the *telos*, of all previous experience. In the historical plot of the *Aeneid*, Aeneas (the *aition*) and Augustus (the *telos*) are joined together as the cause and the purpose, by a mutually self-reinforcing explanatory scheme. Book VIII is the most condensed embodiment of this theme, packed as it is with aetiological explanations of all kinds, and culminating in the image of Augustus as the inheritor of the historical process set in train by Aeneas. The shield which Aeneas receives from his mother at the end of Book VIII, with its depiction of Augustus' triumph over Antony and Cleopatra, is an icon of the poem itself. When the master craftsman, the divine image-maker Vulcan, makes this shield, he works on fluid amorphous stuff ('Brass flows in streams'), and he beats it into meaningful shape. Virgil does the same, making a unified, meaningful shape out of the fluidity of the past, a round shape, the shield, a world, in fact *the* world, the world of Rome and Augustus. The power of the *Aeneid* to impose its meaning and shape upon history is an image of Augustus' power to impose his meaning and shape upon history.

Set against these powerful structures of triumphalism and linear progress, however, are countervailing currents of flux, instability and mutability. Cyclical patterns pervade the poem, of which some are potentially beneficial in nature (the return of the Golden Age), while some destabilise faith in the durability or value of human establishments. When Aeneas goes to the site of the future city of Rome in Book VIII, for example, he sees there ruins of earlier settlements, when Rome is still centuries in the future, and he wanders through scenes of rustic pastoralism that are all too close to the images of post-imperial desolation that Greek poets had associated with the former glories of Mycenae or Argos – all too close, as well, to the fate that overtook the metropolis in the Middle Ages. Similarly, the poem cannot shut out the future beyond Augustus. The parade of Roman history at the end of Book VI closes not with Augustus, but with the death in 23 BC of his designated heir, Marcellus, leaving the forward impetus of Roman history uncontained, as the audience is left wondering what or who will follow Augustus now that this future has been removed.

While celebrating the foundation of the Roman empire and the restoration of peace, the poem refuses to gloss over the catastrophic toll exacted in the process, on both vanquished and victors. The vivid energy and splendour of Camilla and Turnus perish under the Trojan/Roman machine, and for most readers over the last two thousand years the main memory of the poem has been the wreckage of Dido. Virgil invented the story of the love affair of Aeneas and Dido, and it has become the most important Roman myth for later generations. Dido has so much in common with Aeneas, as a leader of refugees and founder of a new city in the West, yet she is destroyed by two goddesses, two gods and the refusal of Aeneas to give up his mission for her sake. Aeneas' abandonment of Dido has earned him the condemnation of most readers. His lost love for Dido is actually one of a series of mutilations inflicted on him by his creator, for in the course of the poem he loses wife, father, lover and protégé (Pallas). He speaks to his son, Iulus, only once in the poem, at the very end, as he leaves him to go and fight Turnus. From this perspective the *Aeneid* appears an extremely bleak and sombre poem, especially in comparison with the Homeric poems, with their wider range of characters and sympathies, their more capacious vision of the human experience. The *Aeneid* acts out a systematic series of exclusions as it constructs its picture of what is involved in being a member of the governing class of the imperial race.

By presenting such a rich and complex range of ways of thinking about the Roman experience through time, the poem makes itself indispensable to the construction of Roman identity. One major element after another of Roman life becomes the focus of the poem's searching scrutiny. Relations between the genders are crucial to the poem, as we see the male civilising process opposed or retarded by a series of female characters (Juno, Dido, Amata, Allecto, Camilla). The religion and mythology of the Mediterranean are an absorbing theme throughout. The first character we meet in the poem, after all, is a goddess, Juno, an emblem of the complexity of divine representation and significance. She is the Homeric goddess Hera, enemy of Troy, and simultaneously she is the Carthaginian goddess Tanit, who fears for the future destruction of her city by the descendants of Aeneas. One day she will be reconciled with her husband and brother Jupiter, the chief god of the Roman state, and nurture the Roman people, but until then she will wreak as much havoc as she can. These mighty creatures are the gods of poetry, of different nations, and of Rome: without their stupendous participation the poem would be weakened beyond recognition.

If the larger thematic strands of the *Aeneid* are multiple and interwoven, any individual episode is likewise made up of numerous genres and layers of meaning, becoming a compound of different ways of viewing the action. The journey to the Underworld in Book VI, for example, culminates in a great revelation of future Roman history, showing Aeneas and the reader what the consequences of his foundation will be. Before we arrive at that point we have journeyed through terrain that is Homeric in origin, but which had been brought into philosophy by the genius of Plato, who constructed numerous underworld myths in the attempt to find the life that was truly worth living for humans. Plato's enquiries had in turn been made part of the Roman intellectual inheritance by Cicero, the great statesman and writer who had been murdered by Octavian and Antony during the civil wars. Virgil's image of Roman history, then, is in dialogue with a Roman and a Greek philosophical and political tradition, even as it is set in a framework which evokes the experience of one of Aeneas' prototypes, Odysseus, the first epic hero to see the shades of Hades.

The descent into Hell to view the dead is a compelling metaphor for an encounter with earlier tradition, and as Aeneas is led through the underworld by the inspired figure of the poet-like Sibyl, meeting figures from the Homeric past, we see Virgil's own encounter with the dead weight of the poetical tradition, which he must reanimate. This is a scene of incalculable consequence for later poets, the archetypal moment of initiation into a poetic inheritance. Dante, of course, actually has Virgil as his guide into the Inferno, and as recently as 1991 Seamus Heaney brackets a collection with translations of these moments: at the beginning of *Seeing Things* stands a translation of the conversation between Aeneas and the Sibyl in Book VI, with the instructions for plucking the Golden Bough, and at the end stands a translation from the third Canto of Dante's *Inferno*, where Dante and his guide Virgil encounter the infernal ferry-man, Charon. In the first poem of the collection which is bracketed in this way, Heaney brings his own allusive tradition to life, as he meets the shade of Philip Larkin, who is quoting Dante.

The examples of Dante and Heaney alert us to another vital dimension of the poem – its rich dialogue with its literary predecessors. The importance of Homer is paramount here, for Virgil adapts Homer from line to line, making the educator of Greece now a collaborator with his Roman equivalent in the education of Rome. The very first line displays the process, for 'battles' (*arma*) looks to Homer's *Iliad*, while 'the man' (*uirum*) looks to Homer's *Odyssey*, whose first word is 'man' (*andra*). Virgil does not try to suppress our awareness of his poem's dialogue with Homer, for he often explicitly reminds us of Homeric passages, using language that calls attention to his poetic operation. When Aeneas speaks to his son for the only time in the poem, for example, as he goes to fight Turnus in the middle of Book XII, he puts on his armour, kisses his son through his helmet, and says, 'Mind you remember ... What sort of people you come from; try to be like/ Your father Aeneas and your uncle Hector.' In telling his son to remember Hector, Aeneas is also instructing the reader to remember *Iliad* Book VI, where Hector likewise kisses his son. As this example shows, however, the departures from Homer are regularly the real point of the imitation. In Homer, Hector's baby son cries when he sees his father, unrecognisable in his battle equipment and helmet, so that Hector takes off his helmet to cradle the boy in his arms and pray for his future glory. In Virgil, this human moment is reversed, as the Roman hero puts on his helmet before he kisses his son, interposing a barrier of iron between himself and his child in an almost exaggeratedly metaphorical gesture. As we may see from the example of the Greekless Dante, to whom Homer was only a name, it is possible to read Virgil without knowing a word of Homer and still penetrate to the core of the poem; but modern readers, who may read Homer in the excellent translations now available, would be depriving themselves of a great deal if they did not do so.

There are also a host of other literary prototypes behind our text. Attic tragedy is of great importance, most famously and obviously in Book IV, which is constructed like a tragedy, with speeches of advice, recrimination and self-defence, culminating in the suicide of the heroine, Dido. Other cardinal models include the post-Homeric epic of Apollonius Rhodius, the *Argonautica*; Callimachus, the great scholar-poet of Alexandria; Catullus, the love-poet of the previous generation; Ennius, the first poet to write Homeric epic in Latin. As this brief discussion has shown, most of Virgil's main models are Greek, and this is a fact of more than literary-historical interest. One of the cardinal themes of the *Aeneid* is Hellenisation, the centuries-long process of symbiosis by which the Romans developed a unique new culture, profoundly Greek in many respects yet always different, and independent. As we see Greek literary culture pressed into service in order to construct a poem about Roman identity, we are simultaneously being educated in a historical understanding of how Roman culture is formed. The profundity of the Greek contribution to Rome is nowhere more vividly demonstrated than in Book VIII, when Aeneas goes to the place where Rome will one day be, and finds living there a group of people who embody the antique virtues of frugality and hardihood that his Roman contemporaries idealised in their ancestors – yet these people, the Arcadians of Evander, are themselves Greeks. In showing us that it is not possible to go back to a period of Roman culture before Greek influence, Virgil is teaching us a lesson that modern historians of Rome have only quite recently begun to absorb.

This discussion of Virgil's literary models may give the impression that his poem is a very scholarly one, and such is indeed the case. He read his models in a scholarly context, with commentaries, and some of his imitation reveals and invites a considerable degree of learning. Yet one of the things I have learnt from compiling the notes for this edition is how little scholarly explanation the poem actually needs in order to be read as the gripping narrative that it is. Early on in the poem, for example, there are many allusions to the treatment of the fall of Troy in Attic tragedy, starting with the frieze in Juno's temple in Book I, and especially in Aeneas' narrative in Book II. Tragedy commonly treats the sack of Troy as the turning-point when Greek victory turned rancid in the very moment of attainment, and anyone who has read Aeschylus' *Agamemnon* or Euripides' *Trojan Women* will appreciate Virgil's ironic mobilisation of this tradition, as Aeneas tells of the Greeks' great triumph in ignorance of the catastrophes that awaited his enemies. Nonetheless, someone who does not know the tragedies will have practically all of this spelled out early in Book XI, when one of the Greek heroes, Diomede, refuses to fight again against the Trojans, giving a catalogue of the humiliating disasters suffered by each of the heroes who sacked Troy.

As with any great work of art, then, the more you bring to it the more you are capable of getting out of it, but just as possession of scholarship is no automatic passport to reading the poem well and enjoyably, so lack of it is no bar. The next step, for anyone who comes to love the poem, is to learn Latin, for only in Latin can one sense the matchless musicality and power of Virgil's verse, and begin to see why he has always been held in such awe by his peers.

# NOTE ON THE TEXT

The text is the translation of C. H. Sisson, originally published in 1986 by Carcanet Press Ltd and the Mid Northumberland Arts Group.

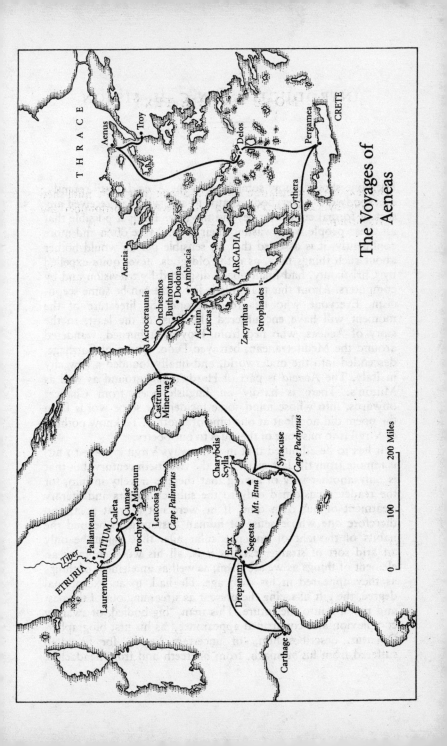

The Voyages of Aeneas

THRACE

Aenus
Troy

Delos

CRETE
Pergamea

Cythera

ARCADIA

Aeneia
Onchesmos
Buthrotum
Dodona
Ambracia
Acroceraunia
Actium
Leucas
Zacynthus
Strophades

Castrum
Minervae

Charybdis
Scylla
Syracuse
Cape Pachynus

Cumae
Misenum
Leucosia
Cape Palinurus
Prochyta

Mt. Etna

Caieta

Pallanteum
ETRURIA    LATIUM
Tiber
Laurentum

Eryx
Segesta
Drepanum

Carthage

200 Miles

100

0

# INTRODUCTION BY C. H. SISSON

Everyone should know something of the *Aeneid*. Until recently, everybody did – everybody, that is to say, who had received any sort of formal education beyond the three Rs. Is it possible that all those people were wasting their time? More often and more confidently, it is asserted that no sensible person would bother about such things now, as if the old gods, never quite expelled by Christianity, had finally been displaced by television and by computers. About this plausible belief there can be some scepticism. Everyone who has read beyond the literature of the moment will have encountered allusions, at the least, to the story of Aeneas, who fled from Troy as it burned, wandered around the Mediterranean, betrayed Dido, Queen of Carthage, descended into the underworld, and finally founded a new city in Italy. The *Aeneid* is part of Hardy's background as well as Milton's. There is hardly an English poet, from Chaucer onwards, into whose mind some incident or some words from the poem did not float at one time or another. To know nothing of Virgil is to miss one of the clues to our poetry.

It has to be admitted that in some ways Virgil (70 BC–19 BC) is remote from the last quarter of the twentieth century, but that is only another way of saying that there is novelty in him, for the reader accustomed only to the subject-matters and literary treatment of our own time. If he were not a great poet, and therefore one whose sense of human destiny goes beyond the habits of thought of any particular age, that might be only an arid sort of strangeness. As it is, all his work contains an element of things as we see them, as well as an element of things as they appeared in his own age. He had, to an exceptional degree, the gift of seeing the present as streaming out of the past and moving into the future. This man, 'big-bodied, of swarthy complexion and countrified appearance,' as his first biographer, Donatus, describes him, 'of uncertain health, for he often suffered from his stomach, from his teeth and from headaches, and spit blood', 'abstemious so far as food and drink are concerned, but given to the love of boys', for the rest had the reputation of being a man of great integrity, and not at all keen to exhibit himself to his fans or to those who made a fuss of him in public. He lived through civil wars, in which he seems to have played no part, and he brooded, as not only the *Aeneid* but the *Eclogues* and the *Georgics* show, on a future age of peace. His vision is at once historical and prophetic. Neither quality is free from suspicion in an age which, like our own, prefers to think of itself as far as may be in terms of the present. Yet the great figures of the poem – Dido, Anchises, Aeneas himself – are presented in traits which mark them more vividly than any figure in a modern European novel, say Madame Bovary, Jude the Obscure, or Kafka's 'K'. They are, however, in no sense people who are 'doing their own thing': the thing they are doing is determined by their part in the destiny of Rome herself. It is on that account that Anchises is carried from the burning ruins of Troy, that Dido is abandoned, to throw herself on her funeral pyre, and that Aeneas himself endures untold hardships and, finally, battles. The fate which hangs over the story of the *Aeneid* is something far closer to us than any determinism based on the abstractions of nineteenth-century German philosophers. At the back of it are the gods of the old world, with their ambitions and jealousies, and the inscrutable Father of All who presides over them and over human affairs. They represent the hopes and fears of the people scattered around the still lightly populated shores of the Mediterranean. The refugees from Troy are pursued by the hatred of Juno; the city itself falls although Neptune built the walls. There is no absolute protection in divine favour, for the gods and goddesses are often at odds among themselves. They are propitiated, like the Christian saints who succeeded them at so many shrines, rather in superstitious hope than in utter conviction. Yet for Virgil, as for the demigod Aeneas who in his greatest need invokes his mother Venus, the Supreme Destiny seems invincible. Small wonder that, in the Christian epoch which began so few years after Virgil's death, these apprehensions were in some sort appropriated by the Church. As we look back, Virgil seems to stand between the ancient world and the mediaeval world which grew out of its decay. He seemed so already to Dante, in 1300, the more convincingly because for Dante the figures of Livy's history and of the Bible had the same sort of vivid reality.

The modern reader is perhaps unlikely to be attracted by Virgil as the poet of imperial Rome. Empires are unfashionable, at least in the west, and in Eastern Europe a different kind of language has been adopted to justify the subjugation of vast stretches of territory. Moreover, no-one is likely now to forget that, if Virgil's father was originally a potter or a labourer, and if the poet himself was turned off his farm near Mantua to make room for the veterans settled in that part of the country after the civil wars, he none the less enjoyed the favour of the Emperor Augustus and died a rich man. Nor is it likely to be forgotten that the era of peace Virgil saw opening before him was, in the actuality, troubled by spectacular corruption and violence. None the less, the *pax Romana* was real enough and laid solid foundations for the civilisation of the western world, and to regard this achievement with retrospective hostility is possible only on a narrow and perverted view of history. To sympathise with the band of refugees driven from Troy, only to withhold one's sympathy when one discovers that Aeneas's destiny was not only to find a new home but to found a city and set it on course to become the centre of a great empire – one that was indeed to dominate the whole of the known world – would be to reject not only the Roman past but all the intervening history and to confine oneself within the limited views of the second half of the twentieth century.

The reader who comes fresh to the *Aeneid* should not bother his head with such, or indeed any, ideas *about* the poem: he should simply read it, and let the story, the scenes, the characters work as they will. He will be plunged at once into the middle of things, with Aeneas and his companions, after long voyaging already, encountering a great storm which drives them on to the coast of Africa. The land proves to be the realm of Dido, who mounts a great feast for Aeneas and asks him to tell her the tale of his adventures. In this way, as by one of those time shifts which are a common device in the fiction of the twentieth century, the reader is taken back several years, and the second book, which moves swiftly, gives an eye-witness account of the stratagems and terrors of the fall of Troy, from which Aeneas escapes with his father Anchises on his back and holding his little son Ascanius by the hand; Creüsa his wife follows but is lost in the confusion. The third book contains the story of the Trojans' travels till they reach Sicily, where Anchises dies: this is the point from which Aeneas started the voyage which landed him on the coast of Carthage. In the fourth book, he sails away to Sicily where, as if to solemnise his return to the course of duty, he celebrates the anniversary of his father's funeral by a series of games in his honour. The Trojan women, tired of travel, fire the ships, and Aeneas leaves, in a new city, all who are reluctant to follow him, and himself sets out once more, this time with only the vigorous remnant who are to found Rome. They sail to Italy and the sixth book – perhaps the most profound and moving of all, and the key if any is to Virgil's thought – tells of Aeneas's consultation of the oracular Cumaean Sibyl, and his subsequent visit to the underworld, where he encounters not only Dido but Anchises, and the future heroes of Rome pass before his eyes. It is as if Aeneas's mind is finally cleared by this journey; after this there is no defection. The little band of Trojans goes on, finding its way in Italy through new friendships and hostilities to the death of Turnus, a tribal king who has stood in the way of Aeneas marrying Lavinia, the daughter of King Latinus. Thus is established, ultimately, that union of Romans and Latins, with the clear predominance of the former, which was the historical basis of the imperial power.

There have been many attempts to re-tell this story in the vernacular of this island; the first, and arguably the best, being that of Gavin Douglas (1474?–1522) in Scots, a version which Ezra Pound claimed – it must be said, with a touch of exaggeration – was 'better than the original'. The first English version was that of the Earl of Surrey (1517?–1547), who translated Books II and IV and in doing so invented 'blank verse'. Since then there has been a series of versions, of which the most brilliant is unquestionably that of John Dryden (1631–1700), in vigorous rhymed couplets which carry the whole argument through at a cracking pace. Of the contemporary versions I will say nothing, except that if any of them satisfied me I should not be offering this further attempt. The problem of translating any poet of a more or less remote epoch is to find a tone in which the translator can give the matter of the original in language which comes naturally to him. This involves a tension between his language and thoughts and perceptions which by definition are unfamiliar to the ordinary reader of the age and differ more or less profoundly from those of the translator himself. This tension must show at every point, not least in the rhythm which is part of the language. It is no use proceeding, as many translators have done, by imagining a sort of solemn dignity and calling it Virgilian. The translator has to discover the work afresh as he goes on, line by line, and gives his findings as best he can, assimilating them in his own speech. There will always be more or less of failure, and there is no such thing as complete success. The degree and kind of assimilation will be different for different translators and for different ages. What Dryden assimilated comes to us not only as Virgil but as some of the best Dryden we have. Only a poet can even begin to perform a similar operation for our own day. It is as someone who has long wrestled with the art of verse in his own poems and, as much at least as any of his contemporaries, with the procedures of translation, that I offer this new version: but above all, as someone who has enjoyed Virgil. If people who have not hitherto been acquainted with the poet, or have read only odd bits of him, are thereby induced to follow the course of Aeneas's story, I shall be content.

C. H. SISSON

# THE AENEID

# BOOK I

# BOOK I

This poem is about battles and the man
Who, fugitive but in the hands of fate,
Came first from Troy to the Lavinian shores,
Tossed to and fro on land as on the sea
By violence from above, the unforgetting
Anger of Juno was the cause of that;
And in war too he suffered much until
He had laid the foundations of his city
And brought his own gods into Latium
– Whence came the Latin race, the Alban fathers
And finally the high walls of Rome.
    Muse, bring to mind the causes, say what injury
To her divinity made the Queen of Heaven
Drive this man, so remarkable for his piety
Through such a circle of misfortune to face
So many drudgeries. Who would have thought
There could be such resentment in the gods?
    There was an ancient city, with Tyrian colonists,
Carthage, across the sea from Italy
And the Tiber delta, a prosperous city it was
With tough fighters who understood their business:
Juno preferred it before all other lands
Even Samos itself; here was her armoury,
Here was her chariot, and her intention was
That it should rule the nations of the earth
If so the fates allowed, with her support.
She had, however, heard of another race
Which had its origin from Trojan blood
And was one day to wreck the Tyrian stronghold
– An imperial people, arrogant in war,
Which would have Libya quaking: it was pre-ordained.
It was that she feared, for she had not forgotten
The old war, and she was Saturn's daughter;

Had she not fought at Troy for her dear Argives?
Nor indeed had the causes of her anger
And all the pain it gave her, gone from her mind;
She had not forgotten the judgment of Paris
That her figure wasn't the best, or how she hated
The race Ganymede came from and how he was taken
To serve as cup-bearer to Jupiter.
That made her wilder still, she threw the Trojans
– Such of them as were left when tough Achilles
And the Greeks had done – out on the wide waters
And kept them far from Latium. They had years
Of wandering, fate would have it so, at sea
This way and that. You see it was not easy;
It was a giant's task to set up Rome.
    They were hardly out of sight of Sicily,
Sails spread, happy, pushing the salt spray,
When Juno, nursing her eternal wound,
Said in her heart: 'Have I to give up, beaten,
Powerless to turn the Teucrian king from Italy?
The fates will not allow it? They allowed Pallas
To burn the Greek fleet and send the crews to the bottom
For the wrong one man did, the son of Oileus,
Demented Ajax! It was Pallas herself
Who launched the thunderflash from the clouds,
Broke up the ships and turned the sea upside down
And while he, pierced to the heart, was spouting flames
With his dying breath, she caught him in the blast
And landed him upon a jagged rock;
But I, who go in first as Queen of the Gods,
Jove's sister and his wife, have to go on
Year after year with war against one small tribe.
Will anyone in future worship Juno,
Let alone beg her favours or dress her altars?'
    This it was the goddess was thinking about
– And her heart burned – as she came to the clouds' home,
The place that is alive with tumbling winds,
Aeolia, where in great caves King Aeolus
Thrusts down the struggling air, the sonorous tempests,
Into obedience, and chains them in his prisons.
Indignantly they crash against the barriers
And the mountain groans; Aeolus sits above them,

Perched in his fortress and holding his sceptre,
Quietening them till their anger is within bounds;
If he did not, the seas, the earth and the skies
Would be carried off by their fury and blow through space.
But the omnipotent Father hid them in caves;
He feared this, and piled the mountains on them;
He gave them a king, with rules and regulations,
One who could handle the reins as he was told.
This was the person Juno had now to plead with:
'Aeolus, you are he to whom the Father
Of all the gods and the Ruler of all men
Has given the power to keep the waves in place
Or to whip them up with a wind: hostile to me,
A people is sailing over the Tuscan sea,
Carrying to Italy Troy and her failed gods:
Put some force in your winds and sink their ships,
Or scatter them and throw the men overboard.
I possess fourteen nymphs, all splendid bodies,
The best of the lot for beauty is Deiopea,
I will allot her to you in permanent marriage;
If you will do what I ask she will stay with you
And make you the father of handsome sons and daughters.'
   Aeolus answered: 'You, queen, have one task only,
To make up your mind what you want; it is my business
To do whatever you say. I owe you my kingdom,
My sceptre, Jove's favour, my seat at the gods' table,
The fact that I am in charge of clouds and storms.'
   Having said this, he turned his spear to the mountain
Where it was hollow, and struck a blow on its side;
The winds rushed out like a column of armed men,
Where the opening was, and blew across the world.
They pressed down on the sea and turned it over,
East and south winds together, the wind from Africa;
Squalls everywhere, the great waves roll on the shore;
Then comes the cry of men and the tackle creaking.
In a moment clouds snatch away the light of the sky
From the Trojan's eyes; black night lies on the sea.
The thunder rolls, there are frequent flashes of lightning,
Everything glares the menace of instant death.
Aeneas's limbs are weak with the chill:
He groans and, stretching both his hands to the stars,

Calls out: 'You were fortunate, more than that,
You who died under the walls of Troy
With your fathers looking on! O Diomed,
Bravest of all the Greeks, could not I have fallen
On the Ilian fields, and been released by your hand?
Fierce Hector lies there, killed by the spear of Achilles,
With gigantic Sarpedon, where Simois
Sweeps shields and helmets and brave men under the waves!'
    As Aeneas called out the storm screamed back at him,
Beating against the sail with a north blast
And lifting sea to sky; the oars were broken;
Then the prow was turned and the side against the waves;
There followed a mountain of water, slap on the deck.
Some men appeared on the crest; others touched the ground
Which suddenly lay bare between the waves,
Nothing but seething sand. Three ships the south wind
Catches and spins against the hidden rocks
The Italians call the Altars, a spine of stones,
Some sticking out of the water. Three of the ships
The east wind forces from the deep to the shallows
Among the banks of quicksand – terrifying! –
Dashes them into a heap and covers them.
One, with the Lycians and loyal Orontes aboard,
Is struck before Aeneas's eyes by a huge sea
Falling astern; the man at the helm is washed
Flat on his face overboard; but the ship turns round
Three times rapidly and goes down straight as a die.
Here and there sailors are swimming on the vast surface,
There are weapons, planks, Trojan valuables everywhere.
Already the storm has the better of the stout ship
Ilioneus had, now Achates's ship has gone down,
Now the one Abas sailed in, now aged Aletes's;
The timbers have sprung at the sides and all of them
Admit the hostile sea and gape at it.
    Meanwhile, by the rising noise of the sea's riot,
Neptune knew a storm was at large; in the depths
Which should be still there were currents, then commotion;
He raised his head from the water and looked around
Calmly, and saw Aeneas's fleet scattered
On the surface far and wide, the Trojans
Hard-pressed by the waves and the tumbling sky.

He knew all Juno's tricks, he was her brother,
He knew she was angry. Quickly he called the east wind,
He called the west wind. Then he spoke to them:
'Who do you think you are? What gives you the right
To turn sky and earth topsy-turvy without my permission
And pile up water like that? I'll show you, you winds!
You won't get off so lightly another time.
Get back to base at once and tell your king
That he has no authority over the sea,
Nor over this sharp trident: that's my affair.
His kingdom is those cruel rocks where you belong.
East wind, the lot of you! Let Aeolus only brag
That what he rules is the prison where winds are confined.'
    In less time than it took him to speak these words
He drove the clouds away and brought back the sun.
Cymothoë and Triton, working together,
Push the ships away from the sharp rocks
While he himself helps with his trident; vast
Sandbanks are opened up, the sea is calmed
And over the top of it his chariot rides.
As when a great nation is stirred to sedition
And the mob are out and raging like lunatics
With torches and stones, anything they can lay hands on,
And then, if they catch sight of some public man
Who weighs with them for what he is or has done,
They fall silent and listen to what he will say
And what he says steadies and makes them calm:
So all the din of the sea dropped to nothing
As the old god, looking round over the surface
And carried on under an open sky,
Wheeled his horses and then gave them their head
So that the chariot flew on an easy course.
    Worn out, Aeneas's men make for the nearest land
Which means turning their ships to the Libyan coast.
There is a place with a deep recess, an island
Which makes a harbour with its reaching arms
And breaks whatever waves come from the deep,
Taking them quiet and broken in its lap.
On one side and the other huge rocks rise,
Menacing twins which stretch into the sky,
While down below the water lies silent;

From above a screen of shimmering woods
Hangs down, and in it a dark grove
Of terrifying shadows, with a cave
Under the brow and on the face of the cliff;
Inside is fresh water and there are seats
Cut in the living rock; the nymphs live here.
No need for weary ships to be tied up,
No need for anchors here for the seven ships
Aeneas has crept into harbour with,
All that is left of his fleet. How glad they are,
The Trojans, to be on dry land again!
They take possession of the delicious sand
And lay their salty bodies on the ground.
The first thing then is flint to strike a spark;
Achates does it, and sets fire to leaves,
Puts other dry stuff round it: there is flame.
Then they bring out the corn that they have salvaged
And, weary as they are, pestle and mortar,
Ready to dry the grain and pound it up.
  Meanwhile Aeneas climbs a pointed rock
To get a view of the sea as far as he can.
Is Antheus there, with his Phrygian galleys?
Or Capys, after the wind has done with him?
Or Caicus with his shield hung at the stern?
There is not a ship in sight, but he sees on the shore
Three wandering stags and whole herds following them,
Strung out along the valley as they graze.
Quickly he takes in hand his bow and arrows
Which – trust him! – Achates has there at his side
And brings down the leaders first, whose antlered heads
Had run so high, and then the common run
Is put to flight, his arrows follow them
Into the leafy covert; he does not stop
Till he has seven large carcases on the ground,
One for each ship. Then he goes back to the harbour
And shares them out with his companions.
The wine the munificent Acestes
Gave them in Sicily as a parting gift
Aeneas now divides, and speaks to them
To mitigate the sorrow in their hearts:

'Comrades, this isn't the first time things have gone wrong,
You have known worse than this: God will end this too.
You have approached Scylla's fury and gone right up
To the barking rocks, you know your way around
To the Cyclops's cave; that courage will serve again,
There is no need to be down-hearted now:
This day too may be one you will look back on.
We have our ups and downs, even disasters,
But we are going to Latium which the fates
Determine is to be our resting-place;
There providence will have Troy rise again.
Keep on, and keep yourselves for better days.'
   Such are his words as, sick with many cares,
He puts on a hopeful look and fights back the pain.
The others attend to the spoil and the feast
They strip the hide from the ribs to get at the meat;
Some cut it in lumps and stab it, still shuddering, with spits;
Some set cooking-pots on the shore and flames underneath.
They have food now to bring back their strength, and they lie
      on the grass
To fill themselves up with old wine and succulent venison.
Their hunger out of the way, and the food cleared up
They miss their comrades and talk of them at length,
Half in hope, half in fear. Are they to believe
They are still alive or are they to think of them
As having suffered the worst beyond recall?
More than the rest Aeneas grieves; he thinks
First of Orontes, so keen a soldier,
Then of Amycus and what has happened to him,
Of disasters to Gyas, who had such courage,
Of Lycus who encountered a cruel fate,
And of Cloanthus, he was a good man too.
   All this had come to an end when Jupiter
From the top of heaven looked down on a sail-flecked sea,
On the countries lying around its shores, the nations
Spread over them: he halted there and his eyes
Settled upon the kingdoms of Libya.
And then it was, as his heart was full of their troubles,
That Venus, with her eyes brimming with tears,
Spoke to him: 'You who govern men and gods
And their affairs in your eternal empire

And terrify them with thunderbolts: what wrong
Has my Aeneas done you so intolerable,
What have the Trojans done that after suffering
So many violent deaths, because of Italy,
They are shut out from every land on earth?
Surely the Romans were in course of time
To spring from them, and call back Teucer's blood,
Holding both sea and land under their sway,
– Commanders, such was your promise. What is it, father,
Has turned your mind away from this purpose?
It was that, when I saw Troy in ruins,
Comforted me, thinking of different fortunes;
Yet now the same fate, after all they have been through,
Pursues them. When, great king, will you let them rest?
Antenor was allowed to escape the Achaeans,
Come up the Illyrian coast and safely penetrate
The inmost parts of the Liburnians' kingdoms
And pass beyond the source of the Timavus
The river through whose nine mouths, underground,
The sea comes flooding up into the fields
While the ground murmurs. Here he set Padua
As a home for the Teucrians, gave his race
A name and here hung up the arms of Troy
Where he is now settled in lasting peace.
But we, your children, whom you beckon up
Into the citadel of heaven, are betrayed,
Our ships are foully lost, and through the anger
Of one person, and we are kept from Italy.
So much for loyalty! So you reward us!'
     He smiles at her, the source of men and gods,
With that look which he uses to calm storms,
And kisses her before he speaks to her:
'Don't be afraid, Cytherean; nothing has changed
For you and yours, and you will see your city,
Lavinium with its walls as I have promised,
And you shall raise Aeneas to the stars,
For he deserves it and I do not change.
Your son – for I will speak, since you are anxious,
And let you see a little more of fate –
Will conduct a great war in Italy,
Crushing ferocious peoples, and establish

The customs of his city and its walls
When he has reigned for three years in Latium
And passed three winters after their defeat.
The boy Ascanius, who is now called Iulus
And was called Ilus when Ilium still stood,
Will rule for thirty years from Lavinium,
Transfer his government to Alba Longa
Which he will fortify decisively.
Here for three hundred years will be a kingdom
Which Hector's family will rule until
A royal priestess, Ilia, pregnant by Mars,
Produces twins of whom one, Romulus,
Wearing the tawny hide of the she-wolf
That suckled him, will take over the line,
Will trace the walls for Mars and call his people
Romans, so naming them after himself.
For these I set no bounds in place or time
But I have given them empire without end.
Turbulent Juno herself, who now shakes up
Both sea and earth with fear, and heaven itself,
Will be of better counsel, and with me
Do what she can for the Roman conquerors,
The people of the toga. So I decree.
And so the time will come with holy steps
When the house of Assaracus will crush
Phthia and clear Mycenae into slavery
And will be master of the conquered Argos.
From this line will be born a Trojan Caesar
With no bounds but the Ocean and the stars,
Julius, a name come down from the great Iulus.
This conqueror, loaded with eastern spoil,
You will constantly receive in heaven
And he himself will be invoked in prayer.
Then wars will cease and centuries grow mild,
And ancient Truth, with Vesta, will return,
Quirinus make laws with his brother Remus.
The savage gates of war will be shut up
With iron bolts; inside, insanity,
Impious and cruel and sitting on its weapons,
Will scream its bloody head off, with its hands
Tied in a hundred knots behind its back.'

   Having said this, he sent the son of Maia
Down from heaven to the Carthaginian territories:
The citadel itself was to open up
And hospitably let the Teucrians in;
Dido, not knowing the future, might shoo them off.
The messenger flew as if rowing with his wings:
In no time he was on the shores of Libya
And did as he was ordered; the Phoenicians
Forgot their anger and did the will of God.
The queen herself looked kindly on the Teucrians
And in receiving them was liberal.
   Aeneas, having thought all through the night
Dutifully, in the morning, at first light
Decides to explore these unfamiliar places
Here on the shores the wind has brought them to.
He will find out what men or beasts live here
(Everything seems deserted) and report
What he discovers accurately to his comrades.
He hides his fleet under a hollow rock
Shadowed by trees and almost shut in:
Then sets out with no company but Achates,
Hunting spears at the ready in his hand.
His mother comes to meet him in the woods,
In the shape of a virgin, carrying a virgin's weapons,
Like a Spartan girl or the Thracian Harpalyce
Who outruns horses and the river Hebrus.
The huntress lets her hair fly in the wind;
Bare to the knee, with her dress knotted up,
She gets the first word in: 'Hi!' she calls out,
'Tell me, you boys, has either of you seen
One of my sisters here wandering about,
Carrying a quiver and in a spotted lynx skin,
Perhaps bawling after a puffed wild boar?'
   Then Venus stopped, and Venus's son began:
'I have neither heard nor seen one of your sisters
– But how do I address you? For you seem
Not to be like a mortal, by your looks,
Nor does your voice sound like a human voice.
A goddess certainly! A sister of Phoebus?
Or perhaps one of the race of Nymphs?
Please help us in our difficulty.

Where on earth are we? And what coast is this?
We are washed up here and are wandering round
Ignorant what this land is or who lives here;
The wind brought us, on enormous waves;
You may count on getting sacrifices from us.'
    Then Venus: 'Not for me honours like that!
But Tyrian virgins always carry a quiver
And wear red boots that stretch right up their calves.
It is the Punic kingdoms that you see;
They are Tyrian; Agenor's children built the city;
Beyond is Libya, a bellicose people they are.
The ruler here is Dido, from the city of Tyre;
She left it, wanting to get away from her brother.
That is a long and complicated story
But I will tell you the most important bits.
Her husband was Sychaeus, the richest landowner
Among the Phoenicians, and the wretched woman
Was mad about him and her father had given her
In marriage to him when she was a virgin.
But in Tyre her brother Pygmalion ruled;
He was a criminal if ever there was one.
Between the two men a violent quarrel
Blew up; the king, blinded by love of gold
And thinking nothing of his sister's loves,
Surprised the other impiously at the altar
And struck him with a knife: for long enough
He kept this from the love-sick young woman,
Inventing various lies to keep her hoping.
But her unburied husband, his ghost rather,
Came to her in a dream, wherein she saw
Him lifting his pale face and saw the altar
Which had been cruel to him, saw him stuck through:
So he disclosed this grim domestic crime.
Then he persuaded her to flee the country;
To help her on her way he showed her where
Great treasures had been buried long before,
A heap of gold and silver. That was enough;
Dido assembled friends and took to flight
With men who either hated the cruel tyrant
Or feared his hatred; there were ships at hand;
They seized them, loaded them with gold; the covetous

Pygmalion's treasure was on the high seas;
All organised by a woman. They came to the places
You see before you now, where these high walls
Rise, and the citadel of new Carthage:
They bought the ground which now they call the Hide
– As much as strips from one skin could encircle.
But who are you, after all this? Where do you come from?
Where are you bound?' Aeneas, at these questions,
Sighed and dragged up his voice from deep inside him:
    'O Goddess, if I started at the beginning
And you had time to hear the whole story
Of what we have done, the day would be over
And the evening star would have shut the gates of heaven.
We have come from ancient Troy, if you ever heard
The name of Troy before, sailing the seas
And storm has thrown us on the Libyan coast;
I am Aeneas, who does what he must;
I carry in my fleet the household gods
Snatched from the enemy: heaven knows my story.
I seek for Italy as my own country,
My race was born there, coming from Jove himself.
With twenty ships I embarked on the Phrygian sea,
My mother, who is a goddess, pointing the way
And I obeying as the fates required.
Just seven are left, battered by wave and wind,
And I, unknown, necessitous, must wander
Over the emptiness of Libya,
Europe and Asia having driven me out.'
    Venus would hear no more of his complaint
But interrupted his dejection with:
'Whoever you may be, it seems to me
You're not forgotten by celestial persons!
You're still alive; and here you are arriving
At the Tyrian city; all you have to do
Is go on and you're on the queen's doorstep.
For I can tell you that your mates are safe,
Your fleet brought back by the wind veering north:
At least if I know anything of augury.
Look at those twelve swans flying single file
Contentedly. Just now Jove's eagle chased them,
Scattering them far and wide; now back in line

They are either landing or looking where to land.
As they are flying home with pounding wings
And first circle and whoop in unison,
So your ships and the young men on board
Are either in port or sailing into the harbour.
Only go on and, where your path leads, follow.'
    She had spoken and, as she turned away, a glow
Came from her lovely neck and from her hair
A fragrance which betokened the divine;
Her robe fell into place and as she moved
It was plain she was a goddess. So Aeneas
Recognised his mother and called out to her
As she receded: 'Why, again and again,
Do you treat your son so cruelly and play tricks
With your disguises? Why can we not take hands
And talk to one another as we are?'
With this complaint he walks towards the city.
But Venus puts a wall of darkness round him,
She is not a goddess for nothing; thick mist cloaks
The traveller so that none can see or touch him
Or hold him up or ask him what he wants.
She herself flies to Paphos and is happy
To see her island and her temple where
A hundred altars smoke with Sabaean incense
And breathe out fragrance from fresh wreaths of flowers.
    They hurried on their way along the path
And so climbed up the hill above the town
Till they could see the towers opposite.
Aeneas was amazed at the huge buildings
Where recently there had been only tents;
Amazed to see gates, and hear clatter from paved streets.
They were at work, those Tyrians, some built walls,
Some heaved up stones to make the citadel,
Some marked out the foundations of a house;
There were meetings, magistrates, a sacred senate.
Here some were excavating docks and others
The deep foundations of a great theatre
And cutting immense columns from the rock
To stand beside the stage when it was built.
As bees in the fresh summer fields of flowers
Work in the sun and show the young the way,

Pack liquid honey, filling the cells to bursting,
Take in what others bring them, or like soldiers
Drive out the herd of drones who do no work;
The heat is on, the honey smells of thyme.
'Happy are those whose walls go up already!'
Aeneas says, looking up at the town's roof-tops.
He is going in now, still in his magic mist;
He walks among the men and no-one sees him.
    In the heart of the town was a grove of shady trees,
The place where the Phoenicians, cast ashore
Had first dug up the sign the regal Juno
Had given them: the head of a battle horse.
This people was to be, through centuries,
Brilliant in war and never lack supplies.
Here was the temple to Juno Sidonian Dido
Was founding, rich in gifts and in the goddess
Herself, who lent her presence to the spot.
The threshold was bronze, and steps led up to it;
There were beams clamped with bronze, and hinges which
      screamed
With the weight of bronzed doors. Among the trees
Aeneas saw something to re-assure him,
A strange sight which first gave him hope
And made him trust he might see better times.
For, as walking below the huge temple,
He waited for the queen, and the city's fortunes
Struck him as marvellous, with so many artists
And so many immense works put in hand,
He saw represented the Trojan war,
Just as it was, with all its battles, already
The fame of it had spread through the world;
There were the Atrides and Priam,
With Achilles who was so fierce against them all.
He stopped and wept. 'Is there any place, Achates,
Anywhere on earth not full of our distress?
Look!' he said, 'there is Priam. Even here
Virtue has its reward, and what is it?
There are tears and men are moved by mortality
Forget your fears; this story may yet serve us.'
    And as he spoke, he let his mind feed
Upon the picture, heaving sighs, and wetting

His face with a river of tears. For he could see
How, in the fight round Pergamus, first of all
The Greeks were in retreat, the Trojans after them,
And then the Phrygians, with a crested Achilles
Chasing them in his chariot. Not far away
The snowy tents of Rhesus are what he sees,
And weeps: caught in their first sleep
And raided by the son of Tydeus,
Covered in blood from head to foot from slaughter;
Then turned the half-mad horses back to camp
Before they could see what the grass was like in Troy
Or drink from the Xanthus. In another place
– In flight – there is Troilus who has dropped his weapons,
The poor boy was unequal to Achilles;
The horses drag him along with the empty chariot,
He has fallen out backwards but still holds the reins,
His head and hair are bumping in the dust
Which is inscribed by his spear, now upside down.
Meanwhile the Trojan women in procession
Approach the temple of the unjust Pallas,
Their hair loose and bearing the ritual garment,
Suppliants who slap their breasts with the flat of their hands;
The body of Hector, lifeless, which Achilles
Had three times dragged round the walls of Troy,
Is now put up for sale. When he sees this
Aeneas groans from the bottom of his heart:
His friend's equipment, chariot, very body
And Priam stretching out with his bare hands.
He sees himself among the Achaean princes,
The eastern levies and black Memnon's armour.
Leading her Amazons with their crescent shields
Is Penthesilea, she blazes among thousands,
Her one breast sticking out, bound underneath
With a golden scarf. She was a warrior,
A virgin who dared do battle with men.
    Aeneas the Dardanian is intent
Upon the marvellous things his eyes are fixed on;
Meanwhile the queen appears, approaching the temple,
A beautiful figure, it is Dido herself
Accompanied by a retinue of young men.
She is like Diana on Eurotas' banks

Or on the top of Cynthus, with her dancers
Followed by droves of Oreads; the huntress
Wears her quiver over her shoulder and she walks
More proudly than any other goddess
So that Latona is glad to be her mother.
Dido carries herself in the same manner
Among her followers, her mind is full of her plans.
At the door of the shrine and under the temple's
Central arch, with her guards in attendance,
She mounts on a high throne and takes her seat.
She was laying down the law to men, deciding
Who should do what, or settling by lot,
When suddenly Aeneas saw approaching,
Surrounded by a mob, Antheus, Segestus,
The undaunted Cloanthus and other Trojans
Whom the black storm had scattered and driven off
To other beaches far along the coast.
He was astonished, and Achates too,
Half hoping, half in fear; they are impelled
To take the new-comers by the hand
But their surprise is such they give no sign,
Only remain concealed in their tent of mist
Wondering what has happened to these men,
Where they have left their ships and why they have come;
For there were some men out of every ship,
Pleading the laws of hospitality
And calling out as they drew near the temple.
    When they were inside and granted audience,
Ilioneus, senior among them, and self-possessed,
Began to speak: 'O queen of this new city
Jupiter lets you found, permitting you
To teach these wild tribes what is meant by justice,
We Trojans, exhausted by the wind-swept seas,
Petition you: stop our ships from being burned;
Spare us, a race under divine protection:
Consider how matters stand with us.
We have not come to spread out over Libya,
To put men to the sword in their own homes
Or drive off slaves and cattle to the shore;
No violence of this kind is in our minds;
Such arrogance is not for the defeated.

There is a place the Greeks call Hesperia,
An ancient land of warriors and rich farms;
The Oenotrians lived there but their descendants,
Apparently, now call it Italy
After the name of their prince. It was there we were going
When suddenly at the rising of Orion
The sea rose high and stormy and carried us
On to hidden shoals and the wind followed
And we were in waves of leaping foam,
Driven against rocks, and so a few of us
Have ended up here upon your shores.
What kind of men are here? What country is it?
So barbarous as to allow such customs?
They will not even leave us on the beaches
But must attack if we so much as touch
Even the very borders of the land.
You may think nothing of the human race
And mortal arms: consider the immortals,
They still know right from wrong. We had a king,
Aeneas was his name; no juster man
Or more religious ever stepped, nor one
Who was a better man in war and arms.
If the fates still protect him and he breathes
The air still and is not among the shades,
We shall fear nothing, nor would you regret
Having been the first to help us. There are in Sicily
Cities and fields we could find refuge in;
The great Acestes there is of Trojan blood.
Let us draw up our battered fleet on shore,
Have access to your woods for planks and oars
And, if our comrades and our king still live,
We will go off to Italy with pleasure
And find our Latium; if safety there
Is not for us and you, Father of Trojans,
Have been devoured by the Libyan deeps
So that no hope remains in Iulus now,
We can at least sail to Sicily,
Find a home there and Acestes for our king.'
So spoke Ilioneus and all the Trojans
Roared their approval.

Then Dido lowered her eyes and spoke concisely:
'Fear nothing, Teucrians, no cause for anxiety:
Things are hard here, and with a new kingdom
I have no choice but to take my precautions
And keep a close guard upon my frontiers.
Who has not heard of Aeneas and his people,
The city of Troy, the courage of its inhabitants,
Or all that that great struggle set alight?
We are not so dull-witted, we Phoenicians,
Nor do we live so far from the track of the sun.
Whether you make your way to great Hesperia,
Saturn's own country, or decide instead
On that of Eryx, with Acestes for your king,
I will see you get off safely and supply
All you need for the journey. Or if you will
You may settle in these kingdoms on equal terms.
The city I am building is your own.
Beach your ships, Trojan and Tyrian are one.
If only the same wind that brought you here
Would bring your king Aeneas! I will send
Search parties all along the coast of Libya
In case he is ship-wrecked and wandering in forest or town.'
   These words went deep: Achates and Aeneas
Had long burned to break through their cloud.
Achates spoke first, addressing his prince:
'Goddess-born, what do you think now?
You see that all is safe, the fleet, our friends;
The only one missing is him we saw
Sink in the waves: otherwise all is as
Your mother said.' The words were not out of his mouth
Before the cloud around them opened up
And then vanished into the wide sky.
Aeneas stood there, shining in the light,
His face and shoulders like a god's; his mother
Gave him that marvellous hair, the brilliant light
Of youth, eyes full of honour and happiness;
He was like some piece of worked ivory
Or silver or Parian marble set in gold.
He addressed the queen, and everybody
Was astonished as he spoke: 'I am here', he said,
'The man you are looking for, Trojan Aeneas,

Saved from the Libyan waves. O you who alone
Have pitied Troy's unspeakable eclipse,
Now offer the few of us the Greeks have left,
Exhausted by mischance on land and sea,
Destitute as we are, to share your city,
Your home: how can we thank you enough, Dido?
We cannot, nor could all the Dardanians
Now scattered far and wide over the world.
If there are powers which mark our acts of charity,
If there is justice anywhere or a mind
Conscious of rectitude, then may the gods
Reward you fitly. What race was so happy
As to bear fruit in you? What parents could
Produce so wonderful a progeny?
While rivers run into the sea, while shadows
Play upon mountains, while sky feeds the stars,
Your name will always have honour and praise,
Whatever lands may call me.' When he had spoken
Aeneas gave his right hand to Ilioneus,
His left hand to Serestus; after that
He greeted one by one his other friends,
Courageous Gyas and courageous Cloanthus.

   Queen Dido was struck first by the appearance,
Then by the plight of this distinguished man.
'O you that are the son of a goddess,
Who is pursuing you in these dangerous ways?'
She asked, 'And what force drives you here? Are you that
      Aeneas,
Trojan Anchises's son, whom bountiful Venus
Bore by the waters of Phrygian Simois?
I well remember Teucer coming to Sidon,
An exile from his native land, and seeking
A new kingdom with the help of Belus,
My father, who was putting Cyprus down;
It was worth the winning and it was he who won it.
From that time I have known of the fall of Troy,
And known your name and that of the Pelasgian kings.
Even among the enemy there was praise
For the Trojans and people boasted of Trojan ancestry.
So come in, gentlemen, under my roof:
I too have had misfortunes of this kind

And know what it is to be driven by events,
Till fate has now brought me to rest here.
Because I know, I have learned to give assistance.'
With these reflections, the queen led Aeneas
Into the palace, and ordered sacrifices
In the temples of the gods: she also sent
The companies which had been left on the shore
Twenty bullocks and a hundred bristling swine
As well as a hundred fat lambs with their mothers,
With wine enough to cheer.
Inside the palace everything was splendour;
In the central hall a banquet was prepared:
The whole place was hung with marvellous purple,
And on the tables massive silver plate
With, in gold, representations of the deeds
Of Dido's ancestors, a long series
With all their exploits from the very beginning.
    Aeneas (for what else could he have in mind
But a father's love?) sent Achates back to the ships
To bring Ascanius as quickly as might be
Within the walls; for it was in Ascanius
His fatherly care was centred. Besides he orders
Presents to be brought, salvaged from Ilium,
A cloak stiff with figures worked in gold
And a veil bordered with yellow acanthus,
Garments which Argive Helen had had on
When she set sail for Pergamus, intent
On her unlawful marriage; they were the gifts,
These sumptuous garments, of her mother Leda:
Besides the sceptre Ilione once used
– She was Priam's eldest daughter – was to be brought,
As well as a pearl necklace, and a coronet
With a double circle of gems and gold.
Achates set off quickly with these orders.
    But the Cytherean thinks up new devices:
Cupid shall change his looks and, so disguised,
Come in the place of sweet Ascanius,
Give Dido the presents and, as he does so,
Render her love-mad to the very marrow:
For Venus fears the house and its uncertainties,
She fears the forked tongues of the Tyrians;

The unrelenting Juno burns her up
So that night finds her restless and she speaks
To the winged Cupid: 'Son, in you alone
Lies my strength and ability to act.
Son, you who do not fear your father's thunderbolts,
I come to you tonight as a suppliant,
I need your powers. You know your brother Aeneas
Is tossed about the sea and thrown on shore
And all because of bitter Juno's hatred:
You have bemoaned this with me often enough.
And now Phoenician Dido has him fast
With flattering talk: I dread to think what turns
Her hospitality may take at Juno's whim;
The wheel of fortune must turn for the worse.
Therefore my plan is to deceive the queen
And circle her with flames so that no power
Can keep her from a fierce love for Aeneas.
How can you make this happen, I will tell you.
The princely boy, at his dear father's bidding
Is making ready for the Sidonian city
To which this boy who is so dear to me
Is to go bearing presents still remaining
From the deep sea and from the flames of Troy.
But I will take him in his deepest sleep
And hide him on the heights of Cythera
Or in the sacred precincts of Idalium,
So that he knows nothing of all these schemes
And cannot get mixed up in them at all.
You must pretend to be him for just one night,
You are a boy yourself, you can change your looks
So that when Dido takes you on her lap,
So pleased to see you, at the royal table
And as the wine goes round she cuddles you
And gives you special kisses, you breathe over her:
She will take fire and poison without knowing.'
Love does exactly as his mother tells him,
She is so dear to him, takes off his wings
And walks off laughing as if he were Iulus.
But Venus pours quiet over Ascanius
And when his limbs are still she picks him up
And carries him in her arms to Ida's groves,

High up the mountain, where sweet marjoram
Embraces him in flowers and scented shade.
   Already on his way as his mother had told him,
Cupid was carrying the royal gifts for the Tyrians,
Delighted to have Achates for a guide.
When he arrived, there was the queen already
In her place on a golden couch hung with tapestries;
The father, Aeneas, appears, and with him the Trojans
And all recline upon purple coverlets.
Men-servants pour water over their hands,
Serve bread from baskets and bring them smooth napkins.
Within, maid-servants – fifty of them – arrange
The dishes in long rows, and tend the great fire;
Another hundred girls and as many young men
Set the food on the tables and put out beakers;
The Tyrians too come crowding through the doors
And they are bidden to embroidered couches.
They admire Aeneas's presents, they admire Iulus,
The little god's fresh face and his feigned words,
The cloak and the veil with the yellow acanthus.
But most of all the lady, the unfortunate
Phoenician who is destined to die soon,
Cannot have enough of looking, and she burns,
Moved at once by the boy and by the gifts.
When he has hung round Aeneas's neck
And satisfied his pretended father's love,
He makes for the queen. She is all eyes, all heart.
Poor Dido, she clutches him and fondles him,
Not knowing what great god is on her knee.
And he, remembering his Acidalian mother,
Bit by bit makes her forget Sichaeus
And tries the effect of a present love
Upon a mind and heart long disaccustomed.
   When for the first time the feast fell quiet
The tables were cleared, they set out great bowls,
Filled them and decked them round about with flowers.
What a noise in the palace! voices rose
And rumbled round the halls; the lamps were lit,
Hung from the golden panels of the ceiling,
And flaming torches drove the night away.
The queen asked for a cup, all gold and jewels,

Her family had used time out of mind.
Silence was called for: 'Jupiter,' she prayed,
'From whom we have the laws of hospitality,
Make this day happy for the Tyrians
And for these who have come to us from Troy,
And may it be remembered by our children.
May Bacchus, who gives happiness, and Juno,
The kindly one, be present with us here;
And you, Tyrians, celebrate with good-will.'
She made a libation on the table;
Afterwards, touching the goblet with her lips,
Gave it to Britias and appealed to him.
He was not backward but took a great draught;
Wine sparkled and the gold shone back at him:
Then other nobles drank, and Iopas
With the flowing hair, took up his golden lyre
And made it twang, Atlas had been his master.
He sang the wandering moon and the sun's course,
Whence men and cattle came, whence rain and fire,
Arcturus and the watery Hyades,
The Great Plough and its twin the Little Bear;
Why winter suns so quickly seek the Ocean,
Or what it is makes winter nights so tardy.
The Tyrians applaud, the Trojans copy.
The ill-starred Dido spends the night in talk
And all the time drinks dangerously of love,
Asking about Priam, about Hector,
What sort of armour had Aurora's son,
How Diomed's horses were, how tall Achilles.
Then she says: 'Come, tell us, you are my guest,
All the Greeks' tricks and all your misadventures
From the beginning, all your wanderings too:
For seven summers now have carried you
A wanderer over every land and sea.'

# BOOK II

# BOOK II

# BOOK II

Then all were silent and they looked at him,
Their faces tense: our ancestor Aeneas,
From his high couch, began to tell his story:
'Unspeakable pain once more! That is what, queen,
Your command is for me: the Trojan power
And all that grievous kingdom brought to nothing
By Greeks – intolerable events I saw
And had a great part in. Could a Myrmidon
Or a Dolopian or any soldier
Of pitiless Ulysses, telling the story,
Keep back his tears? The dews of night are falling
And the stars too are on their way to sleep.
But if you so desire to know these things
And to hear briefly of Troy's final struggle,
Whatever grief it costs me to remember
I will begin.
          The leaders of the Greeks
Broken by war, rejected by the fates
After so many years, devised a horse,
A mountainous construction, workmanship
Pallas herself imagined. All of pine
The ribs were put together. The pretence was
It was a votive offering; that was the rumour.
In it they secretly shut up picked men
Until the dark inside, the huge cavern
Of the beast's womb was filled with armed soldiers.

  'From there you can see Tenedos, a famous island,
Rich in resources while Priam was king,
Now only a harbour and an unsafe one:
Thither they sailed and hid on the vacant shore.
We thought they had gone, the wind was set for Mycenae,
So the whole of Troy felt free of its old troubles;
The gates were flung open and out they trooped,

Going to look at the site of the Doric camp,
Empty now, and the shore the Greeks had left.
Here had been the quarters of the Dolopians,
Here cruel Achilles lay, here the fleet had been,
And here was where the pitched battles were fought.
Minerva's deadly present amazed some.
A virgin's gift! and then, how big that horse was!
Thymoetes first spoke up in favour of bringing
The animal inside the walls of Troy
And putting it in the citadel. Was he a traitor?
Or were our fates already drawn that way?
But Capys, with all men of better judgment,
Would have thrown any present from the Greeks,
Which must be treacherous or at least suspect,
Into the sea, or put a light to it;
He was for boring out the horse's guts
To see what hiding places might be in them.
The crowd's opinion swayed this way and that.
　'Ahead of all, with a crowd at his heels,
Laocoon ran down from the citadel,
Furious, and called out to the citizens:
"Heaven help you, are you mad? Do you imagine
The enemy has gone off in his ships?
Do you think any present from the Greeks
Could come without a trick in it? You know Ulysses.
Either there are Achaeans hidden here
Inside the wood, or this is some contraption
For use against our walls, to spy upon us
And come down on us from above, or else
Some other such deception. That horse, Trojans,
Is not the thing it seems. I fear the Greeks
Whatever presents they may bring to us."
As he spoke he discharged his heavy spear
With all his might into the horse's side,
The round work of the belly. There it stuck,
Shuddering, and in the womb-like space within
The hollow caverns echoed with a groan.
Had fate not been against us, had our minds
Not been so out of tune, Laocoon
Would have pushed home that iron tip and made

A carnage in those Argive hiding-places.
Troy would still stand, and Priam's citadel.
    'But meanwhile, see, here comes a band of shepherds,
Dardans, dragging a youth whose hands are tied
Behind his back, to bring him to the king
And shouting as they do so. He was a stranger
Who had deliberately set himself to be captured
So that he could open Troy up to the Greeks.
He was cool and ready for whatever came,
Whether the ruse came off or he was killed.
From all sides Trojan boys, to see what was happening,
Rushed up, surrounded him and jeered at him.
Now listen what they did, those tricky Greeks;
From this one instance you may know them all.
There he stood in the middle of the crowd,
Roughed up, unarmed, looking around him at
The Phrygian troops. "Well, this is it," he said,
"What country will accept me now, what sea?
What is there left for me, in my condition?
I have no place with the Greeks, and here the Trojans
Are hostile and are calling for my blood."
These words of his made people change their minds;
There was no more disturbance. So we asked him
What blood he came of and what news he brought,
What he expected from us, as a prisoner?
Then he began to speak with confidence.
    '"I will tell you the whole truth, king, come what may,"
He said, "I don't deny I am an Argive:
That is the first thing: if I am unlucky,
Ill luck does not extend to being a liar
In Sinon's case. You may have heard the name
Of Palamedes the son of Belus
– Well spoken of, indeed held in honour
Until, upon a false information,
The Pelasgians, with an ugly pack of lies,
Because he opposed the war, put him to death:
He was innocent and now he is dead they mourn him.
With him, since he was near to us in blood,
My father, who was poor, sent me to the wars
While I was still a boy and I came here.
While Palamedes remained safe and sound

And held his place among the princes' councils,
We too enjoyed some name and some respect.
But when, because of Ulysses' jealousy
(It is public knowledge) he passed from the world,
I was ruined and my life was in the shadows,
I mourned, and in secret I was furious
At what had happened to my innocent friend.
I was out of my mind and did not hold my tongue:
I swore that if ever I had the chance,
If ever I came back a winner from Argos,
I would have vengeance: with my words I aroused
The bitterest hatreds. That was my first slip,
Thereafter Ulysses would terrorise me:
Fresh charges all the time, and he sent out
His whisperers to sow doubts in the crowd,
Seeking ways to destroy me. He did not rest
Until, with Calchas as his agent. . . . No!
Why tell so foul a story to no purpose?
And if you think all Argives are the same,
Why hold you up? You will have heard enough,
You may as well exact the penalty.
It will suit the Ithacan, the sons of Atreus
Will no doubt set a good price on my head."
    'That made us desperate to ask further questions:
We did not know what tricks Greeks could get up to,
Nor half their crimes: so this profound actor,
Looking afraid, then took the story further:
"Often the Greeks wanted to retreat
And see the back of Troy; they were tired of war,
It had gone on too long. Would they had sailed!
But every time they were stopped by rough seas
Or the wind made them think better of going;
Especially was it so when that horse
That they had put together from maple trees
Stood there; the sky was full of clouds and thunder.
Anxiously we sent Eurypylus
To find out what the oracle of Phoebus
Would say to us, and he came back from the sanctuary
With these sad words: "A bloody sacrifice,
A virgin struck down, was what you offered
For fair winds, Greeks, when you first came to Troy:

An Argive life is what is wanted now
For your return." When people heard that
They were benumbed, then a cold shudder ran
Inside their bones. Whose fate was this to be?
Who was Apollo asking for? Then the Ithacan
Hauled the diviner Calchas through the crowd
And set him in the middle. What, he demands,
Do the gods want? Many then guessed that I
Was now the subject of a criminal plot;
They kept quiet but saw what was to come.
Calchas refused to speak for twice five days,
Unwilling to betray anyone
Or fix on one for death. But then at last,
So fierce became the Ithacan's demands,
He spoke as had been planned and picked me out
As destined for the altar. All consented:
What every man had dreaded for himself
Became acceptable for someone else.

   '"Then came the terrible day, with all the rites
Prepared for me, the salt grain, the headband.
I broke out, I admit it, to escape death
And all night long hid in the muddy lake
Among the reeds, hoping that they would sail.
Now I have no hope of ever seeing
My old country, my children, my aged father;
As like as not the Greeks will take revenge
For my flight on them, and expiate
My fault by massacring those innocents.
So I beseech you by the gods above,
By all the powers from whom no truth is hidden,
By any good faith there yet may be
Remaining among men, have pity on me
In my distress, have pity on a mind
Weighed down by trouble that is undeserved."

   'We gave him life for shedding all these tears
And even gave him pity beyond that.
First Priam said his hands should be untied
And all his bonds removed, then he addressed
The prisoner himself with friendly words:

   '"Whoever you are, you can forget the Greeks.
They have gone and now you are one of us.

But I have questions I would put to you,
Tell me the truth: why they did they build that horse
And make it so huge? Who started it?
What are they after? Some religious thing?
Or is it a military device?"
Sinon, as clever as a pack of monkeys,
And full of Greek tricks, held up his hands
– Only just out of hand-cuffs – to the stars:
"O you inviolable eternal fires,"
– He said that – "bear witness for me now,
You altars with the misdirected swords
I fled, you sacred headbands that I wore
As sacrificial victim, it is just
For me to break my Grecian vows;
It is just to hate the Greeks and publish
Whatever they may choose to hold secret;
I have no country now to hold me back.
Only stand by your promises, O Troy,
And you will be secure if what I tell you
Is true, and if I show my gratitude.
  ' "All the hopes of the Greeks have always rested
On Pallas ever since the war began.
But from the time the sacrilegious Diomed
With that father of mischief Ulysses
Sneaked in to carry the Palladium off,
The auspicious image from the sacred temple,
When they had killed the guards of the citadel
And seized upon the sacred effigy
And even dared to touch with bloody hands
The virgin headband of the goddess, then,
From that time on, Greek hopes began to ebb,
They ran away like water, all their strength
Was gone, the goddess was with us no more!
And she gave signs to show her clear aversion.
No sooner was the image in our camp
Than dancing flames were burning in its eyes
As if in fury; over the limbs salt sweat
Poured, and three times – tall story though it seems –
The figure shook, the shield and spear trembled.
Upon that Calchas prophesied; retreat
Across the sea was what the goddess wanted;

Pergamus could not fall to Argive weapons
Unless they once more sought omens in Argos
And so brought back the power they had had
When their curved ships had brought them to this shore.
Now that the wind is right for Mycenae
And they are on their way to their own country
It is to get arms and the help of gods;
They will be back across the sea, to spring
One more surprise. So Calchas reads the omens.
This figure of a horse they have constructed
On his advice, because of the Palladium
And offence to the deity: an expiation
And one much needed. They made the figure huge,
Calchas said how it should be, jointed timbers
That would stretch to the sky, so that no man
Could get it through the gates and within the walls
Where it would give the people the protection
Of the old religion. For if your hand should violate
This offering to Minerva, a great destruction
(May the gods turn the omen against Calchas!)
Would fall on Priam's empire and the Phrygians;
But if the horse should penetrate the city
With a helping hand from you, Asia would live
To see its soldiers under Pelops' walls:
What a fate for our children's children then!"
  'By such devices artful, perjured Sinon
Made us believe him, we were taken by his snares,
His tears which were play-acting, we whom neither
Tydeus's son nor the Larissan Achilles,
Nor ten years nor a thousand ships could tame.
  'But then came something much more terrible,
Poor devils that we were, and startled us.
Laocoon, chosen by lot as Neptune's priest,
Was sacrificing at the appointed altars
A huge bull, when suddenly, from Tenedos,
Across the tranquil water came a pair
(The memory chills me like the event itself)
Of serpents, their immense coils on the sea
And making for the shore, their heads held high
With blood-red crests standing out of the waves;
The rest of them was twisting on the surface,

This way and that and at enormous length;
You could hear them thrashing up the salt spray.
Soon they were on dry land, their eyes blazed,
Suffused with blood and fire, their hissing mouths
Licked by their darting tongues. We were white-faced
And scattered. They, in military formation,
Went for Laocoon; and they first surrounded
The little bodies of his sons, one each,
Embracing them with bites and feeding on them;
Then it was his turn, as he ran to save them
With weapons in his hand; they seized upon him
And tied him in their coils:
Now twice round the middle, twice round the neck
With their scaly length, and looking down on him
With heads and necks held far above his height.
He with his hands tried to wrench loose the knots,
His headband black with poison and with gore
And threw up terrifying shouts to heaven,
Sounding like a bull running away from the altar
Not properly felled and shaking the axe from his neck.
But the two serpents, dragons you might say,
Glided away up to the sanctuary
And disappeared under the goddess's feet.
    'Then indeed into all our fluttering hearts
There comes another terror: Laocoon,
Everyone says, deserved what he got;
He violated that sacred tree
When he threw his spear at the horse's flanks.
The image must be put where it belongs,
They shout, the goddess must be paid with prayers.
We cut through the city walls and throw them open.
Everyone gets to work and they put rollers
Under the horse and tug at its neck with ropes.
Up goes the fatal engine, through the walls,
Full of arms as it is. Around, the boys
And the unmarried girls sing hymns, they cannot
Keep their hands off the ropes, they are so pleased.
Up she comes, there she is with all her menace
Inside the city. So much for our country.
Home of the gods, Ilium, Dardan walls
Famous in war! The horse stuck four times

At the very gates, and four times from within
There was a sound of weapons shaken up:
We press on all the same without a thought,
Blind and mad, and set the monster firm
Inside our consecrated citadel.
And then Cassandra starts to prophesy,
But no word that she spoke was ever credited
By Teucrians: a god saw to that.
And we, whose last day this was to be,
Poor wretches, going up and down the town
Set festal boughs in the gods' sanctuaries.
    'Meanwhile the heavens move round and from the Ocean
Rushes the night, covering with great shadows
The earth, the sky, the Myrmidons' treachery.
Stretched out all over the city are the Trojans,
They are silent now, sleep holds their weary limbs.
And now the Argive host, the ships in line,
Was sailing in from Tenedos, coming to shore
Under the friendly silence of the moon,
When the royal galley signals with a light
And Sinon, favoured by an unjust fate,
Undoes the door of pine-wood secretly
Where the Greeks crouch inside. The opened horse
Gives them back to the outer air. Well pleased
They issue forth, Thessandrus, Sthenelus,
Both captains, and the merciless Ulysses;
A rope is lowered and they all slide down,
With Thoas, Acamas, Neoptolemus
The sons of Peleus, and Machaon,
With Menelaus and with Epeus
Who was the rascal who designed the horse.
They creep into the city, which is buried
In wine and sleep, and fall upon the sentries,
Then open wide the gates, let in their friends:
The plot has worked, the forces have joined up.
    'It was the time when the first quiet comes
To suffering mortals and creeps over them
Pleasurably, as gods' gift. In sleep I saw
Hector before my eyes, profoundly mournful
And shedding floods of tears. At the chariot's tail
When he was dragged round Troy he must have looked

Like that, he was black with blood and dust
And his feet swollen, eaten by the leathers
In which they were tied. How pitiful he looked!
How he was changed indeed from that Hector
Who came back loaded with Achilles' spoils,
Or when he set the Greek ships alight!
His beard was stiff, his hair clotted with blood,
He bore those many wounds he had sustained
Around his city's walls. I saw myself
Weeping and blurting out these mournful words:
"O light of all Dardania, surest hope
Of all the Teucrians, why have you been so long?
From what shores do you come to us now, Hector,
Whom we have so long looked for? So many deaths
There have been, of your own people, so many
Efforts made by your men and by your city,
Now that we see you we are exhausted.
What is it has caused such disfigurement
To what was an untroubled countenance?
Why do I see these wounds?" He did not answer
And took no notice of my empty questions
But, sighing from the bottom of his heart
A long "Oh!" said: "Escape while still you can,
Goddess-born. Take yourself out of the flames.
The enemy are now inside the walls
And Troy is falling from her pinnacle.
Enough has been done for your country
And for Priam: if Pergamus could have been saved
By any man's right hand, it would by mine.
Troy commits to you now her holy things,
Her homely gods: take them to share your fortunes,
Seek walls for them, the great walls you will build
When from long travel you come in from the sea."
And then with his own hands he brought the headbands
Out of the inmost shrine, the great Vesta,
And finally the eternal fire itself
    'Meanwhile the city is in agony
And more and more, although my father's house
Lay far back, covered by a screen of trees,
The noise grew more distinct, the horror greater.
It was the sound of arms. My sleep fell from me;

I climbed up to the highest bit of roof
And stopped and strained my ears. It is as if
A storm wind is blowing through the corn,
Driving a fire; or else a mountain torrent
Is falling on the fields and flattening
The crops, the ploughland, all the quiet work
The oxen have performed, dragging down forests,
While up above, upon a rock, a shepherd,
Not knowing what is happening, scarcely credits
The noise he hears. Suddenly all is plain:
The Greeks have tricked us and this is their treason.
Already Deiphobus's great house
Is nothing but a ruin with huge flames
Towering above it; now Ucalegon
His neighbour is on fire; the straits of Sigeum
Are lit up far and wide. There are men shouting
And trumpets blare. Frantic, I seize my weapons
Although the time for weapons has gone by,
But my mind burns to get a troop together
Of fighting men, and with them to the citadel,
Comrades-in-arms: for I was mad and anger
Carried my mind away. I thought only:
The best thing I can do is to die fighting.
    'But here comes Panthus who has slipped away
From the Greek spears, Panthus the son of Othrys;
He is the priest of Phoebus from the citadel
And in one hand he bears the holy things
And the defeated gods, while with the other
He pulls his little grandson. He is running
And so arrives demented at my door.
"How are things up there, Panthus? What place is there
For us to make a stand?" I had hardly spoken
When with a groan he answers me like this:
"The last day, the inescapable hour
Has come for all Dardania. This is the end:
No more Trojans, no more Ilium,
The glory of the Teucrians is no more;
The lion Jupiter bears all away
To Argos; Greeks reign in the burning city.
Up there the horse stands, right at the centre,
Pouring out armed men; Sinon, triumphant

Is setting fire to everything, and laughing.
Others are by the gates, which are wide open,
As many thousands as ever came from Greece;
Some block the narrow places with their spears;
A whole array of glittering points of steel
Stands by, ready to kill; our men at the gates
Are hardly in the battle and they fight blind."
　'By these words spoken by the son of Othrys
And by the inspiration of the gods
I am swept away into the flames and fighting
Whither the Furies call me and the tumult
And where the shouting rises to the sky.
Some comrades join us, Ripheus, Epytus
– A first-class fighter – they spring up in the moonlight,
Hyspanis, Dymas, and are at my side,
The young man Coroebus, son of Mygdon:
It happened that at that time he had come
To Troy with a mad passion for Cassandra,
Helping the family, Priam and the Phrygians,
Poor devil, not to listen to his sweetheart's warnings!
When I saw these men dared to face the battle
I spoke to them: "Lads, it is all for nothing,
This courage, but if you are sure your last wish
Is to follow one who still dares to go on,
You see how things are. They have left you now,
All those gods on whom the empire rested,
Gone from their shrines and altars: what you are serving
Is a burning city. Let us die in it
And charge into the middle with our arms.
The one hope the defeated have is to fight
And hope for nothing." That made the boys mad.
Then they were like wolves after their prey,
Plunging into the mist blindly, driven
By ignominious hunger and their cubs
Waiting with empty jaws: we waded through
Weapons and enemies to certain death,
Taking the road straight to the city centre;
The black night circles us with hollow darkness.
How can one tell the story of that night,
Its devastation and its many deaths
Or find tears equal to our agony?

The ancient city falls, who was queen so long
And on her streets the dead lie everywhere,
There are dead in all the houses, on the steps
Of all the shrines and temples. Not only Teucrians
It is who have paid the penalty of their blood;
Here and there the defeated have found courage
And Greeks have fallen to them. Everywhere
There is grief, there is fear, and death in many shapes.

'The first Greek we encounter, Androgeos,
With a large company, thinks we are friends
And he addresses us accordingly:
"Hurry, you men, why have you been so long
You idle lot? Your mates are there already
Burning and looting upon Pergamus.
Have you only just got here from the ships?"
As he spoke, suddenly – for the response
Was hardly re-assuring – he perceived
That he had stumbled on the enemy.
With a start he checked his step and checked his voice.
He was like a man who has stepped on a snake
He failed to see among the undergrowth
And jerks back as it raises up its head
Swollen, angry and blue; so Androgeos
Drew back, his face showing what he felt.
We charge and pour around them on all sides;
They do not know the ground and there is panic.
We cut them down. Our first try has been lucky.
Coroebus was wild with the success
Yet he had courage too. "Come on," he said,
"Fortune has shown a way we can be safe,
Let's follow her suggestion; change our shields
For Greek shields and put on the Greek equipment.
An ounce of trickery's worth a pound of courage.
They will supply the weapons." As he spoke
He took the crested helmet of Androgeos
And put it on, and then he took his shield
With the device on it; the Argive sword
He fitted at his side. Then Ripheus
Follows suit, Dymas too and all the lads
Joke as they do the same: so everyone
Equips himself with his new-taken spoil.

So we move on and mingle with the Greeks,
Protected by gods other than our own;
Many we meet in that unseeing night
And exchange blows with; many are the Greeks
Who are despatched to Orcus with Greek swords.
Some scatter to the ships or to the shore
Where they can see who's who, and some of them
Like cowards climb back into the great horse
And hide inside the belly where it's safe.
   'No good to trust the gods against their will!
See there Cassandra, Priam's virgin daughter
With streaming hair dragged from Minerva's shrine,
Turning her blazing eyes to heaven in vain
– Her eyes, because she cannot move her hands,
Those delicate wrists are fastened with a chain.
Coroebus was beside himself at the sight
And threw himself in where he was bound to die.
All of us followed him and on we went,
A walking wall of swords. Here first a shower
Of weapons from our own side fell upon us,
Thrown from the temple roof, a wretched death,
The price of our disguise in Grecian crests.
And then the Greeks let out a furious groan
At having lost their captive, close their ranks
And fall upon us, Ajax at his fiercest,
Atreus' two sons, the whole Dolopian army;
As winds come together in a hurricane,
The west wind and the south, the east wind
Horsed on the dawn; while forests bellow out
And Nereus, all in foam, storms with his trident
And stirs up all the seas to their very depths.
Those too whom, in the darkness of the night
We had dispersed, tricking them in the shadows,
And driven here and there over the city
Appear once more; they are the first to recognise
Our shields and see our weapons are a lie
And to detect our accents are not Greek.
We are overwhelmed by numbers in a flash;
First Coroebus, at Peneleus' hand,
Falls at the altar of the strong-armed goddess;
Ripheus is down too, the justest Trojan,

The man who cared most for what is right
(Though to the gods it seemed otherwise);
There died also Hypanis and Dymas,
Speared by their friends; and you, Panthus, protected
Neither by virtue nor your sacred office.
Ashes of Ilium, last flame of my race,
I call on you to witness that I fought
As a man should, not shrinking from Greek weapons,
And so earned my own death, had the fates willed it.
When I was snatched away, with Iphitus
And Pelias – Iphitus bowed with years,
Pelias lamed by a blow from Ulysses –
It was by shouts coming from Priam's palace.
    'Here indeed the fighting was horrendous,
As if the rest of the slaughter amounted to nothing
And people were not dying all over the town;
Here we see Mars become ungovernable;
Greeks storming the roof-tops, and below
The threshold thick with men under their shields.
There are ladders against the walls, on the rungs
Men are struggling even by the doorways,
Holding their shields against the flying darts
With their left hands while with their right they clutch
Or fumble for the parapet. The Trojans
Opposing them tear down roof-tops and pinnacles;
Anything serves as at the point of death
They struggle to defend themselves; gilt rafters
Their fathers were so proud of, are hurled down
While some, below, stand by the doors in squads
With drawn swords; a new determination
Makes itself felt in us to help the palace,
To relieve the defenders and to bring
A fresh access of strength to the defeated.
    'There was a secret door into a passage
Connecting all the parts of Priam's palace,
A recessed entrance through which, in his day,
Andromache, poor woman, often walked
Privately to her father-in-law's people,
Leading the young Astyanax by the hand.
By this way I managed to reach the roof
From which the wretched Teucrians were throwing

Whatever came to hand, and all was useless.
There was a tower built up from the roof
Right at the edge and stretching to the stars,
An observation post from which all Troy
Could be observed, as well as the Greek ships
And all the Achaean camp: this we attacked
With axes and with crow-bars round the edge
Where joints holding the structure could be loosened,
And so ripped it from its old supports
And pushed it over; it fell a toppling ruin
With a loud rumble and cut through the lines
Of Greeks, but more came up, and more stones
Showered on them, with spears and arrows of all kinds.

'There by the doorway of the entrance-hall
Stands Pyrrhus, insolent in gleaming bronze;
He might have been a snake out in the light,
Swollen with poisonous herbs that it had eaten
After a cold winter underground,
Now, having shed its skin, shining with youth,
Twisting its slippery coils, raising its head
High in the sun, its three-forked tongue darting.
With Pyrrhus comes the giant Periphas,
Automedon who drove Achilles' horses
And was his armour-bearer, all the youth
Of Scyros in attendance: these close in
Upon the building and throw torches up
To fire the roof, while Pyrrhus leads the way,
Seizes a battle-axe and smashes down
The door, ripping the bronze fitments apart;
The hinges give, then he is through the wood
And there is a gaping window where he struck.
The house is wide open, the long halls
Lie there before him, and the inner chambers
Of Priam and the ancient kings of Troy
See armed men standing poised upon the threshold.

'Inside the house is wailing and disorder;
From the back comes the sound of women mourning,
The halls ring, it strikes the golden stars.
Then through the vast buildings, up and down,
Women begin to circulate in terror,
Putting their arms round pillars, kissing them.

With his father's energy Pyrrhus pushes on:
Neither barriers nor guards can block his way.
Doors come down before the battering rams
And the supporting posts fly from their hinges.
A way through has been found, the Greeks break in,
Do their first killing and fill the place with soldiers.
They are more furious than a raging river
Which breaks its banks and sweeps away the dykes,
Flooding the fields and all the level pasture
And dragging byres and cattle in its trail.
I saw with my own eyes Neoptolemus
Out of his mind with slaughter, with the sons
Of Atreus as they came past the entrance;
I saw Hecuba with her hundred daughters
And Priam as his blood defiled the altars
Where he himself had consecrated fires,
The fifty bridal chambers, with their promise
Of such a crop of grandsons, and their pillars
Decked with proud trophies in barbaric gold
Come crashing down. There were Greeks everywhere
And everywhere they were not was on fire.

  'Perhaps you want to know how Priam died.
When he saw that the city had been taken,
The palace gates torn off, the enemy
Right in the central suite of his apartments,
Old as he was he put his armour on,
The first time for years, buckled his sword,
Useless although it was, and off he went
Into the thick of the enemy, to die.
In the middle court of the palace was an altar,
A huge one, with an old laurel near-by
Which leaned against it and you might say embraced
The gods of his house in its shadow.
Here Hecuba and her daughters were huddled;
Helpless like doves blown in by a storm,
They sat there with their arms around the images,
When the queen saw Priam had taken up
The arms that he had used as a young man
She said: "Are you out of your mind, husband,
To put on those weapons, in your condition?
Where are you off to now? The situation

Does not call for assistance of that sort
Nor for protection of that kind at all;
Not even if my Hector were here now.
Come here with us at last; these altars will
Save all of us, or we shall die together."
And so she took the old man to herself
And sat him down in a place beside the altar.

'Then came Polites, a son of Priam's,
Escaping from the murderous hand of Pyrrhus
Through a shower of spears, a crowd of enemies
Along the colonnades, across the courtyards
Which were abandoned now. He was wounded.
Pyrrhus comes after and now catches him,
Holds him and presses on him with his spear.
As Polites appears before his parents
Before their eyes there he falls to the ground
And pours his life out in a river of blood.
Then Priam, although in the midst of death,
Cannot hold back his anger or his words:
"May the gods, if there are any in heaven
Who take notice of such acts as yours,
Your criminality and contempt of them,
Reward you in the manner you deserve,
You who in my presence force me to look
Upon my own son's death, and desecrate
A father's countenance with sight of murder.
It was not thus that the great Achilles,
Whose son you lyingly say that you are,
Dealt with his enemy Priam; he was a man
Who treated honourably with a suppliant
And gave back the lifeless body of Hector
For burial and allowed me safe return."
Those were the words he spoke, the old man,
And then he threw his spear, without effect,
Feebly, it bounced off the bronze with a 'ping'
And hung harmlessly from the edge of the shield.
Pyrrhus addressed him: "Very well, you shall take
A message to my father, Peleus' son;
Tell him of my unfortunate behaviour:
Say Neoptolemus is degenerate.
Now die!" As he spoke he was dragging Priam,

Slithering in his son's blood, up to the altar.
He wound the old man's hair round his left hand
And with his right hand flashed his sword
And buried it deep in the victim's side.
That was the end of Priam's destinies;
So fate would have it, that he departed
Seeing Troy burnt and Pergamus in ruins,
He who had proudly ruled people and lands,
The lord of Asia. He lies upon the shore,
A huge trunk, shoulders without a head,
He is a body now without a name.
    'The cruelty and horror of it all
Came home to me then for the first time.
I was benumbed; my father's image then
Rose up before me as I saw the king,
Of like age with him, dying of his wound;
Creusa rose before me, left alone;
I thought what might befall the little Iulus.
I looked round to see what company
Was still behind me. All had deserted.
Exhausted, they had either jumped down
Or yielded themselves wounded to the flames.
    'So I was on my own there when I saw
Close by the entrance to the shrine of Vesta,
Silent, and shrinking in obscurity,
Helen the daughter of Tyndareus;
The clear fire showed her up as I wandered
Here and there and cast my eyes about me.
She, apprehending danger from the Trojans
Who had just seen their citadel swept away,
As well as the vengeance of the Greeks,
Of the husband she had left, Helen the Fury
Alike to Troy and to her own country
Had hidden her hated self beside the altars.
Fire blazed in my heart; anger emerged.
I would avenge the fall of my country
With a penalty criminal like the crime.
"Shall this woman," I said, "see Sparta again
And Mycenae her native country
Without a hair of her head being hurt?
Shall she go home a queen in triumph, see

Husband, home, parents, children, with a crowd
Of Trojan men and women to attend her?
Now that Priam has fallen by the sword,
Troy been burnt to the ground? The Trojan shore
So often made to sweat with Trojan blood?
Not so. For though there is no reputation
In vengeance on a woman, and no victory,
Yet I shall have some praise for the extinction
Of a great wrong and one that cries for justice.
It will be joy to fill my burning heart
With vengeance and make satisfaction for
The ashes of so many of my kin."
　'Such words I spoke, for I was swept away,
I was in a frenzy, when before my eyes,
More clearly than I had ever seen her before
And shining through the darkness in pure light,
Was my dear mother, every inch a goddess,
Looking as she appeared to the gods.
She took me by the hand and held me still
And spoke these words from the rose of her lips:
"Son, what resentment, great as it may be,
Can drive you to uncontrolled anger?
Have you gone mad? Have you forgotten us?
Should you not think first about your father,
Anchises, at his age, look where you left him?
See if your wife Creusa is still alive,
And the boy, Ascanius? For the Grecian troops
Are wandering everywhere. Had I done nothing
The flames would have carried them off by now
And enemy swords would have had their blood.
It is not the detested face of Helen
Nor is it Paris who is to blame.
It is the gods' lack of mercy, the gods',
Has brought down all this splendour and brought Troy down.
Look now – for I will whip away the cloud
Which, drawn before your eyes like a blanket,
Impedes mortal sight and bathes you in mist;
Have no fear, do as your mother tells you,
You should not refuse to follow her advice –
Here, where you see huge buildings dismembered,
Stones heaved out from among other stones,

Billowing smoke and dust. Neptune is here,
Shaking the walls and foundations, waving his trident
And ripping the whole city from its seat.
Here Juno who is cruellest of them all,
Wearing her sword, stands at the Scaean gate
And furiously calls her allies from the ships.
Now look the other way: Tritonian Pallas
Sits at the summit of the citadel,
Ablaze with storm and with the Gorgon's head.
The Father of the Gods gives the Greeks strength
And courage to go with it, he himself
Urges the gods to fight against the Dardans.
Escape now quickly and have done with it.
I will not leave you till I see you safe
Before your father's house." When she had spoken
She hid herself where night was at its darkest.
Terrible apparitions were before me,
Emanations of gods hostile to Troy.

    'All Ilium seemed to settle in the flames;
The Troy that Neptune built was overturned
As when upon the mountain-tops the woodmen
Try, first one, then another, to bring down
An ancient ash-tree dented by their axes;
The tree looks threateningly and seems to wobble,
Shaking its foliage as it nods its head,
Then at last beaten, gives a final groan
And down it comes and crashes down the slope.
I went down, guided by my divine mother
And made my way among the flames and swords.
The weapons let me go, the flames leapt back.

    'When I arrived before my father's door,
The ancient house, my first thought was for him,
To take him off into the mountains. No,
He would not, Troy was down, he would not live
To suffer exile. "You," he said, "whose blood
Has still no taint of age, who are still solid
And have your strength, it is for you to escape.
If the gods had wanted me to go on living
They would have spared this house. It is enough
Once in a life-time to see one's city fall
And I have survived the capture of Troy once.

So leave my body lying as it is
And say farewell and go, I shall find death
By my own hand: the enemy will have pity
And be content with spoil. Never mind burial.
I have held back the years long enough,
Unserviceable and detested by the gods
Since the time when the Father of gods and men
Breathed on me with the wind of his thunder
And struck at my body with his fire."
    'He talked on in this way. He was stubborn.
We were in tears – my wife Creusa, the boy
Ascanius and all the household servants,
Begging my father not to upset everything
Or to add his weight in the scale against us.
He stuck to what he'd said and would not budge.
My thoughts turned once more towards my weapons;
I longed for death, so wretched was I then.
For what else was there, what could the future hold?
"Father, did you expect me to go away
And leave you here? It is a monstrous thing
To hear from the lips of any father.
If the gods please that nothing shall be left
Of this great city, if your mind is set
On you and yours perishing with Troy,
So be it, the gates of death are open wide;
It won't be long before Pyrrhus is here,
Drenched in the blood of Priam, Pyrrhus the butcher
Who kills the son before the father's eyes
And then kills the father at the altars.
Was it for this, gentle mother, that you brought me
Safely past all those weapons and those fires
So that I could observe with my own eyes
The enemy in the inmost rooms of the house
And see Ascanius, my father and Creusa
Slaughtered and lying in each other's blood?
To arms then, men, to arms! The last light calls
Those who have been defeated. The Greeks can have me.
Only let me see battle once again;
Never today will we die unavenged."
    'I buckled on my sword and took my shield,
Passing my left fore-arm through the strap,

And so I made my way out of the house.
But there on the threshold was my wife;
She lay flat on the ground and embraced my feet,
Then held the little Iülus up to his father:
'If you are going out to die, take us
Wherever you may go; but if you hope
To achieve anything by taking arms,
You who have seen fighting, protect this house,
That is the first thing. To whom is young Iülus,
To whom is your father, to whom am I,
Who once was called your wife, to be abandoned?"
   'So she cried out and filled the house with wailing
When suddenly a prodigy appeared:
Between the hands and eyes of grieving parents
A numble tongue of flame was shedding light
Over the head of Iulus; harmless to the touch
It licked his soft hair and played round his forehead.
We were alarmed and tried to get the flame
Out of his hair and poured water on it,
Trying to extinguish the holy fire.
But Anchises, my father, joyfully
Raised his eyes to heaven, stretched out his arms
And prayed thus: "Omnipotent Jupiter,
If you are moved by any prayers at all,
Look on us now, and this is all we ask:
If we have any merit in your eyes,
Give us a sign, Father, confirm this omen."
   'The aged man had hardly finished when
Suddenly there came thunder from the left
And from the heavens, sliding through the darkness,
Shot a star with a tail, bringing great light.
We saw it glide over the roof of the palace
And bury itself in the woods of Ida,
Marking its course by a brilliant track;
It left a long bright furrow, and around,
Far and wide there was a sulphurous smoke.
At last my father gave way; he stood up,
Acknowledging the gods, and adored the star.
"Now indeed there is no more holding back;
I follow, where you lead, there am I.
Gods of our fathers, save my family,

Preserve my grandson. This omen comes from you
And Troy rests in your sacred power.
I yield, my son, and I will come with you."
   'When he had spoken, all throughout the city
The roaring of the fire was heard more clearly,
The waves of heat rolled ever closer to us.
"Now come, dear father, mount upon my back,
Here are my shoulders, they will not let you down.
Whatever may befall, it will be the same danger
For both of us, and one way out of this.
Let little Iulus come with me, my wife
Follow the way we go, but at a distance.
You of the household, listen to what I say.
As you go out of the city there is a tump
With an old temple of Ceres, long deserted
And nearby there is an ancient cypress,
Our fathers held it sacred and preserved it;
We will go by different routes and join up there.
You, father, hold the holy things in your hand,
The household gods: and take them up now;
For me, coming fresh from war and slaughter,
It would be sin to handle them until
I had washed myself in a running stream."
So speaking, I pulled over neck and shoulders
A tawny lion's skin and then bent down
To take my burden; and the little Iulus
Put his hand in mine, following his father
But hardly keeping up. My wife came next.
We made our way through the darkest places
And I, whom no weapons and no Greeks
However massed against me, discomposed,
Now found that every breath of air was frightening,
Each sound made me start, so anxious was I
Fearing for my companion and my load.
   'Now I was near the gates and felt my journey
Was almost over, when suddenly a sound
Of what seemed to be footsteps struck my ears
And father, looking out into the gloom,
Called out: "Son, hurry, son, they are coming,
I can see light from shields and glittering bronze."
Then in I know not what urge to get on

Some evil influence confused my mind;
It was as if I had none. While I followed
The byways and had left the main road,
Alas, something happened to Creusa.
Did she stop? Did she get lost? Was she so weary
That she collapsed on the way? I never knew;
All I know is, she was never seen again,
And I did not look back or think of her
Until we had arrived at Ceres' temple.
Here they were all assembled, except her;
She had lost everyone, her son, her husband.
Whom did I not accuse, what man, what god?
I was demented. In all the ruin of Troy
I had seen nothing so cruel as that.
Ascanius, Anchises my father, the household gods
I recommended to the company
And left them all in the bend of a valley;
Then I went back to the town, armed once more.
I was determined to retrace my steps
All over Troy, to risk my life again.
First I made for the walls and the darkened gate
By which I had come out, and followed the track
As before; I went up and down with a torch
Through the night, and everywhere there was menace,
The very silences were terrifying.
I went back home, perhaps she had gone back:
The Greeks had stormed in and were everywhere.
All is lost, devouring fire is blowing
About the roof-top; the flames go higher still,
The hot blasts are dancing in the wind.
I go on, Priam's palace and the citadel
Come into view, and in the empty courts,
Under the protection of Juno herself
Are Phoenix and the terrible Ulysses,
Appointed to keep an eye on the plunder.
Here from all parts of Troy had been collected
All her treasures torn from burning temples,
The gods' tables, bowls of solid gold,
And stolen garments. Marshalled round about
Are children and their mothers, a great number.
I ventured to shout out through the darkness;

I filled the streets with my redoubled cries;
In my grief I called Creusa's name
Again and again but all for nothing.
While I was searching, distraught as I was,
The houses of the city, suddenly
The pitiful image of Creusa,
Her ghost indeed, appeared before my eyes,
In form larger than I had known her.
I was thunderstruck, my hair stood on end,
My voice stuck in my throat. She spoke to me
Some words which mitigated my distress:
"What is the use of this extravagant grief,
Sweet husband? For these things do not happen
Without the gods will them; the divine order
Is that you do not take Creusa with you,
Nor will the ruler of Olympus allow it.
For you there is to be a long exile
And there are vast oceans to be ploughed;
Then you will come to the Hesperian land
Where among miles of rich and well-worked fields
The gentle current of the Tiber flows.
There happy times await you, a new kingdom,
A royal bride. Do not weep for Creusa.
For I shall never see the proud houses
Myrmidons or Dolopians inhabit,
Nor go as a slave to any Greek woman,
I who am Trojan, wife to the son of Venus;
The Great Mother guards me upon these shores.
So now farewell: keep well your child I had."
When she had said this she deserted me,
I weeping and with much to say to her.
She vanished in thin air; three times I tried
To put my loving arms about her neck,
Three times her clasped figure escaped my hands
And left them empty. She was like light wind
Or like a dream whose flight cannot be held.
So, the night gone, I saw my friends again.
    'What did I find? A huge company,
A stream of new comrades had flowed in,
The number was remarkable, a crowd
Of mothers, husbands, youths, wretched they looked,

All gathered there for exile. From all quarters
They came, determined and with bits of baggage,
Ready to follow me wherever I chose
To any distant land across the sea.
Already the morning star was climbing up
Over the top of Ida, bringing the light.
It could be seen that the Greeks held the gates.
There was no hope of help. I gave up
And, lifting up my father, took to the mountains.'

# BOOK III

# BOOK III

'When, as it pleased the gods, the Asian power
Had been destroyed, proud Ilium had fallen,
All Neptune's Troy lay smoking on the ground,
Then we were driven by their auguries
To exile where we might find empty lands.
We built a fleet, just there by Antandros,
Under the Phrygian shadow of Mount Ida,
Not knowing where we were fated to go
Or where it was appointed we should rest.
We called our men together. Summer came;
No sooner had it come than my father,
Anchises, ordered us to chance our sails:
Weeping, I left the shores of my country,
The harbours and the plains where Troy had been.
I was an exile as I put to sea
With all our company and with my son
And all the great gods of our household.

'Far away from Troy there is a land
That Mars has made his own, a flat stretch
The Thracians cultivated; fierce Lycurgus
Once ruled there and had been friendly to Troy
And had had household gods allied to ours
When our luck was in. Thither I went
And where the shore curves set my first city
– An ill-fated enterprise, as it turned out –
And called it Aeneadae, from my name.

'Intent upon the rites due to my mother,
The daughter of Dione, and to the gods
Favourable to the work I had begun,
I was on the shore, sacrificing a bull,
A white one, to the high king of heaven.
Nearby there was a hillock and on top
A copse of dogwood and myrtle bristling with shafts

Such as might serve for spears. I went up
And tried to pull the green growth from the ground
To deck the altar with foliage.
What I then saw is something hard to speak of,
A portent that was frightening:
From the first tree whose roots were torn up
Trickled dark drops of blood, which fell about
And stained the earth around loathsomely.
My limbs shook with horror and were like ice;
Indeed my veins began to freeze with fear.
Again I tried, tugging a pliant shoot
From another tree, to find what caused the trouble:
There must be something there. And once again
Dark blood came, from the bark of the second tree.
Turning over many things in my mind
I said a prayer to the country nymphs
And to old Gradivus, the deity
Of all those Getic fields; be you, I said,
But only favourable and avert the omen.
I set to work once more, pressing my knees
Against the sandy soil with greater effort
And tried to pull a third bunch of shoots,
Uncertain whether to use words or be silent.
From deep within the mound there came a groan,
Pitiful to hear, a voice which spoke thus:
"Why do you tear my wretched corpse to pieces,
Aeneas? Rather spare a buried man
And spare your holy hands from an offence.
For I am Trojan-born and not a stranger,
Nor does my blood come from a foreign stock.
Ah, you must get away from these cruel lands
And get away from this devouring shore.
For I am Polydorus. Here I lie,
Pierced by an iron crop of javelins
And so the shafts grow through me, sharp as ever."
At that I was astonished and oppressed
By my uncertainties, I felt my hair
Standing on end, my voice stuck in my throat.
    'This Polydorus, with a pot of gold,
Had been sent secretly by the luckless Priam
To be reared up by the Thracian king

When he already felt uncertainty
About the Trojan army and could see
The city was invested on all sides.
The Thracian, once Troy's power had been destroyed
And fortune had abandoned us, took up
With Agamemnon and the winning side
And broke all faith with us: then Polydorus
Was cut down and his pot of gold was seized.
To what does it not drive human hearts,
That damned hunger for gold! When I recovered
My equanimity, I put the matter
To some few of the leaders of the people,
Particularly my father, telling them
About the portent, asking their advice.
They all were of one mind: we had to go,
The land was criminal and we should leave
The place where hospitality was profaned
And trust our fleet once more to the winds.
So we began the rites for Polydorus,
Raising a huge barrow for a tomb;
Altars to the spirits of the dead
Were set up and decked with dark hangings
For mourning, and with boughs of black cypress,
While all around the Trojan women stood
With their hair loose as the custom was.
We offered bowls of foaming milk and cups
Of consecrated blood; so, put to rest
The spirit in the tomb and said farewell.
As soon as we can trust the sea, the winds
Have given a calm surface, a cracking breeze
But gentle, calls us out to the horizon,
The lads bring down the ships and crowd the shore.
We put out from the port and soon the land
And the last trace of cities are behind us.
  'There is a sacred and most pleasing island,
The mother of the Nereids is its patron
With the Aegean Neptune. Once the Archer,
Devoted to it, caught it as it floated
Along the coast and bays, and tied it up
To Myconos and towering Gyaros
So that it could be still and face the winds.

Thither I went, and in a safe harbour
It took us in to peace when we were weary.
We went ashore, honouring Apollo's city.
King Anius – at once king and priest of Phoebus –
Ran out to meet us with his temples bound
With fillets and with sprays of sacred laurel;
He recognised Anchises, an old friend:
We all shook hands and went up to his palace.

   'Entering the temple built of ancient stone
I prayed: "Thymban Apollo, give us rest,
Our own home and walls for weary men,
Succession and a city that will last;
Vouchsafe to Troy a second Pergamus
For those left by the Greeks and cruel Achilles.
Whom must we follow? Where would you have us go?
Where should we set our resting place? Father, give
An augury and fill us with your spirit."

   'Scarce had I spoken when all seemed to shake
Suddenly, both the entrance to the shrine
And the god's laurel, the whole hill was moving,
The doors flew open, the sacred vessel roared.
We fell flat on the ground; a voice was heard:
"Hard sons of Dardanus, the land that bore
The ancestors from whom you first began
Welcomes you back and offers you her breast.
Seek out your ancient mother, for with her
Aeneas shall find home and rule all shores
With his sons' sons and those who spring from them."
Those were the words of Phoebus: there arose
A murmur of contentment and it swelled
Into a tumult; everyone was asking
What might that city be, to what was Phoebus
Calling the sorry wanderers to return?
My father then turned over in his mind
What he knew of the men of old times
And said: "Listen to me, you who are leaders
And let me tell you where your hope must be.
Crete, which is great Jove's island, lies away
In the middle of the sea; Mount Ida is there
And that is the cradle of our race.
Crete has a hundred cities, the land is rich:

It was from there, if I remember truly,
Our forebear Teucer first sailed to the Troad
And chose the site for his kingdom. In those days
There was no Ilium and no citadel;
There were men but they lived down in the valley.
From Crete too came the Mother Cybele;
Her Corybantic symbols were from Ida,
Her silent mysteries, her lions yoked
For service in the chariot of our lady.
Come on then, let us go where the gods bid us,
Placate the winds and seek the realms of Cnossus.
The voyage is not long; if Jupiter
Favours our enterprise, in three days' time
The fleet should beach upon the Cretan shore."
When he had spoken thus, upon the altars
He offered up the proper sacrifices,
A bull to Neptune and a bull to you,
Lovely Apollo, and to the Storm
A black sheep, to the Fair Winds, a white.
   'A rumour flew around: Idomeneus,
The prince, had been pushed out from his father's lands
And so the shores of Crete were left deserted,
No single enemy in all those houses
Which had been left standing for our use.
We left the harbour of Ortygia,
Flew over the sea past Naxos with its hills
Full of Bacchantes, past green Donysa,
Olearos, and Paros white as snow,
And past the scatter of the Cyclades
We pushed our way through foam and many islands.
The sailors shout, vying with one another;
They urge their mates: "To Crete, and where we came from!"
A wind astern helped us upon our way
And then we sailed up to the ancient shores
Where the Curetes had their mysteries.
I was eager then and began to build
The city I desired; I called it Pergamus,
The people were delighted with the name;
I bid them love their home and build a citadel.
Our ships were hardly drawn up on the beach,
The young men busy settling down with wives

And working at the land; and I was busy
Dividing properties and making laws:
When suddenly a wasting fell on limbs
From an infected corner of the sky
And pitifully seized on trees and crops,
A pestilence; it was a year of death.
Men let their dear lives go or trailed round
In sickened bodies; Sirius burnt the fields
And they bore nothing; all the grass dried up
And the sick harvest brought no food to eat.
Back to the oracle of Ortygia!
My father urged, and back again to Phoebus!
Across the sea so many leagues again!
To pray for mercy and to ask what end
There was to be for us weary people,
What help we were to seek in our labours
And what course he would have us follow now.
   'It was night, sleep held all living things;
The sacred images of the gods I'd carried
With me from Troy, the Phrygian Penates
Brought from the middle of the burning city
I saw before me as I lay asleep,
They showed up in the overwhelming light
The full moon poured in through the deep-set windows.
Then they spoke to me and I was less anxious:
"What, if you sailed back to Ortygia,
Apollo would have said to you, he utters
Here in this place; he sent us to your door.
Dardania was on fire, we followed you,
Followed your arms, and we were with the fleet
Under your charge, as you crossed the wild sea;
So shall we raise your issue yet to come
High as the stars, and give you city and empire.
It is for you to build up the great walls
For those who will be great; you must not shirk
The effort your long wanderings require.
You must leave here, for these are not the shores
Delian Apollo had in mind for you
Nor has he ordered you to settle in Crete.
There is a place the Greeks call Hesperia,
An ancient land, both powerful in arms

And rich for those who farm it. The Oenotrians
Used to inhabit it but new men there
Now call it Italy after their prince:
This is our home, from it came Dardanus
And Iasus who was the father of our race.
Get up and go and tell your aged father
Joyfully, as something not to doubt,
What I have told you, that he should seek
Corythus and the Ausonian lands.
Jupiter will not let you have Crete."
Thunderstruck by the visions and the voice
(It was no dream, I seemed to recognise
The gods, their shapes, their hair dressed with garlands,
Their very faces as they spoke to me
And all my body was in a cold sweat.)
I leapt up from my bed and stretched my hands
To heaven and prayed, and then poured on the hearth
Inviolate offerings and, these honours done,
Joyfully I reported to Anchises
All that had happened and laid all before him.
It came to him that two lines of descent
From two ancestors had been confused
In this way, mixing up the old homelands.
He cast his mind back: "Son, the destinies
Of Troy," he said, "still bear down upon you;
Only Cassandra prophesied these things.
And I remember now that she foretold
How this would be the fortune of our race;
Often she spoke of this Hesperia
And of Italian kingdoms. Who could credit
That Teucrians would land upon those shores?
Hesperia! Who believed Cassandra then?
But let us yield to Phoebus now, and warned
By him, follow a better course at last."
With shouts of triumph we obeyed his orders.
This resting-place too we abandoned,
Leaving a few men only on the shore,
Set sail and once again on the high seas
We ran before the wind in our light ships.

    'When all the fleet was there in deep water
With no more land in sight, but everywhere

Was sky and all that was not sky was sea,
Then overhead a dark blue cloud appeared;
It brought a stormy darkness all around
And the waves shuddered underneath the shadows.
Then came winds that set the waters rolling
And there were huge seas; scattered, we tossed
Up and down over the limitless ocean.
The clouds shut out the light, a pouring night
Took away every glimpse of the sky;
When the clouds parted it was to spit lightning.
We were buffeted off course and wandered on
In utter blindness over the dark waves.
Palinurus himself cannot discern
Day from night or remember the way.
We wander on the sea for three whole days,
So far as we could tell them in the gloom
And for as many nights without stars.
On the fourth, land heaves into sight at last,
Mountains appear, above them curling smoke.
The wind dropped and we took to our oars.
Unhesitatingly the sailors force them
Among the foam and so sweep the waves.
   'When we were through these seas, the Strophades
Had fished us out and I was on the shore.
The Strophades is the name the Greeks give
To islands in the great Ionian sea
Inhabited by the horrible Celaeno
And other Harpies, since they were thrown out
Of Phineus' house where they had once fed.
There are no sadder prodigies than these
And no more cruel or more noxious pest
Was ever raised by gods out of the Styx.
For these birds have the faces of girls
And filthy excrement pours from their guts,
Their hands have claws, their cheeks are pale and drawn
With hunger.
To this place we were carried, found a harbour
And then we saw scattered in open country
Abundant herds of cattle, flocks of goats
With no attendant there upon the grass.
We rushed in with our swords and called the gods

And Jove himself, to share in the plunder.
There on the curving shore we heaped up bedding
And made a solemn feast with the best spoil.
But suddenly, with a terrifying swoop,
The Harpies were upon us from the mountains;
We cowered under the thudding of their wings.
They tore at the food, befouling everything
They touched; a boding screech
Pierced through air thick with their filthy stench.
Again, this time in a deep recess
Under a hollow rock sheltered by trees
And their forbidding shade, we set up tables;
Once more we put fire upon the altars.
But again, from a fresh quarter of the sky,
Wherever they were hiding, down they came,
That flock with all their din, and flew around,
Their claws outstretched, polluting any food
They put their lips to. So I called my comrades
To take their weapons and go into battle
With that ill-omened race. As they were ordered
They covered up their swords in the grass
And also put their shields out of sight.
Then, when the birds came sweeping round the bay,
Misenus gave a sign from his look-out
With his bronze trumpet. My men went in at once:
It was a strange battle they had on hand,
To worst those obscene sea-birds with their swords.
But swords had no effect on those feathers
And the birds' backs were invulnerable;
They flew away quickly into the sky,
Leaving half-eaten prey covered with filth.
One only stayed upon a lofty rock,
Celaeno, to prophesy ill for us;
These were the words which erupted from her:
"Is it war then, as well as slaughtering cattle
And knocking bullocks down, and paying nothing?
And you think nothing of bringing war here
To drive poor Harpies from their natural kingdom?
Hear what I say and fix it in your minds
– Things the Almighty once foretold to Phoebus
And great Apollo then conveyed to me,

I now, who am the chief of all the Furies,
Reveal to you. It is for Italy
That you are bound and when the winds are called
To Italy you will go and find a harbour;
And never shall you build your promised city
Until the injury you did us by this slaughter
Has brought you to a hunger so cruel
That you gnaw your very tables."
With that, borne away upon her wings,
She fled into the forest. My comrades then
Felt their blood chilled and frozen by quick fear;
They were dispirited, thought no more of arms
But wanted me to sue for peace with prayers
Whether the creatures were indeed goddesses
Or only filthy birds. Anchises then,
My father, stretched his hands towards the sea,
Called on the mighty powers and then appointed
What honours we should pay them: "Gods," he prayed,
"Confound these threats, gods, let not such things happen,
Be merciful and keep your servants safe."
Then he gave orders: Cast off from the shore,
Prepare to hoist the sails. Then the breeze filled them;
We got away over the foam-flecked waves
Wherever wind and helmsman might direct.
Already, lying out among the waves,
Appears Zacynthus with its wooded slopes,
Dulichium, Same and then Neritos
With its high crags. We keep clear of the rocks
Of Ithaca, the kingdom of Laërtes
And curse the land that bore cruel Ulysses;
Soon, there before us are the cloudy tops
Of Leucate, where the Apollo is
Sailors have learned to dread. We make for this,
Worn out, and so approach the little town;
There we cast anchor and we beach the ships.
    'Because we are in safety on dry land
Beyond our hopes, we pay for our redemption
With offerings to Jove and light his altars
And honour the Actian shores with Trojan games.
The lads, naked and slippery with oil,
Are occupied with the traditional games,

Glad to have missed so many Argive towns
And to have given their enemies the slip.
So the sun rolled to the turn of the year
And icy winter with its winds from the north
Made the sea rough: I took a shield of bronze,
One that the great Abas had once borne,
And hung it up there between two pillars,
Marking the act with this inscription:
"Aeneas took this from the victorious Greeks."
Then I gave orders that we should leave port
And the lads took their places at the oars,
Dipped them into the sea and raced away.
Quickly we left Phaeacia out of sight,
Its tallest peaks were gone and we were skirting
The coast of Epirus, so we reached
The harbour of Chaonia and went up
Towards the hill city of Buthrotum.

   'Here an incredible rumour reaches us,
That Helenus, one of the sons of Priam,
Is now reigning as king over Grecian cities,
And has possession of the wife of Pyrrhus
The Aeacid, as well as of his sceptre,
And that Andromache has once again
Passed to a husband of her own race.
This tale filled me with more than curiosity
To get to him and find out what had happened.
I went up from the harbour, leaving the fleet,
And there was Andromache, as it chanced,
In a clear space under the city walls,
Among the trees, pouring a ritual offering
Beside a spring that represented Simois,
Mourning gifts to the ashes of Hector,
Calling his spirit to an empty tomb,
A mound of turf, where she had consecrated
A pair of altars. When she caught sight of me
And saw the Trojan arms all around,
She was beside herself and terrified
By such extraordinary appearances.
She froze to her very bones at what she saw,
And fell in a swoon. It was long before she spoke:
"Is your shape what it seems, does it speak the truth,

Son of the goddess, can you be alive?
Or, if the light of day has left us all,
Where is Hector?" With that, her tears came,
She filled the place with her cries. For my part
I could only throw in a few words,
So frenzied was she, and I was so moved
That I could hardly say what I said:
"I am alive indeed, and keep on somehow
Through all extremities; so do not doubt
These are real things you see
But oh, what has happened now to you
After your marriage to so great a husband?
What fortune could be worthy of your past,
Hector's Andromache? Are you still with Pyrrhus?"
She hung her head and spoke quietly:
"Oh, fortunate above all other women
Was Priam's virgin daughter who was ordered
To die at the tomb of an enemy
Under the walls of Troy. No lots were drawn
For her and no victorious master took her
A prisoner to his bed! But I, when Troy
Was burnt, was carried off through distant seas
To bear the scorn and youthful arrogance
Achilles's son showed to a slave in labour;
Then, when his mind turned to Hermione,
Leda's grand-daughter, and a Spartan marriage,
He handed me over to Helenus
As one slave is given to another.
But then he fell foul of Orestes
Who, jealous because Pyrrhus had taken his bride
And driven by the Furies for his own crimes,
Surprised him beside his father's altars
And finished him. After the death of Pyrrhus
Part of his kingdom fell to Helenus;
It was he called these plains 'Chaonian'
And the whole place 'Chaonia', taking the name
From Chaon in our home country of Troy,
And he topped this eminence with a Pergamus,
A citadel that would recall Ilium.
But you? Where have the winds taken you?
What course have the fates set you on? What god

Has brought you here without your knowing it?
How is that boy Ascanius? Did he survive
And does he still breathe in the living air?
Is Troy already . . .
And does he still think of his lost mother?
Does he show signs of following in the footsteps
Of his father Aeneas and his uncle Hector?"
The words poured from her as she wept, she broke
Into prolonged laments, vain though they were,
And as she did so, from the city walls
Emerged the hero Helenus himself,
Priam's son, with a great company.
He knew at once that we were his own people;
Delightedly he led us to the gates
And yet shed tears with every word he spoke.
I went ahead and saw a little Troy,
A citadel copied from great Pergamus
And a dry water-course they called Xanthus;
I hugged the pillars of the Scaean gate;
Indeed all the Teucrians loved the city.
The king received us in a pillared walk
And in the middle of the courtyard there
They tasted cups of wine and they were served
On gold plate and drank from great bowls.
    'Day after day went by and then the breeze
Called to the sails, the south wind filled the canvas.
I went to the seer and enquired:
"Son of Troy," I said, "interpreter,
You who perceive what the god would say,
What is the will of Phoebus, and the meaning
Of tripods, Clarian laurel, and the stars,
The voices of the birds, omens of flight,
Come, tell me now (for I am well assured
By the divine powers where I must go
And all the gods have said: Italy
Is the land I must make for, the territory
That I must prove in place of Troy, is there;
Only Celaeno the Harpy prophesied
Something monstrous to speak of, a new prodigy,
Declaring that, having incurred her anger
All the obscenities of starvation

Were to be ours): what dangers must I avoid?
What course will enable me to succeed
After so many troubles?" Helenus,
Having sacrificed bullocks, as the custom is,
Beseeched the gods that they would give us peace,
Loosened the band around his sacred head
And took me by the hand to your gates, Phoebus,
Under the influence of your great power;
Then, as your priest, he spoke prophetically:
    ' "Goddess-born, since it is evident
It is by greater auspices you go
Across the sea (and thus the king of the gods
Has drawn the lot and so it will turn out),
I shall but tell you few things as I speak
Of many that will happen, that more safely
You may wander over the foreign waters
And come to rest in an Ausonian harbour;
The other things the Fates keep from Helenus
Nor will Saturnian Juno let him speak.
First then, the Italy you think so near
And into whose harbours you would sail,
Is far from you: a long pathless way
And a long journey separates you from it.
You must bend your oars in Trinacrian waves,
Your ships must pass the salt Ausonian deep,
You must encounter the infernal lakes
And Circe's island, before you can build
Your city upon land that is secure.
Signs I will give you; keep them in your mind.
When, in your trouble, you shall come upon,
Beside the banks of a secluded river,
Under the branches of an oak, a sow,
White, lying back on the ground, a new
Litter of thirty tugging at her dugs,
The little ones white like her; then that will be
The place for your city; there you will rest.
Have no fear of having to gnaw your tables
As was foretold: a way will be found
By the Fates, if you invoke Apollo.
But these lands and this new Italian shore
Which is washed by the tide of our own sea

You must avoid; for ill-intentioned Greeks
Inhabit all the towns here. Here the Locri
Come from Narycium have put up walls
And Lyctian Idomeneus has stationed
Soldiers all over the Sallentian plains;
Here is the famous town of Petelia,
Small, but fortified by Philoctetes
The Miliboean captain. When your ships
Have passed all these and crossed the seas and anchored
And you have set up altars on the shore
To pay your vows, pull up your purple cloak
Over your head, lest any hostile face
Should be seen as, in honour of the gods,
You tend the holy fires, for so the omens
May be disturbed. This rule you must keep
In your observances, you and your friends;
In this your children's children should follow you,
Doing as they should do before the gods.
But when you have gone from here and the wind
Has brought you to the coast of Sicily
And the narrows of Pelorus open out,
Then you must keep to the land on the larboard side
And the adjoining sea, wide though it is,
Avoiding both land and water to starboard.
These places were at one time torn apart,
They say, in some vast convulsion
(For such things could happen in old times)
Where before the two countries had been one;
The sea came in between and the waves cut
The Hesperian coast off from Sicily
And washed the fields and cities on both sides
With the draught of the narrow-running tide.
The right side Scylla bars, while on the left
Charybdis is, who never has enough
And who three times a day sucks down vast waves
Into the furthest depths of her abyss
Then splashes them back against the stars.
But Scylla is confined to the recesses
Of a dark cave whence she thrusts out her mouths
To draw passing ships on to the rocks.
Her upper part is human, she is a maiden

With firm breasts, so down to her patch of hair;
Below that she is an immense sea-monster
With dolphins' tails and the sex of wolves.
Better a slow journey round the cape
Of Pachynus in Sicily, a wide circuit
Than once to have seen the shapeless Scylla
In her vast cave and heard the rocks
Resounding with the bark of her watery dogs.
This too I say: If Helenus has foresight,
If there is reason to trust his prophecies
And if Apollo fills his mind with truth,
This one thing, goddess-born, I will proclaim,
This one thing above all, I will repeat it
Over and over and I give you warning:
Before all else address yourself to Juno,
Respect her greatness and her influence,
Freely perform Juno's ceremonies
And by your prayers and offerings win over
That powerful Queen of Heaven: so at last
You will leave Sicily and successfully
Arrive at the confines of Italy.
When you have reached there you will come upon
The town of Cumae and the sacred lakes
Among the rustling forests of Avernus.
There you will see the distracted prophetess
Who, deep inside the rock foretells the fates
And commits words in writing to the leaves,
Sets them in order and puts them in her cave.
They remain in their places as they should be,
Yet when a light wind turns the hinge of the door
It stirs the delicate leaves and blows them about
And never does she think of catching them
As they flutter through the cave, nor of recalling
Where they belong in her prophecies;
So men go away knowing nothing
And hate the Sibyl. But you should not count
Any delay as being of importance
However much your comrades make of it
And though your voyage calls your sails to sea
And there are favourable winds to fill them;
You must go to the prophetess and beg

For oracles, pleading that she herself
Should speak to you, opening her lips freely.
She will explain the peoples of Italy,
The wars that are to come, how you should meet
– Or else avoid – each trouble on your way;
Treated with worship, she will second you.
These are the matters I can warn you of.
Go now, and accomplish such deeds
That Troy will be exalted to the stars."
    'The speaker of these friendly prophecies
Then ordered presents for us, heavy gold
And carved ivory, to be taken to the ships
And made them stow away a lot of silver,
Dodonean cauldrons and a coat of mail
Put together with triple hooks of gold;
There was also a splendid pointed helmet
With a long crest of hair: these were the armour
Of Neoptolemus. And for my father
There were special gifts. Helenus also gave us
Horses, and men to act as guides, more oarsmen,
And equipped all my company with arms.
    'Meanwhile Anchises was making sure the fleet
Had its sails ready, so that when the wind
Was favourable there would be no delay.
The man who spoke for Phoebus then addressed him:
"Anchises, you whom Venus herself thought
Worthy to be her husband, and for whom
The gods have special care, who was twice snatched
From ruined Pergamus, before you now
The land of Ausonia waits for your sails.
Yet this coast you see you must let go by;
It is a distant part of Ausonia
Apollo declares to be your own.
Go now," he said, "you are fortunate
In having so dutiful a son.
But now a favourable wind is rising,
I must not now detain you with my talk."
Andromache, sad at the final parting,
Also brought gifts, garments with golden figures
Woven into them, and for Ascanius
A Phrygian cloak, she too is liberal

And piles upon him presents from her loom.
"Take these, my child, these are my handiwork,"
She said, "They will remind you of Andromache
The wife of Hector and her enduring love.
These are the last gifts from your own kin,
You are the image of my Astyanax
And all that now remains to me of him,
For he had just such eyes, such hands and face
And he would now be just about your age."
   'Going from them, not without rising tears,
I spoke these words: "Farewell and be happy,
O you for whom fortune's work is done;
We are still summoned on from fate to fate.
Your lot is quiet; not for you to plough
Over the great surface of the sea,
For ever making for Ausonian fields
Which always recede further as you advance.
You see before you that image of Xanthus,
Of Troy, which you made with your own hands
– With better auspices I hope and less
Open to Greek attacks. If ever I
Do indeed sail into the Tiber mouth
And walk upon the fields beside its banks
And ever see the walls promised to my people,
We shall be two cities that are akin,
Two peoples still close to one another,
One in Epirus, one in Hesperia,
For both of us have a common ancestor,
Dardanus, and have suffered a common fate.
So we shall be in mind a single Troy
And may our children's children be the same!"
   'Over the seas we sped, down to Ceraunia,
Which was the shortest way to Italy
And also the shortest sea-passage for us.
Meanwhile the sun went down, we saw the mountains
Grow shadowy and dark. We went ashore
And threw ourselves down close to the water's edge
– And glad we were to rest after the voyage.
Distributing the oars among the men
We made ourselves comfortable on dry land
Where sleep would refresh our weary limbs.

The night had not worn out half its hours
When Palinurus – who is not an idler –
Leapt up from the place where he was lying
To test the wind, catching the slightest sound;
He observed all the stars in the silent sky
Riding past, Arcturus, the Hyades
That bring rain, both the Bears, and then he saw
Orion armed in gold. The whole heavens
Were visible, there was not a cloud anywhere.
Then from the poop he gave a clear call;
We shifted everything and went aboard
To try our luck at sea and spread our sails.
The sky grew red with dawn, the stars had gone,
When far off we saw the dark hills
Of the low line that was Italy.
"Italy!" Achates was the first
To shout the name and all the lads joined in
Saluting Italy with ringing voices.
Anchises then, my father, took a bowl,
A great one, and crowned it with a wreath,
Filled it with pure wine and called the gods,
Standing on the high poop:
"Gods of the sea and land who rule the storms,
Send us a wind to make our passage easy
And as you breathe upon us, favour us."
The very winds we wanted freshened then,
A harbour opened for us, close already;
On a hill was a temple of Minerva.
The harbour had the shape of a bent bow
As the winds blown in from the east had made it;
Before it rocks dashed up a salt spray,
The port itself was hidden; from towering crags
Two walls ran down like arms to hold the harbour;
The temple stood back far from the shore.
I saw, as a first omen, four horses
Upon the grass, grazing, and white as snow.
"Strange land!" my father Anchises said,
"It is war you bring; horses are armed for war;
It is with war these herds threaten us.
Yet sometimes these animals are yoked
In a laborious team and are restrained,

Which means hope of peace." Then to Minerva
Of the resounding armour, who first greeted us
As we sailed in with cheers, we say a prayer
And, with our Phrygian cloaks over our heads
As Helenus had taught us we must do,
Sacrificed in due form at the altars
To Argive Juno, omitting no prescription.
   'No time for dawdling; when our vows are paid,
With the last ceremony we turn our sails
Into the wind, leaving behind fields
Not to be trusted because those who live there
Have Greek blood in their veins. Next come into sight
The bay and city of Tarentum where,
So it is said, Hercules once was;
Opposite it the Lacinian goddess
Stands aloft in her temple, there is a fortress
– That of Caulonia – and Scylaceum,
The point where ships are wrecked. Trinacrian Aetna
Is sighted far off, rising from the water:
We hear from far the huge moan of the sea
Beating upon the rocks as the waves break;
The shallows leap up and all the sands
Mix with the surf. My father Anchises
Says: "That surely must be that Charybdis;
The jutting pieces those terrible rocks
Helenus warned us of in his prophecy.
Out of it, lads, put your weight on the oars."
They do as they are bidden; Palinurus
Is the first man to pull his prow round,
It creaks as he does so; the whole line
Follows to port, using both oars and sails.
We are carried up to heaven by one curved wave
And the next draws us nearly down to Hell.
Three times the shelf between the hollow rocks
Gave a loud thud; three times we saw the spray
Falling above us in a shower of stars.
Meanwhile the wind dropped as the sun went down;
Exhausted and not knowing where we were
We drifted gently to the Cyclops' coast.
   'The harbour is large and sheltered from the winds
But close at hand is Aetna thundering

And throwing out its terrifying rubble,
With clouds of black smoke reaching the sky,
Among it whirling pitch and red-hot ashes
And balls of flame which lick at the stars;
Meanwhile it vomits up the mountain's guts,
Collecting huge stones and molten rock
Until it boils up from deep inside it.
The story is that Enceladus,
Half-burnt by a thunderbolt, lies there
With all the weight of Aetna laid on top
And that he breathes out flames from a wrecked smithy;
As often as he turns wearily over
The whole of Sicily murmurs and vibrates
And the whole sky is blotted out with smoke.
That night we took cover in the woods,
Enduring all these monstrous prodigies
Without seeing or knowing what caused the sound.
For there was no glimmer of a star,
No brightness in the upper air at all
But cloud everywhere in a dark sky;
Night without time kept the moon out of sight.
  'The next day was upon us, with first light
The wet mist disappeared from the sky.
Suddenly from the woods, emaciated,
Came the strange figure of an unknown man,
Unkempt and wretched, and stretched out his hands
In supplication to us on the shore.
We looked back. He was squalid and unshaven,
His rags pinned up with thorns: but still a Greek
And one who had been sent to fight in Troy,
And when he saw our Dardanian clothes
And, far-off, recognised our Trojan arms,
He stood stock still, terrified at the sight
But then came on and rushed to the shore,
Weeping and begging us: "By all the stars,
By the gods and the sunlit air we breathe,
I give myself up, Trojans; take me away
To any land you like, it will serve.
I know that I was with the Grecian ships,
I admit I made war on the gods of Ilium.
For that, if it is so great a crime,

Throw me into the sea limb by limb
And let me sink for ever under the waves;
Let me at least die at the hands of men!"
His words ceased and he embraced my knees
And stuck there grovelling. We called on him
To tell us who he was and of what blood
And what had been his fortune till that time.
My father Anchises himself gave him his hand
With only a little hesitation
And re-assured the young man with this gesture
Till he had put aside his fear and spoken:
"Ithaca is my country and I served
With the unfortunate Ulysses, my name
Is Achaemenides, my father was poor
(I only wish I had had no worse fortune!)
So I set out for Troy. I was left here,
My mates forgot me as they rushed in panic
Out of the cruel mouth of the Cyclops' cave.
The place is huge and dark inside and swimming
In filth and blood from the feasting there.
The master of the house is gigantic,
Enough to bump his head against the stars
– O gods, deliver the world from such an evil!
Men cannot get a proper view of him
And no-one can address a word to him.
He feeds upon human flesh and blood.
I myself saw two of our number taken
In his great hand as he lay back in his cave,
Their bodies smashed against a rock; and all
The entrance splashed and swimming in their blood;
I saw their limbs dripping with what flowed from them;
As he munched their warm joints were still re-acting.
It was not unavenged, for Ulysses
Would not suffer such things, an Ithacan
Doesn't forget himself at such a moment.
As soon as, full of food and drowned in wine,
The giant's head nodded and he lay back,
Stretching right through the cave and belching blood
And bits of bodies, all mixed up with wine,
We prayed the gods to be on our side
And drew lots to settle who should venture,

Then we poured in on all sides of him
And with a sharp spear put out his eye,
A huge one set under his shaggy brow
Like a Greek shield or a blazing sun,
And so at last – how glad we were to do it! –
We managed to avenge our comrades' ghosts.
But get away from here, you poor devils,
And cut your cables now.
There are a hundred such as Polyphemus
Who now has driven his great flocks of sheep
Into his cave and there is milking them;
And all these unspeakable Cyclopes
Live on these shores or wander in the mountains.
Three times I have watched the moon fill her crescent
Since I began to drag out my days here
In the woods and in the haunts of wild beasts,
Observing from my rocky look-out post
The huge Cyclopes and, as I heard
The sound of their steps and voices, trembling.
What have I eaten? Stony dog-wood berries
From any branch and the torn-up roots of weeds.
I have kept my eyes skinned but yours are the first
Ships I have seen coming to these shores.
I would give myself up to whoever it was;
Enough to get away from this foul race.
You can take my life whatever way you will."
    'He had hardly spoken when on the mountain-top
We saw a huge bulk moving among the flocks,
The shepherd Polyphemus, coming towards us
– A huge shapeless thing with his one eye blinded.
A pine-trunk in his hand steadied his steps;
His long-haired sheep came with him – all he had
To give him pleasure or to comfort him.
When once he felt himself among the waves
And out in the deep water, he stopped short
To wash the blood out of his eye-socket,
Grinding his teeth and groaning, then strode on
Far out to sea, still without wetting his middle.
In terror we made haste in our retreat
With our suppliant on board, for he deserved it
And silently we cut the cables loose,

Bent over our oars and so away;
The giant heard and turned towards the sound.
But since he had no way of getting at us,
The Ionian sea being too deep for pursuit,
He raised an immense shout, so that far out
The waves trembled and inland, Italy
Was terrified, while from its intricate caverns
Aetna gave forth a roar. Then from the woods
And from the high mountains the race of Cyclops
Was roused and rushed headlong to the harbour,
Filling the whole shore. And there we saw them,
The whole fraternity of Aetna, standing
Each with his single eye gazing in vain,
Savagely, with their heads stretching aloft,
A company it was not good to see:
They stood like great oaks upon a mountain-top
Or dark cypresses, a Jovian forest
Or a grove of Diana. Then indeed
Fear drove us on, we let the sheets go
Wherever our sails would fill with following winds,
And so headlong. Yet Helenus had warned us
Against a course between Scylla and Charybdis
For that meant risk of death on either side;
So back we had to go. Just then it happened
A north wind arose from Pelorus,
The narrow headland. I sailed past the mouth
Of the Pantagia with its natural harbour,
The bay of Megara and low-lying Thapsus.
Such were the places that were pointed out
By Achaemenides, he was retracing
His wanderings with the luckless Ulysses.
    'Stretched at the mouth of the Sicanian bay
There lies an island, facing Plemyrium
On which the waves run in; they used to call it
In the old days, Ortygia. It was here,
The story goes, that the stream Alpheus
From Elis, came up after its secret journey
So that now, Arethusa, it is mingled
With your spring in the waves of Sicily.
Obediently we prayed as we were bidden
To the great spirits of the place and then

I passed by Helorus with its marshes
And its rich soil. Then we skirted the reefs
And the projecting rocks of Pachynus;
Camarina – "never to be disturbed"
The oracle said – appeared far away
And with it the Gelonian levels, and Gela
Which has its name from its immense river.
Next steep Acragas which used to be
A breeding-ground for high-spirited horses
Showed up the full extent of its great walls;
With a good wind behind me I left you,
Selinus, and your palm-trees, and picked my way
Through shallow water by Lilybaeum
With all his hidden rocks, and found a harbour
At Drepanum, but that was no happiness.
For there, after so many storms at sea,
I lost him who had made it all worth while,
My father Anchises, alas: here it was
That you deserted me, you best of fathers,
Exhausted as I was; you, saved in vain
From so many dangers. Neither Helenus,
Seer though he was who warned of many horrors,
Predicted this trouble, nor cruel Celaeno.
This was my final trouble, and so ended
All the long voyages I had undertaken;
When I left there, the god washed me up here.'
  Thus our ancestor Aeneas told
All that had happened as the gods had willed
And explained the whole story of his voyage.
Then he was silent. No more, and no movement.

# BOOK IV

# BOOK IV

The queen, however, has an injury
Which has long troubled her as she listened,
The blood flows to her wound, she is consumed
By a blind fire. Here was a man indeed
And of a noble race: so she reflects;
His looks and what he said stick in her mind,
She is troubled all the night long, and restless
So that she cannot sleep. When the sun rises,
Purifying the whole world with its light
And dawn has cleared the sky of mist and shadows,
Uneasily she speaks to her sister
Who is of the same mind as she: 'Anna!
Sister, I lay awake and I was frightened.
What is it? And who can this new guest be
Who has come into our house and bears himself
So, as he does, so like a great captain?
I do indeed believe there is reason to think
That he is of the race of the gods.
Fear is the mark of degenerate minds.
But how he has been tossed around by fate!
What a story he had to tell of those wars
In which he hung on to the end! If I had not
So utterly made up my mind already
Never to enter into marriage again
After my first love disappointed me
Through death; and if I had not had enough
Of bed and weddings, it is possible
This one occasion might have tempted me.
Anna, I will admit, that since Sychaeus,
My poor husband, was murdered by my brother
At the family altar, this is the one man
Who really has made an impression on me
And caused my resolution to waver.

I recognise the signs of the old trouble.
But I would rather the earth opened before me
Or the Almighty Father sent me spinning
Into the shades with one of his thunderbolts
– The pallid shades of Erebus, the night of nights –
Than go against decent behaviour
And break the rules of what is expected of me.
The man who first married me took away
All my affections, let him keep them now
And have them for his own in the grave!'
As she said this tears welled into her eyes
And fell however she might try to dry them.
    Anna replied: 'You are my sister, dearer
Than life to me. Must you go on alone?
And spend all your years of youth in mourning
Without knowing the pleasure of having children
– And that is not all that love has to offer.
Do you think ashes or shades underground
Bother about such things? All right, till now
In Libya and before that in Tyre
You have been too put out to think of a husband;
Iarbus got short shrift, like the other gentry
And there are plenty of them in Africa
Which is a place for triumphs; will you struggle
Even against a love you find agreeable?
Have you forgotten on whose lands you are?
On one side the Gaetulians have their cities,
There is no defeating them, then the Numidians,
Who are uncontrollable, complete the barrier
Except where the sandbanks of Syrtis lie
– Unfriendly too; on the other side is desert,
The thirsty region where the Barcaeans prowl
And they are desperate. I say nothing of wars
Which might come from Tyre, where your brother threatens.
It is by the gods' will, it seems to me,
And Juno's favour in particular,
These Trojan ships have been blown on this course.
What a city you could have and what an empire,
With such a marriage as this! With the Teucrian forces
What glory there would be for our Carthage!
Only demand the favour of the gods

And give them all the proper sacrifices,
Then pile on hospitality and contrive
That there should be good reasons for delay
While winter wears itself out on the sea,
Orion threatens rain, the ships are damaged
And the sky seems to be unmanageable.'
     With talk like this she made the queen's glowing mind
Burst into flame with love, and gave her hope
Where before doubt had been, and made her shameless.
First they approached the shrines and asked for favours;
They sacrifice sheep with perfect teeth
As the custom is, to Ceres the law-giver,
To Phoebus and then to Bacchus the father
But above all to Juno, for it is she
Who is in charge of the chains of marriage.
Dido herself, the loveliest of women,
Holds the cup in her hand and pours libations
Between the horns of a milk-white heifer
Or, there with the gods looking on,
Moves slowly to the richly smoking altars
To present solemn gifts and then, expectant,
Stares as the animals' bodies are torn open
At the living entrails. But alas, alas,
It matters little what the seer thinks
And neither prayers nor altars can assist
A woman mad with love. A pleasant flame
Eats at the very marrow of her bones
And in her heart the unadmitted wound
Stirs meanwhile. The unhappy Dido burns
And wanders all round the city, distracted,
A doe with an arrow in her side,
Struck when she least expected it by some
Shepherd out hunting in the woods of Crete
Who did not know that he had wounded her;
In flight she runs through the woodland pastures
Of Dicte but the deadly arrow sticks.
So Dido drags Aeneas round the buildings
To let him see the wealth of Sidonia
And what the construction of the city is.
She tries to speak and then stops half-way.
As the day goes she is eager to resume

The banquet as before, and asks again
– She cannot help herself – to hear once more
All that the Trojans have undergone
And hangs on every word as he speaks.
When they have parted and the moon in turn
Has snuffed out her light and the circling stars
Commend the world to sleep, she is alone,
The house is empty and she is weeping
And lies down upon the abandoned couches;
Absent herself, it is that absent man
She hears and sees. Or else she takes Ascanius
Who is so like his father, on her lap,
Trying to trick the love she cannot speak of.
The towers she had started rise no more,
The young men fail to carry on their training
Or to complete the work on the defences
And all is interrupted, mountainous walls
And the cranes topping them are left deserted.
   As soon as Saturn's daughter, Jove's dear wife,
Saw Dido so in the grip of her sweet plague
She approached Venus and addressed her thus:
'You and your boy are becoming famous,
Indeed you are, and winning marvellous prizes;
If one woman is conquered by the stratagems
Of two gods they must be very powerful!
Still I can see that when you look askance
At those who live within towering Carthage,
It is our walls you fear. What are you at?
What is the point of such a struggle now?
Should we not do better to settle for peace
For ever and for a treaty of marriage?
You have what you have set your heart on, Dido
Blazes with love and madness fills her bones.
Let us therefore rule this people jointly,
With equal powers; let Dido take her Phrygian
As husband and the Tyrians for a dowry.'
   In answering her, Venus was well aware
What Juno said was meant to deceive her
And that the object was to turn the power
That should be Italy's, to the Libyan shores.
She said: 'With terms like that it would be mad

For anyone to prefer war with you
If only things turn out as you propose.
But I am left uncertain by the fates
Whether Jupiter wills a single city
For the Tyrians and those who come from Troy
And whether he approves the mixture of races
Or an alliance between the two peoples.
You are his wife; it is for you to ask
What he has in mind. You go ahead
And I will follow you.' The queenly Juno
Answered her then: 'That I will undertake.
Now I will tell you how it can be done;
Listen, a few words only. They go hunting
Tomorrow, Aeneas and the unhappy Dido,
Together, when the sun first shows itself
And draws aside the curtains of the world.
I will pour down a blinding rain upon them,
Rain and hail, while the huntsmen are busy
Harbouring the deer, I will wake heaven with thunder.
The company will scatter and be lost
As if at dead of night. Dido and the man
Who is the Trojans' leader will end up
In the same cave. I will be there and if
I can be certain I have your good will
They shall be joined together in proper marriage,
With bridal then and there.' The Cytherian
Did not oppose what Juno sought to do
And laughed at her evident trickery.

   Meanwhile the dawn rose from the ocean.
Picked youths issue out from the gates;
With nets and snares and broad-tipped hunting spears
Massylian horsemen charge out with their pack
Of hounds keen for the scent. The Punic nobles
Wait for the queen, standing at the threshold
While she still lolls in bed; her horse is ready,
Splendid with purple and gold, stamping his hooves,
And champing eagerly at the foaming bit.
At last she comes, with a great company,
A Sidonian tunic with embroidered borders
Wrapping her up. She has a golden quiver,
It is with gold her hair is bound,

A golden clasp fastens her purple dress.
With her ride a company of Phrygians
And Iulus in high spirits; then Aeneas,
The most resplendent figure of them all,
Advances to join his troop with hers.
It is as when Apollo in the spring
Leaves Lycia and the wintry streams of Xanthus
To visit his mother's home in Delos
And sets the dancers going, while about
The altars Cretans mingle with Dryopans
And painted Agathyrsians raise their voices;
Apollo walks on the slopes of Cynthus,
Twists foliage in his flowing hair and binds it
With gold, while weapons clatter on his shoulder.
Aeneas was no less alive than he
As he went by, so noble did he look.
When they came to the tops of the mountains
Where it was pathless, wild goats jumped
And made off down the slopes; from elsewhere
Stags ran across open moors, kicking up dust
As herds of them in flight came off the hills.
The boy Ascanius, down in the valleys,
Enjoys himself with his skittish horse,
Galloping past first one lot then another
And hoping that in among the quiet herds
He will have the luck to find a wild boar
Foaming with rage, or else a tawny lion
Down from the mountains.

                  Meanwhile above his head
There is a turbulence, a roaring sound is heard
And then begins rain mixed with hail;
The Tyrian company scattered about,
The Trojan youth, Venus's Dardan grandson,
All seek shelter here and there in the fields,
In fear as torrents rush from the mountains.
Then Dido and the leader of the Trojans
Arrive at the same cave. The Earth itself
And nuptial Juno give the sign; lightning flashes
And heaven is awakened for the marriage;
The Nymphs shriek upon the mountain-top.
That day was the first day of death,

The first cause of all the ills that followed.
After that appearance and reputation
Were nothing to Dido, and she thought no more
Of keeping her love secret. She called it marriage
And by that word sought to disguise her sin.

   At once Rumour goes through the great cities
Of Libya, Rumour – and no plague moves more quickly.
She thrives on her ability to move
And gathers strength as she goes along;
Little at first, through fear, soon she is big,
Walking on ground with head hidden in the clouds.
They say that Mother Earth gave birth to her
When she was incensed against the gods
– Her last child, sister to Coeus and Enceladus;
Rumour is swift of foot, quick on the wing,
A terrifying monster, huge: and see!
For each of the feathers on her body
There is a watchful eye underneath;
She has as many tongues and speaking mouths,
As many ears, and all pricked up to listen.
All night she flies between heaven and earth,
Shrieking among the shadows, never closing
Her eyes in gentle sleep; and in the day-time
She perches on guard upon a roof-top
Or on high towers, intimidating cities;
To what is false and wrong she sticks as fast
As to the true things that she announces.
Now her delight was through many tongues
To spread among the peoples of Africa
Stories both true and false without distinction:
Aeneas had come, a man of Trojan blood
Whom lovely Dido deigned now to marry;
Now they are spending all the winter long
In idle pleasure, not caring for their kingdoms;
They are the slaves of their shameless passion.
These things the filthy goddess spread around
Where she might here and there on people's lips.
She then turned her steps to King Iarbas,
Setting his mind alight and by her words
She gave him all he needed to be angry.

This son of Hammon by a ravished Nymph,
A Garamantian, raised to Jupiter
A hundred temples on his wide domains
And in these huge structures consecrated
Fire as eternal watchers for the gods;
The ground was rich with blood of sacrifices,
The entrances flowery with many garlands.
He was beside himself and flared
When he heard the bitter talk, and it is said
That there before the altars, in the presence
Of the gods, he made with hands upturned
Long supplication to Jupiter:
'Almighty Jupiter, to whom the Moors,
Feasting upon their decorated couches,
Pour a Lenaean libation in your honour,
Do you observe these things? Or is it vainly
That we are frightened when you hurl your bolts?
And does the lightning there among the clouds
Terrify our minds only to empty murmurs?
The woman who strayed into my territory,
Set up a small city in return
For payment, and to whom we gave permission
To plough the shore on terms I myself set,
Refused the marriage that I offered her
And took Aeneas as lord of her kingdom.
And now this Paris with his gang of eunuchs,
His chin and scented hair tied in a scarf
Just like a Phrygian, keeps what he stole,
And we are bringing offerings to the temples
Said to be yours: or is that just a rumour?'
The Almighty heard the man who clutched the altars
And prayed in this manner: he turned his eyes
Towards the kingly walls and the two lovers
Who were forgetful of their better fame.
Then he addressed Mercury and gave him orders:
'Rouse yourself, son. Out! and call the Zephyrs
To carry you down to the Dardan prince;
Speak to him as he dawdles in Tyrian Carthage
Ignoring the cities given him by the Fates,
And carry my message through the swift air.
He does not live up to his mother's promises,

The lovely goddess who twice rescued him
From Greek assailants; yet he was to rule
Italy, where the empire waits to be born
Which is alive with arms; Teucer's proud race
Was to continue till the whole wide world
Was subject to its laws. If that is nothing
Or not worth any effort on his part
For his own reputation, let him think
Whether he has the right to grudge Ascanius
A citadel in Rome. What is he up to?
What is he after as he idles there
Among a hostile people, giving no thought
To his Ausonian posterity
Or the Lavinian fields? Tell him to sail,
That is the point: make sure he gets the message.'
   Such was his speech. Then Mercury made ready
To do as his great father had commanded.
First he bound on his feet his golden sandals
Which bear him aloft on their wings
Over seas, over land, like a great wind.
Then he took his wand, with which he calls up
Pale ghosts from Orcus while he sends others
Down to the bitter world of Tartarus,
Gives sleep or waking and opens eyes on death.
With this to aid him, he drove on the winds
And moved easily in the wild clouds.
Now as he flew he saw the steep-sided peak
Of labouring Atlas who holds up the sky,
Atlas, whose great head bristling with pines
Is always in dark clouds and buffeted
By wind and rain; snow falls upon his shoulders,
Rivers flow down the chin of the old man
And on his beard daggers of ice stick out.
Here the Cyllenian hovered on his wings,
Then suddenly swooped with his whole weight
On to the water like a bird who skims
Along the shore, around fish-haunted rocks,
Always close to the surface as he flies.
That was the manner in which Mercury
Flew between land and sky along the shore

Of sandy Libya, and cut through the winds
Coming from Atlas whence his mother came
    When his winged feet first touched the native huts
He came upon Aeneas building forts
And putting up houses of a new kind.
There he was with his sword glittering
With yellow jasper; from his shoulders fell
A cloak that was ablaze with Tyrian purple,
A gift the sumptuous Dido had made for him
And decorated with thread of gold.
He challenged him at once: 'You wife's servant!
So now you are laying the foundations
Of a powerful Carthage, what a lovely city!
So, you have forgotten your own kingdom
And all your own affairs! The god of gods,
The Lord of All, whose power is supreme
In heaven and earth, has sent me from Olympus
Through the swift winds, to say these things to you.
What are you up to? What have you in mind,
To kill your time as you do here in Libya?
If you are not moved by thoughts of glory
At what awaits you, and will not stir yourself
To any exertion for your own good name,
Think of Ascanius who is growing up
And share the hopes of your heir Iülus
To whom the kingdom of Italy
And all the Roman lands should fall by right.'
So the Cyllenian spoke, and as he did so
Left mortal sight, vanishing in thin air.
    But then Aeneas was struck dumb indeed;
His hair stood on end and his voice stuck.
He burned with a desire to get away
And leave the country that was sweet to him,
Astonished to have had such a warning
And that the gods' hands reached out to him.
What should he do? How would he ever dare
To approach and reason with the raging queen?
How should he begin such a discourse?
Rapidly he turned over in his mind,
Now this way and now that, what he should do
And went through all the possibilities.

Having weighed all, he came to this conclusion:
He had best call Mnestheus and Sergestus
And brave Serestus, and instruct them
To make the fleet ready and say nothing,
Ordering all the company to the shore
To collect the weapons while concealing
What was the reason for the change of plan;
He meanwhile, while his dear Dido knows nothing
And has no inkling of any rupture,
Will try to get to her and discover
The moment that is best to speak to her
And how he can get out of this affair.
Quickly and cheerfully his men make ready
And carry out the orders he has given.
    But the queen – for who can deceive a lover? –
Before he gets there, guesses at his tricks.
She is the first to know what is afoot
And is afraid though things still look secure.
It was that evil Rumour brought to her,
Mad with anxiety, some indications
That the fleet was armed and made ready to sail.
She could do nothing but raged furiously
And stormed up and down through the city
Like a Bacchante maddened by the shaking
Of the sacred emblems when the orgies begin
And there is shouting all the night long.
At last she finds her way to Aeneas
And so addresses him:
    'Are you so faithless that you hoped to hide
So terrible a wrong and creep away
Silently from my land? Is not our love,
Nor yet your solemn promise made to me,
Nor Dido who must die a cruel death,
Enough to keep you here? But even in winter
You cannot wait to hurry out your fleet,
So cruel are you? Why? If foreign fields
And unknown destinations were not all
You had to look for and if Troy still stood,
Would you set out for Troy with all your fleet
Over such stormy water? Is it me
That you are running away from? By these tears

I beg you, by the promise that you made me
(When there is nothing else that's left to me),
By our marriage and by its consummation,
If ever I deserved well of you,
If there was ever any pleasure in it,
Have pity now upon a falling house;
If prayers are anything, change your mind now.
Because of you the wandering peoples of Libya
And all their princes, hate me; even the Tyrians
Have turned against me; and because of you
My honour is gone and all that reputation
Which promised once to raise me to the stars.
And to whom are you leaving me – I who must die –
You a guest, for I cannot call you husband?
What is there for me? Either Pygmalion,
My brother, will tear down the walls
Or else Iarbas the Gaetulian
Will lead me home a captive. At the least
If I had had a son before you went,
A small Aeneas playing in my hall,
He would have let me see your face again,
I should not seem so utterly deserted.'
    She had spoken: he, remembering Jove's warning,
Kept his eyes motionless and with an effort
Fought back overt expression of his feelings.
At last he answered in a few words:
'Queen, I never shall seek to deny
That you have deserved more than well of me
For all the benefits you can spell out,
Nor shall I think of you without gratitude
As long as I remember my own life
Or there is any soul left in my body.
I will say little to the matter now.
Do not imagine I had any notion
Of stealing away from you like a thief.
I never went through any marriage ceremony
Nor entered any compact of that kind.
If the Fates ever let me live a life
To suit myself or to assuage my feelings
As I myself preferred, it would be Troy,
The city and the remnant of my people

That would pre-occupy me, Priam's palace
And a new Pergamus would have been built
Again by my own hands, for the defeated.
But it is Italy Grynian Apollo,
Italy that the Lycian oracles
Have ordered me to take as my own;
There is my love and that is my country.
If you as a Phoenician are kept here
By the attractions of a Libyan city
And the towers of Carthage, why should not we,
The Trojans, find a home in Ausonia?
We too may seek to rule a foreign land.
As often as the night with dewy shadows
Covers the earth, as often as the stars
Rise with their nightly fires, my father's ghost,
Troubled Anchises warns and terrifies me
In dreams, and the young Ascanius
Makes me think of the injury to him,
So dear a head cheated of a kingdom,
Hesperia and the fields the Fates intend.
And now the messenger of the gods has come,
Sent, I swear it on your head and mine,
By Jove himself, has brought instructions down
Through the swift winds; and I myself have seen
In the clear light of day, the god walking
Into the house and I have heard his voice
With my own ears. Do not incite me therefore,
Nor yet yourself, with any more complaints.
It is not of my own will that I seek Italy.'
     While he was speaking Dido turned away
But all the time her eyes were upon him,
Looking him up and down with silent glances
Until she could contain herself no longer:
'You never had a goddess for a mother,'
She said, 'Nor Dardanus for an ancestor,
A treacherous man like you! The Caucasus
Begat you upon his flinty rocks
And you were suckled by Hyrcanian tigers.
Why should I pretend any more
Or keep myself in check for worse to come?
Did he mind when I wept? Or as much as look at me?

Did he burst into tears or even pity
The one that loved him? What should I say now?
Not even great Juno or Jupiter
Looks fairly now on all that has happened.
Nothing can be relied upon. I took him,
Washed up on the shore, without anything,
And was insane to let him share my kingdom;
His fleet was lost, I saved it, his companions
I saved from death. I am being driven mad.
Now Apollo prophesies, the Lycian oracles
Have their say and now Jove himself
Sends down the messenger of the gods with orders
To frighten me. This really is something
For gods to worry about and spoil their rest!
I will not keep you or contradict you:
Go off to Italy with the winds and look for
Your kingdom among the waves! And I hope,
If the divine powers can do anything,
That halfway on the rocks you will gulp down
Your punishment calling on Dido's name.
Far away, I will follow you with fires
And ashes and when cold death has severed
Soul and body, I will be near you
Everywhere that you are, as a ghost.
You who are unjust will pay the penalty
And I shall hear, among the kindly dead
The story will come to me.' Here she stopped,
Her speech uncompleted, and escaped
Trembling, turning first from public view
Then going altogether, leaving Aeneas
Frightened, hesitant, still thinking what to say.
Her women catch her as she faints and falls
And carry her into her marble chamber
Where they lay her gently on her bed.
The dutiful Aeneas longed to comfort her
And to say things he knew would ease her trouble;
He groaned, his spirit weakened by great love
But did as the gods said he must do
And went at once to look to the fleet.
    Then indeed the Trojans get to work
And all along the shore they are dragging

Tall ships to the sea, and once again
The tarred keels are afloat.
They bring oars from the woods with leaves still on them
And timbers not yet shaped, so eager are they
To get away. And all over the city
You can see them moving out. They are like ants
Taking plunder from a great heap of corn,
Remembering what the winter is like, and storing;
Over the plain there goes a black column
Carrying their booty now through the grass
On a narrow track; some of them push huge grains,
Setting their shoulders to them, some press the files
And keep the stragglers up; the whole path seethes
With creatures at their work. As you looked on,
Dido, what were your feelings, what sighs
Did you exhale when from your citadel
You saw the whole shore seething far and wide
And heard the whole sea ringing with cries?
Love without measure, is there anything
You do not force the human heart to do?
Again she was compelled to tears, again
Compelled to try the effect of supplication,
Abjectly submitting her mind to love
Lest she should omit any remedy
That might have worked, and go to death for nothing.

  'Anna, you see what is happening on the shore;
They have all collected there; now the canvas
Is flapping in the breeze and now the sailors
Are decorating the ships in celebration,
You can see the garlands. It is as I expected,
This terrible grief, sister, and you will find
That I can stand it. Only one thing, sister,
I ask of you, to help me: you are the one
That rascal really cared for, he told you
What he was really thinking; no-one but you
Knows the best moment to approach the man.
Go, sister, plead with my proud enemy.
I did not join with the Greeks in Aulis
Swearing to extirpate the Trojan people;
I did not send a fleet to Pergamus,
Nor did I break up Anchises' grave

To trouble his ashes and his ghost;
Why is he deaf to all I have to say?
Where is he off to? Let him do one favour,
The last one, to the woman who has loved him:
Let him await favourable winds
To make escape easy. I plead no more
For the old marriage-vows that he betrayed,
Nor that he should forego his lovely Latium
Or give up the idea of a kingdom;
All I ask is a little empty time,
An interval of rest from this passion
Till fortune can teach me how to grieve.
Have pity on your sister, this is the last
Plea I shall make to him, and when he yields
I shall repay in full with my death.'
   Such were the supplications which her sister
Miserably plied him with again and again.
But he was not moved by any tears
And no words could make him tractable;
If he would listen, the gods stopped his ears.
It was as if the north winds from the Alps,
Blowing this way and that, in competition,
Were trying to uproot a stout oak
To which great strength had come with the years;
The trunk is shaken, leaves strew the ground,
The tree itself clings firmly to the rocks
And, far as the top stretches to the skies
The roots descend into Tartarus:
Just so was the hero buffeted
This way and that by ceaseless entreaties
And he felt troubled by them through and through,
Yet his mind was unmoved, the tears meant nothing.
   Then Dido was unhappy, terrified
By the Fates and she prayed for death, weary
Of looking up at the wide arch of the sky.
What drove her on to carry out her purpose
Of leaving the world was that before her eyes
Upon the altars smoking with incense
As she put down her offerings, she saw
What even in the telling is terrible,
The water turn black and the wine poured out

Turn into menacing blood, though no-one saw
Except herself, and she told nobody,
Not even her sister. There was in the palace
A marble temple to her former husband,
She kept it up in all the proper pomp
With snowy fleeces and celebratory foliage;
From here, it seemed to her, there came a voice,
Her husband calling her, she heard the words
When dark night had fastened on the earth
And the owl alone, perched somewhere aloft,
Utters its repeated wild complaint,
Drawing its hoot out to a mourning call;
And besides many of the past predictions
Made by inspired seers came back to her,
Terrible warnings that horrified her.
Aeneas himself appeared in her dreams
With cruel admonitions which made her frenzied;
She seemed to be alone, with no companions,
Going on a long and endless journey,
Looking for the Tyrians in an empty land:
As when Pentheus, driven out of his mind,
Sees the Eumenides pursuing him,
Two suns in the sky, two cities of Thebes,
Or when Agamemnon's son Orestes
Is driven across the stage escaping from
His mother armed with flaming torches
And black snakes, and all the while at the door
The Furies squat and wait for vengeance.

So, when she has the Furies in her mind
And, overcome by pain, decides for death,
Settling within herself the time and manner,
She comes to her grieving sister and speaks,
Hiding her purpose behind a calm appearance
And showing a clear hope upon her brow:
'Sister,' she says, 'I have found a way;
Wish me joy. What I have thought of now
Will either give him back to me or else
Rid me of my love for him for ever.
In the farthest reaches of the Ocean
And by the setting sun, lies Aethiopia.
There the great Atlas turns upon his shoulders

The axis of the sky ablaze with stars:
I have been told of a priestess there,
She is a Massylian, and the custodian
In that place, of the temple of the Hesperides.
It was she who gave the dragon such a feast
And kept watch over the sacred boughs
Of the apple-tree, and sprinkled honey-dew
And soporific poppies. She, it seems,
Can by her charms free any mind from love
Just as she wishes, and trouble others;
She can stop rivers and turn back the stars;
Bring out the ghosts at night; under her feet
The earth will rumble and meanwhile you see
The mountain-ash walk down the mountain-side.
I swear, my dear, by all the gods, by your
Dear head, sister, it is against my will
That I invoke such magic arts as these.
You secretly set up a funeral pyre
In an interior courtyard of the palace,
Where it is open, and then pile upon it
The arms that wicked man left in my chamber
And everything he wore, the bed itself,
The marriage-bed that was the end of me;
The thing is, to get rid of everything
That could remind me of that evil man:
That's what the priestess says.' Then she was quiet
And a great pallor spread over her face.
But Anna did not guess that these new rites
Concealed her sister's funeral preparations;
She did not think there could be such passions
Or fear that things would be any worse
Than when Sychaeus died. And so it was
She did as she was told.
     But the queen, when the pyre had been erected
In the middle of the palace, under the sky,
A towering pile of pine and planks of oak,
Hung the whole space with garlands and the pyre
With yew and cypress; on the bed she placed
The garments and the sword that he had left,
Also his effigy, knowing what would happen.
Around stood altars, there was the priestess,

Her hair about her shoulders. She spoke like thunder,
Calling upon three hundred gods, upon
Erebus, Chaos and the tri-formed Hecate
Who is the three faces of Diana.
She sprinkled water, saying it had come
From the spring of Avernus; herbs were brought,
Cut in the moon-light with bronze sickles
And bursting with a milky black poison;
They brought also a love-charm snatched from the brow
Of a new-born foal before the mare could get it.
Dido herself stood by the altars,
Holding the ritual grain in outstretched hands,
One foot out of its sandal, her garment loose,
And called the gods to witness and the stars
Which know what is to happen, that she would die.
Then she prayed to whatever powers there are
Just and mindful of lovers not well matched.

   Night came, and all across the world the weary
Took quiet sleep and bodies were at rest
With woods and cruel seas, and now the stars
Had glided half-way along their course;
The fields were all silent, herds and bright birds,
Whatever lives on wide stretches of water
Or on the rough land among the briars
Was sunk in sleep under the silent night.
It was not so with the unhappy Phoenician,
She never fell asleep, not ever took
The night into her eyes nor yet her heart;
Her troubles multiplied, her love came back
And raged in her, billowing like a great tide.
In this state she began to turn things over,
Arguing with herself: 'What should I do?
Am I to make myself a laughing-stock,
Trying my former suitors once again,
Numidians I have so often scorned as husbands?
Shall I follow the Trojan fleet and submit
To whatever orders the Trojans care to give me?
Are they so delighted with the help I gave them
That the memory of it will stand me in good stead?
Who – supposing that I wanted them to –
Would let me go aboard and welcome one

They hate so much among their arrogant ships?
You are lost, do you not know even now,
Do you not see, Laomedon means treachery?
What then? Am I to go on my own
In company with those sailors, exultant
Because they are getting away? Or else surrounded
On every side by a great mob of Tyrians
I could hardly tear away from the city of Sidon,
Tell them to hoist their sails and travel again,
Forcing them on to the sea? Better to die,
You have deserved it, deflect the pain with a sword.
And you, sister, beaten down by my tears,
Beside myself as I was, you were the first
To pile all these calamities upon me
And expose me to the enemy. No,
I was not allowed to live my life unmarried,
In innocence like the wild animals
And keep away from all such cares as these;
I have not kept faith with Sychaeus!'
Complaints like these came bursting from her heart.
    Aeneas meanwhile, high up on the stern,
His mind set on departure, was asleep,
Having made all his preparations first.
To him as he slept on a shape appeared;
It was the god come back with the same look,
Who once again seemed to admonish him;
He was like Mercury in everything,
The voice, the colouring, the same golden hair,
The handsome youthful limbs: 'O goddess-born,'
He said, 'And can you in your present straits
Persist in sleeping, while so many dangers
Crowd round about, do you not see them, madman?
Do you not hear the favourable breeze?
That woman is conceiving fresh deceits,
There is evil in her heart; resolved to die,
Her fury bobs on an uncertain tide.
Why not escape quickly while you can?
Soon you will see around you in the water
Ships' timbers jostling and fire-brands ablaze,
Soon the whole shore will be in flames,
If the dawn finds you idling in these territories.

Get up and get to work! No more delays!
Women are always full of chops and changes.'
With these words he melted into night.

   Then indeed Aeneas was terror-stricken;
He started up from sleep and roused his men:
'Quickly, wake up, lads! sit down on those benches;
Hurry there, get the sails up! A god sent
Once more from high heaven is urging us
To escape now and cut the twisted ropes.
We follow you, you holy deity
Whoever you may be, and jubilant
We are ready for command. Be with us now,
Graciously help us, make the stars favourable.'
So saying, he drew his sword like lightning
Out of its scabbard and as he drew it struck
The cable which was all that held them back.
The same enthusiasm seized them all;
They snatch up what they can and do the same;
They leave the shore; the sea is lost in ships;
They turn up foam and sweep into blue water.

   And now Dawn scattered light over the land,
Rising up from the saffron bed of Tithonus.
The queen, as she saw from her look-out towers
The first light whiten, saw the fleet at sea
Moving with steady sails, and realised
There were no oarsmen anywhere in the harbour
Or on the shore, beat herself with her hand
Three times, four times, on her lovely breast
And pulled out handfuls of her golden hair:
'Jupiter!' she called out, 'And shall this stranger
Make this kingdom of mine a laughing-stock?
Will they not bring their arms out, everyone
In the city, and tear those ships from their berths?
Go quickly, bring torches, distribute weapons,
Get to the oars and row! What am I saying?
Where am I? What madness twists my mind?
Unhappy Dido, now your sins come home!
But why not when you offered him the crown?
So this is what he offered as his trust,
He who they said carried his gods with him,
His ancestors' gods, and bore upon his shoulders

His father who had outlived his time!
Could I not have carried him off then,
Torn him apart and thrown the bits in the sea?
Could I not have finished his friends with a sword
And served up Ascanius for him to eat?
It cannot be certain we would have beaten them.
Suppose we hadn't, whom had I to fear?
I was going to die in any case. Torches!
I could have taken them into the camp,
I could have set all the ships ablaze,
Wiped out father and son and all and then
Thrown myself on the heap. O flaming Sun,
You who purify everything upon earth,
And you, Juno, who understand these troubles
And know my plight, and you nocturnal Hecate
For whom there is howling at the city cross-ways
You Furies who are nothing but revenge
And all you gods of the dying Elissa,
Accept my prayers, turn your powers, as is right,
Upon these evils, hear me! If he must,
If that intolerably evil man
Must reach his destination after all
Because the end is fixed and Jove requires it,
Yet let him be harried in his wars
By an audacious people, and expelled
From his new territories, Iülus be torn from him,
Let him know what it is to sue for aid
And may he see his comrades lie unburied.
Then, when he has submitted to an unjust peace,
May he never live to enjoy his kingdom
But let him fall before his time, and lie
Without rites on a lonely stretch of sand.
This I beg, and this final utterance
I pour out with my blood. Then you, O Tyrians,
Vex with your hatred all his race, through all
Generations to come, for you could pay
No better tribute to my ashes. Let there be
No love and no treaties between our peoples.
May some avengers rise from my bones
Who will pursue the Trojan colonists
With fire and sword, now and hereafter,

Whenever there is strength and opportunity.
Let shore be against shore, seas against seas,
I pray, arms against arms, may they have war
They and their children's children for ever.'
    She stopped, then cast her mind this way and that,
Wondering how she could most rapidly
Break from the light of day which now she hated.
Then she spoke briefly to Sychaeus's nurse,
Barce, her own having long been black ashes
In their homeland: 'Dear nurse,' she said, 'fetch Anna,
My sister; tell her to sprinkle river water
Over her body and bring with her the animals
And all the things for expiatory sacrifice.
Let her come like that, and you yourself
Must put on a sacrificial headband.
I have everything ready for the rites
Of Stygian Jove, and have begun already;
I want to finish now and end these troubles
By setting light to the Trojan's pyre.'
She stopped again. With an old woman's fussiness
The nurse hurried away. But Dido, trembling,
Having begun her terrible course, grew wild;
She cast blood-shot glances here and there,
Her cheeks trembled and became blotchy
And she was pale as one about to die.
She burst through the door of the inner court-yard
And scrambled furiously up the funeral pyre.
Then she took from its sheath her Dardan sword,
A present she had begged, but not for this,
Yet when she set eyes on the Trojan's clothes
And the familiar bed, she paused a little
And shed tears for what she was to do,
Then threw herself down upon the bed
And spoke her last words: 'There are his things,
I loved them while the Fates and god allowed;
Take my last breath, release me from these troubles.
My life is over, I have run the course
That Fortune gave me. Now my noble ghost
Will go beneath the surface of the world.
I have founded a famous city, seen my walls;
I have avenged my husband, punished the brother

Who was our enemy. I could have been
Happy, too happy, alas, if Dardan ships
Had never been drawn up upon my shore!'
She stopped and pressed her face to the bed,
Then spoke again: 'I shall die unavenged,
But I shall die. To go into the dark
In that way pleases me. From out at sea
May the cruel Dardan to the very last
Strain his eyes to catch sight of the fire
And carry with him the omen of my death.'
    She had had her say, and while she was still speaking
Her attendants saw her fall upon her sword
Which spurted blood and left her hands bespattered.
A cry went up high above the court-yard
And through the shaken city Rumour danced.
The buildings roared and with a loud wailing
The heavens re-echoed. It was not otherwise
Than as if Carthage or the old town of Tyre
Had fallen and the enemy rushed in
And flames spread uncontrolled over houses and temples.
Anna heard, terror-stricken, and in her fear
Rushed through the crowd like a lunatic,
Tearing her cheeks with her fingernails
And striking her breast with her fists. She called out
The dying woman's name. 'So this was it!
And so you were deceiving me, sister?
This is what this pyre was for, these fires and altars?
Yet what is the first thing that I lament,
Deserted as I am? That you, in dying,
Were too grand to think about your sister.
You should have asked me to share your fate;
One sword would have hurt both at the same time.
And so I built the pyre with my own hands,
Called our ancestral gods with my own voice,
Only to be, when you put yourself there,
The cruel one who kept out of the way?
You have destroyed yourself and me with you,
Sister, your people, their leaders and your city.
Let me at least wash your wounds with water
And if there is a trace of breath still,
Let me take it in my mouth.' And as she spoke

She climbed up the high steps and with a sob
She took her sister, less than half alive,
Put her arms round her and mopped up the blood
Using her dress. Dido tried to look up
But found her eyes were heavy and she could not;
The wound deep in her chest hissed a little.
Three times she tried to raise herself on her elbow;
Three times she fell back on the bed;
With wandering eyes she looked for the sun
And when she found it she let out a sigh.
　Almighty Juno then, pitying the pain
That went on for so long, and the hard exit,
Sent Iris down to her from Olympus
To free the struggling spirit from the limbs.
For since it was not fate that made her perish,
Nor a just death, but she was dying pitiably
Before her day, caught in a sudden madness,
Proserpine had still not taken from her head
The yellow lock she owed to Stygian Orcus.
So dewy Iris on her saffron wings
Flew down from heaven trailing her changing colours
Against the sun, and stopped above her head.
'I take this offering, sacred to Dis, as ordered,
And so, set you free from that body,' she said
And with her right hand cut the lock. At once
All her warmth ebbed, her life went to the winds.

# BOOK V

# BOOK V

Meanwhile far out at sea Aeneas kept
Steadily on his course, cutting the waves
The north wind had darkened. He looked back
And saw the city lit by the flames
Burning up Dido. What caused that great fire
Nobody knew; but what they all knew
Was what grim pains love suffers when dishonoured
And what a woman mad with love can do:
This made the Trojans heavy with forebodings.

　　As the ships sailed on the high seas
With no land in sight anywhere
But sea on all sides, on all sides the sky,
A dark cloud stood above Aeneas's head;
It brought storm, it shut out the light
And all the waves shuddered in the shadow.
The helmsman Palinurus from the poop
Called out: 'Why is the whole sky lost in cloud?
What, Father Neptune, are you doing to us?'
Then he gave orders they should make all trim
And put their full weight behind the oars;
He veered the sails to the wind and spoke:
'Magnanimous Aeneas, not if Jupiter
Himself had promised it, should I have hope
Of reaching Italy with such a sky.
The winds have shifted right across our course,
Rising and roaring from the blackened west;
The atmosphere is thickening into cloud.
We cannot fight against it, all our strength
Is not enough for this. We must trust to luck,
So let us go wherever Fortune calls us.
And if my memory serves and if the stars
Are where I think they are, then not far off
Will be the safe shores of your brother Eryx

And the Sicilian harbours.' Aeneas, calm,
Says: 'I saw long ago that the winds
Require this of us, and that it is vain
To strive against them as you have been doing.
Change course, sail on. Could anything be better,
Or could I hope to find a better haven
For weary ships, than that which has already
Dardan Acestes and, in its bosom,
Clutches the bones of my father, Anchises?'
So they make for port, and favourable Zephyrs
Fill their sails; the sea runs the fleet's way;
Gladly they turn towards the familiar sands.
    But far off from the top of a high hill
Acestes marvels as he sees the approach
Of friendly ships; bristling with javelins
And in the rough skin of a Libyan bear
He runs to meet them, for a Trojan mother
Bore him, the river Crinisus was his father;
He does not forget their old relationship
But wishes them joy on their return;
Welcoming them with all his country treasures,
In friendly fashion he gives them refreshment and rest.
    When with first light the stars were driven away
By a clear morning, Aeneas called his men
From all along the shore and spoke to them
Standing upon a mound, part of an earth-work:
'Great sons of Dardanus, you of a race
Descended from the high blood of the gods,
The months have passed, the circle of the year
Has been completed since we buried here
The bones, the last remains my divine father
Left on the earth, and here dedicated
The altars where he was mourned. Now is the time,
The very day, unless I am mistaken,
Which I shall always honour (so you have willed,
O gods!). This day, even should I pass it
In exile in the Gaetulian Syrtes, or caught
In the Argolic sea, or in Mycenae,
Yet I would carry out the vows I made
Each year to celebrate the proper rites
And pile the altars up with offerings due.

How much more then, when we are gathered here
(It must be the intention of the gods,
It must be through their power) on the very spot
Where lie my father's ashes and his bones
And we have found a friendly harbour here.
Now therefore let us celebrate together
This glad occasion and pray for fair winds
So that one day, when I have built my city,
My father may be pleased that every year
I carry out these rites in his own temples.
Acestes is from Troy and he gives you
A couple of oxen for each and every ship.
Bid to the feast your own country's gods
And also those your host Acestes worships.
Then, if in nine days' time the dawn still brings
Its kindly light to mortals and again
Shows us the world, I will arrange contests,
And first, a contest for the fastest ship;
Then for the fastest runner; a competition
For the best man with javelins and light arrows,
Or for whoever has the guts to try
What he can do with raw-hide boxing-gloves;
Let them all come, they can look forward
To prizes if they deserve them. But now, silence,
And put your crowns of leaves upon your heads.'
　　Having said this, he bound about his brows
His mother's myrtles. Helymus did the same,
So did Acestes, a man of ripe years,
And so did young Ascanius. All the youth
Followed suit. Then Aeneas went away
From the assembly and, followed by thousands,
Made his way to the tomb, where a great throng
Surrounded him. He poured on the ground,
As the custom is, two bowls of unmixed wine,
Two of new milk, two of consecrated blood;
He scattered bright flowers and then he spoke:
'Hail, holy father, once again; and hail
You ashes of him I rescued in vain
And you spirit and shade of my begetter.
It was not permitted, in your company,
To seek where the Italian borders lay

Nor the Ausonian Tiber, whatever that is.'
When he had spoken, from the foot of the shrine
A slippery serpent came, huge with seven coils,
Curling seven times as he dragged himself
Smoothly, circling the tomb, slipping by the altars
And showed his back spotted with blue markings
Which shone also with gold, as in the clouds
A rainbow shows a thousand changing colours
From the sun opposite. Aeneas then
Was staggered at the spectacle. The serpent,
With its long train among the bowls and cups,
Tasted the offerings and again withdrew
Harmlessly to the bottom of the tomb,
Having consumed what was upon the altars
And gone away. Aeneas, all the more
For this occurrence, celebrated anew
The honours he had recently begun,
Uncertain whether to think that this was
The genius of the place or his father's spirit.
As custom is, he killed two young sheep,
As many pigs, as many black-backed bullocks;
He poured wine from the bowls and called upon
The great Anchises's spirit and the shades
Released from Acheron. Then his companions
Joyfully brought gifts, whatever each had,
Heaped up the altars, sacrificed bullocks
While others set the cauldrons in their places
And, stretched upon the grass, blew at the fires
Under the spits, and so roasted the meat.
    The awaited day arrived, the horses
Of Phaethon brought the ninth dawn with clear sky.
The news had got around, the reputation
Acestes had did the rest, the neighbourhood
Was roused; a cheerful throng crowded the shore,
Some come to see Aeneas and his men,
Some set to compete in the games.
The prizes are first laid out on the ground
In the middle of the course; there are sacred tripods,
Garlands of leaves and palms for the winners,
Armour and garments which have been dyed purple,
Together with piles of silver and gold;

Then from a mound thrown up at the centre
A trumpet sounds the opening of the games.
    Entered for the first contest are four ships,
Well-matched, with heavy oars, they are the pick
Of the whole fleet. Mnestheus with his rowers,
A keen crew, propel the *Sea Dragon*;
He will soon be the Italian Mnestheus,
The line from which the house of Memmius comes;
Gyas has the *Chimaera*, a huge ship,
A floating city, three rows of Dardan youths
Send on her way, rowing in three tiers;
Sergestus, from whom the Sergius family
Takes its name, rides high in the *Centaur*;
Cloanthus comes on in the sea-blue *Scylla*;
He was your ancestor, Roman Cluentius!
    Far out at sea there is a rock, standing
Over against the line of foam on shore;
At times it is submerged as it is battered
By swollen waves when stormy north-west winds
Hide the stars; in calm it lies quiet,
Its flat top rising from the sea
And making somewhere for the gulls to bask.
It was here that Aeneas set a marker,
Green boughs of leafy oak, to tell the sailors
Where they should turn and start the long course back.
They chose positions by lot, and the captains
On the high sterns shone out in gold and purple;
The rest of the young men wore crowns of poplar
And their bare shoulders glistened, rubbed with oil.
They took their places on the benches, arms
Stretched out to hold the oars, and so they waited
Until they got the signal; leaping hearts
Drained of blood, they trembled with anxiety,
So great was the desire they had for praise.
Then, when the clear trumpet gives its note,
Unhesitatingly from their starting-places
They shoot out; a roar from the sailors
Hits the sky, they pull on the oars
Turning up foam. Together they cut furrows,
The whole surface of the sea is opened,
Torn by the oars and the three-headed prows.

They are faster than chariots with two horses
Slipping out at the start of a race
And rushing over the course like a flood
While over the backs of the bolting animals
The charioteers lean forward, shake the reins
And lay on the whip. The whole forest rings
With the applause and shouts of 'Come on!'
From the supporters, while from the enclosed beaches
The roar strikes the hills and they shout back.
    It is Gyas who gets away, he slips out
First on the sea through all the press and shouting;
Cloanthus after him, his oars are better
But his ship is heavy in the water.
Then equidistant from him, the *Sea Dragon*
And *Centaur* race to get ahead; *Sea Dragon*
First has the advantage, then the huge *Centaur*
Gets the better of her, now both are riding
Together neck and neck, the salt shallows
Cut by their long keels. Now all draw near
The rock, holding course for the turn. Gyas
First and the winner at the half-way mark,
Calls to Menoetes who is steering for him:
'Why are you going so far to starboard?
Turn this way! Hug the solid side and let
The oar-blades go close to the rock to port!
Leave the high sea to others!' But Menoetes,
Despite the warning, feared the hidden rocks
And turned the prow further out to sea.
'Why are you going off course?' Once again Gyas
Shouted at him, 'Make for the rocks, Menoetes!'
Then looking back he saw Cloanthus coming
And holding a closer course than he.
Cloanthus scrapes his way on the port side
Between Gyas's ship and the sounding rocks,
And suddenly he has shot past the leader
And is in safe water, the half-way mark behind him.
Young Gyas blazes up in high anger
As if his very bones were set alight;
There are tears on his cheeks. Forgetting himself,
Forgetting too the safety of his crew,
He flung the sluggish Menoetes from the high poop

Headlong into the sea, and took over the helm
And still acting as captain urged on his men
As he swung the rudder round towards the rocks.
Menoetes, meanwhile, came heavily up
From the bottom of the sea, he was not young
And his clothes were soaked, he made for the rocks,
Climbed up and sat down where the stone was dry,
The Trojans laughed at him as he fell
And as he swam; they laughed at him again
As he sat coughing up the salt water.
　　　Then the last two, Sergestus and Mnestheus,
Burned with the hope that they would beat Gyas
Who now was lagging. Sergestus took the lead
And drew near the rock, not a length ahead
But part of a length only, the *Sea-Dragon*
Was pressing him so hard. Mnestheus
Meanwhile walked up and down among his crew
Urging them on: 'Come on, rise to the oars!
Comrades of Hector, men that I picked out
In the last hour of Troy! Now show that strength,
That courage which you showed among the quicksands
Off Africa, and on the Ionian sea
And in the following water of Malea.
Though I Mnestheus no longer seek
The first place, and do not hope to win,
Yet still, oh! – but let the winner be
Whoever, Neptune, you would have victorious –
It would be a disgrace to get home last;
Make sure of that at least, my countrymen,
And don't be put to shame!' The men lean forward
To pull back on their oars, a supreme effort;
The great bronze-plated poop rang with their strokes,
The sea sped under them; in quick time
They panted till their limbs shook,
Their mouths were dry; they sweated bucketfuls.
A chance brought them the honour that they sought.
For while Sergestus in a towering rage
Pushed his ship between *Dragon* and the rocks,
Skirting them at an injudicious distance,
He had the bad luck to hit a jutting ledge
And stick to it. There is a bang, the oars

Strike the sharp edge and snap, the prow hangs
Poised there. And the sailors jump up shouting,
They are at a standstill. They reach for poles and boat-hooks
With iron tips and points, and from the swell
They do their best to fish out broken oars.
Mnestheus meanwhile becomes keener still;
Cheered by the way he has got round the point,
With oars in quick time and the wind he prayed for,
He leans over the sea and runs in clear water.
Like a dove suddenly frightened from her niche
Among the hiding-places in the pumice
Where she has her home and newly-hatched young,
And carried in her flight towards the fields
After the noise she made with her wings
When scared from cover, soon skimming
In quiet air with no movement of wings,
But swift, a liquid course: just so Mnestheus,
The *Sea-Dragon* cuts over the surface
In the last stretch momentum carries her on,
She flies. And first he leaves Sergestus there
Struggling on the high ledge, calling for help
Over the shallow waters, but in vain,
And learning how to run with broken oars.
Then he goes after Gyas and *Chimaera*,
With her great bulk, gives way, having no helmsman.
    Now there is no-one but Cloanthus left,
Close by the winning-post, Mnestheus
Following him closely, straining every nerve.
Then indeed there is twice as much shouting
And everyone encourages the pursuer
With cries which make the whole sky re-echo.
The leading crew were furious they might not keep
The honours that they reckoned they had won;
They would die now rather than let it go.
The challengers were pleased with their success;
They can do well because they think they can
And maybe they would have forced a draw
Had not Cloanthus, stretching out his hands
Towards the sea, poured out a stream of prayers
And called the gods to witness as he vowed:
'Gods who command the sea over whose surface

I speed, gladly will I bring to your altars
A white bull if you listen to my prayers,
And cast the entrails into the salt waves
And I will pour out wine in your honour.'
As he spoke, from the deepest floor of the sea
The whole company of Nereids heard him,
The company of Phorcus, Panopea
The virgin; and the old god Portunus
With his great hand sent them upon their way.
Swifter than south wind or a flying arrow
The ship flew to land and rested in harbour.

    Aeneas, as successor to Anchises,
Called all together as the custom was
And declared, through the bawling of a herald,
Cloanthus was the winner; then he crowned him
With bay-leaves and made the presentation:
Three bullocks for each ship at his choice,
With wine and a heavy talent of silver.
Then for the captains he adds special honours:
The winner gets a cloak worked in gold,
Bordered with Meliboean purple in
A double wandering line; and woven in it
The kingly boy upon leafy Ida
Wearying swift stags, pursuing them with javelins,
Eager, as if panting; Jove's armour-bearer,
The eagle who snatched him in his claws
And lifted him high up; his guardians
Stretched out their hands in vain towards the stars
While dogs barked wildly into the air.
But to the runner-up Aeneas gave
A corselet with triple links of gold
Which he had with his own hand stripped from Demoleos
When he defeated him by rapid Simois
Under the walls of Troy when they were high
– A gift for ornament and for protection.
So heavy was it Phegeus and Sagaris,
The servants, carried it with difficulty
Folded upon their straining shoulders, yet
Demoleos once chased and scattered Trojans in it.
The third prize was a pair of bronze cauldrons
And silver bowls cast in heavy relief.

Now everyone had had their prizes and all
Were going away with ribbons round their heads,
Proud of their winnings, when the missing captain,
Sergestus, who with great skill had managed
To get himself off the dangerous rock,
Brought his ship in amidst jeers and derision,
Having lost oars, with one tier out of action.
She was like some snake caught on the side of the road,
Run over by a brazen wheel or left
Half-dead and mutilated by a traveller
With a heavy stone, as it tries, but in vain
To escape by twisting and turning all its length,
Part of it furious, raising its hissing neck,
Its eyes blazing, part of it holding back,
Lame from its wound, struggling in knots, folded
Back on itself: for that is how the ship moved,
Slowly, the oars limping; she came under sail
None the less, and it was with all her canvas
That she entered the harbour. And Aeneas
Made an award to Sergestus as he had promised,
Glad he had saved the ship and brought his men back.
He was given a slave-girl, skilled in spinning and weaving,
Pholoë a Cretan, with twin boys at her breasts.
   This contest over, good Aeneas moved
To a stretch of level grass surrounded
On all sides by a line of wooded hills
Which formed an amphitheatre in the valley.
Thither the hero went with many thousands
And sat down on a daïs in the middle.
It was the turn here for the runners, anyone
Who wanted to show his speed he encouraged
And set the prizes out. From every side
Came Trojans and Sicilians, all mixed up;
The first were Nisus and Euryalus,
Euryalus distinguished for his looks
And in the bloom of youth, Nisus for being
Devoted to the boy; after them came
Diores, princely, from the eminent house
Of Priam, then came Salius and Patron
Together, one of them an Acarnanian,
The other an Arcadian from Tegea;

Then two Sicilian youths – Helymus, Panopes –
Who knew their way in the forests and were followers
Of old Acestes; there were many besides
Whose names are now lost to history.
Aeneas spoke with the whole group around him:
'Hear what I have to say, it is worth hearing.
Not one of you will go away from here
Without a gift from me. To everyone
I will present two Cretan arrow-heads
Of gleaming polished iron, and besides
A double-headed axe chased with silver;
These awards there will be for all of you.
The first three will also have prizes
And will be crowned with wreaths of pale olive.
The fastest man of all shall have a horse
With superb trappings; for the second there is
An Amazonian quiver full of arrows
– Thracian ones – with a broad belt of gold
From which it hangs, with a gem on the buckle;
The third will have to go away content
With this Argive helmet.'
                              When he had spoken
They took their places and on hearing the signal
Suddenly darted out from the starting line,
Streaming away like clouds in a storm
And all with their eyes on the finish.
First Nisus gets away, and flies ahead
Far beyond everyone, faster than wind or thunderbolt;
Next to him, but next by a long interval,
Salius follows; and some distance behind
Euryalus third;
Helymus follows Euryalus; close on him,
Grazing his heel with his heel and, with his shoulder,
Leaning on him, Diores; had there been time
He would have shot past him or at least
Left the issue in doubt. But on the last lap
Now, worn out, they were approaching the finish
When Nisus had the bad luck to slip on some blood
Which had been spilt perhaps when the bullocks were killed
And now had soaked the green grass and the ground.
Here the young man, who was triumphant,

Thinking he'd won, could not retain his footing,
He tottered and fell flat in the filthy muck
And the blood of the sacrifice. But nevertheless
He was not forgetful of Euryalus
Nor of his love; for, as he scrambled up
From the slippery place, he put himself in the way
Of Salius, who went sprawling in the sand
Where the blood was. Euryalus flashed past
And, through his friend's assistance, came in first
Amidst applause and shouted encouragement.
Helymus was the runner-up, then came Diores,
Now in third place.

       Then Salius remonstrated
Before the faces of the row of elders,
Filling the whole vast amphitheatre with cries,
Demanding that he be given back the honour
Which had been taken from him by a foul.
Euryalus however was protected
By popularity; his tears were appealing
And his performance was the more pleasing
Coming as it did in a handsome body.
Diores helped by protesting loudly;
He had won third place but would have lost his prize
If the first honour had been given to Salius.
Our ancestor Aeneas said: 'My lads,
Your rewards will stay just as they are;
No-one alters the order of the prizes,
But let me give some consolation
To a friend who has had undeserved bad luck.'
So he gave Salius a Gaetulian
Lion skin, huge, with claws that had been gilded.
Then Nisus said: 'If even those who lost
Are to be given prizes, and you are sorry
For those who had a fall, what will you give
That would be appropriate for Nisus
Since I deserved to have won the first place
If I, like Salius, had not had bad luck?'
And as he spoke he showed them the wet muck
Covering his face and fouling all his limbs.
The genial leader laughed and gave orders
For a shield to be brought out, Didymaon

Had made it and the Greeks taken it down
From where it hung in the temple of Neptune;
This splendid prize he gave to the young athlete.
    The races were over, the prizes given out:
Aeneas said: 'Now for the boxing. Who
Has strength and guts enough to come forward
And put the gloves on?' There would be two awards;
The winner would get a bullock decked out
With gold and ribbons and, for the loser,
To cheer him up, there would be a sword
And a fine helmet. Then immediately
Dares showed his face; his strength was huge.
There is a loud murmur as he rises;
He alone used to stand up to Paris
And by the tomb where the great Hector lies
Had done for Butes, giant though he was,
The champion from the race of the Bebrycian
Amycus, leaving him stretched out half-dead
On the yellow sand. Such Dares was, who now
Raised his head high, ready for the first bout;
He showed his broad shoulders, threw his arms around
And landed a few blows into the air.
Who would fight him? No-one from all that host
Dared to approach him and put on the gloves.
So, thinking no-one ventured for the prize,
He walked smartly up to the daïs
And stood at Aeneas's feet, then reached out
And caught the bull's horn in his left hand,
Saying: 'If, goddess-born, nobody dares
To trust himself to fight, how long do I wait?
Is it right to keep me here? Tell me to go
And take the prizes with me.' The Dardans shouted
And called for him to be given what was promised.
    Entellus was then blamed by Acestes
Who sat beside him on the green grass:
'Entellus, you used to be a hero,
The bravest of them, is it nothing now?
And will you patiently let these prizes
Be carried off without any contest?
Where do we see our god and master now?
We talk of Eryx but it means nothing.

Were you not famous once all over Sicily?
Are there not spoils hanging in your house?'
He answered: 'It is not because of fear
I seem to care for fame and glory less,
Nor do I; but my blood has grown cold
And age has slowed me up, my strength of body
Is chilled now and exhausted. If I had still
What once I had and what that impudent fellow
So confidently exults in, if I had youth,
I should have come forward, and not because
The prize of a fine bullock tempted me;
I don't need presents.' When he had said this
He threw a pair of heavy boxing-gloves
Into the ring, gloves which the violent Eryx
Used when he fought, binding his arms with hide.
There was amazement, so great were the skins
Of the seven oxen from which they were made
And lead and iron had been sewn in to stiffen them.
And more than any of the concourse there,
Dares himself was shaken and shrank back;
Meanwhile the generous son of Anchises
Tried the weight and turned this way and that
The immense coils of thongs. The older man
Addressed him with these words: 'Had any seen
The gloves that served as arms to Hercules
Or seen the fight upon this very shore!
Your brother Eryx used to wear these gloves;
(You see that there is still blood on them
And they are bespattered with brains); these he wore
When he stood up to great Alcides;
I used to wear them when I had better blood
To give me strength, and when envious age
Had not so sprinkled my temples with grey.
But if the Trojan Dares shies away
From our arms, if good Aeneas thinks fit
And if Acestes my sponsor approves,
Let us fight on equal terms. I will give up
These leathers Eryx used, don't be afraid,
And you can take off those Trojan gloves.'
So saying he threw back the double cloak
That was about his shoulders, and he bared

His great arms and legs and big-boned frame
And stood there like a giant on the sand.
    Anchises' son then, fatherly, brought out
The matching gloves and bound them on their hands.
Both stood on tip-toe and both fearlessly
Raised their arms high in the air, heads up
And drawn well back out of reach of the blows.
First they began to spar and then to fight,
One of them better on his feet and trusting
To youth to keep him going, while the other
Had strength and weight to help him; but his knees
Moved slowly and unsteadily and he panted
Unhealthily so that his limbs trembled.
The two men both threw many useless punches
At one another, fast on their hollow ribs;
Their chests gave out resounding thuds, and round
Their ears and foreheads hands are always busy;
Their cheeks are hit and rattle. Still Entellus
Stands heavily, his stance never changes,
Only his body moves as his quick eyes
Instruct him how he should elude the blows.
The other, like a captain who attacks
A tall city with siege-works or surrounds
A mountain fortress with his men-at-arms,
Tries this approach and that, and with great skill
Makes use of the whole ground and presses home
Varied assaults but still to no effect.
Entellus then rising to his full height
Put out his right and carried through with it;
The other saw the blow descending on him
And quickly slipped aside and so avoided it;
Entellus poured his strength on the wind;
The heavy man fell heavily to the ground,
Carried on by his own enormous weight
As sometimes hollow pine-trees fall on Ida
Or Erymanthus, torn up by the roots.
The Trojan and Sicilian supporters
Rise to their feet wildly; a shout goes up;
Alcestes is the first man to run forward
And sympathetically picks up his friend,
An old man like himself. But the contestant

Is not put out, a hero is not terrified;
He returns to the fight more violently,
His anger gives him energy. The disgrace,
Together with his consciousness of courage,
Sets him on fire: he chases Dares headlong
Over the whole area, laying on
A double rain of blows with right and left.
There is no hesitation, no respite;
It sounds like hail rattling on a roof;
The hero with quick blows from either hand
Hits Dares again and again and sends him spinning.
　　Aeneas then, the father of them all,
Would not allow this fury to continue,
Entellus was so bitter and enraged:
He stopped the fight, pulled Dares out of it
Exhausted as he was, and spoke to him
In words designed to mitigate defeat:
'Bad luck! But it was madness to go on.
Do you not see his strength is not his own
And that divine favour has turned against you?
Do not resist the god!' With these words
He separates the contestants. Then Dares
Was taken off by his loyal mates
And as he went he dragged his wobbly legs
And threw his head from side to side; he spat
Clots of blood from his mouth and with them teeth
Covered in blood; they led him to the ships
While some were called to take his prizes to him,
The helmet and the sword, leaving Entellus
The palm and the bullock. Then the winner,
Proud of the bull he had won and triumphant,
Said: 'Goddess-born, and you Trojans, all of you,
I'll show you what my strength used to be
In my young days, and from what sort of death
You have saved Dares by reprieving him.'
He took his place in front of the bullock
He had won in the fight and, drawing back
His right hand he swung the hardened glove
Plum in the middle of the creature's horns,
Towering above it: so he smashed the skull,
Scattering the brains and the bull collapsed

And lay lifeless but quivering on the ground.
Entellus, standing above it, poured out his heart
In some such words as these: 'I pay you honour,
Eryx, by giving you this better life
Since you have been robbed of that of Dares:
And I the victor lay aside my art.'
   Aeneas then invited those who wished
To try their hands at archery: the prizes
Were set out and then with easy strength
He raised the mast from Serestus's ship
And hung from it, to serve as a target,
A dove attached to the mast by a cord.
Men congregate and a helmet holds the lots;
The first to come out was that of Hippocoon
The son of Hyrtacus; there was applause.
Mnestheus followed, he who had just won
The naval competition, the Mnestheus
Whose forehead was still bound with green olive.
The third was Eurytion – he was your brother,
Renowned Pandarus, you who, receiving orders
To break the treaty, first shot an arrow
Right into the middle of the Achaeans.
The last lot in the helmet was Acestes,
Not afraid to compete in a young man's sport.
   They all bend their bows with all their strength
And each selects an arrow from his quiver.
The first arrow went with a twang
Through the air, it was young Hippocoon's;
It came close and stuck in the mast.
The mast trembled, the bird fluttered, terrified;
The shot was followed by a roar of applause.
Mnestheus then took his position;
He bent his bow and took his aim upwards,
His eye on a level with his arrow.
But, bad luck! he did not hit the bird;
What he did was to cut the knots and cord
Binding her foot, and she made off at once
Into the south wind and the black clouds.
Then rapidly Eurytion, who had long
Held his bow drawn, the arrow ready to go,
Invoked his brother, took aim at the dove

Which was now sporting in the open sky
And pierced her as she flapped against the background
Of a black cloud. The bird fell down dead,
Leaving her life among the stars of heaven;
Falling, she brought the arrow down with her.
Only Acestes, with no hope of the prize,
Remained; he turned his weapon to the sky
In spite of everything, to show the skill
An old man might have when he drew his bow.
A portent full of menace for the future
Suddenly came before their eyes; the event
Proved terrible, as seers in later time
Proclaimed at large. For, flying through the clouds
Without impediment the shaft of the arrow
Caught fire and left trace in a flaming path
Until it burnt out and disappeared
Into thin air, as shooting stars often
Are loosed and cross the sky, their hair streaming.
Sicilians and Teucrians alike
Stood stock-still in wonder and they prayed.
Aeneas did not reject the omen
But took the glad Acestes in his arms,
Heaped gifts upon him and spoke as follows:
'Take them, father; the great king of Olympus
Shows by these portents that it is his wish
That you should be awarded special honours.
You shall have this gift from old Anchises,
A bowl engraved with figures which a Thracian,
Cisseus, once gave my father, a token
Of his affection, to remember him by.'
This said, he crowned him with a wreath of laurel
And declared him the winner of the contest.
The generous Eurytion was not jealous
To see his honour given to another
Though he alone had brought down the bird.
The next prize went to him who sliced the cord;
The third to him whose arrow pierced the mast.
    But while this contest had been in progress
Our ancestor Aeneas had called Epytides
Who looked after Iülus and kept him company
And spoke these words into his faithful ear:

'Go off to young Ascanius: if he is ready
With his troop of boys and has the horses
Drawn up in order for the exercise,
Tell him to bring them in for his grandfather
And show what he can do with his men-at-arms.'
He tells the milling crowd to stand back
From the arena and leave the whole space clear.
The boys ride in before their fathers' eyes,
Keeping their distances, their harness glittering;
As they go by the youth of Sicily
As of Troy give a murmur of approval.
All have their hair decked with trimmed garlands,
As the custom is; they carry spearshafts,
Two each, of dog-wood with an iron tip
And some have polished quivers on their shoulders;
High on their chests there are necklaces
Of twisted pliant gold. There are three squads
Of horses and three boys are leading them,
Each of the leaders followed by two lines
Of six boys each, the whole is divided
Into three parts with three equal commanders;
The whole company shines. One of the squads
Was led triumphantly by little Priam,
Called after his grandfather – your son, Polites,
Famous and destined to increase the strength
Of the Italians. He rode a Thracian piebald
Whose fore-pasterns showed white as it stepped,
White on the forehead too.
The leader of the second squad was Atys,
From whom the Latin Atii claim descent,
Little Atys, Iulus's special friend.
The last and the most handsome of them all
Is Iulus himself, on a Sidonian,
A horse the radiant Dido had given him
To show her love and make him think of her.
The other boys all rode Sicilian horses
Which old Acestes had provided for them.

The boys are nervous, the Trojans are delighted,
Watching them and encouraging with applause;
They see how like their forefathers they are.
The boys rode solemnly past the whole gathering

Before the eyes of fathers, uncles, brothers;
Epytides then bellowed out an order
And cracked his whip. They galloped in formation,
Dividing the company into equal halves;
The three squads broke up and the half-sections
Performed a sort of dance; at the word of command
They wheeled again and charged, their spears lowered.
They formed new figures and then broke them up,
Separated as if they were enemies,
Entwining one circle with another
And exercised themselves in mock battle.
Sometimes they turned tail, sometimes wheeled round
Attacking with their spear-points, then they rode
Peacefully side by side. As in Crete
In the old days, in mountainous country,
The Labyrinth was said to have a path
Hidden from view with many twists and turns
Full of a thousand snares and surprises
Which made it impossible to follow
So that any who entered was lost for ever:
Just so were the many entangled courses
The Trojan boys were set on as they played
At battle and escape from battle, like dolphins
Who, swimming through salt water, make their way
Through the Carpathian or the Libyan seas,
Sporting among the waves. These exercises
And this kind of contest were revived
In Alba Longa by Ascanius
When he first raised the walls, the same he had
First practised with the other Trojan boys;
The Albans taught their sons; great Rome in turn
Took over and preserved the ancient practice;
The lads who take part are now known as Troys,
The company is called the Trojan troop.
Thus far Anchises' games were duly celebrated.
    There was a change of fortune at this point.
While they were celebrating at the tomb
With the successive games, Saturnian Juno
Sent Iris down from heaven to the fleet
The Trojans had laid up and breathed upon her
A fair wind for her journey – Juno still

Full of devices and still venomous,
Iris making her journey rapidly,
A girl in the thousand colours of the rainbow
Descending the sudden arc invisibly.
She saw the huge concourse on the shore,
Passed along and saw the harbour was deserted,
The fleet unattended, while far away
On a lonely beach, there were the Trojan women,
On their own, bewailing the loss of Anchises
And as they wept staring at the horizon.
'Alas! for weary women, what an expanse!
How much sea still to cross!' So they all cried.
They crave for a town; they are sick of being at sea.
So Iris, who knows how to make trouble,
Flings herself into the midst of them
Throwing aside the appearance of a goddess
And turns into Beroë, the aged wife
Of the Tmarian Doryclus who once
Had had family, fame and children, and as such
She slips in among the Trojan matrons:
'O wretched women,' she says, 'you'd be better off
If some Achaean had dragged you to your death
Under the walls of your native city!
O luckless race, what sort of end now
Does fortune hold for you? It is seven summers
Since Troy was brought down and ever since
We have been carried over land and sea,
And what unfriendly rocks have we encountered
And what unfriendly stars! while over the ocean
We chase after Italy and it eludes us,
And we find nothing but the tossing waves.
Here we are upon Eryx's territory,
Our brother's, with Acestes for our host;
Who stops us putting up our walls here
And giving all our citizens a city?
O mother country and you household gods
Snatched in vain from the enemy, shall Troy
And her walls mean nothing for the future?
Shall I see nowhere Hector's dear rivers,
Xanthus and Simois? Rather than that, come
And with me set fire to those fatal ships!

I saw Cassandra's image in a dream,
The prophetess seemed to give me blazing torches:
"Look for Troy here," she said, "this is your home."
Now is the time for action, after such portents
We should not hesitate. Look at those altars,
Four of them, they are Neptune's, the god himself
Gives us the brands and tells us what to do.'
   She spoke first and she was the first to act.
Boldly she seized a branch from the fire,
Raised her right arm and energetically
Whirled the flames round her head and then threw.
The Trojan women were startled, stupefied.
Then one of all that number, the eldest of them,
Pyrgo, the nurse of Priam's many sons,
Called out: 'That is not Beroë you see,
Ladies, that is not the Rhoeteian wife
Of Doryclus; that is a goddess, look!
Her beauty, shining eyes, all point that way,
Her mien, her face, her voice, the way she walks.
I myself have just come from Beroë,
I left her sick, furious that she alone
Would miss the sacrifice and could not honour
Anchises as she should.' At first the matrons
Were in two minds, they gazed at the ships,
Hesitating between their desperate love
For the land they were on and those realms
To which the fates were calling them. Suddenly
The goddess raised herself upon two wings
And as she fled through the sky under the clouds
Cut the great rainbow. These indeed were portents
Which left them thunderstruck, and then they screamed
In frenzy and some of them snatched fire
From hearths indoors while some stole from the altars
And hurled leaves, sticks and brands all together.
So Vulcan raged in unbridled fashion
Along the rowers' beeches and the oars:
The pine of the painted sterns blazed.
   Eumelus brought the news to those who were sitting
In the amphitheatre by Anchises's tomb
That the ships were on fire; they themselves saw
The cloud of black ash fluttering around.

Ascanius was the first to move; as brightly
As he had brought in his troop of horse
And with the same enthusiasm, he rode
To the camp on the shore, troubled as it was,
Nor could his breathless instructors hold him back.
'What is the matter with you, are you mad?
Where are you off to now, you wretched women?
Think of our country! That is not the enemy
Or a camp of hostile Argives, you are burning!
Itis your hopes and I am your Ascanius!'
He threw to his feet the empty helmet
He had put on when he was playing at battles.
Aeneas too hurried forward, with the Trojan troops
But the women, frightened, scattered along the shore
And made for the woods and caves where they could hide,
Hating the light, ashamed of what they had done;
They were themselves again and recognised
Their own kin, for Juno's power had left them.
   But that did not make the flames subside;
The fire still raged; among the wet timbers
The caulking was alive and belching smoke
Slowly, and smouldering heat was at the keels
And the disease went through the whole body;
Neither the heroic efforts of the men
Nor the water they poured on did any good.
Then the mindful Aeneas bared his shoulders,
Tearing the clothes away, calling on the gods
To give their help: he stretched out his hands:
'Almighty Jupiter, if there is one Trojan
You do not hate, if you care as in ancient times
For men's endeavours, grant that the fleet escape
From these flames, and the precarious fortunes
Of the remaining Trojans from destruction:
Or strike us dead with your hostile bolt,
If I deserve no less, destroy us all
With your right hand.' He had hardly finished speaking
When pelting rain came down, a black storm
Raged uncontrolled; the high places were shaken
By thunder, even the plains below shivered;
From the whole sky there descended
The blackest of turbulent storms, in rain

And with great force of wind. The boats fill up
And overflow, and timbers half-consumed
Are drenched until the last heat has gone.
So all the ships, except for four, were saved;
It was as if they had recovered from a disease.

Our ancestor Aeneas was thunder-struck
By this bitter event, and in his heart
Turned over his concerns this way and that:
Was he to settle on Sicilian soil
And think no more of Fate, or should he grasp
The shores of Italy? It was old Nautes,
The one Tritonian Pallas had instructed
And whom she had made famous for his skill,
Who could tell what the anger of the gods
Portended or what course the destinies
Required – he spoke now for Aeneas's comfort:
'Goddess-born, let us always follow Fate
Wherever it may drag us to and fro;
The only way of overcoming fortune,
Be what it will, is to submit to it.
You have a Dardan here, one of divine
Descent, Acestes; take counsel with him,
He is a willing partner: let him take
Those who, now that those ships are lost
Are too many for you, and those
Who have grown weary of the immense task
You have undertaken and of your destinies;
Pick out the old men and with them those ladies
Who have grown tired of putting to sea and all
Who are unfit for and afraid of danger;
Let those who are weary have their city here;
They can ask Acestes to let them call it Acesta.'

This advice from a friendly older man
Roused him, his mind was indeed divided
Between responsibilities which conflicted.
And black night in her chariot had come up
To high heaven, when a figure seemed to glide
Thence downwards – that of his father Anchises
Who suddenly poured out a stream of words:
'My son, you who were dearer to me than life

While I still had life, son exercised
By the destinies of Troy, I come to you
At the command of Jove, by whom the fleet
Was rescued when he drove back the fire
And who had pity on you from on high.
Obey the counsels that old Nautes gives,
They are the best. Take into Italy
The pick of the young men, the bravest hearts.
A hard people, bred up to violent ways,
Awaits your conquest there in Latium.
Yet first you must visit the habitations
Of Dis who reigns below and through the deep
Avernus seek, my son, a meeting with me.
It is not Tartarus which holds me,
I am not in hell among the bitter shades
But in the sweet regions of the blest,
Elysium. It is hither the chaste Sibyl
Will lead you by the shedding of much blood
Of black lambs. It is here that you will learn
What walls are to be yours. And now farewell;
The dewy night turns at the middle point
And the devouring East with panting horses
Has blown upon me.' So he spoke and fled
Like smoke curling away into thin air.
Aeneas said: 'Where are you vanishing?
Snatched away where? Escaping where? Or who
Puts such a distance between our embraces?'
So speaking he stirs up the sleeping embers
And with new fire worships the household god
Of Troy and white-haired Vesta's inmost shrine
With sacred grain and full censer, suppliant.

   At once he calls his comrades – first Acestes –
And tells them what commands Jove has given,
The instructions he has had from his dear father
And how in his own mind the thing was settled.
There was no room for further argument,
Nor does Acestes jib at what was ordered.
They enrol the ladies for the new city
And segregate the ordinary people
Who want to stay, those with no mind to hanker
After great glory. Those who are really with him

Renew the rowing-benches and replace
The timbers which the flames have half-devoured,
Fitting the ships out with oars and rigging:
They are few in number but they are the ones
Who are full of life and capable in war.
Meanwhile Aeneas marks out the city
Using a plough and decides where each shall live;
This place, he ordered, was to be 'Ilium',
These other places 'Troy'. This new kingdom
Delights Acestes, Trojan that he is;
He proclaims and establishes a forum,
Summons a senate and hands down the laws.
On the top of Mount Eryx, near the stars,
A shrine is set up for Idalian Venus
And further, in a broad glade near the tomb,
A priest for the service of Anchises.

  For nine days now all the people have feasted
And altars have been honoured; gentle breezes
Have flattened out the sea and now once more
The south wind, freshening sometimes, calls them out
To the high seas. Along the winding shore
Rises a huge wailing; they hold back
A night and a day, locked in each other's arms.
The very women, the men who before thought
The sea too rough and would not hear of it,
Want to go now and share all the hardships.
Aeneas is kindly and speaks friendly words,
Commending them with tears to Acestes,
One of their own blood. He orders sacrifices,
Three calves to Eryx, a lamb to the Storms
And then, on time, tells them to loose the moorings.
He himself stands aloft on his ship's stern,
His head crowned with a wreath of trimmed olive
And in his hand a goblet. He casts the flesh
Into the salt waves and pours wine upon them.
Wind freshens astern and sends them on their way.
Competitively the rowers pull their oars
And so they sweep out across the water.

  But Venus in the mean-time was alarmed;
Thinking what might happen, she spoke out

To Neptune, pouring forth streams of complaints
Straight from her heart, as follows: 'Juno's anger,
So damaging because she is never satisfied,
Constrains me to descend to every prayer,
O Neptune, for, however long the day,
Whatever vows are paid her, nothing softens her
And she is daunted neither by Jove's commands
Nor by the Fates: she never rests. For her
It is not enough to have devoured the city
The Phrygian people guarded, her wicked hatred
Must drag what little is left of them through torments
Of every kind; the city once destroyed
She pursues its bones and ashes. She alone
Knows why she rages so. You are my witness
What storms she lately raised in Libyan waters;
She made confusion between seas and sky,
Aeolus lending hurricanes to no purpose;
She dared to interfere where you are master.
Criminally working on the Trojan matrons,
By foul play she burnt the Trojan ships
And forced them, because of the fleet's losses,
To leave their comrades to an unknown land.
I pray you, let the remnant that remains
Entrust themselves to you and sail in safety
Through the waves to the Laurentine Tiber:
Let them reach it, if what is asked may be
And if the Fates are giving them those walls.'
Then Saturn's son, the tamer of the seas,
Delivered himself as follows in reply:
'It is entirely proper, Cytherean,
That you should trust yourself to my empire,
To which you owe your birth. I have deserved
Your confidence. How often have I checked
The madness and the rage of sky and sea!
On land too (witness Xanthus and Simois)
Aeneas, being yours, has had my care.
And when in Troy Achilles, in pursuit
Of weary troops thrust them against the walls
And dealt out death to thousands till the rivers
Were choked and groaned, and Xanthus could not find
A way to flow or how to reach the sea,

I saved Aeneas as he fought against
The hardy son of Peleus without either
Having strength enough nor yet divine favour
And hid him in a hollow cloud, although
I wanted to uproot the walls of Troy,
The perjured city built by my own hands.
I am still of the same mind, so have no fear.
The harbour you have chosen he will reach,
Hard by Avernus, with one man lost at sea
And only one, who will give his life for many.'
He soothed and cheered the goddess with these words
Then yoked his horses in their golden harness,
Put the bits in their foaming mouths and let
The reins run through his hands. Lightly he flew
Over the water in his sea-blue chariot;
The waves subside as his thundering axle
Passes, the swollen surface flattens out,
The storm-clouds fly away in the vast sky.
Then comes his retinue, all shapes and sizes,
Huge whales, the aged troop of Glaucus, Palaemon
Ino's son, the swift Tritons, Phorcus's army;
On his left Thetis, with Melite and the maid
Panopea, with Nesaea and with Spio,
Thalia and Cymodoce in her train.
    Then for Aeneas, brooding on the fleet,
It was a time of happiness, his mind filled with it.
Quickly he ordered them to raise the masts
And draw out the sails along the yards.
As one man they made the sheets fast
And let out the canvas to port and starboard;
As one man they manipulated the sails
And so the breezes carried the fleet on.
Heading them all, there was Palinurus,
He led the line, the rest were to follow.
Already the moist night was half-way done;
The sailors stretched out on the hard benches,
Their oars on top of them, were in repose
Resting their arms and legs, when Sleep came
Sliding down gently from the starlit sky,
Cutting the darkened air and dispelling shadows.
It was you he was looking for, Palinurus

And heavy dreams he brought your innocence:
The god sat down upon the high poop.
Pretending to be Phorbas, and poured out talk:
'Palinurus, son of Iasius, the sea
Carries the fleet without your intervention,
There is an even breeze: an hour for rest.
Put your head down and let your weary eyes
Steal from their labour. For a little while
I will perform your watch.' But Palinurus,
Hardly raising his eyes, spoke in his turn:
'Do you tell me to pay no attention
To the smooth face of the sea and the quiet waves?
Am I to disregard what they portend?
Or trust Aeneas to the treacherous winds,
I who have so often been deceived
By a clear sky and found it a pretence?'
And as he spoke he gripped the tiller harder,
He would not let it go nor take his eyes
Even for a moment off the stars he sailed by.
But the god took a weeping branch from Lethe,
A Stygian herb of soporific virtue,
And shook it, first one temple then the other:
The eyes were released from their task,
Flickered and then closed. The unexpected rest
Hardly began to make the limbs fall limp
When Sleep bent over him and threw him down
Into the liquid element, still holding
The tiller, carrying with him part of the stern;
He called his comrades but they did not answer.
Then the god lifted himself on his wings
And flew off to the light air above.
The fleet ran on its course none the less
Safely and without fear, for Father Neptune's
Promises held. Borne onwards, it drew near
The Sirens' rocks, so dangerous in old time
And white with the bones of many men.
(Meanwhile the rocks moaned hoarsely as the salt
Constantly flooded round them.) But Aeneas
Sensed that the pilot was gone and his ship was drifting
And himself steered her through the waves of night,

Sighing and numbed at what had befallen his friend:
'Trusting too much to clear skies and calm seas,
The end is, Palinurus, you will lie
Naked upon an unfamiliar shore.'

# BOOK VI

# BOOK VI

He spoke these words with tears streaming down
And then he let the fleet have its rein;
So it came softly to the Euboean coast
Of Cumae. Swinging the prows round to seaward
They dropped the anchors where they bit firmly;
The rounded sterns lay all along the shore.
The young crews shot out in a flash,
It was the Western Land; some hunted sparks
Hidden in veins of flint, some tore up woods
Which gave a thick cover for wild beasts;
They called out when they came across streams.
But Aeneas thoughtfully made for the summits
Where Apollo presides loftily
And the secret places of the terrible Sibyl,
A huge cave; there the prophetic Delian
Breathes into her a great mind, an intelligence
That lays the future open. Now they approach
The groves of Trivia and the golden roof.
    Daedalus, so they say, escaping from the land
Where Minos reigned, dared on his headlong wings
To trust himself to the sky, he swam out
By this unlikely route to the cold north
And hovered lightly over the top of Cumae.
He first came back to earth in this place
And, Phoebus, it was to you he dedicated
These immense temples and the wings that brought him.
On the doors is the death of Androgeos;
The Cecrops' children ordered, alas, to pay
The bodies of seven of their sons each year
As tribute; this is the urn, the lots are drawn.
Over against this, rising from the sea,
There is the land of Cnossus; here are seen
The cruel love of the bull, Pasiphaë

Set under him by a trick; the issue she had
Of bastard race and of ambiguous shape,
The Minotaur who is a monument
To such prohibited and filthy loves;
Here is the labyrinth where none goes right,
Though Daedalus himself, who built the place
Took pity upon Ariadne's love
And opened up every twist and turn,
Guiding her lover's footsteps with a thread,
You, Icarus, would have had a large part
Upon the sculpted doors, had grief allowed,
But twice your father tried to represent
In gold just how you fell and twice his hands
Dropped and he left the work. All this and more
The Trojans would certainly have studied
Had not Achates suddenly appeared,
With him Glaucus's daughter, Deiphobe,
Priestess of Phoebus and of Trivia,
Who thus addressed Aeneas: 'Sights like that
Are not what such a time as this demands:
It would be better now to sacrifice
Seven bullocks from the still unbroken herd
And seven lambs, chosen as custom requires.'
The priestess having spoken to Aeneas
There was no holding back, the sacrifices
Commanded were at hand: and then she called
The Teucrians to climb with her to the temple.
    On one side of the Euboean rock
Is cut a huge cavern. To it lead
A hundred broad ways, a hundred mouths
From which there tumble out as many voices,
The Sibyl's answers. As they all arrived
Upon the threshold of the cave the virgin
Cried out: 'The time to question fate is now!
The god is here, the god!' As she spoke
Before the temple doors her countenance
Changed suddenly, her colour changed, her hair
Fell loose about her shoulders and she panted
Violently, her wild heart grew great within her,
She seemed taller, her voice was not a mortal's
Because the god's power was breathed upon her,

Closer now, 'Are you holding back, Trojan,
Your vows and prayers? Aeneas, are you holding back?
You must give way before the great doors open
And the house is filled with breath.'
She spoke and fell silent. The Teucrians shuddered,
The marrow froze in their bones, but their king
From the bottom of his heart poured out these prayers:
'Phoebus, you whom the heavy griefs of Troy
Have ever moved to pity; who directed
The hand of Paris when he sent his arrow
Into Achilles' body; I have entered
Upon so many seas that wash around
The shores of vast lands and, at your bidding,
As far as the remote Massylian tribes
And to the fields stretched out against the Syrtes,
And now at last the elusive shores of Italy
Are in our grasp, if only it may be
That Trojan fortunes follow us no further.
And all you gods and goddesses, you too
Whom Ilium and the greatness of the Dardanians
Offended, may now spare the race of Pergamus.
You, O most holy prophetess, who know
The future, grant (I ask what I may ask
And nothing more, the kingdom fate assigns me)
That Teucrians now may settle in Latium
With their homeless gods and all the troubled powers
Of Troy. For you then, Phoebus, and for Trivia
I will build a temple out of solid marble
And appoint festal days in honour of Phoebus:
You too, beneficent lady, a great shrine
Awaits, in my kingdom; there I will set
The oracles you pronounce, the secret fates
You destine for my people, and will ordain
Men who shall serve you. Only, do not trust
Your sayings to the leaves lest the swift winds
Treat them as playthings and they fly away;
I beg you, let us hear them from yourself.'
With this, he let his own lips fall silent.

But Phoebus is not wanted by the prophetess,
Not yet, and so she rages through the cave
Trying to shake the god out of her mind;

The more she does so, the more he wearies her,
Her looks are frantic, he tames her wild heart
And forms her by repression to his will.
Now of their own volition all the hundred
Great doors of the temple fly open.
The prophetess's answer is borne out
On the breathing winds: 'O you who have done at last
With all the great perils of the sea
(Though worse await on land), yes, the Dardanians
Will reach the kingdom of Lavinium,
Never fear, that is certain, they will arrive
But wish they had not come. Wars, menacing wars
I see, and foaming Tiber full of blood.
You will not lack a Simois or a Xanthus
Nor a Greek camp; already another Achilles
Is spawned in Latium, son of a goddess likewise
And Juno will be there to haunt the Trojans,
While you, a desperate beggar,
What tribes of Italy and what cities there
Will you not supplicate! Once more the cause
Of these calamities will be a bride,
The daughter of a man whose guest you are,
Once more a foreign marriage.
Do not give way to these severities
But go on with a greater show of courage
Than Fortune seems to sanction. The best way,
Little as you think it now, to find safety
Will lie before you in a Greek city.'
   So the Cumaean Sibyl from her shrine
Chants her appalling ambiguities
And sets the whole cavern in a roar,
Wrapping up truths in obscurities;
Apollo shakes those reins on her mad back
And turns the spurs in under her mad heart.
The moment that her rage comes to a stop
And her demented lips are quiet at last
Aeneas speaks as a hero should:
'Trouble can show no unfamiliar face
To me, and cannot come unexpectedly,
O virgin, I have seen it all before
And been over all that in my mind.

One thing I beg: since here the King of Hell
Is said to have the gates of his kingdom
In the shadowy marsh where Acheron floods out,
May I pass through and see with my own eyes
The face of my dear father; show the way,
Throw wide the sacred gates. I bore him out,
Through flames and followed by a thousand javelins,
Upon these very shoulders and I brought him
Right from the middle of the enemy;
He kept me company in all my journeys
Through all those seas; and the threatening skies
And deep waters he bore although unfit,
A destiny beyond the strength of age.
Not only that, but it was he who charged me
That I should seek you as a suppliant
And so present myself upon your threshold.
Be gracious to the son and to the father,
Have mercy now, I pray you, gracious lady;
For there is nothing that you cannot do
And not for nothing were you appointed
By Hecate to be keeper of the woods
About Avernus. And if Orpheus
Could summon back the shadow of his wife
By virtue of his Trojan lyre, believing
Music would bring her; and if Pollux could
Ransom his brother, change and change about,
Now one dead, now the other, and for this
Comes and goes often; if great Theseus,
If Alcides – why speak of them? – I too
Am of the race of the supreme Jove.'
    So he prayed, his hands upon the altar,
And then the prophetess began to speak:
'You, with the blood of gods in your veins,
Trojan, son of Anchises; night and day
The door of mournful Dis's house lies open;
But to retrace your steps, to get away
Into the breezes of the world above,
That is the point at which the task is hard.
A few, whom Jupiter has loved and favoured
Or whom a blazing courage has exalted,
The god-begotten – these have found a way.

The ground to be traversed is thick forest
Round which the gliding waters of Cocytus
Make a dark loop. But if your mind is filled
With so much love, if you have such desire
To travel twice across the Stygian lake,
To see black Tartarus twice, if you are pleased
To give yourself the luxury of this madness,
Listen, for there are things you must do first.
In a dark tree there hides a golden bough
With leaves and pliant twigs of the same substance,
And it is sacred to the Juno of Hell;
The whole grove covers it, shadows enclose it
In obscure valleys. But it is not given
To any to approach earth's hidden places
Except that he have first plucked from that tree
Its golden foliage, which Proserpina
In all her beauty set her heart upon
Having brought to her as her special gift;
Tear one bough off, another golden bough
Grows in its place, and leaves of like metal
Sprout from it instantly. Search for it therefore,
Deep hidden though it is, find it you must,
Then stretch your hand and pick it; it will come
Easily and as if of its own will
If it is you whom the fates are calling;
Otherwise no strength will be enough
For you to pull it down, you could not loosen it
Even with a sword. There is another thing:
Emptied of life the body of a friend
Lies waiting for you but unknown to you
And so a death pollutes the whole fleet
While you hang at my door asking for oracles.
Carry him to the place where he belongs,
That is your first task, and bury him.
Take black sheep first for your expiation.
So at last you will see the Stygian groves,
The kingdom where there is no road for the living.'
With that she closed her lips and was dumb.
 Aeneas, with his looks cast down in mourning,
Went on, leaving the cave and turning over
In his mind the obscurities that had come from it.

Beside him the reliable Achates
Walked heavily, absorbed in the same cares.
They talked, trying to pull the threads together.
Which of their comrades had the prophetess meant
When she said one was dead, whom must they bury?
Then there he was, on the dry beach, Misenus:
They came up to the spot and saw that death,
Cruel death, had finished Aeolid Misenus
Who had excelled all others with the trumpet,
Moving men by his music to the wars.
He had been the great Hector's companion,
With him he had faced battle, notable
For his spear-work as well as for his bugle.
And when Achilles took the life of Hector,
This hero, so courageous, would have none
But Dardan Aeneas for his company,
No lesser man would do. Yet on that day
He blew a hollow shell till the seas rang,
Playing insanely, challenging the gods,
Till emulous Triton, if the tale is true,
Took him and plunged him in the foaming waves
Among the rocks. And so it was that all
Trooped round him with a great shout of rage,
His loyal friend Aeneas above all.
The Sibyl's orders then were executed
Without delay as, hurriedly and weeping
They piled up trees as altars and as tomb
And tried to make it reach up to heaven.
There was a movement into the ancient woods,
Deep in, where the wild beasts had their lairs;
Pitch pines came down, flex rang as the axe struck,
Wedges drove into ash and oaken logs,
The splittable wood was split, huge mountain ash
Were rolled down the mountain side from where they fell.
    In this work too Aeneas was the first,
Urging his comrades, like them carrying tools
And he besides had a heavy heart,
Was thoughtful as he looked at the huge forest
And so it came about that he prayed:
'If only, somewhere in this vast wood
That golden bough would show itself! For all

The prophetess told me of you, Misenus,
Was true.' He had scarcely spoken when two doves
As if by chance came flying from aloft,
Settling before his eyes upon the grass.
Then the great hero understood the birds
Were from his mother; joyfully he prayed:
'O be my guides, if there is any way,
And through the air set your course to the grove
In which the shadow of that precious bough
Falls on productive ground. And you, mother,
Goddess, do not desert me in my need!'
Speaking so, he stood still and watched the birds,
What signs they gave and whither they would go.
Now feeding and now flying – but no further
Than the observer's eye could follow them –
They came up to the jaws of Avernus.
The smell is pungent. Then they rose quickly
And dropping through the liquid air they perched
In the desired place on the ambiguous tree
Through whose leaves shone a strident gleam of gold.
As in the winter cold the mistletoe
In the woods flourishes with strange foliage
Not seeded from the tree it grows upon
And decks the rounded trunk with yellowy fruit,
So looked the golden foliage in the shadows
Of that ilex, so crackled in the light breeze
The leaves of metal. Aeneas snatched the bough,
It hesitated, then he broke it off
And carried it back to the prophetic Sibyl.
    Meanwhile upon the shore the Teucrians
Were weeping for Misenus as before
And were proceeding to the last rites
For his uncaring dust. And first they built
A huge pyre of oak logs livened with pitch-pine,
Covering the sides with dark foliage
And setting funeral cypresses in front;
On it they laid a heap of glittering arms.
Some heated water in a brazen pot
Until it bubbled in the flames, and then
They washed the dead man's body and anointed it.
There was lamenting. Then, when that was done,

They laid him out upon a bed and threw
Purple robes over him such as he had worn.
Some took upon themselves the heavy duty
Of shouldering the bier; then, as their ancestors
Had done before them, with averted eyes
They set a torch under the pyre. It blazed
With frankincense and offerings of food
And bowls of streaming oil from the olive.
When the ashes had fallen and the flame died down
They washed in wine all that was left and doused
The thirsty ashes; and then Corynaeus
Gathered the bones into an urn of bronze.
Three times he paced around the company
Bearing pure water, sprinkling it like dew
From a bough of fruitful olive and so purified
The mourners and then spoke the final words.
But good Aeneas set up a great tomb
With the man's arms and armour, oar and trumpet
Under a lofty mound which is still called
Misenus after him, and so it is
His name is kept undying through the centuries.
    When these things had been done he executed
As quickly as he might the Sibyl's orders.
There was a deep cave with yawning entrance,
Barbed rock safe by the dark lake, in the shadow
Of woods; above the spot no bird could keep
A steady course without fear of falling,
Such was the vapour that poured up from it
Out of those black jaws to the roof of the sky:
The Greeks call it the birdless place, Aornos,
For that reason. Here the priestess first set
Four black-backed bullocks, then she poured wine
Over their foreheads and took from between their horns
A bunch of thick hairs and put them in the flames
As a first offering while she called upon
Hecate who has power in heaven and hell.
Others thrust knives up from below and caught
The blood, still warm, in bowls. Aeneas himself
Struck with his sword a lamb of fleecy black
For the Eumenides' mother and her great sister
And for you, Proserpine, a barren cow.

Then for the Stygian king he began
Nocturnal celebrations, laying on the flames
Whole carcases of bulls, pouring rich oil
Over the entrails as they burned away.
Then, at the first touch of the rising sun,
The ground gave a roar under their feet;
The outline of the wooded hills changed
And dogs were seen howling in the shadows;
The goddess was at hand. 'O keep away!'
The prophetess cried out, 'O keep away
All you who are unsanctified, leave the grove free!
But you, Aeneas, set out on your journey,
Snatch your sword from its scabbard:
Now you need all the courage that you have;
Be of good heart.' With this, she threw herself
Like a mad woman into the cave-mouth
And he with no sign of hesitation
Followed her lead and kept hard on her heels.

   You gods whose empire is over spirits,
You silent shades, you Chaos and Phlegethon,
You lands spread out in silence and in night,
Suffer me without blasphemy to tell
What I have heard, and by your powers reveal
Things which are buried deep in earth and darkness.

   Invisibly they walked in the lonely night,
Through shadow, through the empty halls of Dis,
His kingdom where there is nothing but nothing;
It was like a path in woods, with uncertain moon-light
Giving no re-assurance, when Jupiter
Has covered the sky with shadow and black night
And taken the colour out of things. The entrance
Was there before them; there in the jaws of Orcus,
Sorrow and gnawing cares make their beds;
There live pallid Disease, dejected Age,
Fear, Hunger the bad counsellor, ugly Want,
Terrible spectres, Death and Decline,
With Sleep akin to death, Concupiscence
And by the doorway opposite, threatening War
And the barred cages of the Eumenides,
Lunatic Discord with her snaky hair
Laced through with blood-stained ribbons.

In the middle of the courtyard a dark elm
Of vast proportions spread out its arms,
Agèd, and branched and under every leaf
Clings a false dream and there they have their home,
Or so it is believed. And at the gate
Are stabled many beasts shaped out of kind,
Centaurs, half-human Scyllas, with Briareus
Who has a hundred arms, and then the monster
Out of the marshes, whose hiss terrifies,
Chimaera armed with flames, Gorgons and Harpies,
The three shapes in one shadow, Geryon.
At this Aeneas, suddenly afraid,
Grasped his sword tightly and presented the blade
Against all comers; and had his companion,
Wiser than he, not warned that these were lives
Of subtle substance with no body, flitting
Behind hollow appearances of shape,
He would have rushed in and to no purpose
Cut unresisting shadows with his sword.
    And here that road begins, which leads to Tartarus,
Acheron and its waters; here the foul cess-pit
Gurgles and boils over the vast abyss
And throws up all its sands to Cocytus.
A terrifying harbour-master serves here
In hideous mourning, Charon, his grey beard
Tangled, untrimmed, eyes alive with flame;
A filthy, knotted cloak hangs from his shoulders.
He himself pushes the boat out with a pole,
Handles the sails and in that dusky skiff
Conveys the figures over; though he is old,
The old age of a god is hale and green.
To this point on the bank all the crowd flows,
Mothers and husbands and shapes of great heroes
From which the life has gone, with young boys,
Unmarried girls, young men set on a pyre
Before their parents' eyes: so many they were
They were like leaves falling in a forest
In autumn at the first touch of frost,
Or like great flocks of birds coming to land
In from the sea when the cold season drives them
Over the water to seek sunnier lands.

They stood there pleading to be carried first
And stretched their hands out as if love drew them
To the further shore. But the sad boatman now
Takes some but fends others far from the sand.
Aeneas marvelled: what was this tumult?
'Tell me,' he asked, 'What is the meaning, Virgin,
Of all this crowd pressing towards the river?
What do these spirits seek? What is the reason
Some leave the water's edge, others are rowed
Across the livid current?' Then the priestess,
Who had lived long, gave him this brief answer:
'Son of Anchises, offspring of the gods,
As certainly you are, what you are seeing
Is the profound pools of Cocytus
And the Stygian marsh, a name by which the gods
Fear to swear and then to break their word.
And that crowd you see so helpless there
Are those who are unburied; the harbour-master
Is Charon: those he takes aboard are buried;
He may not carry them over the choking stream
From these grim banks until their bones find peace.
A hundred years they wander and flutter here
About these shores; then at last they may come
And once more visit the pools they so long for.'
Anchises' son stood still, his feet were heavy,
He thought of many things and in his heart
Pitied their fate which seemed to him unjust.
He sees there, grieved at their unhonoured death,
Leucaspis and the Lycian fleet's commander,
Orontes, both sunk by the south wind
As they sailed over the stormy sea from Troy,
And the ship went down and all the crew with it.
    Then Palinurus came by, the helmsman
Who on the Libyan voyage, watching the stars,
Fell from the stern and was lost among the waves.
Aeneas had hardly recognised this sad ghost
Among the shadows when he spoke to him:
'Palinurus, which of the gods was it
Snatched you from us and plunged you into the sea?
Tell me. For I was tricked by one I had never
Found deceitful before; with this one answer

Apollo cheated me; his prophecy was
That you would be unharmed by the sea
And reach the land of Italy. Is it thus
That he fulfils his promises?' The other
Answered him: 'No, the oracle did not fail you,
Captain, son of Anchises, no god drowned me.
The helm was wrenched from me with great force
By chance, while I as one in duty bound
Was clinging to it as I steered our course;
I fell, and dragged it with me. And I swear
By those rough seas that no fear for myself
Seized me like that I felt for your ship
Lest, having lost its gear and lost its master,
It might go down among the mountainous waves.
For three nights of storm the south wind
Drove me on violently upon the surface
Of the immense deeps; at the fourth dawn
I could, from the top of a wave,
Just discern Italy. Slowly I swam to land;
I was already safe or should have been
Had not a savage race slashed me with knives
As, weighed down by wet clothes, I was clawing
At the top of a jagged rock; so mindless were they
They thought I was a prize. And now the waves
Had me indeed, the winds blew me on shore.
I beg you, by the glad light of the sky,
By the air; in your father's name, your son's,
The hopeful Iülus; from these evils
Rescue me, you who never have been worsted:
Either throw earth upon me, you can do it
If you go to the harbour of Velia;
Or, if there is a way, if your divine mother
Will show you (for indeed I believe without
Divine assistance you would not attempt
To travel on these rivers and this marsh),
Give your hand to a wretched man and take him
Across the waves, so that at least in death
I may rest in peace at last.' When he had spoken
The seer then began: 'O Palinurus,
Whence does it come, this wild wish of yours?
Shall you, unburied, see the waters of Styx

And the Eumenides' grim stream, or approach
The bank although unbidden? Give up hope
That prayer will change the gods' determination.
But hear what I say and remember it,
It will console you in your hard misfortune:
For all the neighbouring cities shall be roused
By heavenly portents to appease your bones.
They will erect a tomb and to that tomb
Will send their solemn offerings, and the place
Shall be called Palinurus, and for ever.'
With these words his anxieties were ended
And grief was quickly driven from his heart,
Happy that this land should bear his name.
    So they went on their way towards the river.
The boatman saw them from the Stygian waters
As they passed through the silent grove and turned
Their steps towards the bank: he spoke first,
Bawling at them: 'Whoever you are, who come
Armed to my river, tell me what you come for!
Answer from where you are: not a step further!
This is a place of shadows and of dreams,
Of night, which brings sleep; and it is evil
For the Stygian boat to have a living cargo.
I was not pleased to have taken Hercules
To travel on this lake, nor Theseus
Or Perithoüs, though they were all sons of gods
And no strength had ever conquered theirs.
One came to chain the dog of Tartarus
And dragged him shaking from under the king's throne;
The others were set to take our lady off
Out of her bed-chamber.' Apollo's prophetess
Gave him a short answer: 'We play no tricks;
Calm yourself; these arms offer no violence;
The huge dog at your door can howl for ever
To frighten bloodless shadows; Proserpine
Can stay chaste behind her uncle's door.
Trojan Aeneas, no less dutiful
Than he is famous in the wars, goes down
To seek his father in the deepest shades
Of Erebus. If this example of his truth
Leaves you untouched, this branch' (here she pulled out

The branch from the folds of her garment)
'Is something you will recognise.' At this
Charon was quiet and his anger left him.
No more was said. He marvelled at the gift,
So holy and kept from his sight so long,
The appointed bough. He turned his dark craft
And came close in to shore, the other spirits
Seated upon the benches he turned out
And, clearing the gangways, took Aeneas aboard,
Huge cargo though he was. The vessel groaned
And the marsh water crept in through the seams.
They made the crossing at last and he set down
Priestess and man unharmed upon the shore
Among the formless mud and glaucous sedge.

   Gigantic Cerberus makes these realms ring,
Barking from his three throats as he lies there
In the cave opposite, so huge he fills it.
The prophetess, seeing his collar of snakes
Already bristling, throws him a biscuit,
Honeyed and made of flour drugged with sleep.
Opening his three throats wide, mad with hunger,
He catches it and gobbles, then his great back
Subsides, he stretches on the ground, the whole
Floor of the cave is covered. Then Aeneas,
The guard-dog so disposed of, jumps to the entrance
And swiftly makes away from the bank
Of that river from which no-one returns.

   Immediately voices are heard, a loud wailing,
The weeping spirits of infants, just by the gate:
They were those whom a black day had carried off
Without their share of what is sweet in life,
Torn away to bitter death as they sucked.
Near these were those who were condemned to die
Upon false charges: these places are not given
Without lots cast nor yet without a judge.
Minos presides and shakes the urn; he calls
A silent council and informs himself
Of men's lives and their faults. The next places
Are occupied by those unfortunates
Who innocently died by their own hands,
Who loathed the light and threw their lives away.

How they would wish now for poverty
And their worst troubles in the air above
In preference to this! It is forbidden;
The repulsive marsh with its dejected waters
Binds them; Styx holds them in its nine circles.
    Not far away and stretching far and wide
The fields of mourning lie; they call them that.
Here those whom a brutal love has gnawed and wasted
Are hidden in secret paths by woods of myrtle;
Their troubles do not leave them even in death.
In these retreats he sees Phaedra and Procris;
Eriphyle grieves there and shows the wound
Her cruel son inflicted; and with her
Evadne and Pasiphaë; Laodamia
Goes with them and Caeneus, once a young man
But now a woman as she was before,
In the form that her destiny required.
Among these women was Phoenician Dido,
Her wound still fresh, wandering in the great forest.
The Trojan hero, when he first stood near her,
Saw who it was, shadowy among the shades,
As one might see the new moon when it rises
Or think that one has seen it through the clouds;
Then his tears fell, he spoke with tenderness:
'Unhappy Dido, so the messenger
Spoke truly in reporting you were dead
And that your own sword brought you to this end?
Was it then I who was the cause of it?
By the stars I swear it, by all the gods above,
By any truth there may be in these depths,
It was against my will I left your shores.
O queen, the gods commanded me to go
As now to travel here among the shades;
They force me here through these forsaken places,
Through the dark night; they drove me irresistibly;
I could not know what pain my going caused you.
Stay still and do not go out of my sight.
Who are you running away from? Those words
Are the last fate will let me speak to you.'
Aeneas with such talk was mollifying
Her blazing heart and her glaring looks

And moving her to tears. She turned away
And kept her eyes firmly on the ground;
Her face changed no more when he spoke
Than if it had been flint or Parian marble.
She rushed off, retreating like an enemy
Into the shady grove in which her husband
Of earlier times, Sychaeus, loving her
As she did him, comforted her. Aeneas,
Shaken by the injustice of her fate,
Followed her with his eyes and, as she went,
His tears streamed out and he pitied her.

    He struggled on his way. Now they had reached
The distant fields in which there were assembled,
A group apart, those once famous in war.
Here Tydeus met him; here was Parthenopaeus
Renowned in war; the pale shade of Adrastus;
Here much bewailed and fallen in the war
The Dardanids – as he saw the long file
He groaned – Glaucus, Medon, Thersilochus,
Antenor's three sons; Polyboetes
Dedicated to Ceres, Idaeus
Still with his chariot, his weapons in his hand.
The spirits stand around him to left and right.
They are not content just to catch sight of him;
They want to stay with him, to walk with him,
To learn the reasons for his coming there.
But the Greek princes and Agamemnon's cohorts,
When they saw the man with his burnished armour
Among the shadows, fear made them tremble:
Some fled as they had once fled to their ships;
Some raised their voices, almost inaudibly
– What should have been a shout became a yawn.

    And here he saw Deiphobus, Priam's son,
His body mangled, face cruelly slashed
– His face and both hands – his head without ears
And hideously cut back at the nostrils.
Aeneas hardly knew him as he cowered
Hiding the fearsome penalty he had suffered
But spoke to him in a voice the other knew:
'Deiphobus, mighty in battle, descended
From the high race of Teucer, who was it

Chose to inflict on you this cruel revenge?
Who could do such things to you? On that last night
I heard that, tired with killing so many Greeks,
You lay stretched on a bloody heap of them.
Then I myself set up an empty tomb
Upon the Rhoetean shore and three times
Called out in a loud voice to your shade;
Your name and arms now mark the place. But you,
My friend, I could see nowhere; when I went
I could not leave you in your native earth.'
Priam's son answered: 'You left nothing undone;
You have paid everything that could be paid,
My friend, to Deiphobus and his ghost.
It was my fate and the destructive fate
Of that woman from Sparta that pushed me
Into these horrors; she left these marks upon me.
You know well we passed that last night
In celebrating what had not come to pass;
Impossible not to remember it.
When fate sent that horse jumping up to Pergamus,
Its gravid belly full of infantry,
She, making out the dance was a ritual,
Led Phrygian women with a Bacchic yowling
In a troop round the town; she herself held
A huge torch and from the top of the citadel
Called to the Greeks. Meanwhile I was asleep,
Exhausted with anxieties, in that
Ill-fated marriage-chamber; a repose
Sweet as it was deep and very like death,
So peaceful was it, held me as I lay.
Meanwhile my careful wife took all the weapons
Out of the house, taking even my sword
From underneath my pillow; called Menelaus
Into the house and opened the door wide;
She thought she was doing her lover a great service
No doubt and that in this way the memory
Of her old crimes would be stamped out. They came,
Nothing to stop them, into the bed chamber,
With them that old counsellor of evil
Ulysses. Gods, do the same to the Greeks
If I speak truly who make this demand!

But tell me now what chances brought you here
While you are still alive. Was it the wind?
Was it the seas that washed you up here?
Did the gods send you? Or were you so weary,
Your fortunes such that you must come here
Where we live sunless in this troubled place?'
    The rosy horses of the dawn had passed
Half-way over the sky during this talk;
They might have spent all the time given them
On such matters had not the Sibyl spoken,
Laconically warning her companion:
'Aeneas, night is on the way while we
Spend the hours weeping. This is the place
Where the track splits itself into two:
The right-hand path here runs under the walls
Of the great Dis and leads to Elysium,
But the left is the way of punishment
And sends evil men to Tartarus.'
Deiphobus intervenes: 'Do not be angry,
Great priestess! I will go on my way
And make up the number of those in darkness.
Go, flower of Trojans, go and may you meet
A better fate than mine.' So far he spoke
And as he spoke he turned his steps away.
    Aeneas looks round. Under a cliff to the left
He sees an extensive keep and round about it
Three lines of walls; the whole is encircled
By a fast river formed of raging flames,
Tartarean Phlegethon with spinning boulders
Roaring among its flood. The other side
Stands a great gate with columns of solid adamant,
Such that no human strength, nor even the gods'
Could shift them from their base in an attack;
There is an iron tower, high in the air;
On top of it there sits Tisiphone,
Her blood-stained gown hitched up. Unsleepingly
She guards the entrance day and night. Inside
Are heard groans, the cruel sound of the lash,
The squeal of iron as of chains being dragged.
Aeneas stopped, the terror of the noise
Held him transfixed: 'What crimes can these be?

What punishments do they suffer? Speak, Virgin!
What does it mean, this cry that fills the air?'
The prophetess began to speak: 'O Trojan,
Famed leader of the Trojans, no honest man
Can pass this polluted threshold; but when Hecate
Set me over the groves of Avernus
She taught me all the pains the gods inflict
And led me through them all. These merciless realms
Are those of the Gnosian Rhadamanthus;
It is he who corrects the faults of men.
Listening, and forcing a confession
From anyone who in the world above,
Thinking himself lucky with his lies,
Put off making amends to his last hour.
Tisiphone is there to take revenge;
Armed with her whip she comes down on the guilty,
Reviling them and, with her left hand,
Menacing them with hideous snakes; she calls
Her train of sister Furies to assist.
At last the sacred gates are opened wide
Upon their screeching hinges! Do you see now
What sort of keeper sits in the entrance
And what form guards the approaches?
The monstrous Hydra, her fifty black throats gaping,
Is further in, and fiercer than Tisiphone.
The pit of Tartarus itself lies open
After that, stretching down into the darkness
Twice as far as we look up to heaven.
The ancient dwellers upon earth, the Titans
Cast down by thunderbolts, writhe at the bottom.
And here I saw the twin sons of Aloeus,
Gigantic shapes who had assaulted heaven
And tried to tear it down with their hands
And to push Jove out from his realms above.
I saw too Salmoneus who copied
Jove's lightning and the thunder of Olympus
And now suffers the cruel penalty.
He went in triumph drawn by four horses
And brandishing a torch, through the city of Elis
With all the races of Greece crowded about him,
Out of his mind, thinking that he could imitate

The storm-clouds and the inimitable thunder
With bronze and with the clatter of horses' hooves.
But the Almighty Father hurled his weapon
Through thick clouds – not for him torches or smoky pitch-
        pine –
And sent the upstart headlong in a whirlwind.
Tityos was to be seen there too, fostered
Once by the universal mother Earth,
Now lying, his body stretched over nine acres,
A huge vulture with a crooked beak
Pecking at his indestructible liver,
Rummaging for food in entrails always
Feeling new agonies; the bird lives
Inside him, the tissue grows and hurts again.
Why speak of the Lapithae, of Ixion,
Of Pirothoüs over whom hangs a flinty rock,
Black and always on the point of falling?
They see the golden furniture of high couches
As for a banquet, and before their eyes
Is dressed a feast of royal luxury,
But the most terrible of the Furies lies
Close by and will not let them touch the tables
But leaps up, fends them off with her torch, and screams.
Here are those who, while they were still alive,
Hated their brothers or attacked a parent
And those who implicated subordinates
In their own crimes or, having acquired wealth,
Gave nothing to their families (these are numerous),
And those who were killed for adultery;
With those who took up arms disloyally
And did not fear to fail their own prince:
All these are shut in here awaiting punishment;
Do not enquire of me what punishment
Or what their fortune may be after this.
Some roll great rocks or hang racked on wheels;
Theseus is here in his unhappiness
And will remain for ever; Phlegyas
In utmost misery warns everyone,
Calling them all to witness through the shadows:
'Now learn what justice is, be warned by me,
And do not treat the gods with contempt.'

This one has taken gold and sold his country,
Imposing on her a tyrannical master;
He made and unmade laws as he was paid;
This one has forced his daughter and joined with her
In a forbidden marriage; all who are here
Ventured upon some unspeakable crime
And carried out the evil they intended.
If I had a hundred tongues, a hundred mouths,
A voice of iron, I could not recount
All these misdoings nor yet name the penalties.'
        When she had finished telling all these things,
The ancient priestess of Phoebus, she paused
Then said: 'But come now, you must be on your way
And finish what you undertook to do;
Let us be quick. I see the battlements
Which were forged in the Cyclops' furnaces
And the gates with the archway opposite
Where we must set down the appointed offerings.'
As soon as she had spoken they set off
Briskly and kept pace with one another
Through the dark ways across the space that lay
Before them and so they approached the doors.
Aeneas leapt ahead to the entrance;
He there sprinkled his body with fresh water
And set the bough up right on the threshold.
        This act discharged their duty to the goddess
And so they came to the happy places,
The pleasant green of the Fortunate Grove
Where the blest dwell. The air here is freer
And dresses all the fields with brilliant light;
They have their own sun, their own stars.
Some exercise upon a playing-field
– Games on the grass or wrestling on yellow sand;
Some keep time with their feet upon the ground,
Dancing and singing songs. The Thracian priest
With his long robe accompanies the beat
With seven strings each with its several note,
Now plucking with fingers, now with ivory.
Here is the ancient family of Teucer,
A handsome lot, heroes in the great style
And born in happier years, Ilus, Assaracus

And Dardanus himself, who founded Troy.
Aeneas from far off admires their arms
And empty chariots; their spears stick in the ground,
While here and there upon the plain their horses
Are feeding at their leisure; for the same
Delight they had in arms when they were living
The same attention to their horses, still
Is with them now that they are underground.
Aeneas sees others to left and right
Taking a meal upon the grass, or singing
A hymn of praise in chorus, in a grove
Of scented bay, from which the Eridanus
Rolls in full flood through woods to the upper world.
Here is the company of those who were wounded
While fighting for their country; those who, while alive
Were priests of upright life; those who were seers
And spoke the things Phoebus would have them speak;
With those who, by the arts they discovered
Made life more civilised; and some again
Who merited remembrance by their conduct:
These all wore snowy ribbons round their brows.
As they thronged round the Sibyl spoke to them,
Addressing in particular Musaeus
Who stood head and shoulders above the crowd
That hemmed him in: 'Tell us, fortunate spirits,
And you, best of poets, in what direction
Are we to find Anchises? What place holds him?
It is because of him that we have come;
Crossing the great rivers of Erebus.'
The hero answered her with these few words:
'No-one has a definite home; we live
In shady groves, on swelling river-banks
And meadows which are watered by fresh streams.
But, if your heart is so inclined, ascend
This hill-side to the ridge and I will show you
An easy foot-path.' Then he led the way
And from the high ground showed them shining fields.
So down they went from the eminence.
    Anchises was there, the father, pondering
On spirits who were shut in a green valley
But were to come back to the light above,

For it so happened he was telling over
His dear descendants and their future fortunes,
What sort of men they were to be, what actions
Were to be theirs. But when he saw Aeneas
Coming over the grass in his direction,
He stretched out both his hands eagerly,
Tears started on his cheeks, he cried out:
'You have come at last, and filial devotion
Has found the hard way as I knew it would.
I am permitted, son, to see your face,
Hear the familiar voice and talk with you!
I had concluded that it would be so,
Calculating how long it would take,
And I was right. What lands and what seas
You had to travel before I could greet you!
What dangers you encountered to be here!
How I feared that the powers of Libya
Might harm you in some way!' Aeneas answered:
'It was your image, father, your sad image,
So often seen, that brought me to these limits;
My fleet stands now upon the Tuscan salt.
Give me your right hand, father, give and do not
Now slip from my embrace!' As he was speaking
He loosed a flood of tears and three times
He tried to throw his arms about his neck,
Three times in vain, the form evaded him
Like a breath of wind or a fleeting dream.

    And then Aeneas sees a secluded grove
Far up the valley, with rustling forest-shoots
And the river of Lethe which is swimming past
These placid haunts. All round about there fly
Unnumbered clans and peoples, as in meadows
Bees in a cloudless summer come to settle
On many-coloured flowers and pour around
The shining lilies, while the whole plain murmurs.
Aeneas is startled at the sudden vision.
What causes lie behind it? He does not know,
Nor what that river is ahead of him,
Or who those men are who line the banks.
His father Anchises says: 'These are spirits
Who are fated to put on a second body

And from the current of the river of Lethe
They drink the quiet waters of forgetfulness.
So long have I wanted to tell you this
And show you face to face this race of mine,
One by one, so that with me you may
Rejoice the more to have found Italy!'
'Father, and is it then to be thought
That there are spirits who will go from here
To the world above and once more return
To drag in heavy bodies? Are they wretched,
To entertain so baleful a desire?'
'I will tell you how it is, son, and not keep you
Long in suspense.' Anchises answered him,
Explaining point by point by point why it was so.
    'First you must know that the heavens and the earth,
The great waters, the bright ball of the moon
And Titan's star itself are nourished by
A soul within them, a mind which is infused
Through every limb and agitates their matter,
Mingling itself with the whole mass. It is this which makes
The race of men and beasts, gives life to birds
And to the strange creatures which inhabit
Below the marble surface of the ocean.
The energy that is within their seed
Is from fire, its origin is divine,
So far as they are not held back by bodies
Harmful to them, and they are not made stupid
By earthly limbs and parts which are to die.
It is from these that fear and desire come,
Grief and joy, it is because of them
That men shut in the gloom of their dark prison
Cannot discern the air. And when at last
Life leaves them with the final light of day,
Not all the evil even then goes from them,
Not all the ills of the body, but there must
Be some that have long grown hard upon them
In a strange manner. Therefore they undergo
Penalties and their old faults are punished:
Some are hung stretched out in the empty winds
And there are others the stain of whose crimes
Is washed away under a swirling gulf

Or burnt out with fire. We all suffer,
In death, our own spirits. Then we are sent
Into the broad fields of Elysium.
A few of us stay in that happy place
Till the long day, in time's completed circle,
Has taken out the hardness of corruption
And so leaves the ethereal senses pure
And with them the fire of life itself.
All these spirits, when they have rolled away
A thousand years, the god calls from the throng
To the river Lethe, so that without memory
They may go back under the vault of heaven
And begin to wish they had bodies again.'
    Anchises finished speaking and he drew
His son and the Sibyl with him through the crowd
Which hummed with talk. In the middle of that company
He took his stand upon a little hillock
From which he could pick out each of the spirits
As the long line came by, and know each face.
    'Come now and I will tell you what glory
Will follow the continuing Dardan line
And what descendants there will be for you
From the Italian stock, illustrious spirits
Carrying our name forward. Be taught by me
What destinies await you. That lad there,
You see, the one who has the headless spear
And stands in the place allotted nearest the light,
Will be the first to reach the upper air
Who has Italian blood mixed with our own:
That is Silvius – it is an Alban name –
The posthumous child of your old age; Lavinia,
Your wife, will bring him up in the woods, a king
Followed by a line of kings; through him our race
Will rule over Alba Longa. Next to him Procas,
Pride of the Trojans, Capys, Numitor;
Then there is one who will bring your own name back,
Silvius Aeneas, a man as excellent
In scrupulous conduct as in arms, if ever
He manages to take possession of Alba.
What lads they are! See, how strong they look,
And with their brows shaded with civic oak!

Those are the ones who are going to build Nomentum,
Gabii and the city of Fidenae
And then the mountain stronghold of Collatia,
Pometii, Fort Inuus, Bola and Cora.
These will be names in lands which have no name.
    'Yes, and a son of Mars will join his grandfather:
Romulus of the blood of Assaracus;
Ilia will be his mother. Do you see now
The twin crests on his helmet? And how his father
Distinguishes him now for the world above
With his own emblem? Under these auspices
Great Rome will match her empire with the world,
Her pride and courage only with Olympus,
And circle her seven strongholds with one wall,
Happy in the men she breeds: as the Great Mother
Rides in her chariot with her crown of towers
Through all the Phrygian cities, glad to have borne
The progeny she has, and she embraces
A hundred of her children's children, all
Inhabitants of heaven, all with their places
In the world above. And now turn your eyes.
Look at that family, they are your own
And they are Romans. Here is Caesar, here
The progeny of Iulus who will come
Under the bending sky. This man who is here
Is he who has so often been promised you,
Augustus Caesar, son of the deity,
Who first will bring back the Golden Age to Latium
In fields where once Saturn himself ruled;
He will extend his empire far and wide
Beyond the Garamantians and the Indians
To lands beyond the passage of the stars,
Beyond the annual journey of the sun
To where Atlas revolves on his shoulders
The entire heavens, set with shining jewels:
Against his coming the Caspian realms already
Shudder at the oracles of the gods,
The Maeotian land too; the Nile's seven mouths
Shift in terror. Not even Hercules
Travelled so far over the earth, not when he shot
The hind with the bronze hooves, or pacified

The woods of Erymanthus and with his bow
Made Lerna tremble; nor did triumphant Bacchus,
Holding the reins of vine to guide his chariot
When he drove tigers down from the top of Nysa.
And do we doubt our courage should go further
Or our deeds show it is not fear that stops us
Taking our place upon Ausonian soil?
    'But who is that, far off and crowned with olive,
Who carries sacred vessels? I know that hair,
That white beard, it is the Roman king
Who will be first to settle the city's laws,
Sent from the poor ground of little Cures
To great dominion. He will be succeeded
By Tullus who will break the country's rest
And move to arms men who have settled down
And troops which have become unused to triumphs.
Ancus follows him close, a boastful man,
Even now too pleased with his popularity.
And do you wish to see the Tarquin kings
And the proud spirit of the avenging Brutus
Who will win the fasces back? – the first consul,
The first who will call his sons to suffer
For stirring up fresh wars, and so will serve
The cause of liberty: himself much grieved,
However later ages view his action;
But love of country wins, and lust for praise.
    'See how the Decii and the Drusii
And there, Torquatus, cruel with the axe;
Camillus who will bring the standards back.
But those you see together in gleaming armour,
Alas! if they attain the vital light
What wars will they make between themselves,
What battles and what carnage they will start!
A father-in-law comes down over the Alps
From the fort at Monoecus, his son-in-law
Waits for him with the armies of the East!
My lads, never allow yourselves the thought
Of wars like those, and never turn the strength
Your country has, against her own heart;
You above all, spare her, you whose descent

Is from Olympus; throw your sword away
Rather than that, you who are of my blood!
  'And there, a spirit who will triumph over Corinth
And drive his chariot up to the Capitol,
The famous victor who killed so many Greeks;
That other will turn Argos upside down
And Agamemnon's Mycenae, kill the Aeacid,
Of the race of Achilles though he be,
And so avenge his ancestors and Troy
And the desecrated temple of Minerva.
Who would leave you without a word, Cato,
Or you, Cossus? Or indeed the Gracchi
Or the two from Scipio's family, martial thunderbolts
Who will wreck Africa; Fabricius,
Poor, but a great man; or you, Serranus,
Sowing your fields when you were called to office?
I am weary now, Fabii, what shall I say?
Only that you, the greatest of them, alone
Will restore the state by waiting for the moment.
Others, I have no doubt, will do better
At making breathing figures out of metal
Or giving lumps of marble living faces;
They will be better orators, better astronomers;
But you, Roman, remember, you are to rule
The nations of the world: your arts will be
To bring the ways of peace, be merciful
To the defeated and smash the proud completely.'
  Such was the speech Anchises made; he added
While they stood there amazed: 'Look now, Marcellus
Advances with spoils taken from a prince,
Splendid, victorious, towering over everyone.
It is he will re-assert the Roman cause
In a time of tumult and, by riding out
Against Carthaginian and rebel Gaul,
Will flatten them and for the third time
Dedicate captured arms to Quirinus.'
  Aeneas then saw, walking beside the hero,
A youth of great beauty in shining armour
But not looking happy, not looking up:
'Who is that, father, beside the other?
Is it a son or some other descendant

From a long line? How those around applaud him!
And what a figure he is! Yet black night
Hovers around his head, a mournful shadow.'
His father Anchises, with tears in his eyes,
Answered: 'O son, do not seek to know
The sorrow that will fall upon your family.
The fates will show this young man to the world
But give him no existence after that.
Great gods! the Roman line would be too great,
As you see it, if this gift were really theirs.
What groans from men upon the Campus Martius
Will sound through the great city! What obsequies
Will you see, Tiber, as you travel past
That recent tomb. No boy of Ilian race
Will ever raise such hopes as this one will
Among his Latin ancestors; in none
Will Romulus's country take such pride
Alas for old loyalties and virtues
And for a hand unconquerable in war!
No man would have put himself in his way
And not suffered for it, whether on foot
He made his way among the enemy
Or spurred his foaming horse into their midst.
Pitiful boy, alas, if you can break
The brutal fates that bind you, you will be
Marcellus! Give me hands full of lilies;
I will strew purple flowers and so at least
Give what I can to my descendant's spirit,
Performing this vain rite.' And so they wander
Here and there in these broad, misty lands,
Seeing what they can see. At last Anchises,
Having guided his son through every scene
And set his mind ablaze with the desire
For future glories, told him of the wars
He must now wage and gave him an account
Of the Laurentine peoples, of Latinus
And his city, and how each task ahead
Is to be circumvented or performed.

   Sleep has two gates, one said to be of horn
From which true shadows have an easy exit;
The other is of shining ivory

Perfectly polished, but through that the dead
Send false dreams into the world above.
When he had finished speaking old Anchises
Accompanied his son, with whom was the Sibyl,
And sent them out through the ivory gate.
Aeneas hurried back to his ships
And rejoined his comrades; then he sailed
Along the coast to the harbour at Caieta.
The anchor is let down; the sterns are ashore.

# BOOK VII

BOOK VII

# BOOK VII

You too, Caieta, nurse of Aeneas,
Dying, have given our shores undying fame
And now we honour your last resting-place;
Where your bones lie, your name is recalled:
Is that not glory in our great Hesperia?
    The dutiful Aeneas carried out
The rites he owed you, raised your funeral mound;
Then, when all was quiet out at sea,
Set sail and left the harbour. Into the night
The gentle breezes blew and the bright moon
Showed up the track across the glittering water.
They sailed close to the shores of Circe's country
Where she, the daughter of the Sun, all day
Makes inaccessible woods ring with her song
And in her jewelled palace lights up the night
By burning fragrant cedar, while she shoots
Her deft shuttle across the fine-strung frame.
From this direction could be heard the growl
Of angry lions shaking at their chain
And roaring as the night covered them,
The sound of raging swine, the noise of bears
Furious at being penned, howls from the huge
Wolves: these were the shapes into which Circe,
The cruel goddess, using powerful herbs,
Had changed what once had had a human appearance
Into the face and figure of wild beasts.
So that the godly Trojans should not suffer
Any such portents, be carried into the harbour
Or approach these fell shores, Neptune blew up
Favourable winds that would fill their sails;
So they escaped through the boiling surf.
    And now the sea was reddening with new light
As from high heaven Aurora in her chariot,

A saffron figure in a rosy mist,
Shone out; the wind dropped, every breath was still
And the oars strained upon a marble surface.
Aeneas then, from far out at sea,
Caught sight of a great forest through which Tiber
Flowed pleasantly and broke to the coast
In rapid eddies filled with yellow sand.
Around and up above a host of birds
Of various kinds found in the estuary
Touched the air with their song and circled the forest.
A change of course was ordered by Aeneas;
The prows were turned to land and joyfully
He was carried up to where the stream was shady.

   Work on me now, Erato, I am to tell
What kings there were in Latium, what events
Happened at what times, and how things stood
When first a foreign army beached its ships
On the Ausonian shores; I will recall
How the fighting first began. Instruct me, goddess,
It is not for nothing that I am your poet.
I shall recount the horrors of these wars,
The battles and the kings whose courage drove them
To a solemn end; the fighters from Etruria
And all Hesperia answering the call to arms.
A greater order of things is born to me,
I move to greater tasks.
                   The king Latinus,
Advanced in years already, ruled in peace
Over those fields and undisturbed cities.
He was, so we are told, the son of Faunus;
His mother was a Laurentian nymph, Marica:
Picus the Woodpecker was Faunus's father,
Who himself claims he sprang from you, Saturn;
It is you who are the founder of this line.
Latinus had, for so the gods determined,
No son to be his heir, his male issue
Having been snatched away as they grew up.
One daughter was all that remained to him
To save his great house; she was ripe for marriage,
Already being fully old enough.
Many in Latium and throughout Ausonia

Were asking for her. The most handsome suitor
Of all that sought her was Turnus, a strong claimant
Because of his ancestors and because the queen,
The mother of the girl, greatly desired
To bring about the match; but divine portents,
Many and menacing, stood in the way.
There was a laurel far inside the palace
In a high inner court, a sacred tree
Which had been tended with awe for many years;
Father Latinus had found it, it was said,
When he began to build his citadel
And he had dedicated the tree to Phoebus,
Calling his settlers after it, Laurentes.
A great cloud of bees, astonishingly
Had settled on the tip and hung in a swarm
On the green bough, tangled in each other's legs.
The soothsayer said at once: 'I see a foreigner
Coming towards us, his army marching in
From the same direction as the bees have come;
I see him lording it on the top of the citadel.'
Moreover, while the virgin Lavinia
Stood by her father as with holy torches
He waited on the altars, a monstrous thing:
Her long hair appeared to catch fire
And all her fine head-gear was burnt up
In crackling flames, all was alight,
Her queenly tresses, her crown with all its jewels:
Then wrapped in smoke and yellow brilliance
She scattered Vulcan all around the palace.
This horror was reported everywhere
As a miraculous sight; what could it mean?
The talk was that it meant she would be famous
But for the people it portended war.

　　Yet the king, rendered anxious by these portents,
Visited the oracles of his prophetic father
Faunus, questioning the groves that lie
Below Albunea, where a huge forest
Fills with the noise of the sacred spring which darkly
Exhales a deadly breath. From this place
The tribes of Italy and all the Oenotrians
Seek answers to their uncertainties.

Here will a priest bring offerings
And stretch himself under the silent night
Upon the skins of slaughtered sheep and pray
For sleep in which he sees many images,
Floating, incomprehensible, hears many voices,
Enjoys the conversation of the gods
And speaks with Acheron deep in Avernus.
Here then the father Latinus himself goes
Searching for answers; he kills a hundred sheep
In the ritual manner, then lies propped on their skins.
Suddenly from the depths of the grove a voice
Which says: 'My son, do not seek a Latin marriage
For your daughter; the bridal chamber is ready
But do not credit it, for foreign sons will come,
Their blood will carry our name to the stars;
Descendants of that stock will see the world
Under their feet, turning at their command,
Wherever the sun re-visits, east or west.'
This reply which his father Faunus made,
This warning given in the silent night
Latinus did not keep behind tight lips,
But Rumour had already spread the tale
Through the Ausonian cities when the Trojans
Tied up their ships upon the grassy river-bank.
    Aeneas, his great captains and pretty Iülus
Lay down under the bough of a tall tree
And set out their picnic, putting cakes of meal
Upon the grass to set their food on (this
Was an idea from Jupiter himself);
On this bread they piled the country fruit.
When they had eaten what was put on top
The insufficiency drove them to get their teeth
Into the little wheat-cakes, finger them
And pick bits off and then munch them up
Until the crusty rounds had disappeared
To the last quarter: that was destiny.
'Whew!' said Iulus and, simply as a joke,
'We are even eating up the tables now!'
His words were taken as an indication
Their troubles were over; his father stopped his mouth,
Overcome by a sense of the divine.

Without hesitation he spoke out:
'Welcome the land the fates have destined for me!
And honour to the faithful gods of Troy!
This is our home: this is our country now.
I now can tell you, my father Anchises
Revealed these secrets to me for he said:
"When you have sailed, son, to an unknown shore
And, short of food, are driven to eat your tables,
Then, weary though you are, hope you are home;
Remember then to find a site and build,
First of all labouring at the defences."
This is the hunger he was talking of,
This is the last hunger that awaits us;
It is the way out of our calamities.
Come then, and with the first light of the sun
Joyfully let us find out what is here,
Who are the inhabitants, where the towns are,
Exploring in various directions from the harbour.
But now you must pour out bowls for Jove
And call upon Anchises in your prayers
And set more wine upon the tables now!'
    When he had spoken he wound about his brow
A leafy spray, and prayed: to the spirit of the place,
To Earth, who is the first of all the gods,
To the nymphs inhabiting yet unknown rivers;
Then to Night and the rising stars of Night,
To the Jupiter of Ida, to the Phrygian Mother,
And to his parents, one of them in heaven
And one in Erebus. The Almighty Father
Then thundered three times from a clear sky
And with his own hand shook out from above
A cloud ablaze with rays of golden light.
Then suddenly through the Trojan ranks a rumour
Is spread about that indeed the day has come
When they must found their city. Once again
They set to feasting with enthusiasm
And, happy at the greatness of the omen,
Bring in the bowls and crown the wine with leaves.
    The next day, when the first light has risen,
Purifying these regions with its torch,
On different tracks the Trojans started exploring

To find what city, boundaries and shores
This nation has: they come upon the pools
Filled up from the spring of Numicius,
The River Tiber and the habitations
Of the courageous Latins. Anchises's son
Orders a hundred orators, who are chosen
From every rank, to go to the king's great walls,
All of them wearing sprays of Minerva's olive
And bearing presents for him, to request
Peace for the Trojans. They do as they are told;
There is no delay, they go with rapid steps.
Aeneas himself marks out with a shallow trench
Where his walls shall be, works on the site,
Surrounding the first settlement on the coast
With stakes and ramparts that will form a camp.
And now his young men reached their objective;
They saw the towers and high roofs of the Latins;
They were drawing near the walls. Before the city
Boys and men in the first flower of youth
Were exercising on horseback or mastering
The management of chariots in clouds of dust,
Training with bows and arrows or else hurling
Useful javelins, and some were competing
In running or in boxing: riding up,
A messenger reports to the aged king
The arrival of a party of tall men
Whose dress no-one can recognise. He ordered
That they should be admitted to the palace
And took his seat on his ancestral throne.
      The palace was majestic, vast, a hundred
Pillars supported its high roof; it was
At the top of the town; Laurentian Picus built it;
Set among fearsome trees and fearful also
As haunted by ancient observances.
Here it was, by divine authority,
That kings received their sceptres and first raised
The rods and axe, here in this Latin temple
Was too a senate-house, here sacred banquets
Were held, here rams were sacrificed and here
In unbroken line the senators took their places
At the long tables. In the entrance-court

There stood old statues made of cedar-wood
Of ancestors in order as they came.
There was Italus and Sabinus the father
Who planted the vine, shown with his pruning-hook,
Old Saturn, and Janus with two faces;
With other kings back to the beginning
And men wounded while fighting for their country.
There were besides, hanging on sacred pillars,
Many arms, huge chariots and curved axes,
Crests of helmets, huge bars from broken gates,
Javelins and shields and beaks torn from ships.
There was Picus himself, the breaker of horses,
Sitting with his Quirinal staff and dressed
In the striped toga, the shield in his left hand;
It was he whom his golden bride, Circe,
In the heat of passion struck with her wand
And gave a potion to, so that he changed
Into a bird with barred and spotted wings.
  Such was the temple of the gods in which
Latinus was now seated as he called
The Trojans to his presence within doors.
It was he who spoke first when they came in,
Saying: 'Now tell me, sons of Dardanus
(For I well know your city and your race
And have heard of your journey over the sea),
What are you looking for? For what reason
Or what need had you to be carried so far
Over blue waters to Ausonia?
Whether it is you were driven off course by storm
Or by miscalculation – as often happens
To sailors who are out on the high seas –
You have come up the river and you are in harbour:
Do not elude our hospitality,
But know we Latins are of Saturn's race,
Just not because we are slaves or under laws
But of our own free will as men who keep
The customs of their ancient god. Indeed
I can remember (though the story is
A little dimmed by time) the Aurancan elders
Used to tell, how Dardanus came from here
And then went all the way to Phrygian Ida

And the cities there, and those of Thracian Samos
Which is now called Samothrace. It was from here,
From his Etruscan home, from Corythus
That he set out, he who is now enthroned
In the golden palace of the starry heavens,
Another god with an altar of his own.'
    When he had finished Ilioneus spoke:
'King, noble son of Faunus, no black storm
Drove us across the waves to your territory,
No star or landmark made us lose our way:
Intentionally and with most willing hearts
All of us here have travelled to your city,
Refugees from a kingdom which was once
The greatest the Sun saw in all his journeyings.
It is from Jove our race has its beginnings,
It is in Jove our Dardan youth take pride;
From Jove's supreme race comes our king himself:
Trojan Aeneas has sent us to your door.
How fierce that storm was which issued out
Over the plains of Ida from cruel Mycenae;
What fates impelled the clash of the two worlds
Of Europe and of Asia, all have heard,
Even the dwellers at the ends of the earth
Where the Atlantic Ocean ebbs and flows,
And those who dwell where the blazing tropics
Extend between two zones on either side.
Swept by the flood on to the high seas
We ask a modest home for our country's gods,
A harmless shore, a little air and water
Which are free to all. We shall not disgrace your kingdom
Nor will your reputation be the less
Nor our gratitude grow less with time;
Ausonians will have no cause to regret
They took Troy to their heart. I swear indeed
By the destinies of Aeneas, by
His right hand, strong both in loyalty
And in arms in the wars: many are the peoples,
Many – and do not think lightly of us
Because we offer you garlands of peace
And suppliant words – are those nations
Who have besought us for an alliance,

But the immortal gods have fated us;
It is by their commands we find your land.
Dardanus came from here; he comes again;
Apollo's high decrees drive us towards
The Tuscan Tiber, the sacred spring of Numicius.
Besides, Aeneas offers you these gifts,
Small but the relics of his former fortunes,
Snatched out of burning Troy. In this gold cup
His father Anchises offered wine at the altars;
These are the accoutrements Priam wore
When he gave laws to the assembled nations
– His sceptre, holy crown, and the robes
The Trojan ladies embroidered.'
    Listening to this speech of Ilioneus
Latinus remained motionless, his head bent,
Only his eyes moving as he looked round.
The king is moved less by the sumptuous purple
Or by the sceptre, than by the thought of his daughter,
Her marriage and whom she should marry,
Reflecting on the oracle of old Faunus:
This must be that son-in-law who is destined
To come from a foreign country and to reign
Under the same auspices as himself;
Whose descendants would be famous for their valour
And so strong as to capture the whole world.
He was contented and at last he spoke:
'May the gods favour what we have begun
In accordance with their auguries! What you ask
Is granted, Trojan! I accept your gifts.
And now, while I am king, you shall not lack
For fertile fields or all the wealth of Troy.
But let Aeneas if he truly wishes
To share our hospitality and alliance
Come here, for friendly faces will not frighten him:
To seal the treaty I must shake his hand.
Take back this message from me to your king:
I have a daughter I may not give in marriage
To a man of our own race, the oracles
From my father's shrine forbid it, heaven itself
Has shown by many signs they are opposed.
What is predicted is that sons shall come

From foreign shores and shall exalt our name
Among the stars. Your king, I think, is he
On whom the fates are calling; if there is truth
In my augury, it is him I choose.'
   When he had finished speaking the old king
Chose horses from among the whole three hundred
Who waited glossily in his high stables;
He ordered them to be led out immediately,
One each for all the Teucrians in turn:
Fast animals with purple saddle-cloths,
Embroidered all of them, with golden chains
Hanging over their chests, and golden armour;
They champed at bits that were yellow with gold.
And for the absent Aeneas there was a chariot
With a pair of horses of celestial breed
Puffing fire from their nostrils, they came of the blood
Of those the clever Circe had bred up
From the mare mated by stealth with her father's stallion.
Such were the gifts and such the messages
Aeneas's young men brought back with them,
Riding high on their horses: it was peace.
   But see! the fierce wife of Jupiter
Is coming back from Argos, in the air,
From Inachus: and from the skies she sees
– While still at Pachynus in Sicily –
The jubilant Aeneas and his fleet.
She sees his men already building houses,
Already confident this is their land,
Their ships deserted: she stops, grieved to the heart.
Shaking her head she pours out this speech:
'Ah hated race, and Phrygian fates, hostile
To my fates! Did they fall on Sigeum?
Could they be prisoners once they had been taken?
Did burning Troy burn them? No, through the battle
And through the fire they found a way out.
It seems my powers are exhausted now,
My hate is satisfied and I must rest.
When they were driven out of their own country
Over the waves, I boldly followed them,
Confronting them even on the high seas:
All the forces of the sky and water

Were spent against the Trojans. Neither the Syrtes
Nor Scylla nor the great gulf of Charybdis
Would serve my purpose. Between the banks of Tiber
They are safe from the sea and me. Yet Mars had strength
To ruin the great race of the Lapiths;
The father of the gods himself allowed
Calydon to be at the mercy of Diana:
And had the Lapiths or had Calydon
Committed crimes that could deserve such treatment?
But I, Jove's high consort, who dared everything
That I could do, unhappy as I was,
Who turned to every trick, Aeneas still
Has got the better of me. But if my powers
Are insufficient, I can ask for help
And find it where I will. If heaven denies it
I will persuade Acheron. I am not allowed
– So be it – to prohibit this Aeneas
From holding sway in Latium; if Lavinia
Is still to be his bride, fate being stubborn:
Yet I can drag things out and cause delays
In all these great events; I can destroy
The peoples of both kings; father and bridegroom
May come together but only at a price.
Your dowry, girl, will be paid out in blood,
Rutulian and Trojan, while Bellona
Will wait upon you as matron-of-honour.
For Hecuba is not the only one
To dream of firebrands and give birth to flames;
No, Venus has herself produced another,
Another Paris, another funeral torch
For Troy as Troy is coming back to life.'

    When she had given vent to these words
She swooped to earth, a terrifying figure,
Then summoned up the trouble-maker Allecto
From where the Furies dwell among the shades
– And with Allecto what is dear to her,
Wars with their griefs, angers and treacheries
And dark recriminations. Even Pluto
Her father hates her, her Tartarean sisters
Hate her, she is a monster: so many shapes
She has, all cruel, so many black serpents

Sprout from her. This is she Juno incites
Now by this speech: 'Daughter of Night, Virgin,
Grant me this labour after your own kind,
This service, lest my name should be injured
And I without honour, while Aeneas's men
Succeed in their designs for intermarriage
Or make themselves at home in Italy.
You can set brother against brother in war,
Turn families upside down with mutual hatreds,
Bring within doors whips and funeral torches,
You of a thousand names and ways to hurt.
Your mind is fertile, shake it up a bit:
Spread accusations, they are the seeds of war:
Let young men wish for arms, demand them, seize them!'
    At once Allecto, full of Gorgon poison,
Made for Latium and came to the lofty palace
Of the Laurentian king: and there she waited
Upon the threshold of the queen Amata
Who was already seething, as women will,
Troubled and angry that a Trojan had come
To upset Turnus's marriage. The goddess threw
One of the snakes from her blue-green hair
Into the queen's bodice, about her heart,
So that she, rendered furious by this viper,
Should turn all the palace upside down.
It slipped between her clothes and her smooth breasts
So quickly that she did not notice it
And breathed a viper's spirit into her;
The monstrous snake became the twisted gold
About her neck; became the long ribbons
Falling from her headband; tangled itself
Into her hair and all its slippery length
Wandered over her limbs. While the corruption
Trailed its moist poison deeper, stole her senses
And wound its fire all about her bones
And still her mind was not yet quite in flames,
She spoke softly, weeping as mothers do
Over her daughter's fate and the Phrygian wedding:
'Is it then to refugees from Troy
That Lavinia is to be given, and you her father?
Have you no pity for her or for yourself?

Nor for her mother whom, at the first north wind,
The traitor will abandon, putting to sea
And taking the girl with him as a prize?
Yet was that not the way that Phrygian shepherd
Got into Sparta and made off with Helen,
Taking her back to Troy? Did you not promise?
You used to care for us and again and again
You pledged her hand to Turnus, one of the family!
If our son-in-law is to be a foreigner
And not a Latin, and what your father Faunus
Told you you had to do, has to be done,
Well, I think anyone not one of your subjects
Is a foreigner; that's what the gods meant.
And Turnus, if you go back far enough,
Has Inachus and Acrisius for ancestors
And they came from Mycenae, the middle of Greece!'

　　When, having wearied him with all these words,
She sees Latinus still stand firm against her,
And when the serpent's poison has gone deep
Into her innards and all over her,
Driving her mad, she is indeed unhappy;
Goaded by these portents she rages madly
Through the great city. She is like a top
Which boys intent upon their game whip round
Through empty halls: it is driven by the thong
Upon its circling course while ingenuous boys
Marvel at the spinning of a bit of box-wood
Animated by blows. So she no less
Is driven on her way through streets and squares
Among the turbulent people. She even flies
Out to the woods as if possessed by Bacchus
For the evil grows as her madness grows,
And hides her daughter in the leafy hills
To rob the Teucrians of the intended marriage
And put off the ceremony. 'Evoe Bacchus!'
She cries, howling then: 'The virgin is yours;
Only you are good enough for her!
For you she takes up the gentle thyrsus,
She dances round you, dedicates to you
Her sacred head of hair!' The news gets round
And every mother's heart blazes with fury;

They all determine they must go elsewhere.
And leave their homes with their unbound hair
Blowing about their shoulders, and some of them
Fill the air with tremulous ululations,
Dressed in skins and trailing vines on spears.
In the middle of these women the queen herself
Furiously holds a torch aloft
And sings a wedding chant as if her daughter
Were marrying Turnus; she rolls bloodshot eyes
Then suddenly calls out fiercely:
'Mothers of Latium, wherever you may be,
Listen to me! If you have any kindness
For poor Amata when she is unhappy
Or any religious feeling, if a mother's rights
Mean anything to you and you feel for them,
Untie your headbands and join in the orgies.'
Such is the queen as with a Bacchic goad
Allecto drives her all over the forest
And in among the coverts of wild beasts.
   When she had, as it seemed to her, done enough
To provoke this insanity in the women,
Unsettling all Latinus had in mind
And his house with it, then the ill-humoured goddess
Spread out her cloudy wings and flew away
To the walled city of the brave Rutulians
– A city founded, or so it was said,
By Danaë and her Acrisian colonists
When she was blown there by a southerly gale.
The place was called Ardea by our forefathers
And the great name of Ardea remains
But that is all. Here Turnus in his palace
Lay asleep in the darkness of the night.
Allecto put aside her savage looks;
No more did she appear as a Fury
But gave herself the face of an old woman
And drew ill-boding wrinkles on her brow;
She gave herself white hair, put on a headband
And wound a spray of olive into it;
She had become the ancient Calybe,
Priestess of Juno, guardian of her temple.
So she appeared before the young man's eyes

With these words: 'Turnus!
So you let all your efforts go for nothing
And stand by while your sceptre is made over
To the Dardanian colonists? The king
Refuses you the bride and the dowry
To which your blood entitles you, he seeks
To give his kingdom to a foreign heir.
Go now, they are mocking you, expose yourself
To dangers without getting any thanks!
Defeat the Tuscans, go, protect the Latins!
Saturn's all-powerful daughter ordered me
To speak to you thus plainly, while you lie
Peacefully in your bed. Get up, take heart,
Make preparations, arm the young men,
Order them out, the Phrygian captains rest
By our fair stream: set their smart ships ablaze.
The great might of the gods gives this command.
The king himself, Latinus, if unwilling
To allow the marriage and to keep his word,
Must hear of it, and face Turnus in arms!'
     At this the young man, jeering at the prophetess,
In turn opened his mouth: 'This news that a fleet
Has sailed up the Tiber has not escaped me;
I'm not the man to be forgotten by Juno!
But you are old, mother, worn out, decayed
And past the time when you know what you're saying;
You worry all the time about nothing,
What pointless fears about kings in arms!
Your function is to dust the gods' statues
And look after the temple; it is for men
To make war and peace, war is their business.'
     Allecto blazed with anger at such talk.
But, as the young man spoke, a sudden trembling
Passed over his limbs, his eyes fixed in a stare,
The Fury hissed at him with all those serpents
And looked so terrifying: her rolling eyes
Made him start back as he was hesitating,
Thinking what he should say; and then she made
Two of the snakes in her hair stand up aggressively
And cracked her whip; and so she continued,
Raving at him: 'So I am worn out, am I?

I don't know what I'm saying, have pointless fears
About kings in arms? Then look at me now!
I am here from where the Dread Sisters live
And in my hand I carry war and death.'
    So speaking she threw her torch at the young man
The brand stuck in his heart and smouldered there,
Giving off black light. A great fear
Broke up his sleep, his bones and muscles seemed
Limp with the sweat that poured all over him.
He roared for his weapons, he was out of his mind
He searched his bed for them and then the house;
The lust to kill, the criminal lunacy
War can bring raged in him, but most of all
Anger: as when crackling sticks flare up
Against the sides of a boiling cauldron
And the water leaps from the heat, gets out of hand
And a smoky steam bursts from the rising foam;
The liquid is no liquid any more,
A dark cloud flies away into the air.
Peace is betrayed: he tells his young captains
They must collect their weapons and prepare
An expedition against King Latinus;
Defend Italy, drive the enemy out;
He could take on the two of them at once,
The Teucrians and the Latins. After this speech
He called the gods to witness to his vows;
The Rutuli egg one another on:
One is excited by the young man's beauty,
Another by his regal ancestors,
Another by his personal skill in battle.
    Turnus encouraged the Rutulians;
In the meantime Allecto flew away
On Stygian wings, to be with the Teucrians.
Here was a new trick: upon the coast
She found the place where pretty Iülus
Was busy netting and chasing wild animals.
The virgin from hell set the hounds in a frenzy
All at once, with a scent they recognised,
And they were away after a stag.
That was what first roused the country-folk
And caused the war. The stag was a special beauty

With huge antlers, taken while it sucked its mother
And brought up by the young sons of Tyrrhus
And by their father, keeper of the king's herds
Who looked after their pastures wherever it was.
Their sister Silvia had trained him to obey her
And used to decorate the creature's antlers,
Weaving pliant twigs among them; she combed him too
And washed him in the finest spring water,
Wild though he was. He allowed her to do it
And used to feed at her father's table;
He would wander in the forest and yet at night
Would come back home, though sometimes it was late.
    This was the wanderer the rabid hounds
Of huntsman Iulus started, as by chance
He floated down the stream and came to rest
On a cool shady bank. The huntsman himself,
Ascanius, who always wanted to be first,
Drew his bow at once and aimed an arrow;
His shaky hand had some divine assistance;
The shaft went whizzing through the stag's flanks
Into his guts. Wounded, the animal
Made his way home and crept into his stall
Moaning and there, bleeding, he filled the house
With his complaints as if asking for something.
Silvia, the sister, was the first to hear
And called for help, beating her arms with her hands
And summoning the rough country-people.
They came – for death hides in the quiet woods –
As men expecting an emergency,
One with a stick hardened in the fire,
One with a cudgel full of knots;
For anything that comes to hand will serve
To make a weapon for an angry man.
Tyrrhus called out his gangs; and as it happened
That he was splitting up an oak in four,
Driving in wedges, breathless, picked up an axe.
    But the cruel goddess, always on the look-out
For opportunities for doing harm,
Took her place on the stable roof
And from there gave the call the shepherds give
– A voice from Tartarus on a crooked horn.

Every grove trembled, the deep woods re-echoed;
The lake of Trivia heard it far away,
The white and sulphurous river Nar heard it,
Velinus' springs too and frightened mothers
Hugged their young children closer. Then indeed
Came running to the voice of the fell trumpet
The stubborn peasants, snatching up their arms;
The Trojans came pouring from their camp
To help Ascanius. All lined up for battle.
No longer was it just a country quarrel
With heavy clubs and stakes hardened with fire;
They fought with two-edged metal; far and wide
Sprang up a deadly harvest of drawn swords.
Bronze gleamed as the sun struck it and reflected
Its light against the clouds: as when white flecks
Appear upon the waves as the wind rises
And the sea grows big and throws the waves higher
Until it pitches them up to the sky
From its lowest depths. It was here Almo fell,
Tyrrhus's eldest son, as he stood out
In front of the first rank; a whistling arrow
Wounded him and, sticking below his throat,
Choked his wind-pipe with blood and his young life
Was gone. All round him there were many dead
Including old Galaesus who was killed
Trying to bring the parties to their senses:
He was the one outstandingly just man
In Italy in those times, a rich man too;
On his land were five bleating flocks, and five
Herds of cattle came home to him each night;
It took a hundred ploughs to plough his land.
    While indecisive battles were fought out
In the flat country, the goddess, who had done
What she had promised and had drawn first blood
And brought about some deaths in the first fighting,
Abandoning Hesperia, flew away
Into the air of heaven and spoke to Juno
With the arrogance of one who had got her way:
'See, there's your quarrel capped with war at last!
Now tell them to make friends and seal alliances
Since I have spattered blood over the Trojans,

Ausonian blood at that. I will do more
If you assure me that is what you want:
I will spread rumours till the neighbouring cities
Are drawn into the war, and set alight
All their minds with a lunatic bellicosity
So that men come from everywhere to help:
And all over the fields I will scatter arms.'
Juno however answered: 'Terror and crime
Are there in plenty now, with reasons enough
For going to war, there is hand-to-hand fighting:
The arms they took by chance are stained with blood.
Venus's precious son and king Latinus
Can celebrate the marriage in this way.
But you should not wander too freely here
In the air of heaven, the Father and the Lord
Of high Olympus would not have it so.
Give way. I will manage the rest myself
If there's a chance of trouble.' Saturn's daughter
Stopped at this point; Allecto flew away,
The hiss of serpents sounding in her wings,
And made off to her haunts in Cocytus,
Leaving heaven far above her. In Italy
There is a place, in the middle, under high mountains
– Well-known, they talk of it in many lands –
The valley of Ampsanctus: on either side
The dark edge of the forest closes on it;
A roaring torrent falls in the middle,
Crashing on rocks and turning to a whirlpool.
Here is a dreadful cavern with deep holes
Through which cruel Dis can breathe, and a huge gorge
Opens the baleful jaws through which Acheron
Belches out. It was here that the Fury
Hid her hated power and the whole earth
And heaven itself were the better for it.
    In the meantime Saturn's daughter like a queen
Gave the war a final push. So one and all
The shepherds from the battle crowded in
Bringing the dead back with them to the town,
The boy Almo, Galaesus with his smashed face:
They called on the gods and appealed to the Latins.
Turnus was there and while the accusations

Of fire and bloodshed raged all around
He frightened people more by saying that Trojans
Were being called in to run the kingdom;
Phrygians would make a family of half-breeds
And he himself be hounded from the door.
Then those whose wives and mothers had gone out
Dancing the orgies in the trackless forest
– Amata's name could not be treated lightly –
Came together, shouting Mars must decide.
And so it was for, going against the omens,
Against what the gods had determined,
All of them, under some malign influence,
Joined in demanding an iniquitous war.
They jostled all around Latinus's palace:
He stood against them like a rock at sea,
Like a rock at sea with water crashing against it
When it stands firm among the breaking waves
And it is for nothing that the foam roars
Over the jutting fingers, or sea-weed floating
Against its side is drawn back again.
But he is powerless against ignorant voices
– A nod from Juno and everything goes her way.
The old man calls on the gods and the empty air:
'Alas,' he says, 'the fates are breaking me;
I am swept away by the storm. O wretched people,
You will pay for this sacrilege with your blood.
You, Turnus, and your criminal intent
Will find a bitter punishment, it will be too late
When you turn to the gods. And as for me,
It is time for quiet now, at the harbour mouth
I am denied a happy burial.'
He said no more but shut himself in his palace
And so let the reins of office fall.
        There was a custom in Hesperian Latium
Which was observed later in Alban cities
As now in Rome the mistress of the world,
When she makes up her mind to a campaign,
Whether the purpose is to carry war
And weeping with it, in among the Getae
Or Arabs or Hyrcanians, or to travel
East to the Indians or hunt down the Parthians

To get our standards back: what they now call
The double Gates of War are held sacred
In ordinary observance and because
The cruelty of war inspires such terror;
A hundred bolts of bronze and all the strength
Iron can give, are used to close them up;
Their guardian Janus never leaves the threshold.
Here, when the senators are resolved on war,
The consul himself, formally arrayed
In the Quirinal toga with Gabine cincture,
Unbars the creaking doors and so announces
Hostilities have begun: the fighting men
Take up the cry and the bronze trumpets then
Breathe out a hoarse assent. And so it was
Latinus was now told to declare war
Against Aeneas and his followers
And open up the melancholy gates.
The old man would not touch them, he recoiled
Before an office that would bring dishonour
And so hid himself among blind shadows,
Then down from the sky came the queen of the gods
And pushed the tardy doors with her own hand;
The hinges turned for Saturn's daughter, the gates
Flew open in despite of iron bands.
Ausonia, where before life had been quiet,
Where nothing seemed to stir, was soon ablaze.
Some turned out at once in marching order,
Some rode on high horses, kicking up dust;
All called for arms. Some of them polished shields
And gleaming spear-heads with great lumps of fat
Or sharpened up their axes with a stone;
What pleasure as they carried out the standards
And heard the sound of trumpets! Five great towns
Erected anvils and renewed their weapons
– Powerful Atina, proud Tibur, Ardea,
Crustumeri and turreted Antemnae.
They hollowed out coverings for their heads
And plaited withies to make frames for shields;
Others made bronze breast-plates, or leg-armour
Smoothed with a covering of malleable silver;
Their pride in blades and sickles, their love of the plough

Gave way to this and their fathers' swords
Were newly fashioned in the furnaces.
The trumpets sounded to battle and the password
Was issued, meaning that this was war.
One snatched up his helmet and ran out,
Another forced a team of snorting horses
Into place in a chariot, then assumed
His shield, his coat of mail trimmed with gold
And buckled at his side the sword he trusted.

   Now open the gates of Helicon,
You goddesses, and so begin your song,
Telling what kings were roused to go to war,
What companies of soldiers followed each,
Covering the plains, and what sort of men
Then sprang up in the fertile land of Italy
And how she blazed in arms. For you indeed,
You goddesses remember all these things
And can tell the tale, while to me hardly more
Than a faint rumour of them has descended.

   The first to arm his men and go to war
Was rough Mezentius from the Tuscan coast;
He scorned the gods. With him there came his son,
Lausus, than whom none was more good-looking
Except, in body, Turnus the Laurentian
– Lausus who tamed horses, fought with wild beasts:
He led a thousand warriors from Agylla
But that did him no good, he deserved better
Than to have had Mezentius for a father
And to have had to follow his instructions.

   Next, in a chariot decked for victory
With prize horses, appeared a son of Hercules,
Aventinus, impressive like his father
Whose device was emblazoned on his shield
– A hundred snakes, a Hydra with its serpents;
He had first seen the daylight in the woods
Of the Aventine, secretly born to Rhea,
The priestess who had been mated with a god
When the Tirynthian had come in victorious
After Geryon was killed, and having reached
The Laurentine fields and the Tuscan river,
Watered his Iberian cattle there.

His men were armed with javelins and ugly pikes
And used slim swords and Sabellian darts,
He went on foot himself, dressed in a lion skin,
A huge one which swung from his shoulders,
The bristling mane uncombed, the white teeth
Drawn over his head; it was thus he approached
The palace and terrifying he looked,
As well he might, in the cloak of Hercules.

  Then twin brothers leave the walls of Tibur
Whose people bear their brother Tiburtus's name;
These are Catillus and the eager Coras,
Young men of Argos: they are carried on
In the first ranks amidst a host of spears,
Like two cloud-born Centaurs coming down
From a high mountain, Homole perhaps
Or snow-capped Othrys, at a fast gallop
So that the great woods made way for them
As they came crashing through the undergrowth.

  The founder of Praeneste was there too,
The king called Caeculus who, as men think
And have done for ages, was discovered
Upon a hearth, after being born, they say,
Somewhere among the country herds of cattle.
He was accompanied by a straggling army
Of rustics, dwellers upon high Praeneste
Or in the fields the Gabine Juno held
Or on cold Anio, the rocks of Hernica
Bedewed with rivulets; and by those reared
In rich Anagnia or by old Amasenus.
Not all of them came with a clatter of arms,
With shields or chariots: most of them had slings
From which they sent a shower of leaden bullets;
But some of them carried a couple of spears
And had brown caps of wolf-skin on their heads;
Their left foot leaves its bare print on the ground,
The right is covered with a raw-hide boot.

  But Messapus, tamer of horses, Neptune's son
Whom none might down either with fire or sword,
Calls to arms tribes long immersed in peaceful ways,
With troops grown unaccustomed to the wars,
And takes his sword again. These are the men

Who form the army of Fascennium
Or live on the Faliscan plains or on
The high slopes of Soracte, fields of Flavinia
Or by the lake and mountain of Ciminus
Or the groves of Capena. With measured tread
They marched and sang the praises of their king:
Like snowy swans among the liquid clouds
When they come back from feeding, their long necks
Emitting notes in time so that the stream
And the marsh lands of Asia feel the pulse.
No-one would think this was a bronze-clad army,
Rather a cloud of hoarse-voiced birds returning
From the high seas and coming home to shore.

   And see, Clausus, of ancient Sabine blood,
Urging a great troop forward, he himself
Was equal to a troop; from him there issued
The Claudian family and clan, now spread
All over Latium since the Romans shared
Their city with the Sabines. With him came
A huge contingent, some from Amiternum,
Some the original Quirites, then
The whole band from Eretum and Mutusca
That has the olive groves; then the inhabitants
Of the city of Nomentum, of the country
Around Velinus, the Rosean district,
The jagged rocks of Tetrica, Mount Severus,
Casperia, Foruli, Himella valley,
With those who drink the Tiber and the Fabaris,
Then more from icy Nursia,
The Ortine squadrons and the Latin peoples
And those who lived divided by the Allia,
The river with the name of ill omen:
As many as the waves which turn and play
Upon the surface of the Libyan sea
When cruel Orion sets in the wintry water,
Or as the ears of corn packed together
In the early sun upon the plains of Hermus
Or yellowing fields of Lycia. The shields bang,
The earth trembles under the marching feet.

   Next Halaesus, a son of Agamemnon,
The enemy of everything called Trojan,

Sets horses to his chariot and for Turnus
Brings out a thousand tribes of desperadoes,
The men who ply their mattocks on the soil
Of Massica which is so good for wine:
Men from the high hills sent down by their fathers,
Auruncans, or from the Sidicine plain close by;
Men from Cales, those who live beside
The shallow river Volturnus, with rough bands
Of the Saticulans; there were Oscans too.
Their weapons were high-polished javelins
To which they used to fix a thong of leather;
They wore a buckler on their left arms
And fought hand to hand with swords like sickles.

  Nor shall you be unmentioned in our songs,
Oebalus, you whom Telon begot, they say,
On the nymph Sebethis when he, already old,
Ruled in the Teleboan Capreae;
A son not content with his patrimonial fields
Already seeking to hold under his sway
The Sarrastian peoples and the plains watered
By the Sarnus; those also who dwelt
In Rufrae and in Batulum, in the fields
Of Celemna, and those from the apple-orchards
On which Abella's battlements look down:
These men had weapons which they sent spinning
In the old Teuton fashion; on their heads
They wore a covering torn from the cork trees;
Their bronze-dressed shields glittered, their bronze swords
    glittered.

  And you whom mountainous Nersae sent to battle,
Ufens, so famous and successful in war,
Whose clan the Aequiculans were such toughs,
Accustomed to much hunting in the woods;
Their hard soil gave them little and they worked it
With weapons at their sides, always delighted
To carry off fresh booty; they lived by plunder.

  There came too from the Marruvian tribe
A priest with leaves of olive on his helmet,
Sent by their king Archippus – Umbro, he was called,
A brave man he was – and it was his practice
With spells and by his touch to call down sleep

Upon all serpents and all water-snakes
That breathe out harm; he calmed their fury
And by his art also he cured their bites.
Yet he had no power to heal the wounds
Inflicted by the spear-points of the Dardans
Nor did his soporific charms avail
Against them, nor the herbs that he sought out
Upon the Marsian hills. Ah, you were mourned
By the grove of Angitia, the glassy water
Of Fucinus, and the clear lakes.

   Hippolytus's son went to war too,
Virbius, and fine he looked, it was his mother
Sent him out looking so, Aricia
Who had brought him up in Egeria's grove
On the marshy verge of the lake where Diana's altar
Waits for rich offerings and she is gentle.
The story is, Hippolytus, when he died
A victim to the wiles of his step-mother
And with his blood assuaged his father's anger
– Stampeding horses tore him limb from limb –
Came back alive to the upper air and the sky
Restored by Apollo's healing herbs
And by Diana's love. The almighty Father,
Furious that any mortal should rise up
From the dark shades into the light of life,
Thundered and sent the finder of such cures
Hurtling down into the water of Styx.
But kindly Trivia hid Hippolytus
In secret haunts and put him out of the way
In the grove of Egeria where he might live,
In solitude in the Italian woods,
A life without distinction, changing his name
To Virbius. That is why horse's hoofs
May not go near Trivia's temple or grove
Because it was horses, frightened by sea-monsters,
Which left the young man and his chariot
Dismembered and abandoned on the shore.
But there was his son driving spirited horses
In a chariot and galloping to the war.

   Turnus himself among the first of them
Walked to and fro with weapons in his hand;

He towered above them all, his lofty helmet
Topped by a triple crest had underneath
The face of a Chimaera breathing fire,
Its jaws like Aetna's; it would roar more loudly
And throw out flames which were more menacing
The more the fighting grew in violence
And the more blood was shed. His polished shield,
However, carried the device of Io
When she had sprouted horns and grown her bristles
And was a heifer: it was a marvellous theme,
With Argus who was set to watch the girl
And Inachus her father, his stream pouring
From a decorated urn. There followed him
A cloud of infantry and all the plain
Was packed with troops with shields, the Argive youth,
Bands of Auruncans, old Sicanians,
Rutulians, Acranians in formation
And Labicans with painted shields; and others
Who ploughed your lowlands, Tiber, and the banks
Of sacred Numicus, or drove their teams
Over the promontory of Circeii; men from the fields
The Jupiter of Ansur has in keeping
And from Feronia with her lovely woodlands;
Or where the black marsh of Satura lies
And chilly Ufens winds through green vallies
And makes its way at last into the sea.
    On top of them there came the fighting girl
Camilla of the Volscian tribe, commanding
A troop of horse, squadrons brilliant in bronze;
She who had never trained her woman's hands
To spinning and weaving but to tough battles;
A girl who could run faster than the wind.
She might have flown over the standing corn
Without hurting the delicate ears as she ran,
Or made her way swiftly over the sea
On top of the waves without wetting her feet.
All the lads pouring out of the houses
And coming in from the fields, watched in amazement;
A crowd of mothers too, stared as she passed;
Open-mouthed with astonishment they see

How well the royal purple looks on smooth shoulders
And how her golden clasp winds in her hair;
How she carries her own Lycian quiver
And a shepherd's myrtle with a point of steel.

# BOOK VIII

# BOOK VIII

As soon as Turnus raised the flag of war
In the Laurentian citadel and the raucous
Horns sounded a blast and high-spirited horses
Were brought out amidst a clash of arms,
There was a great agitation in Latium;
All rose at once in alarm, the young men
Exasperated, furious. Their chief captains,
Messapus, Ufens and he who scorned the gods,
Mezentius, called up their auxiliaries
From every quarter, they stripped the fields of labourers.
To the great Diomed's city in the south
Venulus was sent to ask for assistance:
He was to tell them that the Trojans had come,
That Aeneas had sailed in with his fleet
Bringing his defeated household gods
And saying he must be king, the fates required it;
This was the message and he was to add
That many tribes had joined the Dardan hero
And that his name was spreading throughout Latium.
What he was about, with these beginnings,
What would happen if Fortune went his way
And how the battle that he sought would end,
Would surely be plainer to Diomed than it could be
Either to Turnus or to King Latinus.

So much for Latium. Meanwhile the hero
Descended from the family of Laomedon,
Seeing all this, drifted uncertainly
Upon a tide of troubles, casting his mind
Rapidly first one way and then another,
Seizing all sides of the question, thinking of remedies:
It was as when a flickering light reflecting
Sunlight or else the bright round of the moon

From water in a basin, plays here and there
And swings up now and then to cross the ceiling.
   It was night and, over all the world,
The birds and beasts were held in a deep sleep;
Aeneas, father of his people, lay
On the river bank under a chilly sky,
Troubled at heart by this unhappy war,
And let rest have its way with him at last.
To him there then appeared the god of the place,
Old Tiber himself rising from his pleasant stream
Among the poplars (a thin linen stuff
Covered him with a glaucous cloak and reeds
Like shadows were his hair); and then he spoke
In words which could not but assuage his troubles:
'Seed of a race of gods, you who bring Troy
Back to me from the enemy and save
Her citadel for ever, you whom this ground,
Whom Laurentine and Latin fields have long
Looked for, this is your purposed home and here
The place of your true gods, so do not falter
Nor yet be fearful of the threat of war
For all the swelling anger of the heavens
Is at an end.
And now, to convince you that this dream is real,
I tell you, you will find under the oaks
Fringing the banks, a huge sow with a litter,
Just born, of thirty piglets at her teats;
She is white, lolling back, and they are white.
That is the spot where your city is to be,
The end of all your troubles. When thirty years
Have come and gone, Ascanius shall found there
A famous city to be called Alba.
This is my certain prophecy. In what way
You shall proceed on your victorious course,
Listen, I will explain. Upon these shores
Are the Arcadians, a race sprung from Pallas,
Comrades of King Evander who, following him,
Chose a site in the mountains for their city,
Calling it, after their ancestors, Pallantium.
These men are always at war with the Latin tribes;
Take them into your camp, they are your comrades;

Join with them. And I will show you the way
Along the banks and enable you to row
Straight up the stream although against the current.
So rise up, goddess-born, as the first stars
Are setting make your solemn prayers to Juno
And by your supplications and your vows
Overcome all her anger and her threats.
To me you can pay honour when you have won.
I am he whom you see touching the banks
And cutting through the rich ground in full flow,
The blue Tiber, heaven's most favoured stream.
This is my great palace, and from my spring
There will arise many lofty cities.'

    When he had finished, the river hid himself
In a deep pool and made his way to the bottom
And night and sleep departed from Aeneas.
He rose and, looking at the rising sunlight
Already in the sky, religiously
Raised his two hands with water in the palms
And his lips poured prayers upwards to the skies:
'Nymphs, Laurentine Nymphs, the race from whom
Rivers have birth, and you, Father Tiber
With your hallowed stream, receive Aeneas,
Protecting him at last from all perils.
Whatever springs may feed the pool that holds you,
Whatever ground may see you first appear
In all your splendour, you who are pitiful
To our misfortunes shall be celebrated
For ever with my worship and my gifts:
You horned river, lord of Hesperian waters,
Only be with me and give proof of your powers.'
So saying he picked out from the fleet
A pair of galleys, fitted them out with crews
And issued arms to them at the same time.

    But there was suddenly before his eyes
A marvellous portent: shining through the trees
And of like colour with her snowy litter,
Upon the green bank there lay a sow.
And here Aeneas, doing the right thing,
Sacrificed, great Juno, to you, to you
And set her with her young before the altar

With all else that was needful. All night long
Tiber smoothed out the ribbing of its current,
Flowing back till it stopped altogether
And the water was silent, gentle like a pool
Or a placid marsh, so smooth did he lay it
That rowing on it became effortless.
So they went on their journey speedily
Amidst contented murmurs: greased pine-timbers
Slid on the shallow water which itself
Wondered at them, the trees standing together
Wondered too at the brightness of their shields
And at the painted boats swimming past.
They wore out night and day with their rowing,
One after another the long bends went by;
Trees cover them with their changing greens, they skim
Through woods reflected on the smooth surface.
The burning sun had reached the point of noon
When they caught sight of the walls of a citadel
And roofs of scattered houses – those which now
The power of Rome has raised to the sky
But in Evander's day a poor kingdom.
Quickly they turned the prows towards the bank
And so it was that they approached the city.
   It happened that day that the Arcadian king
Was paying solemn honours to great Hercules
Son of Amphitryon and to all the gods
In a grove outside the city. With him was Pallas,
His son, with him were all the fighting men
And the meagre senate, they were offering incense
And warm blood was smoking at the altars.
They saw high ships gliding among the trees,
The rowers leaning forward on their oars;
The sudden spectacle made them afraid,
They rose and left their banquet. But brave Pallas
Forbade them to break off the sacred rites:
He seized a weapon and he went to meet them
And from a tump he called: 'You men-at-arms,
What drives you here to try out unknown ways?
Where are you going? And what people are you?
Where do you come from? Do you bring peace or war?'
Our ancestor Aeneas answered him

From the high stern and held an olive branch
In his extended hand: 'The men you see
Are Trojan-born, the weapons that they bear
Are turned against the Latins, who forced them to it
When they were fugitives from a great war.
We are looking for Evander. Tell him so
And say that here are captains from Dardania
Appointed to request alliance with him.'
At that great name Pallas was astonished:
'Disembark, then,' he said, 'whoever you are;
Have a talk with my father face to face;
Come as a guest and welcome to our gods.'
Together they advanced into the grove
And turned away from the river-bank.

      Aeneas then spoke friendly words to the king:
'Noblest of all that come of Greek stock,
You whom Fortune has willed that I entreat,
Offering you olive branches dressed with ribbons!
I did not fear you as a Grecian prince
And an Arcadian, nor because you are kin
To the two sons of Atreus; my own courage,
The holy oracles of the gods, the common blood
Our fathers had, your fame, so spread abroad
Served to conjoin us and have brought me here
Willing as fate has willed. The Dardanus
Who was the first father of the Trojan city
And founder, born, the Greeks say, of Electra
The Atlantean, came to the Teucrians
When he set sail from here; and this Electra
Was daughter to great Atlas, who holds up
Upon his shoulders all the spheres of heaven.
Mercury is your father, he was born
To dazzling Maia on the icy top
Of Mount Cyllene; if we may believe
The stories that we hear, Atlas begat Maia
– The same Atlas who bears the stars aloft.
So both our families come of the same blood.
Trusting in this, I sent no embassies
And used no ruses for my first approach
But I exposed myself and my own life
And came here as a suppliant to your door.

The same Daunian people as harries us
Harries you too in a like cruel war;
If they drive us out they think nothing will stop them
From subjugating the entire Hesperia
And holding the seas that wash about her coasts
To east and west. Accept our loyalty
And give us yours. We have stout hearts in war;
The courage of our men has been well tried.'
    Aeneas finished speaking. While he spoke
Evander had regarded him intently,
Eyes, face and all his body; the reply he made
Was brief and to the point: 'Gladly indeed
I welcome you, the bravest of the Teucrians.
I recognise you, for I well remember
Your father's words, the voice and countenance
Of great Anchises. I recall the visit
Of Laomedon's son, Priam, to Salamis
To see his sister's kingdom, and how he went on
To visit our cold land of Arcadia.
I was then a youth with the first down on my cheeks;
I admired the Teucrian nobles, I admired
Laomedon's son, and yet it was Anchises
Who walked tallest of all. I doted on him,
I was young, I longed to speak to him
And to put my right hand in his right hand;
I went up to him and then eagerly,
Conducted him into Phineus's city.
He gave me, when he left, a marvellous quiver
With Lycian arrows, a gold-embroidered cloak
And a pair of golden bits which Pallas now has.
So, when you ask for my right hand, I give it;
We are allies, and when day dawns tomorrow
I will send you off happy, with an escort
And I will help you also with supplies.
Meanwhile, since you have come to us as friends
Favour us by joining in celebrating
Our annual rites which may not be deferred
And make yourselves at home at our banquet.'
    This said, he ordered that the food and drink
Which had been cleared should be set out again
And he himself showed the men to their places

On seats of turf; Aeneas he distinguished
Particularly, inviting him to sit
On a shaggy lion's skin on a throne of maple.
Then chosen youths and the priest from the altar
Brought roasted bull-meat and piled up the baskets
With bread that Ceres gives to human labour
And poured out wine. Aeneas and his Trojans
Feasted together on a great chine of beef
And had their share of sacrificial meat.

   Their hunger satisfied, their pleasure in eating
Gratified, King Evander said to them:
'These rites of ours, this customary feast,
This altar which invokes so great a presence
Are not imposed on us by superstition
Or by a disregard of the old gods.
The honours that we pay here have been earned
And we repeat them as men who have been rescued
From cruel dangers, O you guest from Troy.
Only look at that overhanging cliff
With great lumps of it scattered far and wide
And see how the cliff-dwelling is deserted
And rocks have come down in a vast ruin.
There was a cave here, going a long way back;
The hideous Cacus, half human in shape,
Lived there, the sun's rays never reached it;
The ground was always warm from fresh slaughter
And on the doors were arrogantly hung
Pale faces of men left to rot.
The monster had Vulcan for a father:
Vulcan's smoking fires belched from his mouth
As he lumbered around. Time in time brought help
Even to us who had so long desired it,
The advent of a god. The great avenger –
Proud with the spoil he had won by killing
The triple Geryon – Hercules came,
Driving huge bulls his victory had brought him;
His cattle filled the valley and the stream.
The savage mind of Cacus in his fury
Would leave no crime or trick undared or untried;
He drove from their stalls four splendid bulls
And a like number of good-looking heifers.

So that their foot-marks gave nothing away
He dragged them by their tails into the cave
And hid them in the darkness of the rock,
The clues to where they might have gone reversed;
Anyone looking for them could find nothing
To lead them to the cave. Meanwhile their owner,
Amphitryon's son, preparing his departure,
Was moving the sleek cattle from their stalls
And as they went they lowed, filling the grove
With their complaints, it was a noisy parting
From these hills. The lowing of one heifer
From deep within the cave, answered the call;
Imprisoned though she was she cheated Cacus
Of all his hopes. For Hercules's anger
Blazed and the black bile within him boiled:
He snatched up arms and took in his hand
His heavy knotted club and doubled up
The steep side of that towering hill. It was then
We first saw Cacus frightened, his wild eyes
Showed it; faster than the wind, he fled
And made for the cave; fear winged his feet.
    He shut himself in, breaking down the chains
Holding the great rock which his father's iron-work
Had hung there; down it fell and jammed the entrance
From side to side; then look! in a fury
The Tirynthian was there, scanning each access,
Peering this way and that, grinding his teeth.
Three times, boiling with rage, he went round
The Aventine Mount, three times he tried in vain
To pass the rocky entrance and three times
He sank down in the valley wearily.
There was a sharp flint, left when the rock
Had been cut away on every side, and tall,
Standing high on the ridge above the cave,
A fit nesting place for birds of prey.
He shook it; it was leaning to the left
On the slope over the river; he pushed from the right
And loosed it far down into its roots
Then shoved it suddenly; and at that point
There was a crash of thunder from the sky,
The banks jumped apart, the terrified river

Flowed backwards. But Cacus's huge palace
Was left without a roof, his lair was open,
The shady cave in all its depth exposed;
It was as if the earth, through some violence
Yawned and unlocked the habitations below,
Revealing the pallid kingdom the gods hate
So that the vast abyss was visible
And the ghosts trembled at the sudden light.
Hercules then, catching Cacus in a brightness
So unexpected, shut in the hollow rock
And roaring as he never roared before,
Pressed on him with his weapons from above,
Calling in aid whatever arms he could
And hurling branches and huge rocks like mill-stones.
Cacus, unable to escape the danger
In any other way, belched from his jaws
Tremendous smoke hardly to be believed
And wreathed the hide-out with a heavy pall
Making it quite impossible to see;
He piled up in the cave a smoky darkness,
Black clouds concealing flames. But Hercules
Would not put up with that; with a quick jump
He threw himself through the fire at the point
Where the smoke billowed thickest and a cloud
Of utter blackness rolled through the cave.
Seizing Cacus who in the darkness there
Still vomited flames although they served for nothing,
He tied him in a knot, clung to him, choked him
Till his eyes started from his head, his throat
Was dry and bloodless. Then down came the doors,
The black lair was revealed immediately;
The stolen cattle, the plunder denied to Cacus,
Came to the light of day, his shapeless carcase
Was dragged out by the feet. The onlookers
Could never have enough of looking at it,
The terrible eyes, the face, the bristling chest
Of the half-human monster, the extinct fires
Still smouldering in his jaws. Ever since then
This day has been honoured, those that came after
Have kept it as a happy festival
– Potitius first, who introduced the rite

And the Pinarian family who were guardians
Of all the rites of Hercules. Potitius
Established this altar in the grove, the principal
Altar it will always be called and be.
Come then, my lads, and dress your hair with leaves
In honour of so laudable an action;
Hold out the cup with your right hand and call
Upon our common god, proffering the wine
In unity of purpose.' When he had spoken
He hung in his hair the double-coloured
Poplar leaves, the shade Hercules loved,
And filled the sacred goblet in his hand.
Unhesitatingly and joyfully
They all poured out libations on their tables
And as they did so prayed to the gods.
     Meanwhile the evening star came down from Olympus
And drew nearer; the priests then, in procession
In ritual skins, Potitius leading them,
Went by with torches. The feasting was renewed
And all brought offerings for the second banquet
And heaped the loaded dishes on the altars
Round which, once they were lit, the Salii
Came singing, poplar leaves about their brows:
Two troops, the one made up of young men,
The other of the old men, each with a hymn
In praise of Hercules and of his deeds:
How, as an infant, he had gripped two snakes,
The evil portents his stepmother had sent,
And strangled them with his bare hands;
How he pulled down two great martial cities,
Troy and Oechalia; how, under King Eurystheus,
He carried out a thousand hard tasks
Which Juno, being hostile, destined for him.
So they sang: 'You who are invincible
And slew with your own hand the cloud-born centaurs
Hylaeus and Pholus, and the Cretan bull
And the huge lion under the Nemean rock;
Who set the Stygian lakes shivering with fear,
The janitor of Orcus, as he lay
On half-eaten bones in his blood-splashed cave;
No looks could frighten you, not Typhoeus himself

At all his giant height, weapon in hand;
Nor did you lack ingenuity
When the snake of Lerna with its many heads
Hissed all around you. Hail, true son of Jove,
You who have added glory to the gods!
Approach us now with favourable foot,
These rites are yours, be gracious!' To this hymn
They added as a crowning praise the tale
Of Cacus and his cave, and of the monster
Breathing out fire, until the whole grove rang
With music the hills shouted again.

   Then all of them, the sacred office finished,
Walked back to the city. The king, slow with age,
Kept at his side Aeneas and his son
And as he went beguiled the way with talk.
Aeneas with his quick eyes looked around him
At everything, and was taken with the place,
Happily asking questions and being told
About the old inhabitants of the country
And the traces they had left. Then King Evander,
He who founded the citadel of Rome,
Said: 'Once native Fauns and Nymphs had these groves
And a race of men whose mothers were tree-trunks
Of solid oak; these people had no manners
Or any sense of anything, why, they could not
Put oxen in a yoke or store provisions
Or save from what they had; they fed upon
Whatever game or fruit chanced to their hands.
Then Saturn first came down from high Olympus
Escaping from Jove's armoury, as an exile
From his lost kingdom. It was he brought together
The untaught savages scattered hitherto
Up in the hills and showed them what law is;
And he first chose to call the place Latium,
– A name that meant originally 'a hiding place' –
Because this was the place he found to hide in.
When he was king here it was what they call
The golden age, he ruled so peacefully
All these tribes: gradually, however,
Times grew worse, the shine was taken off them;
Then came lunatic wars and love of gain.

The Ausonian gang and the Sicanian tribes
Came in and Saturn's country more than once
Changed its name; there were kings, there was Thybris,
A gigantic fellow – that is how we Italians
Afterwards came to call our river "Tiber"
And so the old name Albula was lost.
I myself, driven out of my own land
And seeking refuge where the sea would take me
Was fixed in this place by omnipotent Fortune
And ineluctable Fate; the admonitions
I could not but obey, of the nymph Carmentis,
My mother, impelled me, it was Apollo's doing.'
    He paused and then moved on to show the altar
And what the Romans call the Carmental Gate,
So named of old in honour of Carmentis,
The nymph who was soothsayer and prophetess
And first celebrated Aeneas's sons,
Their greatness and the glory of Pallanteum.
He indicated next the vast grove
Restored as a refuge by the shrewd Romulus
And, under a chilly rock, the Lupercal,
Named, in accordance with Arcadian usage,
After Lycean Pan. He showed the wood
Of holy Argiletum, calling the place
To witness how his guest Argus had died
As he recounted it. Then he led them on
To the sanctuary above the Tarpeian rock,
Now golden but then bristling with undergrowth.
The ominous spirit of the place even then
Filled the terrified country people with awe;
They shuddered as they passed the wood and rock.
'This grove,' he said, 'this hill with trees on top
Is haunted by a god, we don't know which,
But a god certainly; the Arcadians
Think they have seen Jove himself there,
Shaking his dark shield as he often does
To call up storm-clouds. These two towns you see
With broken walls are monuments left behind
By the men of old. This citadel was built
By Father Janus, Saturn founded the other;
Saturnia and Janiculum they call them.'

   As they so talked they came upon the house
Of a poor man, it was Evander's palace,
And saw the cattle wandering round about it.
There were moos in the Roman forum and smart quarters.
He had reached home, and said: 'This is the entrance
Hercules came to after his victory;
This is the royal residence that received him.
You are my guest now, dare to scorn riches,
Enter, and model yourself on the god,
Do not disdain the poverty you find here.'
Having said this, he showed the great Aeneas
In under the roof-trees of his narrow dwelling
And set him down upon a heap of leaves
Covered with the skin of a Libyan bear.
Night fell, folding the earth in her dusky wings.

   But Venus, as a mother well might be,
Alarmed and prompted by the Laurentines'
Threatening and by the violence of their riot,
Spoke to Vulcan as they lay in bed
In their golden chamber, divine love in her breath
And in her words: 'When the Greek kings at war
Were sacking Troy's high citadel and fire
Was raging through it, then I asked no help
Nor any arms your skill might have produced
For those poor people, nor did I, dear husband,
Want you to labour when it might be vain,
However much I owed to Priam's sons
Or often wept for all Aeneas's troubles.
But now he stands upon Rutulian soil
By Jove's commands and for this cause I come
To beg the god who is a god to me
For arms, a mother asking for her son.
Nereus's daughter, the wife of Tithonus,
Could move you by her tears. Look now, and see
What nations are assembling and what cities
Behind closed gates are sharpening their swords
Against me for the ruin of my people.'

   Having said this the goddess, as he hesitated,
Threw snowy arms about him and so warmed him
Until he melted. He felt the usual fire
And the familiar heat entered his marrows

And ran on till his bones seemed to be liquid;
It was like lightning racing through the storm-clouds
And bursting out with thunder. His wife felt it,
Then Vulcan, mastered by eternal love,
Said: 'Must you ask in such a roundabout way?
Goddess, do you not trust me any more?
If you had shown the same anxiety
In those days I should have had to arm the Trojans;
Neither the Father Almighty nor the Fates
Were against Troy standing or Priam living
Another ten years. And now, if you want war
And this is really what is on your mind,
Whatever help I can promise through my skill,
What can be done with iron or molten metals,
What fire and bellows can achieve, I'll do it,
So stop asking as if you doubted your powers!'
With that he gave her the embrace she wanted
And, pouring himself out into her lap,
Found sleep and quiet in his every limb.

When Vulcan woke refreshed from his first sleep,
The night half-gone, at the hour when the housewife
Who has to keep life going by her spinning
Stirs up the ashes of the sleeping fire,
Adding the night's work to the day's, and sets
Her maids to their long task by lamp-light, only
To keep her husband's bed free from disgrace
And bring her little sons up, at that hour
The god of fire was no idler himself
But rose from his soft couch to seek his workshop.

There is an island near the Sicanian coast,
By Lipari, one of the Aeoliae,
It stands up high and from its rocks comes smoke.
Underneath are the caves and hollow places
Of Aetna, scooped out for the furnaces;
They rumble, from the anvils comes the sound
Of heavy blows, re-echoing; in the caverns
Worked metal hisses, fire is heard panting;
It is Vulcan's home, they call it Vulcan's land.
Thither he went, down from the heights of heaven.

In the vast cave the Cyclops were at work
Forging their iron, Brontes and Steropes

And Pyracmon who was stripped for the job.
There was a thunderbolt, their handiwork,
Such as the Father often hurls to earth
From heaven above; part was already polished
But part of it remained unfinished still.
They affixed to it three shafts of twisted storm,
Three clouds full of water, three of brilliant fire
And a flying wind from the south. They mixed together
For this piece terrifying lightning flashes
With fearful sounds and flames that carried vengeance.
Elsewhere they had in hand a chariot
For Mars, and pressed on with its racing wheels
Designed to stir up men and trouble cities;
With snaky scales of gold they were burnishing
The dreaded shield of the unquiet Pallas,
Her breast-plate with its interwoven serpents
And Gorgon's severed head with rolling eyes.
Vulcan said: 'Put all that away! You Cyclops
Of Aetna, leave the work you have begun
And turn your minds to this: Arms must be made
For a brave soldier. There is employment here
For strength, quick hands and all the skill you have.
No dawdling now!' He said no more, but they
Set to at once, sharing the work equally.
Brass flows in streams and mines of gold are melted
In the vast furnace with the wounding steel.
They hammer a vast shield to stand alone
Against all weapons that the Latins may bring
And work seven circular plates one into the other.
Some heave the bellows up and down, and blow,
Some dip the hissing brass in the lake-water.
The cave groans as the anvils in it are struck.
The Cyclops all in turn and time lift up
Their arms and reverse the metal with their tongs.

    While on the Aeolian isle the lord of Lemnos
Speeds on this work, the welcome light returns
And with the song of birds under the eaves
Wakes up Evander in his modest dwelling.
The old man gets up, puts on his tunic
And binds his Tuscan sandals on his feet;
Then to his side and shoulder he fastens on

His sword, flinging back his panther skin
Out of the way. The two dogs guarding the threshold
Advance to keep their master company
As he goes out. He makes his way at once
Towards the quarters of his guest, Aeneas,
Remembering what has been said and what promised;
Aeneas is up and stirring no less early.
With the one walks his son Pallas, the other
Is accompanied by Achates. They clasp hands,
Then sit down in the space between the buildings
And speak freely at last to one another,
The king first:
    Greatest of Teucrian captains, while you live
Never will I admit that Trojan power
Has been defeated or its empire gone;
For such a name indeed my strength is small
And I can offer little help in war,
On this side shut in by this Tuscan stream,
On the other hard-pressed by Rutulians
Whose arms clang noisily against our walls.
But I propose that you should join forces
With powerful tribes and camps thronged with kings
– A fortunate delivery which chance offers.
Not far from here and built in ancient stone
There is a city called Agylla where
The Lydian people who were famous warriors
Long ago settled on the Etruscan ridge.
For many years this once flourishing kingdom
Was held with brutal force by King Mezentius.
Why should I tell what murderous ways he followed
Or what were his oppressions? May the gods
Keep such reports for him and those like him!
He would even bind dead bodies on the living,
Hands tied to hands and face set against face,
A kind of torture in which blood and flesh
In putrefaction oozed through the embrace
And brought the man at last to lingering death.
Weary of this in the end the citizens
Took arms and formed a circle round the palace
And round that madman, cut his followers down
And set fire to the roof. He slipped away

Through all the slaughter to Rutulian soil
And there took shelter under the protection
Of his host Turnus. All Etruria
Has therefore risen now in righteous fury
And in a sudden insurrection
Demands to have the king for punishment.
Of all these thousands I will make you leader,
Aeneas. For now, thick along the shore,
Their ships lie, they are furious and give orders
For the standards to advance. An aged soothsayer
Restrains them as he gives voice to the fates:
"O you who are the picked youth of Maeonia,
The flower and promise of an ancient race,
Whom just resentment sends against the enemy
Blazing with proper anger at Mezentius.
None of Italian blood can master you
But you must choose your leaders from abroad."
Then the Etruscans drawn up on the plain
Were quiet, awed by what the gods advised.
Tarchon himself has sent ambassadors
To put the crown and sceptre in my hands
And bid me to accept these marks of office,
Entering their camp as king of the Tyrrhenes.
But my age is slow and blood runs cold,
My strength is too exhausted for great deeds;
Empire is not for me. I might persuade
My son but he is half of native blood,
His mother is a Sabine, so he has
A share of the country from her. You are the one
The fates have favoured both in years and race:
Set out upon this course, O valiant captain
Of Trojans and Italians. Pallas here,
My hope and comfort, shall join up with you;
Under you he will learn how to command
And bear the heat of war; seeing your deeds
He will look up to you from his first years.
I will give him two hundred Arcadian horse,
Pallas himself will give you as many more.'
    When he had finished, with their eyes cast down
Anchises' son Aeneas and Achates
Who followed him so faithfully, with hearts

Full of foreboding thought of many difficulties,
But from the cloudless sky the Cytherean
Gave them a sign. A flash of quivering lightning
Came from the sky which seemed to threaten nothing
And a clap of thunder, everything was shaken
While Tyrrhene trumpets sounded high in the air.
They looked up: again and again
There was a mighty crash; between clouds,
In a serene corner of the sky
They saw arms gleaming red against the blue
And heard them clash. The others were amazed
But the Trojan hero recognised the sound
And knew his mother had fulfilled her promise.
Then he said: 'Do not ask, my friend, what fortune
These portents indicate; for it is I
Olympus summons and the goddess my mother
Prophesied that the sign which she has sent
Would appear if war was at hand: she would bring
Arms made by Vulcan through the air to help me.
Alas what slaughter now awaits the Laurentians,
Poor devils! And you, Turnus, what a price
You have to pay! How many shields and helmets
Of how many warriors, how many strong bodies
Will you turn over, Tiber, under your ripples.
So let them call for war and break their treaties!'
    This said, he heaved himself down from his throne
And first of all stirred up the sleeping fire
On Hercules' altars, and joyfully approached
Yesterday's Lar and the poor household gods;
As custom is, they sacrificed together
The chosen ewes – Evander first and then
The Trojan youth a like number of victims.
Aeneas then went down to his ships
And finding his men again picked out the best
To follow him to war; the rest of them
Were carried gently downstream to report
His doings to his son Ascanius
And how things stood with him. The Teucrians
Who were to make for the Tyrrhenian country
Were given horses; for Aeneas they brought

A specially chosen mount whose back was covered
In a tawny lion's skin with golden claws.
    The news flew quickly through the little town:
The cavalry were off to Tarchon's camp
Down on the shore. The mothers, out of fear,
Said twice as many prayers, for close on danger
Terror follows, and they already see
The figure of Mars looming. And a father,
Evander, gripped his son's hand as the boy
Was going, and in tears addressed him thus:
'If only Jupiter would give me back
The years that have gone by and I were now
As I was when, under Praeneste's walls,
I struck the front rank down and then, victorious,
Burnt their shields in a heap; when this right hand
Sent King Erulus down to Tartarus
In spite of the three lives his mother gave him
When he was born: it is terrifying, Feronia
Gave him also his threefold armour to wear;
He had to be laid dead three times, yet then
This hand took all his lives and as many times
Stripped off his armour: had I still been such
I should not now be torn from your embrace
Nor would Mezentius have insulted me,
His neighbour, nor have killed so many here,
Widowing the city of her citizens.
But you, O gods above, you Jupiter,
Great governor of the gods, pity, I pray
The Arcadian king and hear a father's prayers:
If by your power and the influence of fate
Pallas is to be safe; if I am once more
To see him, if he is to come back,
I pray for life: I could bear any troubles.
But if, Fortune, you threaten a mischance
Not to be spoken of, may my life now,
This instant, now, be cut off, while uncertainty
Hangs over our affairs, while hope is blind
To what the future holds, while you, dear boy,
My late and only pleasure, are held still
In my embrace, and let no worse news come
To hurt my ears.' These words the father

Poured out at this last parting and his servants
Carried him back unconscious to his palace.
    Already indeed, through the open gates,
The cavalry was riding out, Aeneas
Among the first, the loyal Achates with him,
Then other Trojan princes, Pallas himself
In the middle of the squadron, plain to see
With his cloak and coloured armour, he was like
The Morning Star bathed in the ocean waves
Whom Venus loves above all other stars
As he lifts up his sacred head to heaven
And sends the shadows flying.
Within the walls the mothers anxiously
Follow with strained eyes the cloud of dust
And, as the troop rides on, the flash of bronze.
They take the shortest way to their objective,
Through the brushwood, they are fully armed;
A shout goes up, they form in fighting order,
The crumbling ground shakes under galloping hoofs.
    There is a vast grove near an icy stream,
The Caere; in our ancestors' religion
Held sacred far and wide; on all sides hills
Enclose it in a circle of dark pines.
The story is that the old Pelasgians
Who were the first inhabitants, long ago,
Of these Latin lands, dedicated the grove
Establishing a feast-day for Silvanus,
The god of fields and cattle. It was near here
That Tarchon and Tyrrhenes were encamped
In a sheltered place, and from a high hill
The tents of the whole army could be seen,
Spread out wide. To this place came Aeneas
With his picked warriors and here they rested
Tired men and horses and refreshed themselves.
    But then the brilliant Venus came that way,
The goddess, bringing presents through the clouds;
She saw her son in a secluded valley
By the cool stream, and spoke these words to him,
Making herself visible: 'Here they are,
The presents that I promised that my husband
Would use his skill to make; you need not fear

Now, son, the challenge of the Laurentines,
Proud though they are, to battle, no, nor Turnus.'
She spoke, the Cytherean, and then sought
Her son's embrace and put the glittering armour
Under an oak before him. He, delighted
By these gifts from the goddess and the honour
She did him, could not look at them enough;
His eyes sought first one piece and then another;
He wondered at them and he turned them over,
First left, then right; there was the helmet
With the terrifying crest spouting out flames,
The sword a single touch from which was fatal,
The corselet stiff with brass, blood-red and huge
Like a dark cloud set alight by the sun
And flashing its rays into the distance; then
There were the polished leggings of silver and gold,
A spear, a shield of inexplicable texture.

   Into the shield the furnace-god had worked
The tale of Italy and the Roman triumphs;
He was not ignorant of the prophecies
And the times that lay ahead, and showed there
Every generation from Ascanius
And all the wars in series. The work included
The she-wolf with the twin boys at her teats,
Playing and hanging on and without fear
Putting their lips to the mother, whose handsome neck
Curved back as she licked them both in turn
To coax them into shape. Not far from this
He had depicted also Rome herself
With the Sabine women roughly carried off
From the great circus where they were spectators;
Which started up fresh war between the Romans
And Tatius with his tough men in Cures.
Next there appeared the same kings when the war
Had been abandoned, standing fully armed
Before Jove's altar with the ritual cups,
Sacrificing a pig and swearing mutual peace.
Not far away were rapid four-horse chariots
Tearing Mettus apart to teach the Alban
To keep his word, and then there was Tullus
Dragging the liar's body through the woods

And leaving blood spattered all over the brambles.
There was Porsenna, too, demanding that Tarquin
Should be taken back, and laying siege to Rome
While Aeneas's descendants threw themselves
Against the attackers for the sake of liberty.
You might have seen Porsenna then depicted
Menacing them in fury as he saw
Cocles cutting the bridge down and Cloelia
Swimming the river when she had broken her chains.
    At the top Manlius, warden of the fort
On the Tarpeian rock, was standing firm
Before the temple, guarding the Capitol;
The palace was still thatched as by Romulus.
Here was a silver goose flapping along
The gilded colonnades and giving warning
That the Gauls were on the threshold; the Gauls were creeping
Through the brushwood and had ringed the citadel.
They were protected by shadows and were lucky
In finding the night full of them: their hair
Was golden and their clothes were golden too;
Their striped cloaks showed up and their milky necks
Had chains of gold about them; each had in hand
A pair of glittering Alpine javelins,
Their bodies were protected by long shields.
Then there were Salii leaping about
And naked Luperci with shepherds' headgear
And shields which had fallen down from heaven;
Chaste matrons in cushioned carriages
As they went through the city in procession.
Then there was shown, far off, Tartarus,
The gates of Dis, the punishment of crime
And you, Catiline, hanging over a cliff,
Threatened and trembling at the face of the Furies,
And in a separate place, the virtuous
With Cato who was laying down the law.
    Between these scenes there was represented
The sea in flowing gold but with blue waves
Capped by white foam; all about it dolphins
Gleamed in silver, sweeping over the surface
And cutting into the surf with their tails.
In the middle of all this appeared the fleet,

Plated with brass: it was the battle of Actium
And you could see all Leucate alight
With marshalled ships and waves shining with gold.
Augustus Caesar, leading the Italians,
The senate and the people, the Penates
And the great gods, to war, stood on the poop
High up, his helmet flashing joyfully
And on the crest his father's star was dawning.
Elsewhere Agrippa, favoured by the winds
As by the gods, commanded his line of ships,
Standing out prominently with his special trophy,
The naval crown flashing with shining beaks.
Here too was Anthony in barbaric splendour
With a diversity of arms – the conqueror
Of eastern nations to the Indian Ocean;
He brought all Egypt, oriental forces
Even from distant Bactria; he was followed,
To his disgrace, by an Egyptian wife.
All the ships came together at full speed;
The pull of oars and the three-pointed beaks
Set the waves in commotion and made foam.
They made for open water; you would think
The Cyclades were loose and floating there
Or high mountains struggling with one another,
So bulky were the vessels, so high the poops.
Blazing torches were hurled from ship to ship,
With showers of iron missiles; Neptune's fields
Were reddened by ever fresh streams of blood.
In the middle of it all there was the queen
With her exotic rattles rousing her forces
And not yet thinking of that pair of asps
She had left behind in Egypt. There were strange gods
Of many shapes, such as barking Anubis,
With weapons in their hands, opposed to Neptune,
To Venus, to Minerva. In the middle,
Embossed in iron, was Mars at his fiercest
With bitter Furies peering from above
While Discord went rejoicing, her dress ripped
From neck to toe; Bellona followed her,
Wielding a blood-stained whip. Actian Apollo
Looked down upon the scene, bending his bow

At which all Egypt and India, the Arabians
And the Sabaeans, turned tail in terror.
The queen herself was pictured calling the winds
And sailing away, we see her loosening the sheets.
The furnace-god had shown her amidst the slaughter,
Pale at the approach of death, borne on the waves
Before a gale from the north-west; and opposite her
Was the great Nile in mourning, all the folds
Of his wide robe thrown open to receive
The fugitives in the blue water of his bosom
And all his hidden streams. But Caesar was shown
Entering the walls of Rome in triple triumph
And there dedicating to the gods of Italy
His votive gift, three hundred great shrines
All over the city. The streets re-echoed
With shouts of joy, with games and with applause;
In all the temples choruses of matrons
Were seen, and all of them beside dressed altars;
Before the altars there were slaughtered bullocks.
Caesar himself sat on the snowy threshold
Of shining Phoebus and received the gifts
From all the nations, hanging them on proud pillars
While in a long column the conquered peoples
Moved past, with all their many languages,
Their varied dress and weapons. Nomadic people,
The loose-robed Africans, the Leleges,
Carians and the Gelonians with their arrows
– Vulcan had shown them all. Euphrates now
Flowed the more humbly; the Morini who
Lived on the edge of the inhabited world
Were there; there was the Rhine with its bull's horns,
Scythians who had never before submitted,
The Araxes indignant that a bridge had crossed it.
　　Such were the scenes Aeneas wondered at
Upon this shield that was his mother's gift
And Vulcan's handiwork; of the events
He knew nothing, but what was represented
Gave him great pleasure as upon his shoulder
He took the fame and fates of his descendants.

# BOOK IX

# BOOK IX

While these things were happening far away
Saturnian Juno sent Iris from heaven
To the high-spirited Turnus. At that moment
Turnus, as it happened, was sitting in a grove
Dedicated to Pilumnus, his father.
With rose-bud lips the daughter of Thaumas spoke to him:
'Turnus, the passing hour has brought to you
Something no god would dare to promise anyone
In answer to a prayer. Aeneas has left
His new city, his comrades and his fleet
To seek the kingdom of the Palatine
And the palace of Evander. More than that,
He has made so much progress as to reach
The furthest cities of Corynthus, the country-folk
Are mustering and he has given them arms.
Why hesitate? Now is the time, this instant,
To call for horses and to call for chariots.
With speed you can surprise and take the camp.'
When she had said her say, balancing herself
Upon her wings she soared into the sky
And as she flew cut an enormous rainbow
Against the background of cloud. The young man
Recognised her and raised his hands to heaven,
Palms upwards, and his words followed her:
'Iris, ornament of the upper regions,
Who was it sent you to me in the clouds,
Down here to earth? What has caused this sudden brightness?
I see the sky split open in the middle
And the stars at the zenith reeling. I will follow
These omens, whoever you may be
Who are calling me to arms.' And with these words
He went to the river and, scooping up clear water

From the eddying surface, prayed for many things
And charged heaven in return with his vows.
  Now in the open country the whole army
Was on its way, a brave sight it looked
With all the horses, the coloured and golden cloaks;
Messapus led the van, the sons of Tyrrhus
Managed the rearguard, in the main body
Was Turnus who commanded the whole host.
It was like great Ganges with its seven quiet streams
Rising in silence, or the fertile Nile
Flowing back from the fields into its channel.
Then suddenly a cloud of black dust
Was sighted by the Teucrians, a rising darkness
All over the plain. Caïcus first gave the alarm
From the ramparts of the camp: 'What is that mass
Moving there where the blackness billows up?
Everyone, quick! fetch your swords, issue weapons,
Man the walls. Hi! the enemy is here.'
There is shouting everywhere, the Teucrians
Take cover, withdrawing through the gates
And take up their positions on the walls.
Those were the orders that the bravest of them,
Aeneas, had given before he went away:
If anything happened they should not risk battle
Nor venture into the open but guard the camp
And keep themselves secure behind defences.
They barred the gates, therefore, and obeyed,
Ashamed and angry not to come to grips,
But waited for the enemy, holding themselves
In readiness under cover of their towers.
Turnus, who with twenty chosen horse
Had gone ahead of the slow main column,
Was unexpectedly before the city,
Riding on a white-spotted Thracian horse
And wearing a golden helmet with a red crest.
'Lads, is there any one of you,' he cried,
'Who with me will be the first against the enemy?
Here we go' – and, whirling his javelin
He sent it flying to show the fight had begun;
Then, drawing himself up, advanced in the open.
His men took up the cry and between them

Set up a terrifying din, amazed
To find the Teucrians had so little spirit,
Not to come out fairly into the open
– Warriors who dared not come to blows with the enemy
But stuck inside the camp. Hither and thither
He rode round the walls seeking an entrance
And finding none. He was like a wolf lurking
Outside a crowded sheep-fold, howling at it,
Facing wind and rain in the middle of the night
While safe under their mothers the lambs keep bleating;
In wild fury that he cannot get at the prey
He has so long been hungry for, and because his jaws
Are not dripping with blood: so the Rutulian
Is furious as he stares at the camp's defences,
And his resentment burns into his bones,
How should he force an entrance? By what ruse?
In what way can he get the Teucrians out
And so attack them on the level ground?
The fleet lay there on one side of the camp,
Protected by an earth-work and the river:
He attacked, calling on his cheering men
For fire and took a blazing pine himself.
Then they weighed in, and Turnus being there
Whetted their appetite; and all of them
Were soon equipped with smoky torches torn
From any hearth they found; a pitchy light
Glares up among the smoke which Vulcan sends
Into the sky with the glowing ashes.

　　Muses, what god was it turned away
So cruel a fire when the Teucrians were threatened?
Who swept those great flames from the ships?
Tell me. Belief in the event is ancient
But the story does not die. Back in the time
When first upon Phrygian Ida Aeneas
Was hammering up his fleet and getting ready
To put to sea and make for the deep waters,
The Mother of the Gods, so it is said,
The Berecyntian, so addressed great Jove:
'Grant, son, to your petitioner what she asks,
She is your mother, you rule in Olympus.
There is a pine forest I have loved

For many years, and at the top of it
I had a grove where men brought offerings,
A place made obscure by darkening pitch-pine
And trunks of maple: these I gladly gave
To the Dardanian youth who needed ships;
And now I fear what may become of them.
Banish my apprehensions and allow
A mother's prayer to weigh with you so far
That they are neither shaken nor destroyed
By any wind or storm; may it avail
That it was upon my mountain that they grew.'
    Her son replied, the son at whose behest
The stars roll on their courses: 'O my mother,
What is it that you ask the Fates to do?
What favours are you seeking for those ships?
They were made by mortal hands, can they be immortal?
Or should Aeneas on his certain course
Meet no uncertain perils? To what god
Is so much power allowed? It may not be.
But when they have done what they were built to do
And lie at last in an Ausonian harbour,
Then all that have escaped from the waves
And brought their Dardan captain to Laurentia
I will strip of their mortal shape,
Transforming them into sea-goddesses
Like Doto who was Nereus's child
And Galatea, breasting the foaming sea.'
So he spoke and swore by the Stygian waters
His brother rules, by those banks where pitch boils
In a swirling black abyss; as he nodded assent
The whole Olympus trembled at his nod.
    So now the promised day had come, the Fates
Had done all in due time, and the great wrong
Turnus was doing warned the Mother of the Gods
To rescue her dear ships from the blazing torches.
Then first there flashed on the eyes a strange light
And from the east was seen a huge cloud
Which raced across the sky and brought with it
The dancing choirs of Ida; a terrible voice
Broke through the air and fell upon the ears
Of all the ranks of Trojans and Rutulians:

'Have no fear for my ships: sooner shall Turnus
Have leave to burn up the seas themselves
Than these sacred timbers. So, ships, go free,
Go, now sea goddesses; the Mother wills it.'
So forthwith every ship tore from its moorings
And dolphin-like dipped nose-first in the sea
Down to the bottom. Then they rose again
In the form of maidens, one for every ship
And marvellously they swam into deep water.

  The Rutulians were staggered by these happenings,
Messapus was in terror, horses stampeded,
The river Tiber stopped and with a roar
Turned back and would not fall into the ocean.
But Turnus did not lose his assurance;
Indeed, he gave his men encouragement,
Calling out: 'See, it is against the Trojans
That these portents are aimed; Jupiter himself
Has snatched away the help they have relied on;
They did not think that they would have to face
Rutulian fire and sword. The seas are now
Closed to the Teucrians, they cannot hope to escape:
They have lost half the world, the other half,
The land, is in our hands: so many thousands
From the Italian tribes are now in arms.
Nor do I fear the oracles of the gods,
Whatever boasts these Phrygians may make:
It is enough for Venus and the Fates
That these Trojans have reached the shores of Italy
And found our fertile fields. Now is my turn,
My fate, opposing theirs, is to cut down
This race of criminals who have taken my bride:
It is not only Greeks who have been so wronged,
Nor only Mycenae that can take up arms.
"But surely one destruction is enough;"
So should a single crime have been enough
To teach them not to meddle with women again.
These are the men who now get their courage
From trusting on a rampart to divide us,
Ditches to hold us back – small things indeed
To stand between them and death. Have they not seen
The walls of Troy, made by the hand of Neptune,

Go down in flames? But you, the pick of my men,
Which of you is prepared to cut a way through
And with me make a dash into the camp
While they are in confusion? I do not need
Arms made by Vulcan or a thousand ships
To face the Trojans. Why, all the Etruscans
Can join them if they will. They need not fear
The darkness or a miserable set of thieves
Carrying off their Palladium, with the guards
Killed on the very citadel, nor shall we
Hide ourselves in the belly of a horse:
I have decided to set fire to the walls
All the way round, openly in broad day-light.
I will see to it that they do not fancy
They have to do with Danaans and Pelasgians
Whom Hector kept at bay for ten years.
But now, the better part of the day has gone,
Things have gone well so far, now take it easy;
Look forward to the fight you'll have tomorrow.'
   Messapus has orders to set a watch
Upon the gates meanwhile, to keep them blocked
And make a circle of fire around the fort.
Fourteen Rutulians are picked to guard the walls,
Each with a hundred men under his command,
All of them purple-crested and glittering with gold.
They double here and there and then watch by turns
Or rest, stretched on the grass to drink their wine,
Empty their brazen pots and turn them up.
The fires burn brightly, the guard passes the night
Without a wink of sleep, absorbed in play.
   From their stockade the Trojans watch all this,
Standing to arms and not leaving the parapets,
But none the less anxiously check the gates
For fear of what might happen, and construct
Gangways between outer defences and battlements
And have their weapons on them as they do so.
The work is supervised by Mnestheus
And by Sergestus, a sharp commander
– The two Aeneas left in charge of things
In case anything untoward should happen.
The whole legion is stationed round the walls,

All share the danger, turn and turn about
Now keeping watch and now on sentry-go,
Each in the sector that's entrusted to him.
    Nisus was captain of the gate, a keen soldier,
The son of Hyrtacus whom the huntress of Ida
Had sent to bear Aeneas company,
Swift with his javelin and his polished arrows;
Bearing him company was Euryalus,
Than whom there was among Aeneas's followers
Or all the Trojan force, no-one more handsome,
A boy with the first down on his cheeks.
In these two there was a single love
And they would charge the enemy side by side;
So now they were together, at the gate.
Nisus said: 'Is it the gods who give us this ardour,
Euryalus, or do our fierce desires
Severally turn themselves into gods?
My mind has long been spoiling for a fight
Or wanting to be in some feat of daring
And is not happy in this peace and quiet.
You see how confident the Rutulians are.
They have few lights showing, wine and sleep
Have left them lying stretched out on the ground
And everything is silent far and wide.
Listen to me, I will tell you what I am wondering:
This is the plan that has surfaced in my mind.
Everyone – both the people and the council –
Is clamouring for Aeneas to be sent for
Or men to be sent to tell him how things stand.
If they will promise what I ask for you
– For me the glory of it is enough –
I think that underneath that hillock there
I could make out a track to Pallanteum,
To the very walls and the fortress itself.'
Euryalus is taken aback, he too
Is seized by a sudden desire for fame
And so addresses his impatient friend:
'So you don't want to have me at your side
In such a daring enterprise as this?
Am I to send you to face such dangers alone?
That is not the way my father brought me up

Amidst the troubles of Troy and the Grecian terror,
Nor is that how I have behaved with you,
Following the noble Aeneas to the end.
I am not the person to fear death
And I would think it cheap enough to buy
Honour for you at the price of my own life.'
   Nisus replied: 'I had no fears about that,
It would not be right, no – I swear by Jupiter,
May he bring me back and back to you in triumph,
Great Jupiter or whoever looks with favour
Upon my enterprise. But if, as often
Happens on like occasions, if anything,
If any god or chance should carry me off
I should want you to survive; you are young enough
To be more worth saving. Let there be someone
To commit my body, salvaged from the battle
Or bought back, at a price, to the care of the earth:
Or if, as happens often, heaven forbids that,
To carry out the last rites for the absent
And raise an empty tomb. Nor would I wish
To be a cause of grief to a wretched mother
Who has, as yours has, unlike the rest
Dared to follow you here and has not cared
To stay secure in great Acestes' city.'
But he: 'Well, make excuses if you will.
I shall not change my mind, I shan't give way.
Come on, let's hurry.' That is what he said
And thereupon he called out the guard
Who took his place turn and turn about.
He left his post and walked off with Nisus
And both went to look for their commander.
   The wide world over creatures were asleep,
Anxieties at rest, troubles forgotten:
The Trojan leaders with the pick of the officers
Were met in council upon state affairs,
What should be done and whom sent to Aeneas.
They stood on the parade ground of the camp,
In the middle, leaning on their long spears
And holding their shields fast. Without delay
Nisus, accompanied by Euryalus
Eagerly asked permission to approach;

The matter was important, so they said
And it would justify the interruption.
Iülus first agreed they should be seen
Then ordered Nisus to say what he had to say.
The son of Hyrtacus spoke up: 'You captains
Aeneas has appointed, give us a hearing
And do not judge our offer by our years.
Sleeping their wine off, the Rutulians
Are silent now: we have seen with our own eyes
A place where there might be an opening,
On the forked way by the gate nearest the sea;
The fires have gone out and black smoke
Is billowing up there; if you will allow us
To make the most of it, we'll find Aeneas
And the fortress of Pallanteum; you will see us
Back soon enough, and loaded up with spoil,
But not before making a pile of dead.
There is no risk that we shall lose our way:
Often out hunting in those dark vallies
We have caught sight of the town, and we can say
The whole course of the stream is known to us.'
    Aletes, bowed with years but yet still ready
In heart and mind, spoke up: 'Gods of our fathers
Whose power is still watching over Troy,
You do not mean to leave us after all
To our destruction, for you still bring us
Young men of such spirit and such courage.'
With these words he took the pair of them
By their right hands and fell about their shoulders;
Tears streaming down his cheeks covered his face:
'How can I think ever to repay you,
Or what rewards could equal your deserts?
The first and best must be those the gods give,
And your own conduct; for the rest Aeneas
Will answer instantly, so will Ascanius,
Whom age has not touched, for he will never
Allow such service to pass out of mind.'
'I swear to both of you it never shall,'
Ascanius answered without hesitation.
'I know too well my only safety lies
In fetching father back: by the gods, Nisus,

The gods of home, Assaracus's Lar,
The ancient Vesta's shrine; into your hands
I put my fortune and I put my trust:
Tell father to come back, we want him here;
There is no being sad if we have him.
I will present you with two silver goblets,
All worked on the outside, the two my father
Took from Arisba when he conquered it,
A pair of tripods, two great talents of gold
And the ancient bowl Sidonian Dido gave him.
If we take Italy and as rulers here
Determine who has what – you have seen how Turnus
Is horsed and how he goes in golden armour;
His horse, his shield and all his crimson plumes
Shalt be kept for you, they are yours now, Nisus.
Besides, father will give you a dozen women
And men captives with all their armour on
And all the property of King Latinus.
But you, who are more than my own age,
You marvellous boy, I take you to my heart
And you shall be my comrade come what may;
No glory shall be mine without you share it;
Whether I am at peace or making war
Your deeds and words shall be what I most trust.'
Euryalus said: 'The day will never come
When I am not fit to dare so much,
If only fortune now will favour me
And be not adverse. Yet above all gifts
I beg one thing of you: I have a mother
And she is one of Priam's ancient house,
An unfortunate lady neither the land of Troy
Nor King Acestes' city could dissuade
From following where I went. I leave her now
Without her knowing what danger I incur,
I have not said good-bye – I swear by the night
And your right hand, I could not bear her tears.
I beg you, give her comfort if she needs it
And help her if she is left on her own.
Allow me then to hope this much of you
And I shall face all chances the more boldly.'
So moved were the Dardanians they shed tears,

The pretty Iülus more than any of them
For he knew what it was to love a parent.
He spoke at last: 'Be sure that everything
Will be as your great enterprise deserves.
Your mother shall be mine, only the name
Creüsa will be lacking; no small honour
Awaits one who gave birth to such a son.
Come what may of your action, still I swear
Upon the head my father used to swear by:
All I have promised you if things go well
Will fall to her and to her family.'
He wept as he said this, and from his shoulder
He took the gilded sword the Gnosian
Lycaon had made with such marvellous skill,
With it the ivory sheath it fitted into.
Mnestheus gave Nisus the shaggy skin
He had won from a lion, loyal Aletes
Changed helmets with him. So they went forth armed
And the whole group of leading officers,
Both young and old, accompanied them to the gates
With vows for their success, while pretty Iülus,
With mind above his years and the concern
A man might show, sent many messages
To be given to his father, but the breezes
Scattered them to the ineffectual clouds.

   They went out, crossed the ditches and in darkness
Made for the enemy camp, yet first to be
The death of many others. Here and there
Upon the grass they see bodies stretched out
In drunken sleep and, by the shore, chariots
Tilted up, their crews propped against wheels
Or tangled in the harness, lying there,
Their arms scattered, their wine-jars scattered too.
The son of Hyrtacus looked on, and spoke:
'Euryalus, now my right hand must dare;
This is the moment. This is where our way lies.
You keep your eyes skinned, watch that nobody
Comes at us from behind; and I will make
A wide path for us both and lead the way.'
He spoke, then checked his voice, and with his sword
At once fell on the haughty Rhamnes who,

Lying stretched out upon a heap of rugs,
Was snoring from the bottom of his heart
– A king himself and King Turnus's augur,
But augury could not prevent his death.
Then he came down upon the three attendants
Who lay close by with weapons scattered round them
And on Remus's armour-bearer and charioteer,
The latter caught stretched underneath his horses;
He slashed their lolling necks with his sword,
Then had their master's head off and left the trunk
Spurting out blood; the ground and the pile of rugs
Were wet with dark warm gore. He killed Lamyrus
And Lamus and Serranus – still a youth –
Who had played most of the night, a fine lad
Lying defeated already by the wine:
It would have been well for him if he had played
All the night long until the day appeared.
Nisus was like a lion short of food
Rioting through a sheep-fold full of sheep,
Driven on by a hunger that had made him mad,
Mauling the unresisting animals,
Tearing them while they stood dumb with fear,
And roaring, with blood dripping from his mouth.
Euryalus slaughtered as many as his friend;
He was beside himself and raged on
Through the anonymous mob of commoners,
Through Fadus, Herbesus, Rhoetus and Abaris,
Most of them unconscious, Rhoetus, however,
Was on the watch and saw everything
But in his terror hid behind a pitcher:
As he rose up Euryalus's sword
Went into him, and blood followed it out.
He vomited his red soul and, dying,
Brought up wine mixed with blood; the other,
Boiling with rage pursues his stealthy work,
Approaching now Messapus' followers.
The fires are burning low there, and he sees
The tethered horses cropping at the grass.
Then Nisus put a word in, for he saw
His friend carried away by too much killing
And too fond of his sword; 'Let's leave it now,'

He said, 'Daylight is coming and is hostile.
We have had vengeance enough, and cut our way
Right through the enemy camp.' They leave behind them
Much armour, many arms, with solid silver
And bowls and fine carpets. Euryalus
Takes Rhamnes' trappings, the sword-belt studded with gold,
Gifts that once wealthy Caedicus had sent
To Remulus of Tibur, as a token
Of friendship for him when he was far away;
Remulus, dying, gave them to his grandson,
From whom the Rutulians captured them in battle:
Euryalus seized these trophies and – all for nothing,
As it turned out – put them on his strong shoulders,
Then found Messapus' helmet fitted him
And put that on too, liking the fine crest.
The pair then left the camp and made for safety.

   Meanwhile from the Latin city the cavalry
Were sent ahead, while all the rest of the legion
Was still waiting, drawn up in the open;
The horsemen carrying reports to King Turnus,
Three hundred strong, with shield, Volcens commanding.
They were under the walls when, far away, they saw
The two men making off by a path to the left
And in the shadows of the glimmering night
The helmet gave Euryalus away,
For he was careless, it flashed reflected light.
It was spotted at once and Volcens from his column
Called out: 'Halt, you two! Why make off? And who are you
In that armour? Where are you going?' No answer:
The two of them hurried the faster into the woods,
Trusting the night. The cavalry blocked the cross-way
And threw a cordon round the possible exits.
The wood bristled with undergrowth and dark ilex;
Everywhere there were briars, and here and there
The path showed up among cattle-tracks.
The shadows from the branches, and the booty,
Which seemed heavy now, impeded Euryalus,
And fear made him lose trace of the path.
Nisus was gone, without thought he had escaped
The enemy and found himelf in what was called
In later times, after Alba, the Alban stretch,

Where King Latinus at that time kept his herds.
He stopped and looked back for his missing friend,
But to no purpose: 'Euryalus!' he said,
'Unfortunate boy, where have I left you behind?
How shall I find you now, through all this tangle
Of treacherous woodland?' And immediately
He picked his way back as well as he could
And wandered in the silent undergrowth.
He heard horses, shouts, the sound of pursuers;
A moment later a cry came to his ears.
He saw Euryalus seized by the whole band
In that dark and tricky place and carried off
Doing all he could to escape, but in vain.
What should he do? How force the boy away?
What weapons should he use to rescue him?
Should he throw himself upon the enemy
And die a fine death in the middle of them,
A quick end, covered with wounds? Then suddenly
He threw back his arm and poised his spear,
Looking up at the moon and praying to her:
'You goddess, be with us now, and in our trouble
Help us, Latona's daughter, glorious
Among the stars and in your sacred groves.
If ever my father Hyrtacus for my sake
Brought presents to your altars, or if I
Have ever added any from my hunting,
Hung offerings under your dome or at your door,
Let me now scatter this troop, guide you this weapon
As it flies through the air.' When he had finished
He strained his every nerve and threw the spear.
It whistled through the shadows of the night,
Went into Sulmo's back and there it snapped,
The wood fixing itself in his diaphragm.
He rolled over, cold, but vomiting
A warm flood from his chest, his flanks throbbed
With great gasps. His comrades looked around them.
Nisus meanwhile, encouraged by success,
Balanced another weapon in his hand,
Level with his ear. Before they had recovered
The spear went hissing into Tagus's head
And stuck out the other side, the blade lodged snugly

In his pierced brain. Volcens raged like a bull
But could not make out who had thrown the weapon
And did not know on whom to vent his anger.
'But you shall pay for both with your hot blood,'
He said, and with sword drawn made for Euryalus.
Then indeed Nisus was terrified,
Out of his mind, he came out of hiding,
He could not bear the anguish any more
But shrieked: 'I did it, here I am, strike me!
Rutulians, all this crime is mine alone;
He neither dared nor could do anything,
So heaven can witness and the watching stars;
He only loved his luckless friend too well.'
But even as he spoke the sword went in
At full force, passing through the ribs and smashing
The gleaming chest. Euryalus rolled over;
He is dead, blood streams on his handsome limbs,
His neck droops on his shoulders, like a flower
Cut by a ploughshare, growing limp as it dies,
Or poppies, weary-necked, bowing their heads
Weighed by a shower of rain. But Nisus rushes
Right in among them and he only seeks
Volcens and does not stop till he gets at him.
The enemy group themselves round their captain;
Nisus goes in, whirling his sword like lightning,
And buries it in the face of the screaming Rutulian;
So dying, he takes his enemy's soul with him.
Then, riddled through and through he hurled himself
Upon his friend and so found peace in death.
　　Fortunate both of them! And if my lines
Can achieve anything, no day shall pass
Ever, which lets their memory pass from view
While on the Capitol's unshaken rock
The family of Aeneas holds its own
And the Roman Father guards the power it has.
　　The victors, the Rutulians with their spoil,
Carried their prizes and the lifeless body
Of Volcens amidst tears into the camp.
Inside the camp itself there was mourning too,
For Rhamnes had been found, empty of life,
And all those captains lost in one great slaughter,

Serranus, Numa too. A mighty throng
Went to be by those bodies, by the dying,
The place where slaughter was still warm and blood
Still flowed in foaming streams.
They recognised the spoil, the gleaming helmet
Of Messapus and all the precious trappings
Won back at such high cost.
   And now the Dawn sprinkled fresh rays of light
Upon the earth, as she came from the bed
Of Tithonus, saffron on the horizon;
And as the sun streamed in and daylight shone
Turnus, himself in arms, called up his men
To take their weapons, every lesser commander
Roused his particular group to battle order,
Shining in bronze, and sharpened up their mettle
With this or that tale of the night's events.
Then on uplifted spears (a ghastly sight)
They stick the heads of Nisus and Euryalus
And follow them with shouting. On the walls
– The left side, for the stream circles the right –
Aeneas's tough men draw up their line;
They man the great ditches, on the high towers
They stand in grief; they are moved by the heads
Raised up before them, they know them too well,
Defaced by the coagulated blood.
   Meanwhile winged rumour flies through the frightened town,
Reaching the ears of Euryalus's mother.
At once the wretched woman's bones are chilled,
Her hands let fall the shuttle, which unwinds.
She flies out, in her unhappiness
Shrieking as women do, tearing her hair;
Demented she makes for the walls, the front
Pushing past the men, not caring for danger
Or weapons flying her way, fills heaven with her cries:
'Euryalus, is it you that I see?
You came late to comfort my old age,
Could you so cruelly leave me on my own?
Could you, when you were sent to such dangers,
Go without saying a word to your poor mother?
In a strange land you lie, the Latin dogs,
The birds have you for prey! while I, your mother,

Have not, as I should, headed your funeral,
Closed your eyes or even washed your wounds
Or covered you with the garment I was working at
With all the speed I could both day and night
– Weaving to comfort myself in my old age.
Where shall I go? What ground has taken you,
Your body with the limbs torn to pieces?
Is this all of yourself you have brought back?
Son, was it for this I followed you
Over land and sea? O you Rutulians,
If you have hearts, then throw your darts at me,
Transfix me, let me be the first to feel your iron;
Or you, great Father of the gods, have pity,
And with your bolt thrust down my head unseen
Below Tartarus, if in no other way
I can divest myself of this cruel life.'
This wailing so affected the men's courage
That all began to utter cries of mourning,
Their stomach for the battle was dismayed.
As she provoked such grief, Idaeus and Actor,
Ordered by Ilioneus and by Iülus
– Himself in tears – caught her up in their arms
And put her on a bed inside a house.

   The eloquent bronze of a trumpet sounded
Its terrible note afar: a shout followed
And the heavens bellowed back. The Volscians
Push forward in line, shields over their heads,
To fill the ditch and pull down the stockade.
Some try to force an entrance, some with ladders
To scale the walls where the line is thin
And light shows through among the packed defenders.
The Teucrians for their part pour down a shower
Of weapons of every kind, and with long poles
Dislodge the climbing enemy, they have learned
In a long war how to defend their walls.
Stones of destructive weight are rolled down
To see if they can break the covered line,
But the shields linked above the attackers' heads
Are proof against them all. Yet now they give;
For where a mass of troops crouch menacingly
The Teucrians push over a huge lump

Which flattens the Rutulians far and wide
And breaks the interlocking of their cover.
The brave Rutulians no longer try
To fight blind, but come out with their missiles
Aimed at clearing the ramparts. In another place
Mezentius, a menacing spectacle,
Was brandishing a torch of Etruscan pine
And flames and smoking brands were tossed over,
While Messapus, tamer of horses, Neptune's son,
Broke the stockade and called for scaling ladders.

O Calliope, now inspire the singer
You and your sisters, while I tell what havoc
Turnus effected, what deaths he brought about,
And whom each warrior sent down to Orcus;
Be with me and unfold the scroll of war.

There was a tower which looked huge from below,
Out from the walls and linked by high gangways;
It was a strategic point, and the Italians
Attacked at full strength to overturn it.
The Trojans for their part defended it
By hurling rocks and darts through the openings.
First Turnus threw a blazing torch, which stuck
Upon the side and fired it,
Then, fanned by the wind, caught on the flooring
And so attacked the exit. In the interior
There was panic as men tried to get away.
They crowded to one side to escape the fire;
Suddenly, under their weight, the tower lurched
And fell down with a crash that filled the sky.
Half-dead, and followed down by the whole ruin,
Men reached the ground pierced by their own weapons
Or with the splintering wood stuck through their hearts.
Helenor and Lycus escaped, by the skin of their teeth:
And Helenor, the younger of the two,
Born secretly to the Maeonian king
By Lycimnia a slave-girl, who had sent him
In arms to Troy against his father's wishes,
With only a light sword and a blank shield.
He found himself among a multitude
Of Turnus's men, with lines of Latin troops
Before him and behind; like a wild animal

Caught in the closing circle of the hunt
Turning in desperation against their spears
And with a bound leaping to certain death;
So the young man rushed at the enemy
Where they were thickest and where death was certain.
But Lycus, better on his feet, ran back
Among the enemy, among their weapons,
To the walls where he tried to grasp the coping
And stretched his hand to reach those of his comrades.
But Turnus followed him, running as fast
And with his spear ready, and jeered at him:
'Did you think you could get away from me? You're mad!
Not from these hands!' With that he pulled him back
And brought a great piece of the wall down with him:
He was like an eagle seizing in his claws
A hare or some white swan, or like a wolf
– The beast Mars counts as his – snatching from the fold
A lamb that leaves a bleating mother behind it.
There is shouting everywhere, his men pour in
To fill the ditches with earth, while others toss
Their torches over the walls to fire the roofs.
Ilioneus crushes Lucetius with a rock,
A piece like a great mountain, as he approaches
Loaded with fire-brands. Liger fells Emathion,
Asilas Corynaeus, one with a javelin,
The other with a clever shot from a bow;
Ortygius is killed by Caenus who,
Victorious once, is quickly killed by Turnus;
Turnus destroys Itys and Clonius,
Dioxippus and Promolus and Sagaris,
And Idas as he stands up on a tower;
Capys makes an end of Privernus,
Who just before had been grazed by a light spear
Thrown by Themillas and had stupidly
Let fall his shield to put his hand to the wound;
So the arrow pinned his hand to his left side
And went through his chest and so choked him.
Arcens's son – marked out by his fine armour
And by his cloak embroidered with fine work,
A bright Iberian blue – a handsome youth
Sent to war by his father, but whose mother

Had brought him up in her grove beside the streams
Of Symaethus, where Palicus' altar stood,
Laden with gifts and gracious: dropping his spears
Mezentius three times whirled his sling tautly
Above his head, then sent the molten shot
Through his opponent's temples and so laid him
Stretched out at his full length in the deep sand.
   Then first, so it is said, Ascanius,
Who hitherto had frightened only animals
– For he was a hunter – drew his bow in war,
And with his own hand laid Numanus low,
A brave man, also called Remulus,
Who recently had taken as a bride
Turnus's younger sister. He strutted there
Before the front line and shouted out
A mixed-up rigmarole of boastful talk
And serious challenges: too big for his boots,
So proud was he of his new royalty.
He stuck his chest out and his voice carried:
'Aren't you ashamed to be besieged again,
You Phrygians who have already twice been captured,
And to rely on walls to keep you safe?
So that's the sort of people that you are
Who threaten us and want to take our brides!
What god, or rather what insanity,
Drove you to Italy? You will find here
No sons of Atreus, no Ulysses,
The liar with the mouth: for we are tough,
We take our new-born boys to the rivers
And harden them in the icy water;
Our lads give up their sleep to go hunting
And wear the forests down; they play on horse-back
Or else with bows and arrows; none the less,
Used to hard work and short commons, young men
Are kept at the hoe or on active service;
Our whole life is spent with iron in hand,
We goad our oxen with reversed spears;
To us, old age does not bring any weakening
Or change of heart; and when our hair is white
We still put on a helmet; we are always glad
To carry off fresh plunder and we live by it.

You dress yourselves up in embroidered saffron
And shining purple; you love idleness
And pass the time in dancing; why, your tunics
Have sleeves in them, and your head-gear has ribbons!
Oh, you are Phrygian women, not even men;
Go away on the heights of Dindymus
Where flutes go high and low for those who like it;
The timbrels and the Berecynthian box-wood
Call you out to the frolics of Cybele;
Leave arms to men and lay aside your swords.'
   Ascanius could not bear such boasting talk
Or such ill-boding but, drawing his bow
Upon the speaker pulling the string far back
And paused, that first he might supplicate Jove:
'Almighty Jupiter, be on my side,
Second the courage in which I begin;
I will myself bring solemn gifts to your temples
Present a fine bullock with gilded horns
At your altars, a shining white one, already
Tall enough to hold his head with his mother's,
Already butting and stamping the sand with his hoof.'
The Father heard; from the left of the clear sky
There was thunder; at the same time a whirring
From the fateful bow. The arrow leapt away
With a whistle and went through the head of Remulus,
The point splitting his temples. 'Go,' said Ascanius
And added only: 'Jeer at our courage now
With your big talk. This arrow is the answer
Twice-captured Phrygians send to the Rutulians.'
The Teucrians cheered approval then, delighted,
Shouted again and again, their hearts in the stars.
   It happened that the long-haired Apollo
Was looking down from a tract of sky
Over the Ausonian lines and the town;
Sitting on a cloud, he addressed Iülus
In the moment of triumph: 'Bless you, my boy,
With your young courage: that is the way to heaven,
Child of the gods and father of gods to come.
Justly will all the wars that fate must bring
Subside under Assaracus's line;
Troy could not hold you.' As he spoke he leapt down,

Parted the moving winds and sought Ascanius.
Then he altered his shape, and his appearance
To that of ancient Butes, who was once
The armour-bearer of Dardanian Anchises,
His faithful door-keeper, until Aeneas
Gave him the young Ascanius to look after.
Apollo walked on, a complete old man
In voice, in colouring, with white hair
And armour that clanked with an air of menace.
Iülus was burning to do more,
But the old man addressed these words to him:
'Son of Aeneas, by your hand Numanus
Has perished unavenged, let that suffice:
Apollo praises this your first encounter
And is content your skill should equal his;
For the rest, boy, keep away from the fighting.'
So he began, Apollo, but as he spoke
Withdrew from human sight into thin air.
The Dardan captains recognised the god
And his divine weapons; they heard his quiver
Rattle as he departed. So, though Ascanius
Was eager to fight on they would not let him;
Phoebus had spoken, it was the voice of a god;
They themselves went back where the action was
And once more exposed their lives to danger.
A shout rang all along the battlements,
They drew their bows and whirled their slings around.
The ground is strewn with spears, while shields and helmets
Sound hollowly as they are struck, the fight grows rougher:
It is as when a downpour from the west,
Led by the Charioteer, beats on the ground
Or heavy hailstones lash a sheet of water
When Jupiter, driving the gales before him,
Wrings out the watery storm and empties the clouds.
    Pandarus then and Britias, whom Alcanor
Of Ida fathered and the nymph Iaera
Bore in the grove of Jupiter – young men
Tall as their native pines, tall as their hills –
Opened the gates they had been told to guard;
So confident were they of their own weapons
They bade the enemy come in and try.

Inside they waited, standing before the turrets
To right and left, armed in their iron gear
And with crests dancing way up on their heads;
They were like a pair of oaks with untouched crowns,
The tips nodding, raised far into the sky
Among the breezes beside flowing rivers,
By Padus' bank or pleasant Athesis.
Seeing the gates wide open the Rutulians
Charged in. At once Quercens and Aquicolus,
So splendid in his armour, hare-brained Tmarus,
And Haemon son of Mars, with all their troops
Were made to turn tail or breathe their last
Upon the very threshold of the gates.
At this the anger of the contestants grew
And now the Trojans crowded on the scene
And fought hand to hand in prolonged sorties.
     It was reported to the general, Turnus
– Furiously engaged elsewhere in the field
And making havoc – that the enemy
Was hotting up the slaughter and had opened
The gates up wide. Turnus at once deserted
The fight he had in hand and, beside himself,
Rushed to the Dardan gate and the presumptuous
Brothers who guarded it. Antiphates,
Who was the first man he came across
– The bastard son of the great Sarpedon,
Born of a Theban mother – he laid flat
With one throw of his javelin; the dogwood shaft,
Italian-grown, flew lightly through the air,
Stuck in his belly, then upward through his chest;
From the deep wound came out a rush of blood
And the blade was left warming in his lungs.
He brought down Meropes next, then Erymas,
His hand accounted too for Aphidnus;
Then Bitias, though his eyes flashed and his heart
Raged bitterly against him; it was no javelin
Deprived him of his life but a fiery missile
Hissing and whizzing like a thunderbolt,
Which neither the two ox-hides of his shield
Nor the gilded double plating of the corselet
He trusted so, could anyhow withstand.

His huge limbs slipped and fell, the earth groaned,
His great shield crashed on top of him. So it is
On the Euboic shore of Baiae where
Sometimes men tip into the sea a pile
Of massive rocks, erected for the purpose,
And down it goes, crashing into the shallows
Where it comes to rest and leaves the water heaving
And black mud rising up and billowing out;
Then at the noise Prochyta's summit shakes
And the hard bed of Inarime, laid
By Jove's command on top of Typhoeus.
   Then Mars the god of war gave further strength
To the Latins, added courage, he goaded them
Sharply under the ribs, while to the Teucrians
He sent the spirits of Fear and Retreat.
Wherever the fight was fiercest, the Latins gathered,
The warring god was master of their hearts.
Pandarus, when he saw his brother lying
Stretched on the ground, and saw the turn of fortune
And how the situation had developed,
With great strength set the weight of his broad shoulders
Against the gate and swung the hinges round,
So leaving many of his men shut out,
Before the walls and heavily engaged;
But some he shut in as they retreated,
Enclosing them with himself; he was mad
Not to observe that the Rutulian king
Was in the middle of this company
And – the last straw – to shut him in the town,
An immense tiger among helpless cattle.
A new light flashed from the eyes of Turnus,
His armour gave out terrifying sounds,
The blood-red crest of his helmet bobbed
And he sent sparkling lightning from his shield.
Suddenly the Trojans recognise him
And are appalled. Then from the crowd leapt out
The huge shape of Pandarus, blazing with anger
At his brother's death: 'This is the wrong place!'
He jeers, 'This is not Amata's palace
Or her bridal chamber: Turnus will find he's not
Safe in the market-place of Ardea

With his native walls all round him. What you see
Is the enemy camp; no power can get you out.'
But Turnus answers him with a calm smile:
'You can begin, if you have the courage,
Show what your hand can do for very soon
You will be telling Priam you have found
A new Achilles.' He finished, and the other,
Summoning all his strength, let fly his spear,
A heavy one with knots and bark still on it:
The breezes took it up; Saturnian Juno
Deflected it, the spear stuck on the gate.
Turnus then spoke: 'But you will not escape;
The weapon which is poised in my right hand
Is wielded by a different kind of man
And when he strikes he wounds.' With that he rose
To his full height behind his sword; the blade
Split Pandarus's forehead down the middle,
The great wound went so far a beardless cheek
Fell away on each side. There was a crash,
The ground was shaken by a huge weight
As the limbs slithered down with the armour
Spattered with brains; as he lay dying his head
Hung one half from one shoulder, one from the other.

   The Trojans turned and scattered, anxious, afraid
And if the thought had crossed the victor's mind
That he might break the bars upon the gate
And let his comrades in, that would have been
The last day of the war and of our race.
But so mad was he with desire to kill
He was driven on against his adversaries.
First he caught Phalaris and Gyges, the latter
Cut through the knees from behind; he seized their spears
And threw them after those who were in retreat;
Behind his strength and courage there was Juno.
The next to go was Halys, and then Phegeus
– The spear went through his shield and then through him –
Then men on the walls, who were fighting on
Without knowing what had happened, as Alcander,
Halius and Noemon and Prytanis. The turn
Of Lynceus was next as he moved up,
Calling out to his comrades, to face Turnus

Whose sword flashed to the right where the rampart was
And so killed him; a single blow at close quarters
Sent his head flying with the helmet on it.
Amycus was the next, the man wild beasts
Dreaded, the man who excelled everyone
At priming darts and poisoning the tips;
Then Clytius, the son of Aeolus,
And Cretheus, the friend of the Muses,
Cretheus the Muses chose as their companion,
Who never tired of songs and instruments
From which he called notes to accompany them
And was for ever celebrating horses,
Arms, men and battles, all the array of war.
    At last news of the slaughter reached the ears
Of the Teucrian leaders, of Mnestheus
And of Serestus, always quick to act:
They saw their comrades scattered and the enemy
Within their gates. Mnestheus spoke out:
'Where do you think that you are running to?
What other defences are there further on?
Will you, my countrymen, let a single stranger,
Hemmed in on every side by your own walls,
Go on to massacre the whole city?
Is he to send all our best men to Orcus?
Have you no pity for your luckless country
Or for your ancient gods, no shame? Aeneas
Is your great captain and yet you do nothing?'
    With exhortations of this kind he roused them;
They pulled themselves together and closed ranks.
Step by step Turnus drew back from the fighting
And made for where the river circled round.
As he did so, the Teucrians closed on him
With a great shout, and massed all around;
They were like a crowd of hunters with levelled spears
Closing upon a man-eating lion
While he, terrified but still furious,
Glares at them and retreats step by step
But does not turn back, which neither his anger
Nor courage will let him do, yet he is not able,
Desire it as he may, to break through
The line of spears and hunters ranged against him.

So Turnus falls back, but ever more doubtfully,
And still not hurrying, his mind boiling with rage.
Even so, twice he threw himself on the enemy,
Twice sent them scurrying along the walls:
But the whole force came quickly from the camp,
Nor did Saturnian Juno dare to bring
Sufficient strength against them, for Jupiter
Sent Iris down from heaven and she brought
No very gentle message for his sister
If Turnus should not leave the Teucrian camp.
So it was that he did not hold his own
Either with shield or sword, a cloud of darts
Fell on him from all sides. There was continual
Rattle upon the helmet round his brows,
His crest was knocked off his head, the boss of his shield
Gives way under the blows; the Trojans and
Mnestheus himself, like a thunderbolt,
Redoubled the shower of spears. Turnus then feels
Sweat pour all over his body, a dark river,
He cannot breathe, he shakes, sick and exhausted.
Then only does he with a headlong jump
Throw himself, fully armed, into the river
Which welcomes him among its yellow ripples
And, bearing him on gentle waters,
Washes the marks of slaughter from his limbs
And gives a happy man back to his comrades.

# BOOK X

# BOOK X

Meanwhile the palace of supreme Olympus
Has been thrown open: the Father of the gods,
The king of men, has called his council in
As, from that starry place, high over all,
He casts his eyes on the Dardan camp below
And all the Latin peoples. The gods sit down
Between the eastern and the western doors
And he begins to speak: 'Children of heaven,
Great spirits, wherefore now this change of heart,
And why this contest and this bitterness?
I forbade Italy to take up arms
Against the Teucrians. Why this quarrelling,
Which flouts my prohibition? What is the fear
On one side or the other, which provokes
Recourse to arms and brings out all these swords?
There will be time enough for fighting later,
No need to hurry it, when savage Carthage
Will open up the Alps and send her armies
To bring destruction to the Roman citadel;
There will be no forbidding contests then,
Or hatred; but at this time give assent,
And gladly, to the peace I have detern..ned.'
    Jupiter was content with these few words;
But few were not enough for golden Venus,
Who thus replied:
'O Father, O eternal power that rules
The affairs of men (for what superior
Authority exists for us to turn to?)
You see how the Rutulians are behaving,
How Turnus with his chariot rushes on
Surrounded by them, borne on a tide of war
That runs for him. Already now the Teucrians
Enjoy no more protection from their walls;

Within the gates and on their very ramparts
There is battle, the ditches are full of blood.
Nothing of this is known to Aeneas,
Who is away. And will you never allow
The siege to be raised? Once more an enemy,
Another army batters at the walls
Of a fresh Troy; a son of Tydeus
Comes up out of his Aetolian Arpi
Against the Trojans again. Nor have I seen,
I think, the last of my own wounds; your daughter
Can put off only for a little while
The touch of mortal weapons. If the Trojan
Came into Italy without your blessing,
In defiance of your power, then expiation
Is indeed called for and you need not help them;
But if they followed all the oracles
Given by the gods above or shades below,
Then why should anyone be able now
To overturn your orders, why should anyone
Establish a new order of fatality?
Need I remind you how the fleet was burnt
Upon the shore at Eryx, how the king of storms
Woke all the raging gales from Aeolia,
Or how Iris was sent down from the clouds?
Now Juno stirs even the world below,
A province hitherto left to itself;
Allecto, suddenly among the living,
Dances through all the towns of Italy.
I have no thought of empire any more;
That was my hope when fortune went my way,
Now let the conqueror be whom you prefer.
Is there no land that your bitter wife
Will let the Teucrians have? I beg of you,
And may Troy's smoking ruins be my witness,
Father, allow at least Ascanius
To come out of this warfare without hurt,
Allow at least my grandson to survive.
Aeneas may be tossed on unknown waves
And find whatever way Fortune may give him:
Let me at least have influence enough
To save the boy from this ill-omened conflict.

Amathus is my own, Paphos and Cythera,
My temple at Idalium: let him live there,
Having put aside his arms, ingloriously.
Bid Carthage exercise its powerful sway
Over Ausonia and crush them all:
He will not meddle with the Tyrian towns
While he is on my territory. What has been gained
By their escaping from the plague of war
And from a Troy lit up by Argive flames,
Through all the perils that the sea can offer
Or desolate lands, to seek out Latium
And a new Pergamus? The Teucrians
Would have done better, would they not, to settle
On the last embers of their native city
And on the soil where Troy once was? I pray you,
Give back to these unfortunates their Xanthus,
Their Simois, and let them once more, Father,
Know the misfortunes that they knew in Ilium.'
  Queen Juno then broke out in sullen rage:
'Why are you forcing me to break my silence
And to tell everyone how hurt I am?
Did anyone, either a man or a god,
Compel Aeneas to resort to war
Or make an enemy of King Latinus?
It was the fates brought him to Italy?
Suppose it was, it was Cassandra's ravings
That set him on: but when he left his camp,
Was it we who told him to go? Was it we who told him
To trust his life to the winds? To leave a boy
To run his war and keep watch on his walls?
To tamper with Etruscan loyalties
Or stir up peaceful nations? Who was the god
Who made him do these wrongs? Was I pitiless?
Where in all this is Juno, where is Iris,
Sent down from the clouds? It is a scandal
For the Italians to light up their fires
All round this budding Troy, as it is for Turnus
To stand so firmly on his native soil
Although Pilumnus was his grandfather
And the divine Venilia his mother!
But what about Trojans attacking Latins

With smoking brands, ploughing in others' fields
And driving off the stock? Picking up brides
And taking those already promised to others?
Offering to shake hands and make peace
While all their ships are dressed with arms for war?
You smuggle Aeneas out of the Greeks' hands
And leave them with the mist and empty air,
Or turn his ships into a fleet of nymphs:
Yet to give the Rutulians help is infamous?
"Nothing of this is known to Aeneas,
Who is away": well, let him be away.
"Paphos is yours, Idalus, Cythera":
Then why must you meddle with a city
Which is the mother of wars and violent men?
Is it I who have tried to overthrow
Your tottering Phrygian fortunes? Or was it he
Who so exposed the Trojans to the Greeks?
Why was it that Europe and Asia clashed?
Whose was the offence against hospitality?
Did I lead the Dardan adulterer
To the sack of Sparta? Did I give him weapons?
Was it my lust that stirred up those wars?
Then was the time for you to be concerned
About your own: it is too late now
To come here with complaints, they are unjust,
And all your bitter talk is pointless now.'
      So pleaded Juno: the company of gods
Murmured, each taking one side or the other;
It was like the first gusts of a storm
Rising in a forest, the unseen murmurings
Which sailors take as a hint of winds to come.
Then the almighty Father, first in power
Over all things, began: and as he spoke
The lofty palace of the gods fell silent,
Earth shook its ground, the upper air was quiet,
The Zephyrs rested, the sea smoothed its surface:
'Hear what I say and take it to your hearts.
Since the Ausonians and the Teucrians
Are not to be allies, since your disagreements
Are not to have an end, whatever fortune
May fall today to Trojan or Rutulian,

I will remain impartial, whether this siege
Is meant to prosper the Italians,
Or comes about through the maleficent error
Of Trojans following misleading prophecies.
I am not letting the Rutulians off;
Everyone in the end shall find his fortunes
Accord with his endeavours. Jupiter
Is king of everyone without distinction;
So fate will take its course.' With that he swore
By the dark waters of his Stygian brother,
The swirling pitch between the burning banks,
That he would have it so, and all Olympus
Trembled as he inclined his head. So was it
The council ended. From his golden throne
Jupiter rose, the gods crowded round him
And so accompanied, he crossed the threshold.

   Meanwhile round all the gates of the camp
There are Rutulians, pressing home the slaughter
And setting flames all about the walls.
The legion of Aeneas, without their captain,
Are everywhere hemmed in inside their fort,
There is no escaping. High up in their towers
Or scattered here and there upon the walls
There stand dejected men who can do nothing.
Facing the enemy are Asius,
Son of Imbrasus, and Hicetaon's son
Thymoetes, and the two Assaraci
With Castor and old Thymbris; and beside them
Sarpedon's two brothers, Clarus and Thaemon
Who come from the hills of Lycia.
One, straining every muscle, lifts a rock
So huge, it looks more like a piece of a mountain;
The man is Acmon of Lyrnesus, big
As Clytius his father or his brother Mnestheus.
Some try to keep the enemy at bay
With darts, and some with stones, while others struggle
With burning brands or shoot arrow after arrow.
Protected by them all there stands the one
Venus cares most about, the Dardan boy,
His fine head bare, he glitters like a jewel
Deep set in yellow gold, an ornament

To gleam from collar or from coronet,
Or like the ivory inlay of a casket
Of box-wood or Orician terebinth;
Around his milky neck his hair streams down,
A ring of pliant gold holds it together.
Among this noble company was seen
Also, Ismarus, you, priming light shafts
With poison and delivering them to wound;
You who come from a noble Lydian house
And from a country of rich ploughland where
Pactolus waters with a stream of gold.
Mnestheus was there, still glorying
In having the day before sent Turnus flying
Down from the walls; and there was Capys, too,
Whose name survives in the city of Capua.
    That is how things stood in this stubborn war
While in the middle of the night Aeneas
Was sailing steadily along the coast.
He had left Evander, entered the Tuscan camp,
Approached the king and told him who he was
And who his people were; then, what he wanted
And what assistance he himself could bring,
And how the armies of Mezentius
Had rallied to his side; he spoke of Turnus
And the trouble that was brewing in that quarter,
Adding what grounds there were for mutual trust
And asking for the king's help. Without delay
Tarchon agreed that they should join forces
And become allies; then the Lydians,
Released from their doom and following
The gods' commands, embarked, having placed themselves
Under a foreign leader. The first ship
Was that of Aeneas, under her beak
Were the Phrygian lions, above them rose Ida,
A sight to make the Teucrians think of home.
Here great Aeneas sat, reflecting on
The various issues that the war could bring;
Close at his left side, Pallas, questioning him
Now about how the stars stood to their course
Through the dark night, now about how Aeneas
Had fared in journeying over land and sea.

Now goddesses, open your Helicon,
Move me to sing what company it is
Comes with Aeneas from the Tuscan shores
And mans the ships which sail upon that sea.
    Massicus first, he ploughs through the water
In the bronze-plated Tiger, and commands
A thousand young men who have left their fortress
In Clusium, and the city of Cosae;
Arrows are their weapons; over their shoulders
Hang the light quivers and the deadly bows.
With him is Abas: all his followers
Have splendid armour, the stern of his ship
Blazes with the gilt of his Apollo.
The city of Populonia had given him
Six hundred of her sons, all battle-hardened;
Three hundred more came from the island, Ilva,
Whose iron mines are inexhaustible.
The third is Asilas who stands between
Men and gods, the seer who commands
The entrails of beasts, the stars in the sky,
The tongues of birds, prophetic lightning-flashes,
He sweeps to war with a thousand men
In close-packed line that bristles with their spears:
Pisa, a city of Alphean origin
Set in Etruscan soil, provided them
To serve as he thought best. Then Astyr follows,
A handsome sight indeed, proud of his horse
And many-coloured armour. Three hundred men
Besides, all of one mind in their obedience,
Came from diverse places, with homes in Caere,
The farmlands of Minio, in ancient Pyrgi
Or in Graviscae where men die of fever.
    Nor would I pass you over, Cinyras,
The bravest captain the Ligurians have,
Nor you with your little band, Cupavo
With swan-feathers on your crest to tell the world
What shape your father took, to love's disgrace.
The story is that Cycnus, in despair
For love of Phaëthon, sought a mournful comfort
Among the shadows which the boy's sisters,
The leafy poplars, cast and, as he sang,

Drew on instead of age with its white hairs
A soft plumage, and so left the earth
And, singing still, followed the way of the stars.
His son now sailed with young men like himself,
Rowing the huge Centaur on her course;
The figure-head towered high above the waves,
Threatening them with a rock held in its grasp,
And the long keel ploughed its way through the sea.

    From his own country there was Ocnus, too,
Son of the seer Manto and the Tuscan stream,
Who gave you, Mantua, his mother's name,
Mantua, so famous for its ancestry,
Diverse although that was, from three races
Each owning four cities, Mantua herself
Drawing her main strength from her Tuscan blood.
The same region sent five hundred more
Mezentius had provoked against himself,
Men whom the Mincius – child of Benacus –
Covered with glaucous reeds, bore on their way
In their pine ship into the hostile waters.
Then, moving heavily, there was Aulestes
Rising upon a hundred heavy oars
Which beat the waves in time, the smooth surface
Turned up in foam. It was the great Triton
That carried him, its shell terrifying
The blue tracks of the sea, its front shaggy
Down to the flanks, the belly downwards fish-like;
Under this half-human breast the waves
Murmured and foamed. So many picked captains
There were, who travelled in the thirty ships
To give Troy their assistance, the salt water
Cut by bronze prows as by so many knives.

    Now day had gone from the sky and the moon,
Her chariot and horses loosed upon the night,
Thundered across the mid-point of the sky:
Aeneas, whose cares allowed his limbs no rest,
Sat at the tiller and managed the sails himself.
So, as he sailed on his way, a chorus
Not strangers to him, met him: nymphs Cybele
Had graciously transformed from the ships they were
Into sea-goddesses; they swam abreast

Advancing through the waves, as many of them
As there had once been bronze prows moored on the beach.
They recognised their king from far away
And circled in procession round his ship.
Cymodocea, the most eloquent,
Put her right hand upon the stern and rose
Waist-high out of the water, with her left
Paddling the quiet surface. Then she spoke
To him who was still unaware of her:
'Do you keep watch, race of the gods, Aeneas?
Watch, slacken the sheets and let the sails go.
We are they who were once pines upon Ida,
Now nymphs of the sea, we were your fleet.
The treacherous Rutulians pressed on us
With fire and sword and so, unwillingly,
We broke your ties and searched the seas for you.
It was the Great Mother who in pity
Gave us this new appearance, made us goddesses
And bade us to live on under the waves.
But young Ascanius is the prisoner
Of walls and trenches, all around him Latins
Bristling with weapons and intent on war.
Already the Arcadian cavalry
Have joined with a strong Etruscan force
And stand by to attack; Turnus however
Has made his mind up to send in his squadrons
To stop the Arcadians getting to the walls.
Hurry then, and be ready at first light
To order your companions into action.
And take the shield the Fire-worker gave you;
Trimmed with his gold it is invincible.
At dawn tomorrow, if you listen to me,
There will be great piles of Rutulian dead.'
When she had spoken she gave the stern of the vessel
A mighty shove, as only she knew how,
And sent it on its way: the tall ship fled,
Swifter than arrow or javelin or the wind.
Then the rest speeded up. Anchises' son,
The man from Troy, was dazed at these events
But yet the omen lifted up his heart.
Looking towards the circling heavens he prayed,

In few words: 'Lady of Ida, Mother of gods,
To whom Dindymus, castellated cities
And your yoked lions, are dear, command me now
In this battle, may the omen prosper;
March in step with the Phrygians, I pray,
Goddess whose steps are ever favourable.'
That much he managed. Meanwhile day came on
Headlong, the light ripened, and night fled.
    First he gave orders to the men with him
To form behind their standards, hold themselves ready
And make sure their weapons were in order.
Already, standing on the high poop,
He had the Teucrians and his camp in view;
At once he held up his left arm to show
His blazing shield. The Dardans from the walls
Raised a shout to high heavens, and the fresh hope
Brought their anger to life, they threw their spears
Which were like cranes on the Strymon, under dark clouds,
Signalling they are home, and cutting through
The air with cries following in their wake,
Driven on by the south wind. To the Rutulian king
And his Ausonian captains all of this
Was inexplicable till they looked round
And saw the fleet already turned to shore
And the whole sea moving forward with ships.
The gleaming helmet on Aeneas's head
Blazes and flames pour out from its crest;
The golden boss of his shield spews fire:
It is as when on a clear night comets
Glow blood-red with ill-omen, or hot Sirius
Rising with parching fever for the sick
Makes the sky sad with a foreboding light.
    But the brave Turnus still is confident
That he can reach the shore before the enemy
And drive them from the land as they arrive.
'The moment that you prayed for now has come;
Now you can smash through them hand to hand.
Mars is with those who have enough courage.
Remember now your wives and your homes,
The deeds and glories of your ancestors.
Let us now meet them where the waves lap in,

And they take their first stumbling steps on land.
Fortune favours the brave.' That was his speech,
And as he spoke he was considering
Which men to lead forward to the attack
And which to leave on guard below the walls.
   Meanwhile Aeneas gets his men ashore
From the high ships down gangways. Many of them,
As the waves draw back, jump into the shallows;
Others slide down the oars. Tarchon, watching the shore
To see where the shallows are calm and there are no breakers
But the water runs quietly in on the swell,
Suddenly turns his prow and appeals to his men:
'Now, you are the best crew, your oars are strong, pull!
Lift her up now and carry her forward;
Let the beak cut into this enemy land,
The keel will plough a furrow for herself.
I don't mind breaking up in a place like this
As long as we get the land.' Tarchon had spoken
And so his comrades rose upon their oars,
Driving the ships through the foam to the Latin fields
Till the prows were high and dry, with all the ships
Undamaged. Or all but one, for yours, Tarchon,
Which hung uncertainly on a hard shelf,
Washed by the waves, and broke, and all her men
Were thrown among the waves; fragments of oars
And floating benches got in their way as their feet
Were caught by the tow of the receding waves.
   Turnus was not backward, he did not dawdle
But threw his battle-line against the Teucrians,
Disposing his men to hold them on the shore.
The trumpets sounded. Aeneas was the first
To move against the other's troop of peasants;
A good start, he brought some Latins down,
Killing the tall Theron, who had thought
The great Aeneas was a suitable quarry.
The sword went through the bronze links of his armour,
Through his tunic stiff with gold, and pierced his side.
Aeneas then struck Lichas, who had been
Cut from his dead mother's womb and therefore was
Sacred to you, Phoebus, as one who, when small
Already knew how to escape the sword.

Close by, he sent others to their deaths
– The tough Cisseus and the immense Gyas
As they felled ranks of men with their clubs.
The arms of Hercules did nothing for them,
Nor their strong hands, nor yet their father Melampus
Who used to be the companion of Hercules
When he was on earth at his famous labours.
And then Pharus, opening his big mouth
To say what he would do, received a javelin
Aeneas threw at him, right in his words.
You too, unhappy Cydon, as you followed
Your latest pretty boy, young Clytius
With all that golden down upon his cheeks,
You would have fallen by the Dardan's hand
And been released from amorous anxieties,
Lying broken on the ground, if your seven brothers
Had not interposed themselves, Phorcus's sons,
Who threw their seven spears of which some
Glanced harmlessly from Aeneas's helmet and shield,
While some the kindly Venus turned aside
So that they did no more than graze his body.
Aeneas spoke to the loyal Achates:
'Bring me a pile of weapons, every one
That my hand throws will find its Rutulian,
These weapons which, upon the plains of Ilium
Were lodged in Grecian bodies.' Then he seized
A great spear and threw it: it crashed through
The bronze of Maeon's shield and broke at once
His armour and his chest. Alcanor ran
To help his brother, supporting him as he fell
And then the arm he helped him with was pierced,
The spear flying on, bloody but still on course;
The arm itself hung dying from the shoulder
By a few sinews. Numitor wrenched the lance
From his brother's body and aimed it at Aeneas,
But yet it might not strike at him directly
And only grazed the thigh of great Achates.
    At that moment Clausus of Cures appeared,
Full of confidence in his youthful strength
And from far off struck Dryops under the chin
With a heavy spear which, as he was speaking,

Pierced his throat and took his voice with his life:
He hit the ground with his forehead and spat thick gore.
Three Thracians too, from the great house of Boreas,
And three more sent out by their father Idas,
Natives of Ismarus, one way or another
Were struck down by Clausus. Halaesus then
Came up quickly with a band of Auruncans:
Then Neptune's son approached, Messapus
With his fine team of horses. Each side in turn
Tries to drive back the other, for this struggle
Is on the very doorstep of Italy.
They are like opposed winds high in the heavens
Battling with one another with equal strength
And equal force; nothing will give way,
Not winds, not clouds, not sea; the issue hangs
Uncertainly and for a long time
They stand poised in their mutual resistance;
So the Trojan ranks and the ranks of Latium
Close with each other, foot to foot, man to man.
    In another part of the field, which a torrent
Had covered with loose boulders and shrubs torn from the
        banks,
Pallas caught sight of his Arcadians,
Unused as they were to fight on foot
(The rough ground had made them all dismount)
Beginning to retreat before the Latians.
The one thing he could do in such difficulties
He did: he sought to rouse their failing courage,
Now begging and now using bitter words:
'My friends, why are you giving way before them?
By your own heads, by your courageous deeds,
By King Evander's name, by all the wars
That you have won, and by the hope I have
This day of equalling my father's fame,
Don't trust your legs! Think rather of your swords
And smash a way through the enemy's line.
There, where you see the concentration thickest,
That is the spot your country bids you make for
With Pallas at your head. They are not gods
The enemy are mortals like ourselves,
We have as many lives and hands as they.

And look! on one side the high sea
Closes upon us, there is no more land
By which we can escape; for us the choice
Is between the deep water and the Trojans!'
With that he flung himself upon the enemy.

    The first man in his way was Lagus whom
Ill-luck had placed there. As he tried to loose
A great rock from the ground, Pallas let fly
His javelin and pierced him in the back
Just where the spine divided ribs from ribs,
Then tugged it out from where it stuck in the bone.
Hisbo who came down on him as he did so
Failed to surprise him, for as he rushed forward
Pallas caught him blind with rage and reckless
At his friend's cruel death, and buried his sword
Deep in his bursting lungs. The next he went for
Was Sthenius, and then Anchemolus
Of the ancient house of Rhoetus, he who ventured
Incestuously into his step-mother's bed.
And you too fell in the Rutulian fields,
Larides and Thymber, twin sons of Daucus,
A source of pleased confusion to your parents
Who did not know you apart, though now Pallas
Has made a bitter difference between you;
Evander's sword has cut off Thymber's head
While, Larides, your severed hand is ownerless
And the dying fingers still twitch on your sword.

    Furious and ashamed, the Arcadians,
Roused by Pallas's reprimand, and seeing
His own brilliant exertions, found heart
To face the enemy. Pallas then struck
Rhoetus as he was dashing past in his chariot,
Which gave just that much respite to Ilus
At whom he had aimed the spear from afar;
Ithit Rhoetus instead, as he made his escape
From you, noble Teuthras and your brother Tyres
And so he rolled over and fell from his chariot,
Kicking the Rutulian fields with his dying heels.
And as in summer, when the wind rises,
A shepherd waiting for it starts his fires
Here and there in the woodland, and suddenly

They spread to cover all the ground between them
Till all the crackling lines join in one blaze
While he sits looking on, admiring his handiwork:
So all the roused Arcadians come together
And rally round you, Pallas. But Halaesus,
A keen man in a fight, drew himself up
Behind his shield and confronted them.
He killed Ladon, Pheres, Demodocus
And in a flash his sword cut off the hand
Of Strymonius, who tried to throttle him;
He had struck Thoas in the face with a stone,
Scattering bits of his skull amidst blood and brains.
His father who had second sight had hidden
Halaesus in the woods: and when old, he turned
His paling eyes to death, the Fates took over
And sacrificed his son to Evander's arms.
As Pallas sought him out he said a prayer:
'Suffer me, Father Tiber, so to aim
The steel I hold poised that it is fortunate
And finds its way to Halaesus's hard heart;
Then shall this weapon and the victim's spoils
Hang on your sacred oak.' The god heard him;
Halaesus moved his shield to cover Imaon
And so his luck left him; he exposed
His heart, defenceless, to the Arcadian spear.
     But Lausus, who was a great man in this war,
Would not allow his men to be terrified
Even by the slaughter of so great a hero:
First he picked out Abas and cut him down
As he stood in the way, Abas who was
One of the mainstays of that knotty battle.
The youth of Arcadia then fell before him,
The Etruscans fell, and even you Trojans
Whose bodies had escaped the Grecian blows.
The armies close one upon the other,
Each with brave captains and with equal strength.
Those in the rear push on the men in front
Until it is impossible to move
Or handle weapons. From the one side Pallas
Heaves and shoves, while Lausus does the same
From the other side. The two are much of an age,

Both fine young men, yet Fortune will let neither
Return to his native land. But the king of Olympus
Will not allow them to do battle with each other;
Each of them must meet a yet greater enemy.

   Meanwhile Turnus's sister, the gracious nymph,
Warned her brother to go to help Lausus
And so he drove his chariot fast through the ranks.
Seeing his comrades, he cried: 'Leave it to me:
I will deal with Pallas alone, he is my man;
I wish his father were here to see what happens.'
The Rutulians drew back as they were bidden
And when they had retired his young opponent,
Wondering at the high tone of his commands,
Stood in amazement, Turnus was so huge.
He ran his eyes over him and from afar
Observing everything with a resolute look,
Answered those royal words with words befitting
The king's son that he was: 'I shall win glory
Either by now taking these kingly spoils
Or else by a famous death; neither of these
Will give my father cause for discontent.
So much for threats!' With that he made his way
Forward into the open. The Arcadians
Felt their blood gather coldly round their hearts.
Turnus leapt from his chariot and on foot
Advanced to meet his man; he was like a lion
Who from some vantage point observes a bull
Spoiling for battle on the plain below him
And rushes forward: so Turnus seemed
To his opponent as he drew nearer.
When Pallas judged his enemy had come
Within range of his spear, without waiting
He closed in first, hoping that if he were bold
Some chance might make up what he lacked in strength;
He cried to high heaven: 'Hercules,
I pray you, by my father's hospitality
When you came as a stranger, help me now!
May Turnus see me rip his bloody armour
From his half-dead body, may his eyes
As they fade, see the man who defeated him!'
Hercules listened to the young man's prayer

And groaned from the heart, the tears he shed were useless.
For gently the great Father said to his son:
'Every man's day is fixed; for everyone
His time of life is brief and irreparable;
All courage does is to extend his fame
Because his deeds deserve it. By the walls of Troy
Fell many who were children of the gods,
Yes, Sarpedon who was my own child.
The fates are calling Turnus too and he
Has now come to the limit of his life.'
With that, the Father turned away his eyes
From the Rutulian fields. But Pallas then
Threw his spear with full force and drew his sword
From its hollow scabbard, it flashed in the sunlight.
The spear flew on its way and struck the armour
Of Turnus where it rose on his shoulder,
Then through the rim of his shield and even grazed
His mighty body. Turnus at this
Raised his oak lance and held it long balanced
With its sharp iron pointing at Pallas, and threw it.
And as he did so he said: 'Watch this, you'll see
Which of our weapons is the better piercer.'
Then all the iron plates of Pallas's shield
All the bronze, and all the layers of hide
Were pierced through the middle by the point
And quivered at the impact; then the mail
Protecting him was holed, then his broad chest.
He tore the weapon out hot from the wound:
It was no good, for out by the same route
His blood and spirit followed. He crashed down,
Falling upon his wound, his armour rang
Over him as he lay on hostile ground
And, dying, bit it with his bloodied mouth.
Turnus said, standing over him: 'Arcadians,
Remember what I say and tell Evander:
As he deserved, I send back Pallas to him.
Whatever honour may be in a tomb
Or consolation in a burial,
I will allow him: he entertained Aeneas
And he will pay dearly.' As he spoke
He put his left foot on the dead man

And tore from him his heavily-weighted belt
On which was pictured the unspeakable crime
– On one bridal night forty-nine youths
Foully done to death in their marriage beds
Which streamed with blood: Clonus, son of Eurytus
Had embossed the whole story in thick gold:
Now Turnus has the whole as his spoil
And triumphs and rejoices to have got it.
The mind of man is ignorant of fate
And fortunes still to come; when things go well
It does not understand moderation.
The time will come for Turnus, but too late,
When he will wish Pallas alive and well
And would give anything to have him so,
Hating the very spoils he won this day.
Pallas's comrades then, lamentingly,
Crowding around his body, took him up
And bore him home stretched upon his shield,
A great crowd following. What pain, what pride
Will be your father's when you come back thus!
This was your first day at the wars, the day
Also that took you from him, yet you left
Heap upon heap of the Rutulians dead.

   A surer messenger than mere rumour
Rushed to Aeneas news of this calamity
And told him that his men were close to death
And that the routed Teucrians needed help.
He cut a swathe through the nearest ranks,
Blazing with anger, making a path with his sword,
Looking for you, Turnus proud with fresh slaughter.
Pallas, Evander, the table to which he came
A stranger once, appeared before his eyes,
He saw the hands extended in amity.
He took alive the four young sons of Sulmo
And four Ufens had called his own, to offer
As sacrifices to the dead Pallas
Whose funeral pyre called out for prisoners' blood.
Next he had aimed his spear to kill Magus
Who ducked so that the spear quivered over him,
Then threw his arms around the thrower's knees
And cried out for mercy, pleading with him:

'I beg you by the spirit of your father
And by the hopes you have for Iülus
As he grows up, now spare this life of mine
For my son and my father. A great house
Is mine, I have, buried deep in it,
Talents of silver, all engraved, and gold
Wrought and unwrought, in huge quantities.
The victory of the Teucrians does not turn
On my death, one life will not make that difference.'
The answer that Aeneas gave was this:
'That gold and silver that you tell me of,
You may save it for your son. Such deals as that
Turnus has henceforth made impossible
By killing Pallas. That is the reply
My father's spirit, Anchises', gives and Iülus
Is of the same mind.' He seized the helmet
With his left hand, bent back the suppliant's neck,
And put his sword in right up to the hilt.
Not far away there was Haemon's son
Who was the priest of Phoebus and Diana,
The sacred band tied around his head,
His whole array brilliant, his armour splendid:
Aeneas met him, drove him across the field
And when he fell he stood over him,
Offering him as a sacrifice and drew over him
The shadow of death: Serestus took his armour
On his own shoulders, a tribute to you, Mars.
  Caeculus, born of Vulcan's race, and Umbro,
Coming from the Marsian hills, rallied the troops.
The Dardan charged in fury. With his sword
He had cut off the left hand of Anxur
And the shield with it. (Anxur had been mouthing
Some big talk and thought perhaps his strength
Was equal to his words, perhaps imagined
He would live many years and grow white hair.)
Then, proud of his shining armour, Tarquitus,
Whom the nymph Dryope had borne to Faunus,
A dweller in the woods, crossed the track
Aeneas blazed before him. So it was
That, drawing back his spear, the Trojan stuck him
Right through his corselet and his heavy shield

And, as he pleaded and was full of words,
Cut off his head and sent it to the ground
Where the trunk, which was still warm, rolled over,
Then, standing over him, spoke bitter words:
'Lie there now, you who we were supposed to fear!
Your dearest mother will not bury you now
Or build a family tomb over your bones:
You will be left a prey to wild birds
Or, sunk beneath the waves, you will drift on
Where only hungry fish will suck your wounds.'
Then he pursued Lucas and Antaeus,
Both front-line men for Turnus, and the brave
Numa, the auburn Camers, son of Volcens
A nobleman who was the wealthiest
In all Ausonia reigning in quiet Amyclae.
Like Aegaeon, of whom it is told
He had a hundred arms, a hundred hands
And fifty fires burned in his mouths and hearts
When in the face of Jove's thunder he clashed
His fifty shields and drew his fifty swords:
So was Aeneas in victorious fury
Once his sword-point was blooded. Even the chariot
With four horses Niphaeus drove against him
He went to meet head-on. But when the animals
Saw him taking long strides in their direction
And heard his shouted threats, they turned and bolted,
Throwing the driver out, and swept the chariot
Through the ranks and away to the sea shore.
   Meanwhile, with a pair of white horses,
Lucagus and his brother Liger drove on
Into the midst of the battle; but the brother
Kept his hands on the reins while Lucagus
Whirled his drawn sword against any opponent.
Aeneas would not tolerate their insolence;
He went in to attack and appeared before them
A tall figure with a spear. Liger called out:
'What you see now is not Diomede's horses,
The chariot of Achilles, you are not in Phrygia:
You are in the country that will see the end of you
And of your war.' Such were the words which flew
From Liger in his madness. The Trojan hero

Did not reply in words but hurled his javelin
Against his enemy. Lucagus, as he hung
Whipping his horses with the flat of his sword,
Advanced his left foot to be ready for combat;
The spear went through the bottom of his shield
Which flashed as it entered his groin on the left;
He was thrown out of the chariot and rolled on the ground
A dying man. Aeneas jeered at him:
'Lucagus, it's not the horses that let you down,
They didn't run away nor did they swerve
Because they'd seen a ghost; you jumped out
Over the wheels of your chariot and deserted them!'
With that he pulled the horses up; the brother
Slid down from the platform and unhappily
Stretched out his helpless hands: 'Hero of Troy!'
He pleaded, 'By your own head, by the parents
To whom so great a son owes his life,
Spare this life, have pity on a suppliant!'
He would have gone on but Aeneas said:
'Just now your talk was rather different;
Die, for a man should not desert his brother.'
Then with his sword he opened up his breast
And let his spirit from its hiding-place.
Such were the deaths the Dardan leader brought
To many in that field, his rage resembled
That of a torrent or a dark whirlwind.
At last they broke out and left the camp,
The young Ascanius and the fighting men:
The siege had served no purpose in the end.
    Jupiter meanwhile had said to Juno:
'O you who are my sister and my wife,
My dearest, it is, as you supposed
Venus who keeps the Trojans going, not
– You are right again – their ready way
Of handling weapons, their gallantry, nor yet
Their fortitude in danger.' Juno replied
– She was all submissiveness – 'My sweetest lord,
Why, when I am already sick and fearful
Of the commands which, sadly, you have given,
Do you distress me now? If you still loved me
As once you used to do and as you ought,

You would not, I am sure, deny me this,
You who are almighty: you would allow me
Somehow to take Turnus out of the battle
And bring him safely to his father Daunus.
As it is, let him perish to satisfy
The Teucrians by shedding his innocent blood.
Yet he is one of our own lineage,
Pilumnus was his great-great-grandfather,
And often has he with a generous hand
Loaded your altars with a pile of gifts.'
   The high king of Olympus answered shortly:
'If what you ask is to delay his death
And give him time before he has to die
Yet understand that so I have determined,
Take him, let him escape, snatch him away
From his immediate fate. There is yet leisure
For that much indulgence. If, however,
Your prayers conceal some thoughts of higher favours
And you are thinking the whole course of the war
Can be diverted and the issue altered,
You nourish hopes which will come to nothing.'
   In tears Juno replied: 'But what if really
You had in mind to grant what your words deny
And Turnus can still expect his span of life?
As it is he awaits a bitter end,
Innocent though he is, or else your wife
Has no grip on the truth. Yet had I rather
You tricked me into fearing what I need not
And you, who can, would change the course of things!'
With that she left the high court of heaven
And, wrapped in cloud, driving a storm before her,
Made for the Trojan line and the Laurentine camp.
Out of a hollow cloud the goddess then
Fashioned in the likeness of Aeneas
A strengthless shadow, marvellous apparition,
Decked it with Dardan arms, with shield and crest
As if it were the goddess-born himself;
She gave it empty words, sound no mind formed;
It walked exactly as Aeneas did:
It was like one of those shapes they say flit
Here and there after a man has died

Or such as delude sleepers in their dreams.
The happy image strutted before the troops,
Shaking its weapons and uttering challenges.
Turnus rushed at it and when still far off
Threw his spear; the image turned and fled.
Then indeed Turnus thought that Aeneas
Refused to face him and was in retreat;
He was beside himself, drunk with false hope:
'Where are you off to?' he shouted, 'Aeneas!
You have agreed to this marriage, you should stick to it!
You're going to get the land you came to seek,
Six feet of it, from me!' Hot in pursuit
He drew his glittering sword and did not see
His triumph was a plaything of the winds.
   It happened that the ship which king Osinius
Had sailed in from the coast of Clusium
Was moored up against a high rock
With ladders down and gangway in position.
The fleeing image of Aeneas hastily
Sought shelter there and Turnus followed it
With no less speed, no obstacle could hold him:
He sprang along the gangway. He had hardly touched
The prow of the ship before Saturn's daughter
Broke the rope and sent the ship flying
Far out to sea on the retiring waves.
So, while Aeneas sought his absent enemy
To challenge him in battle and many warriors
That he encountered were sent to their deaths,
His bodiless image left its hiding place,
Flew upwards and dissolved into black cloud:
But a gale carried Turnus out to sea.
He looked back to shore, not understanding
How these things could be and not grateful
For having been rescued, raised his hands and prayed:
'Almighty Father, do I stand condemned
For such great crimes that you would punish me
In such a manner? Whither am I going?
Where did I come from? For I am in flight
Without my knowing how or why it is so.
Shall I ever again see that camp
Or the walls of Laurentium? What about my men,

All those who followed me in battle?
Ignominiously I have abandoned them
To an appalling death, I see them now
Wandering up and down, I hear their groans
As they fall one by one. What shall I do?
If the earth opened it would not be deep enough
To hide my shame! Rather, you winds,
Grow pitiful for me now; carry the ship
Against cliffs, against rocks – and willingly
I will go, I Turnus beg you – destructive shoals
Where no Rutulians, no rumour of my doings
May follow me.' And as he speaks, his mind
Bobs this way and that. Shall he for shame
Throw himself dementedly on his sword
And stick it through his ribs, or shall he swim for it,
Battling among the waves to the curved shore
To show himself once more against the Teucrians?
Three times he tried first one course, then the other,
But each time Juno had pity on him
And held him back. He drifted on, the ship
Cutting through deep water till the waves
And current took him back to Ardea
The ancient city of his father Daunus.

    Meanwhile Mezentius, whom Jove has warned,
Takes up the fight and the triumphant Teucrians
Find he is on the attack. The Tyrrhene ranks
Close on him and they all go for one man,
The one they all hate, dart after dart
Is showered upon him. He stands like a cliff,
A vast cliff jutting far into the sea,
Open to all the fury of the winds,
Exposed to the sweep of the sea, and bearing all
The force and all the threats of sky and waves,
Itself unmoved and motionless. Yet he fells
Hebrus the son of Dolichaon and with him
Palmus and Latagus as they make their escape:
But Latagus he faces none the less
And strikes him in the mouth with a great stone,
A chip off a mountain, you might say:
Palmus he cuts off at the knees and leaves him
Floundering ineffectually on the ground

And then presents his armour to Lausus, to wear
Upon his shoulders, with the crest for the top of his helmet.
Then he brings down Evanthes the Phrygian
And Mimas who was his close companion,
Just of an age with Paris, for when Theano
Had borne him to Amycus, that very night
Queen Hecuba, who was pregnant with a fire-brand,
Gave birth to Paris: Paris who now lay
In the city of his fathers, while Mimas
Fell as a stranger on the Laurentine shore.
Mezentius was like a wild boar
Driven down from the mountains by the teeth
Of the dogs set on him, after many years
In which he had found shelter among the pines
Of Vesulus, or in the Laurentine marshes
Where he had fed among crowding reeds;
A boar who, at the last trapped in a net,
Comes to a stop, emits a savage grunt
And raises the bristles on his shoulders
While no-one has the courage to come closer
To vent his anger but, from a safe distance,
Everyone attacks him with javelins:
So with Mezentius, all their just anger
Gave no man courage to draw a sword against him;
Missiles from a distance and loud shouts were their weapons.
He was without fear and turned this way and that
Without haste, but ground his teeth and picked
The javelins from the leather of his shield.
   There had come from the ancient territories
Of Corynthus, a Greek named Acron, banished
So that his marriage was not consummated:
From far away Mezentius caught sight of him,
With his crimson plumes and the purple coat
His bride had given him, as he laid about him
In the middle of the battle. Then as a lion
Famished and searching through the deep coverts,
Driven mad by hunger, if he sees before him
A shy roe or a high-antlered stag,
Is suddenly happy, opens his great mouth,
Sets his mane on end and stands over the carcase,
His cruel mouth awash with the foul blood:

So was Mezentius who as instantly
Rushed into the thick of the enemy.
Down went the luckless Acron and, expiring,
Drummed the dark earth with his heels, bloodying
The broken weapon. The same Mezentius
Was too proud to bring Orodes down
While he was running away, and with his spear
Gave him a wound he could not see coming;
He ran round in front so as to face him
And meet him man to man, to get the better of him
Not by stealth but openly by strength.
With one foot on him as he pulled the spear out
He said: 'Look, soldiers, there lies Orodes,
Who counted for something in this war.'
His comrades joined in with shouts of triumph;
The dying man, however, had his say:
'Whoever you are who defeated me,
I shall not go unavenged; you have not long
To enjoy your triumph; a like fate awaits you
And you and I will hold these fields in common.'
Mezentius smiled, but a smile mixed with anger:
'Now you can die. The Father of the gods
And king of men, will look after me.'
With that he pulled the weapon from the body.
The eyes were glazed in an iron sleep,
Then the light closed into eternal night
    Caedicus cut Alcathous down, Sacrator
Hydaspes; Rapo killed Parthenius
And Orses, one of the toughest fighters there;
Messapus finished Clonius and Lycaon's son
Ericetes, the former as he lay on the ground
When he had fallen from his bridle-less horse,
The latter he fought hand to hand on foot.
Then Lycian Agis had come out in front,
But Valerus, with courage like his ancestors'
Got him down, while Salius killed Thronius
And was himself then hit by Nealces,
So skilled with javelin and long-distance arrow.
    Now Mars was dealing with an even hand,
Equally to both sides, distress and death.
In both armies alike men were killing,

In both alike falling, victors and vanquished;
On neither side was there thought of retreat.
The gods in Jove's palace pitied both
The empty anger and the weight of suffering
Men must endure. On one side Venus watched
And on the opposing side Saturnian Juno;
Among the thousands at war Tisiphone raged.
But over the flat ground Mezentius
Advanced stormily. Huge as Orion
When he wanders through the great pools of Nereus,
Making a path for himself, his shoulders protruding
Out of the waves, or when, with an ancient ash
Torn from some high mountain he strides on,
Feet on the ground and head hidden in the clouds:
Such was Mezentius in his gigantic armour.
Over against him there stood Aeneas
Who picked him out in the long line of men
And made ready to meet him. Mezentius
Remained motionless, he had no fear
But waited for his noble enemy,
Firm as a rock, his eye measuring the distance
At which he should throw his spear. 'Assist me now,
My own right hand and the weapon I hold poised
Ready to throw, for you two are my god!
I vow that you, Lausus, dressed in the spoils
I shall take from the body of this robber,
Shall be my living trophy from Aeneas!'
With that he threw from far his whistling spear,
But it flew on, glancing from the shield
And some way off fixed itself in Antores
Just above the hip – the excellent Antores,
He who had been Hercules's companion
And, sent from Argos, had attached himself
To king Evander and so had settled
In an Italian city. He fell now
By a chance wound intended for another
And, looking up at the sky, remembered Argos
As he lay dying. Then the good Aeneas
Threw his spear: it went right through the shield
– Three layers of bronze, but hollow, three hides
Worked into the circles – and so dropped

To the groin where it was almost spent. Quickly
Aeneas pulled his sword out – he was pleased
To have drawn Tyrrhene blood – and when Mezentius
Was still confused he pressed his attack hard.
Seeing all this, Lausus let out a groan,
For he loved his father, tears ran down his cheeks.
So hard a death as came to you, such deeds
As we may credit only in antiquity,
I will not pass in silence, youthful Lausus,
Who well deserve remembrance for what you did.
  Mezentius gave ground, he was useless
Encumbered as he was by Aeneas's spear
Trailing from his shield as he withdrew.
His young son rushed forward into the fighting
And, as Aeneas's hand went up to strike,
Lausus caught the point and so prevented him;
The young men with Lausus crowded round,
Following Mezentius so that he could escape
Protected by his son's shield; they hurled javelins
And tried to keep their enemy at a distance.
Aeneas was beside himself with rage
But kept under cover. As in a storm,
When clouds fall down in hail-stones, every ploughman
And every farmer, hurries from the fields
And every traveller takes shelter where he can,
On a river bank or in the cleft of a rock,
As long as the earth is rained on, so that afterwards
When the sun comes out, they can resume their business:
So Aeneas, with javelins pouring on him,
Put up with the storm of weapons while it lasted:
But he called out to Lausus and threatened him:
'Where are you going? This is the end of the road
And you are daring more than you have strength for.
Your duty to your father makes you reckless!'
The boy none the less leaps at him madly;
The anger of the Dardan leader mounts
Cruelly, while for Lausus the Fates pick up
The last threads. Aeneas drives his sword
Irresistibly through the young man's body,
Burying it to the hilt. The point has passed
Clean through the shield, too light for one so daring,

And through the tunic his mother had woven for him
From soft gold thread; the folds filled with blood.
Then life left the body and, through the air,
Made its way sorrowingly to the shades.
But when Anchises's son saw the boy's face
With its astounding pallor as he died
He groaned and, pitying him, stretched out his hand,
This likeness of his own love for his father
So touched his mind. 'Poor boy, what can Aeneas
Do for you now equal to your deserts
And worthy of so fine a character?
No-one shall take your arms or your armour
In which you took such pleasure; for yourself,
You shall go back to your ancestral dead
And to their ashes, if that is any comfort.
Unfortunate boy, you have this consolation
In your sad death, that it is by the hand
Of great Aeneas himself that you have fallen.'
Then, blaming the boy's friends for being slow,
He raised him from the ground where he lay,
His hair, so lovely once, matted with blood.
    Meanwhile his father, on the banks of Tiber,
Was cleaning up his wounds in the water
And propped himself against the trunk of a tree.
Above him in the branches hung his helmet,
Bronze, like his armour resting on the grass.
Around him stood the pick of his young men,
But he himself was sick and panted somewhat,
His neck lolled back, his long beard was smoothed out
Over his chest; he asked again and again
About Lausus, sending more than one messenger:
They were to bring him back, such were the instructions
Of his sorrowing father. But, weeping,
His comrades were carrying the lifeless Lausus
Upon his shield, a great figure indeed
But vanquished by a wound from one yet greater.
Mezentius in his heart foreknew this evil
And recognised the wailing from afar;
He sullied his white hair with heaps of dust,
Stretched out both hands to heaven and then,
Hugging his son's body, he said: 'Son,

Was life so much to me, was it so pleasant,
That I allowed the child that I begot
To suffer for me at the enemy's hands?
Am I, your father, saved by your wounds,
Alive because you are dead? Alas, now indeed
I know all the bitterness of exile
And now at last my wound is deep indeed!
It is I, son, who have defiled your name
By my ill-doing, driven out in hatred
From my throne and from my ancestral sceptre.
I owed it to my country to have suffered
For the resentment that my people felt:
I should have yielded up my guilty breath
To any death they chose. I live on still,
I have not yet left the world of men
Or the light of day. But now I will leave.'
With that he raised himself on his wounded thigh
And though the wound was deep and his strength ebbed
He did not falter as he asked for his horse.
It was his pride and joy, he had ridden victorious
From all his battles on it. The animal grieved
As he spoke to it: 'For a long time, Rhoebus,
We have lived together – if, for mortal creatures,
Anything can be long. But today, either
You will with me bring back those bloody spoils
And the head of Aeneas, so avenging
The sufferings of Lausus, or if strength
Is lacking now to open up the way,
You shall die with me: for I think, old friend,
You could not bear submission to a stranger
Or to have Teucrian masters.' And with that
The horse's back felt the familiar load
And both his master's hands held sharp javelins,
His head shone in its bronze, the helmet bristled
With its crest of horse-hair. So Mezentius
Charged into the battle. A tide of shame
Rose in that one heart which was mad with grief.
    And three times then he called out 'Aeneas!'
Aeneas knew who it was and joyfully
He made his prayer: 'The Father of the gods
So bring this thing about, so great Apollo!

Now let us come to grips!' He moved forward
To meet his enemy, threatening him with his spear.
The other spoke: 'Why try to frighten me
When you have dealt so cruelly with my son?
That was the only way you could destroy me.
Death has no horrors for me and I care not
For any of your gods. No need for threats;
I have come to die, and bring you these gifts
Before I go.' With that he hurls a javelin
Aimed at his enemy, then plants another
And yet another, wheeling in a wide circle;
The gold boss of the shield sustains them all.
Three times he gallops round him on the left,
Throwing dart after dart, three times the Trojan
Slews round to catch the great forest of weapons
On his bronze shield. When he could bear no longer
To let things drag on so and do nothing
But pick darts from his shield, standing as he did
At a disadvantage, he thought what he would do
And then broke out at last: he hurled his spear
Straight between the eyes of the fighting horse.
The animal reared, pawing the air, then threw
His rider and came down on top of him,
Putting his own shoulder out as he did so.
Trojans and Latins lit the sky with shouts.
Aeneas flew forward, drawing his sword
And, towering above his enemy, he cried:
'Where is Mezentius now, who was so keen,
Where has his savage strength gone?' To which the Tuscan,
Looking up as if he would drain the sky
And coming to himself, replied softly:
'My bitter enemy, why do you taunt me
And threaten me with death? There would be no wrong
In killing me; in coming here to battle
I had no such thought, and Lausus certainly
Made no such bond with you on my behalf.
I ask one thing only, if there can be
Any grace asked by a conquered enemy:
Allow me burial. I know my people hate me:
I ask you only, keep their fury from me

And let me share a tomb with my son.'
So, and quite consciously, he let the sword
Run through his throat and poured out his spirit
In wave after wave of blood over his armour.

# BOOK XI

# BOOK XI

The dawn rose from her bed in the ocean:
Aeneas, with the men to be buried
Much on his mind, and troubled most by one death,
At first light paid what he owed to the gods
Who had given him victory. Upon a mound
He set up a great oak with branches lopped
On every side, and dressed it with the arms
Gleaming as he had taken them from Mezentius,
A prince's trophies for the god of war.
He fitted on the crests dripping with blood,
The warrior's broken spears, his battered breast-plate
Pierced in a dozen places; the bronze shield
He fastened on the left side, and the sword
With its ivory sheath he hung as from the neck.
Then (for his captains gathered close about him)
He urged his comrades to confirm their triumph:
   'Much has been done, my friends; now have no fear
For what remains to do. The first-fruits here
Are these spoils taken from the arrogant king;
Here is Mezentius as my hands have made him.
The way is open now to King Latinus
And the walls of Latium. Be of good heart
And see your arms are ready. Now the war
Looks hopeful, if we push on immediately
When the gods give the word to raise our standards;
The lads from the camp must follow us
Without time for fear or hesitation.
Meanwhile let us commit our comrades' bodies,
Dust to dust, it is the only honour
There can be for them now in Acheron.
Now go,' he said, 'and pay the last rites
To those great souls who with their blood have won
Our country for us; first to the mourning city

Of King Evander, Pallas must be sent,
For he did not lack courage, a black day
Carried him off and his was a bitter death.'
　　He wept as he spoke, then walked back to his tent
Where, by the entrance, Pallas's lifeless body
Had been laid out and old Acoetes watched by it,
He who had once been the armour-bearer
Of the Parrhasian Evander and afterwards,
With less fortunate auspices, had been made
Companion to the ward he dearly loved.
All the attendants and a crowd of Trojans,
The Ilian women with their hair dishevelled
According to the ritual of mourning,
Stood round the body. As Aeneas came
In through the high opening of the pavilion
They beat their breasts and a great lamentation
Rose to the heavens, and with the sound of mourning
The royal precincts rang. When he saw before him
Pallas's propped head, his snow-white face
And, on his smooth breast, the open wound
Made by the Ausonian spear-point, tears welled up.
'Had it to be you,' he said, 'pitiful boy,
That Fortune, when at last she smiled, denied me
And would not let you live to see my kingdom
Or to ride back in triumph to your father?
It was not this I promised to Evander
When I went from him and he sent me out
To win an empire and, as he embraced me,
Warned me in apprehension that our enemies
Were a brave people, hard men in a battle.
Now, maybe, he is full of empty hope,
Making fresh vows and piling up the altars
While we stand here with this lifeless youth
Who has no further debt to any in heaven
And whom we mourn when all honour is vain.
Unhappy king, a cruel funeral
Is all that you will see now of your son!
This is how we come back and how we triumph:
This is the way I carry out my pledge.
And yet, Evander, what you will see here
Is not a fugitive whose wounds disgrace him,

Nor are you a father who, his son safe,
Has reason to desire the sting of death.
Ausonia has lost a great protector:
Iülus, the loss is yours too.'
    When he had finished his lament, he ordered
The poor corpse to be raised on the shoulders
Of chosen troops, a thousand of whom he sent
To be with the body at the last rites
And share the father's tears, small consolation,
A debt to be paid, none the less.
Some quickly plait up a wicker bier,
Covering the high couch with a layer of leaves.
They lift the youth up on this rustic litter:
He is like a flower delicately picked
By a young girl, a tender violet
Or drooping hyacinth, whose shape and splendour
Are still unspoiled, but which the mother earth
No longer feeds, to which she gives no strength.
Aeneas then brought out two matching robes
Of purple and gold in a stiff brocade,
Work which the Sidonian Dido with her own hands
Had done delightedly for him, weaving the gold;
With one of these, as a final act of mourning,
He covers the boy's body; with the cloak
He hides that hair which soon the fire must burn;
Then, sending for a long trail of prizes
Taken from the Laurentians, he piles them up;
He adds horses and weapons which the enemy
Had yielded up to him. The prisoners
He sends as offerings to the shades below
Have their hands tied behind their backs, their blood
Is to be sprinkled on the funeral flames.
His own captains are to bear the tree-trunks
Dressed in enemy arms with the names on them.
Acoetes, bowed with age and misfortune,
Is helped along, now bruising his breast with his fists,
Now digging his nails into his cheeks
And sometimes falling and lying stretched on the ground.
They draw the chariots splashed with Rutulian blood;
After them comes Pallas's charger, Aethon,
Weeping, his face wet with monstrous tears.

They carry his spear and his shield, as for the rest,
Turnus, as victor, has them. Then there follow
A phalanx of mourners, first the Teucrians
Then all the Tuscans and Arcadians
With their arms reversed. And when the whole procession
Had gone some distance, Aeneas came to a halt.
With a deep sigh he spoke once more: 'For me
The same fates have other tears in store:
They are calling me. So now, from me, great Pallas,
Hail and farewell for all eternity.'
He said no more but turned in the direction
Of the high walls and marched towards the camp.

    Now there came spokesmen from the Latin city;
They carried olive-boughs and came as suppliants
Asking Aeneas to return the bodies
Of those the sword had left stretched on the field
And to allow them honourable burial;
There could be no contest with the defeated
Who no longer enjoyed the light of day;
Let him spare men who had entertained him
And whom he had once called his bride's people.
Aeneas was not the man not to accord
A favour it was so proper for them to ask
And he had something more to say: 'What fortune,
Which you so little deserved, involved you Latins
In this hard war, so that you shun your friends?
You ask for peace for the dead whom the chance of war
Has cut off? Why, I would give it to the living.
Had not the fates bade me to make my home here
I would not have come; I make no war on your people;
It was your king broke the laws of hospitality
And chose to trust to Turnus and his armies.
Better had Turnus faced this death himself!
If he now thinks to end this war by force,
Driving the Teucrians out, he should have tried
His weapons against mine; one of us two
Would have lived either by divine favour
Or by the courtesy of his own right hand.
But now go, and under your luckless countrymen
Set the fire alight.' As Aeneas finished

They were benumbed and silent and they stood
Looking at one another, not at him.
   Then Drances, an older man and always hostile
To Turnus, full of hatred and reproach,
Spoke up by way of answer: 'Hero of Troy,
Great in your fame and greater still in arms,
How can I praise you as highly as I should?
Is it your justice I should most admire
Or your achievements in war? We will indeed
Report with gratitude what you have said;
Let the city hear, and if fortune favours us,
You shall have king Latinus for an ally.
Let Turnus try to make his own treaty!
For our part, we shall be happy indeed
To raise the massive walls which fate ordains
And bear the stones of Troy upon our shoulders.'
All murmured their assent to what he said.
They made a twelve-day truce and in that peace
Teucrians and Latins wandered harmlessly
With one another on the wooded heights.
The sound of the two-handed axe rang out
As giant ash, and pines that touched the stars
Came down and were carried, oak and cedar
Were split with wedges and gave off their fragrance;
Creaking carts bore away the mountain trees.
   Now rumours of the mourning that was to come
Had reached Evander, filled Evander's house
And the town from wall to wall, as just before
Rumours of Pallas's triumphs in Latium
Had been borne home. Then the Arcadians
Rushed to the gates, snatching up funeral torches
Which, as the old way was, they carried with them
Making a line of flame across the fields,
Lit up on either side. The Phrygians
Advancing in procession met the mourners
To form one troop, beating their breasts and wailing,
And so approached the houses where the women,
Seeing them coming, cried aloud; the town
Was a blaze of sorrow. At this point Evander
Could no more be restrained but ran out
Into the crowd. They set the bier down;

He threw himself on the body of his son,
Clinging to him with mingled tears and moans
And hardly able to find a voice for grief:
'It is not this, Pallas, you promised me;
You were to have been more wary, trusting less
To the cruel god of war. Yet well I know
How keen, in the first martial encounters,
The sense of glory can be, and how sweet honour.
Pitiful were the first-fruits of your youth!
Hard your beginnings, with war brought so close!
And no prayer of mine heard by the gods,
My vows neglected! Ah, you were lucky, wife,
To die when you did, now set apart
And so saved from the grief I suffer here
While I have gone beyond my natural span
Only to be a father without a son.
Would it had been I with our Trojan allies,
Brought down by Rutulian spears! Would I had given
My life, and that this funeral procession
Were bringing me and not Pallas home!
Not that I blame you, Teucrians, nor our treaty,
Nor my right hand which took your proffered hand:
Destiny had this marked from the beginning
For my old age. If my son had to die
Before his time, it helps that he was leading
The Teucrians into Latium after killing
Thousands of Volscians. Nor could I wish for you,
Pallas, a nobler burial than this,
With the devout Aeneas, the great Phrygians,
The Tyrrhene captains and the Tyrrhene army.
Those you sent to their deaths have brought us trophies,
Great ones, and you, Turnus, would stand among them,
A monstrous tree-trunk decorated with arms,
If your age had been the like of Pallas's
And years had given you a like strength with his.
But why do I, in my unhappiness,
Keep Teucrians from their battles? Now you must go
And take back this message to your king:
The life I dawdle in is hateful now
Pallas is gone, it is for your right hand
To pay the debt you owe to father and son

By killing Turnus. This is the only action
Open to one of your deserts and fortune.
I do not ask for any joy in life,
The gods forbid it, only to bring some joy
To my son in his place among the Shades.'
   The dawn meanwhile had raised her kindly light
To shine on the poor world, calling men back
To toil and trouble. Along the winding shore
Aeneas now, the father of his people,
And Tarchon too, set up the funeral pyres.
To these, each in the manner of his forefathers,
They brought the bodies, starting dark fires below
Until the sky was hidden in the gloom.
Three times they marched around the blazing piles
With all their armour winking; three times
They rode their horses round the mourning fire
And from their mouths came the sound of wailing.
The earth is wet with tears, their armour is wet,
A cry goes up to heaven, and a noise of trumpets.
Here some throw spoils stripped from the slaughtered Latins
Upon the fire, helmets, beautiful swords,
Bridles and burning chariot-wheels, while some
Offer familiar gifts, the dead men's shields,
The weapons which had brought them no good fortune.
Many the bulls death claims as sacrifice,
And bristling boars and herds of cattle taken
From all the fields around, have their throats cut
To feed the flames. Then all along the shore
They watched their comrades burning, guarded the pyres
While they were half-consumed; only when night
Through the mist showed the stars blazing in the sky
Could they be torn away from where they stood.
   Elsewhere the down-hearted Latins too
Set up innumerable pyres. Some of their dead
They buried in the earth where they lay;
Some they bore off to the neighbouring fields
Or sent them to the city; all the rest,
A huge pile of indistinguishable bodies,
They burned uncounted and without honours
And all around the fields were lit up
By fires burning one against the other.

On the third morning, when the light had cleared
The cold mist from the sky, the mourners gathered
A great heap of ashes and of bones
And built a mound still warm from the fires.
But it was within doors, among the splendours
Of King Latinus' city that the noise
Was greatest and the mourning wails the loudest.
Here mothers with their sons' unhappy brides,
Sisters dear to the dead and sorrowing,
And boys who had lost their fathers, joined together
To curse the war and curse Turnus's wedding,
Demanding that he should settle things himself
With his own sword, since it was he who claimed
To be the foremost king of all Italy.
Drances, still hostile, made the point more sharply,
Confirming that Turnus alone was wanted,
That he alone was challenged by Aeneas.
Yet many people took the other side
And were in favour of Turnus, and the name
Of the great queen protected him, as also
His own reputation and the trophies he had won.

   To crown it all, into this confusion
And in the middle of the altercations,
The ambassadors came back from Diomede's city
Mourning because of the answers they had brought:
Nothing had been achieved by all their efforts;
The gifts of gold and all their urgent pleas
Have gone for nothing; all the Latins can do
Is seek for arms elsewhere, or try what peace
The Trojan king will give them. Even Latinus,
A king himself, weakens under such grief.
The anger of the gods, the recent graves
Before his eyes, give warning that Aeneas
Comes by a manifest divine intent.
Therefore Latinus summons his great council,
His foremost men are ordered to appear
In his high chamber. So they assemble,
Hurrying through crowded streets to the royal palace.
He sits there in the midst of them, the first
In age as he is first in power among them,
His face shows no pleasure. Then he orders

His spokesmen, sent back by the Aetolian city,
To speak, reporting all Diomede's replies
– The whole matter, he says, just as they had it.
All tongues are silent then, while Venulus
Begins to speak and opens the debate.
    'We have seen Diomede, fellow-countrymen,
We have seen the Argive camp and made the journey
In spite of all the difficulties on the way
And we have touched the very hand by which
The land of Ilium fell. The conqueror
In the Apulian fields of Garganus,
Was founding his new city, to be called
Argyripa, after his father's family.
As soon as we went in and were permitted
To speak, we offered the gifts we brought with us,
Told him our name and said from what country
We came, what strangers had invaded it
And for what reason we had come to Arpi.
He heard us out and then calmly replied:
    '"You peoples so fortunate as to dwell
Under Saturn's rule, you the old stock of Italy,
What fortune is it now disturbs your calm,
Persuading you to plunge yourself in wars
You understand so little? All of us
Whose swords violated the fields of Troy
– I say nothing of what sorrows we tasted
Fighting beneath her walls, nor of the men
Over whose bones the Simois still runs –
All of us, scattered over the face of the earth,
Have suffered unspeakable penalties
For the crimes we committed, even Priam
Could not but find us a pitiable band:
The sad star of Minerva, the Euboean promontory
And the avenging Caphereus know
How things were with us. After all that fighting
We were separated and cast on different coasts;
Menelaus the son of Atreus
Went as far as the pillars of Proteus
For his exile, Ulysses on the other hand
Saw the Aetnaean Cyclopes.
Why tell of Neoptolemus's kingdom

Or how the household gods of Idomeneus
Had to shift? Or how the Locrians
Come to live upon the coast of Libya?
Why, Agamemnon who led all the Greeks
Was no sooner over his own doorstep
Than he fell by the hand of his infamous queen,
Conquering Asia only to find an adulterer.
And the gods envied me my return home
To the patriarchal altars; I was not to see
The wife I longed for, nor the sweet land of Caledon.
I am pursued even now by portents
Horrible to see, my lost comrades rise
On wings to the upper air as wandering birds
(So cruel is their punishment), haunting the rivers,
Filling the cliffs with cries that sound like weeping.
These things I had to look for, from that time
When I insanely turned my sword against
Celestial limbs, and so violated
The right hand of Venus with a wound.
No indeed, no, do not try to incite me
To such battles again. Since Pergamus fell
I have finished with war against the Trojans
And when I think of the old wrongs inflicted on them
It is without pleasure. The gifts you bring me
From your country, take rather to Aeneas.
I have stood against the full force of his weapons
And fought him hand to hand: believe me,
I know what I am saying now, he rises
Gigantically behind his shield, his spear
Comes like a whirlwind when he throws it.
Had the land of Ida borne two other heroes
Like him, we should have seen the towns of Inachus
Stormed by the Trojans, Greece would then have mourned,
The fates would have changed sides. In all that time
Wasted under the stubborn walls of Troy
It was by the hands of Hector and Aeneas
That victory was kept from the Greeks
And so escaped them till the tenth long year.
Both had outstanding courage, both alike
Excellent in the management of their arms;
Aeneas had the keener sense of duty.

So make such treaties with him as you may
But do not try his arms against your own."
Now you have heard, great king, a king's reply
And know what he thinks of this heavy war.'

    The ambassadors had hardly finished speaking
When all along the line of troubled faces
A murmur ran, for the Ausonians
Were not all of a mind: it was as if
Rocks were impeding the rapid flow of a river
And the nearby banks murmured as the water
Rumbled against them in a pent-up flood.
As soon as there was calm and the restless lips
Were quiet, the king, after invoking the gods,
Began from his high throne: 'I could have wished,
Latins, to have concluded earlier
What measures we had best take for our country
And it would have been better not to call
This council at a time when the enemy
Lie all around our walls. The ceaseless war
We wage, my countrymen, is against men
Of a divine race, unconquered heroes whom
No battles tire, who even in defeat
Cannot let fall their swords. If you had hope
Of an alliance with Aetolian forces,
Abandon it. Everyone shared that hope
But you can see now how slender it was.
That our affairs otherwise are in ruins
You can see for yourself, your hands can prove.
I am not blaming anyone, what courage could do
Was done; the whole body of the kingdom
Was engaged in the conflict. But listen now:
I will tell you, though my mind is not made up,
What thoughts I have, and put the matter briefly.
There are old lands of mine on the Tuscan river,
Stretching far west beyond the Sicanian borders;
Auruncans and Rutulians farm those territories,
Ploughing the stubborn hills, grazing their flocks
Even on the roughest of them. Let the whole district
With the high stretch of pines in the mountains
Pass to the Trojans as a friendly gesture;
Let us set down the terms of a fair treaty

Inviting them into the country as allies;
Let them settle, if they like, and build their city.
But if they have a mind to go elsewhere
And try another nation, if they are free
To leave our soil, then let us build for them
A score of ships out of Italian oak;
Or if they can fill more, all the material
Is there, close by the water; they can say
The number and the kind of ships they want,
We can provide bronze, workmen, and the yards
For their construction. Further, to let them know
What we propose and settle the treaty with them,
I would have a hundred ambassadors
From the best Latin families, go to them
Holding out olive-branches in their hands
In sign of peace, talents of gold and ivory
And all the emblems of our royalty.
Now you may say what you think openly
And so help to repair our wasted fortunes.'
　　　Then Drances, hostile as he was before,
A man of envious indirections, goaded
To bitterness by the repute of Turnus,
Free with his riches, better with his tongue
But not a quick hand when it came to fighting,
Willing enough to speak up in council,
Influential in faction (his mother's rank
Gave him a proud place, but of his father
Little was known): he rose now and spoke,
Giving weight to their anger and making much of it:
　　　'The matter is clear enough to everyone,
No need for my opinion, gracious king:
All know well enough what the general good
Calls for, but yet they are reluctant to speak.
If only one of us here would pocket his pride
And leave us free to say what we think
(As I will, though he threaten me with death):
I mean the man whose luckless auspices
And perverse conduct have brought us to this pass,
With so many of the luminaries
Among our top men fallen, and the whole town
Sunk in mourning while he, confident

That he can get away, attacks the camp
Where the Trojans are and threatens heaven itself.
Add one more gift, you best of kings,
To those which you have ordered to be sent
Or promised, and let no man's violence
Get the better of you or stop you giving
Your daughter to the best of sons-in-law
In a fit marriage as a father may,
And bind the peace with an eternal treaty.
For if our hearts and minds are terrified
Let us plead with the prince himself and beg him
Of his indulgence to give way and yield
His own rights to the king and to the country.
Must you so often cast your fellow-citizens
Into such patent dangers, you who are
The source and cause of all the woes of Latium?
In war there is no safety; all of us
Demand peace from you, Turnus, and the one
Inviolable pledge which can bring peace.
I am the first to come on bended knee
– I whom you make out to be your enemy,
As I will be, if that is what you want.
Pity your own people! Put aside
Your vanity, admit you are defeated!
In retreat we have seen enough of death
And we have made great areas desolate.
Or if you want glory and really are
So stout-hearted, or so keen on a palace,
Show your courage and confidently expose
Yourself in combat with the enemy.
Are we whose lives are good for nothing, we
The crowd of the unburied and unwept,
To lie out on the fields to allow Turnus
To touch a bride who is a king's daughter?
Surely you, if you have anything in you,
Any trace of your father's war-like ways,
Will want to face the man who challenges you?'
   These words put Turnus in a blazing fury;
He gave a cry, the words that broke from him
Came from the bottom of his heart: 'Drances!
Always the same, you have plenty of talk

When the wars call for hands; when the senate is called
You are the first there. But there's no need
To fill the council-chamber with big words
Which fly from you when you are safe enough,
While piled-up walls keep off the enemy
And blood is not yet filling up the trenches.
Thunder away then with your eloquence
(Your usual way), say that I am afraid
When you, Drances, with your strong right arm
Have piled up heaps of slaughtered Teucrians
And scattered fine trophies over the field.
Whatever energy and courage can do
Is there for you to try: our enemies
Are not so far away; around the walls
They are standing everywhere. Shall we take them on?
What are you waiting for? Is Mars for you
The god of windy words and flying feet?
Always will be, perhaps.
So I am defeated? Can anyone, you louse,
Call me defeated when he sees the Tiber
Rising because swollen with Ilian blood,
The house of Evander and all his line
Brought so low, the Arcadians disarmed?
That was not how Bitias and the gigantic
Pandarus found me, nor those thousand men
Whom in a single day I sent to Tartarus,
I was the conqueror although shut up
Inside their walls, inside the enemy's ramparts.
"No safety in war!" You lunatic,
That prophecy had much better be kept
For the Dardanian's life and for your future.
But go on, upset everything with your funk,
Cry up the strength of a race twice defeated
Then say that Latin arms are good for nothing.
Now of course all the Myrmidon princes
Must tremble at the sight of Phrygian arms,
Diomede now and Achilles of Larissa!
The Aufidus retreats from the Adriatic!
And he pretends that it is quarrelling with me
That he is afraid of, devious old rascal,
And makes his charge against me worse like that!

You'll never lose a life like yours – don't worry –
By my right hand; no, keep it for yourself,
Snug in your cowardly heart. But now, father,
I turn to you and to the great matters
You lay before us. If you hope for nothing
From our arms, if we are so abandoned
And, after one reverse, have gone down
Completely and our fortune cannot change,
Let us sue for peace and hold our hands out helplessly.
Yet if we have some trace of our old courage
I should count that man fortunate
And of noble mind who, not to see such things,
Fell dying to bite the dust once and for all.
If we still have the means, young men still fit,
Cities and peoples of Italy who will help us,
If glory has come to the Trojans at the cost
Of much blood – and they too have had their dead,
The storm has blown on all of us equally –
Then why must we so shamefully give up
Just on the threshold of our enterprise?
And why before even a trumpet has sounded
Must our arms and legs begin to tremble?
Many are the things time has repaired
With effort in the course of changing years;
Many are the men whom fortune has mocked,
Now with them, now against, and in the end
Has put on solid ground again. The Aetolian
And Arpi will not be of any assistance,
But Messapus will be, and Tolumnius
Whose auguries are good, and all those captains
So many nations have sent us; no little fame
Will attend the picked men of Latium,
The Laurentines no less. There is Camilla,
Who comes from the noblest of the Volscians,
Leading her troop of horse, resplendent squadrons
In bronze armour. But if it is me alone
The Teucrians are challenging and if that
Is as you wish, and I stand in the way
Of what is good for everyone, victory
Has not disliked or yet eluded me
So much that with such great hopes as I have

I should decline to try what I can do.
I shall be in good heart when I go to meet him,
Even if he is a better man than Achilles
And wears like armour, made by Vulcan's hands.
I have vowed this life of mine to all of you
And to Latinus as my bride's father,
I, Turnus, not inferior in courage
To any of my forebears. So Aeneas
Seeks me alone. Let him seek me then,
I wish for nothing better, nor shall Drances
Go in my place, whether to satisfy
The anger of the gods by death or else
To carry the day with valour and in glory.'
    While they were occupied with this contention
Aeneas moved his men from camp to field.
The news runs through the palace, there is uproar,
It fills the city with a general terror:
The Trojans, drawn up in battle order,
And the Tyrrhene force, are bearing down on them
From the river Tiber and are all over the plain.
Immediately the minds of the common people
Are thrown into disarray, they are dumb-founded
Then roused to anger by these violent shocks.
In agitation they call for arms to be issued;
The young men shout for arms, their fathers weep
And murmur, full of grief. On every side
There is much shouting, one against the other,
It rises to the heavens, as in some grove
Of lofty trees when flocks of birds are settling,
Or as beside the mouth of the Padus
Where fish are plentiful, the raucous swans
Are heard whooping over the answering pools.
'That is it, fellow-countrymen,' says Turnus,
Seizing his moment, 'Call a council now
And sit talking of peace; the enemy, armed,
Are swarming into our territory.'
He said no more but, with a sudden movement,
Went swiftly out of the high conference hall.
'Volusus, you,' he says, 'tell the Volscian companies
To get their armour on. Take the Rutulians
As well. Messapus, the horse, all armed,

And with your brother Coras, spread them out
Widely over the plain. See that detachments
Hold the gates of the city and man the towers;
The rest will go to the attack with me,
I'll give the orders.' From all over the city
There is a rush to the walls. Old Latinus
Himself leaves the council and postpones
The weighty matters he had broached, troubled
By the sad turn of events; he blames himself
That he did not at once give a welcome
To the Dardanian Aeneas, or
Take him as a son-in-law for the city.
Before the gates, men are digging trenches
While some bring stones and stakes. The raucous trumpet
Gives the bloody call to war. Upon the walls
There appear then a miscellaneous crowd
Of women and boys; everyone is needed
For the final preparations. The queen herself
With a great crowd of matrons makes her way
Up to the temple of Pallas on the heights,
Bearing gifts. At her side walks Lavinia,
Unmarried, and the cause of all the trouble,
Her lovely eyes downcast. Having reached the temple
The matrons fill it with the smoke of incense,
Then as they stand on the high threshold utter
These sorrowing words: 'You who are strong in arms,
Lady of battles, O Tritonian maid,
Suffer the weapons of the Phrygian pirate
To snap under your hand, and cast him down,
Stretching him out before our lofty gates.'
    Eagerly meanwhile Turnus equips himself
For battle, filled with fury. Now already
He has fitted on his flaming breast-plate, bristling
With bronze scales, and enclosed his shins in gold;
He is bare-headed still, but has his sword
Buckled at his side. So, in a blaze of gold
He runs down from the high citadel,
Exultant, brave and in his mind already
He is at grips with the enemy; he is like a horse
Who, having torn the rope that tethered him,
Escapes from the stable, free at last

And with the open country all before him
Either makes for the pastures and herds of mares
Or splashes into a familiar river,
Then streaks on his delighted way, neighing,
His head held high, with his long mane
Streaming out over withers and shoulders.
    Camilla comes to meet him at a gallop,
Accompanied by all her troop of Volscians;
At the gates she leaps down from her horse,
A queen, and all her company do likewise,
Sliding from their horses to the ground.
Then she speaks to him: 'Turnus, if the brave
Have any right to trust themselves, I dare;
I undertake to face Aeneas's squadrons
And, on my own, to meet the Tyrrhene cavalry.
Allow me the first honours of the war;
Stay by the walls on foot and guard the town.'
To this Turnus, his eyes fixed upon
The undaunted girl, answered her: 'O virgin,
You who are the glory of Italy,
What thanks can I give you, how can I repay you?
But since your courage is above all thanks,
Share the command with me. Aeneas who,
As rumour had it and as spies confirm,
Has in his insolence advanced his horse,
Lightly armed, to harry us in the plains;
He is himself advancing along the ridge,
Through the steep mountain slopes where no-one is,
To take the town. It is my intention
To lay an ambush on the wooded path
Along the side of the hills, with armed men
On both sides of the defile. You meanwhile
Should meet and engage the Tyrrhene cavalry;
Messapus will be with you – he is enterprising –
With the Latin squadrons and Tiburtus's troop;
You will lead them and you are in command.'
That said, he also spoke encouragingly
To Messapus and the confederate captains
And then moved off to meet the enemy.
    There is a valley, winding as if made
For treachery and every ruse of war,

The sides press like dark walls, so dense the leaves.
The entrance is along a narrow path
In a deep gorge, the approach is forbidding.
Above all this, and where the look-outs would be
On top of the mountain, lies a concealed plain
Offering safe cover enough, whether the plan
Is to charge from the right or from the left
Or to keep to the ridge and roll down rocks.
To this point the young man made his way,
He knows the roads and soon takes possession,
Establishing himself in those nefarious woods.

Meanwhile in heaven's mansions Latona's daughter
Addressed herself to Opis the fleet of foot,
One of the virgins of her company,
One of that holy band, in these sad words:
'Camilla, dearer to me than any other,
Is off to this cruel war, assuming, Virgin,
Our arms in vain. It is not new, this love
That I, Diana, have for her, my mind
Is not moved by any sudden sweetness.
When, through his arrogant abuse of power,
Her father Metabus was driven out,
Leaving his ancient city of Privernum
He took her, still an infant, into exile
Through all the dangers of a running battle;
She was to be his companion, he would call her
After her mother, with a name like hers
Camilla, from her mother's name, Casmilla.
Carrying her folded in his breast, he sought
The long high ridges of the lonely woodlands;
On every side the Volscians pressed them hard,
Everywhere there were soldiers and cruel weapons.
Then, in his flight, her father came upon
The Amasenus in spate across his path,
Foaming from bank to bank, so great a storm
Had broken from the clouds. He made ready
To swim across but, through love of the child,
He hesitated, fearing for his dear burden.
Quickly then he reviewed all expedients
And with reluctance came to this conclusion:
He took the huge spear that he was carrying

In his strong soldier's hand – a solid weapon
Of knotted, seasoned oak – then took his daughter,
Well wrapped in wild cork bark, and cleverly
Bound her round the middle of the shaft,
Then, poising it in his great hand a moment,
Prayed: "Gracious dweller in the woods, this child
I dedicate to you, Latonian Virgin,
I who am her father; and it shall be yours,
The first weapon she holds; she flies from the enemy
Supplicating you. Accept her therefore
I beg you, as your own, as she is committed
To the uncertain wind." With that he drew
His arm far back and sent the spear spinning:
The waters roared, and over the rushing stream
Flew poor Camilla on the whizzing spear.
But Metabus, as his pursuers pressed on him,
Entrusted himself to the river then, triumphant,
Tore from the grassy turf both spear and child,
His offering to Trivia. As for himself,
No city would receive him under its roofs
Or within its walls, and he in his wildness
Would not surrender: so he passed his days
Among the shepherds upon lonely mountains.
Here, in the bushes among wild beasts' lairs
He nursed his daughter at the teats of a mare
From a roving herd, himself squeezing the milk
Between her tender lips. And when the child
Was taking her first steps with her small feet
He armed her, putting a sharp javelin
Into her hands and over her little shoulder
He slung a bow and quiver. Instead of gold
To deck her hair, and a long trailing robe,
A tiger skin hung down from her head
Over her back. Young as she was, even then
She threw toy spears and whirled around her head
A sling with smooth thongs, and so brought down
Strymonian cranes and swans white as snow.
Many a mother in the Tyrrhene towns
Uselessly longed to have her for a daughter-in-law;
Diana only could give her content;
She cultivated an eternal love

Of spears and virgin life. I wish indeed
She had not been swept into this soldiering
And that she had not tried to challenge Teucrians:
She who is dear to me would then still be
One of my company. But come now, nymph,
Since she is driven on by bitter fates,
Glide down from heaven and visit Latin country
Where with unhappy omens a sad battle
Is on the point of starting. Take these, draw
From my own quiver an avenging arrow:
Whoever, whether Trojan or Italian,
Shall violate her body with a wound
Shall in like manner pay with his own blood.
Afterwards, in the hollow of a cloud,
I will take up her body and her arms
Unspoiled to the tomb, so lay her to rest
In her own country.' Diana said no more
And Opis could be heard on her way down
Through the light air, hidden in a black storm-cloud.

The Trojan force meanwhile, the Etruscan captains,
All the cavalry marshalled in their squadrons,
Are drawing near the walls; upon the plain
Horses are stamping and whinnying a challenge,
Struggling this way and that against tight reins.
The ground is bristling with the tips of spears
Far and wide, and over the wide spaces
Uplifted weapons blaze. Over against them
Messapus and the fast-moving Latins,
With his brother Coras and Camilla's wing,
Come into view and face them,
Their right arms drawn back in readiness;
The advancing men and the neighing horses
Sweep on like fire. But now within a spear's throw
Of one another, both the armies halt:
Then with a sudden shout they break loose,
Urging their maddened horses; at the same instant
From all sides there is a shower of weapons
Falling like snow-flakes; the whole sky is shadowed.
Immediately Tyrrhenus and Aconteus
From opposite sides charge fiercely with their spears;
They are the first to meet and go down

With a loud crash, their animals collide
Chest against chest and fall; Aconteus
Is thrown off like a thunderbolt, or a stone
From some great engine, he flies through the air,
His last breath falling from him as he goes.
    At once the lines are thrown into confusion;
The Latins sling their shields over their backs,
Wheel their horses and make for the walls.
The Trojans, with Asilas at the head,
Pursue them, still in squadrons, but the Latins,
Once near the gates, again raise a shout
And pull their horses round; the Trojans retreat;
With a loose rein they are carried back again
Far to the rear: it is as when the sea,
With waves now advancing, now retreating,
First rushes in to land, breaking over rocks
With boiling waves, and runs on to the sand,
Drenching the furthest inlets,
Then rapidly runs back again, with the surge
Sucking out loose pebbles as it retreats
To leave the shore covered with ebbing shallows.
Twice the Tuscans drove the Rutulians
Flying back to the city; twice, repulsed,
They looked round and slung shields over their backs.
But the third time the two lines came together
They stood interlocked and man marked man,
And then indeed there were groans from the dying
As, deep in blood, arms and bodies pell-mell
Of men and horses only half alive
Wriggled in confused slaughter: the fighting was rough.
Orsilochus, not daring to approach Remulus,
Whirled his spear at his horse and left the point
Under the animal's ear; his chest thrown forward,
He threw his forelegs high into the air;
Remulus was thrown and rolled on the ground.
Catillus brought down Iollas, and Herminius
Whose courage was not less than his giant frame
And giant arms; a shock of yellow hair
Covered his bare head, his shoulders were bare;
Wounds did not frighten him, so powerful
He was against attack. Yet now a spear

Is driven through his shoulders, broad as they are,
And he is doubled up, transfixed by pain.
Dark blood flows everywhere as struggling men
Work with their swords to kill and in their turn
Are killed, finding the glorious death they seek.
   But through the middle of this slaughter rides
The Amazon, with one breast bared for the fight,
Camilla with her quiver at her side:
And now her hand sends showers of javelins,
Now with no sign of weariness she seizes
A powerful battle-axe; her golden bow
Twangs from her shoulder with Diana's weapons:
Even when she is forced to withdraw,
Turning her bow, she looses arrows in flight.
Her chosen virgin comrades all around her,
Larina, Tulla, and Tarpeia wielding
A bronze axe, daughters of Italy,
Were chosen by the divine Camilla herself
As maids of honour who are fit to serve
Either in peace or war: they resemble
The Thracian Amazons who gallop across
The streams of Thermodon in their brilliant armour
When they are warring, whether as attendants
Upon Hippolyta, or when accompanying
Penthesilea, daughter of Mars, as she
Rides back from war in triumph in her chariot
And with tumultuous cries her army of women
Exult, raising aloft their crescent shields.
   Whom did you first bring down with your spear,
Ferocious virgin, and who was the last?
Euneus, son of Clytius was the first,
He faced her with his breast unprotected,
She stuck her spear through him. As he fell
Rivers of blood flowed from his mouth, the ground
He bit was bloody; he turned upon his wound
As he lay dying. Then she brought Liris down
And Pegasus on top of him: the former
Rolled from his horse as the beast was stabbed
And as he gathered up the reins, the other
Held out his free hand to break his fall
And both went down together. After them

She killed Amastrus, son of Hippotas,
And lunging forward with her spear pursued
Tereus, Harpalycus and Demophöon
And Chromis; every dart from her hand
Brought down a Phrygian. Some way off Ornytus,
A hunter, unfamiliar with war,
Rode on an Iapygian mount; he fought
With only a bullock's hide on his broad shoulders,
His head was covered with the head of a wolf
With gaping jaws and white teeth, his hand
Bore nothing but a kind of country weapon;
He rode in the middle of his troop
But showed head and shoulders above the rest.
She caught him (and it was not difficult,
The troop was in retreat) then stuck him through
And standing over him she spoke to him
With all the malice of an enemy:
'Did you think you were still in the forest
Chasing wild beasts, you Tyrrhene? The day has come
When all the big talk of you and yours
Will find its answer in a woman's weapons.
Yet it is not a light boast you will make
Among the shades of your ancestors:
It was Camilla's spear that brought me down.'
    Then she killed Butes and Orsilochus,
Two of the toughest of the Teucrians:
Butes she caught on her spear-point from behind,
Between his corselet and his helmet, where
A rider's neck shows white and his shield hangs
From his left arm below. Orsilochus
She first retreats from, chased in a wide circle,
And so eludes him, and then she pursues him
Catching up with him in a smaller circle.
Rising up in her stirrups, she drives her axe
Powerfully, more than once, through armour and bones,
However much he begs for mercy; the wound she gives
Is such that she spatters his face with his brains.
Then suddenly the warrior son of Aunus,
Who lives upon the Apennine, crosses her path
And stands stock still in terror, seeing her;
He was not the least of the Ligurians

While he had breath to lie. And when he saw
That he could not in any way escape
Nor stop the queen from bearing down on him,
He tried what trickery and cleverness
Could do and started with this little speech:
'What is so wonderful if you, a woman,
Have a great horse and trust yourself to him
To get away from me? Try giving him up
And see how we get on then hand to hand
On equal terms; you will learn soon enough
Whom windy vanity will bring to earth.'
That's what he said to her and it made her smart
But, furious, she handed her horse over
To one of her companions and then faced him
With the same weapons as he had, standing there
With naked sword and ordinary shield.
The young man thought he had won by trickery
And darted away without a moment's pause;
Pulling the reins round sharply, he spurred his animal
Into a gallop and fled. The virgin screamed:
'Fool of a Ligurian, it is no good
To be so proud of yourself, you will get nothing
By trying all your family tricks on me;
Cheating will never take you back safe and sound
To the liars of Aunus.' Then, moving like lightning,
She threw herself across his horse's path,
Faced him and seized his reins, and so her vengeance
Took its due measure of her enemy's blood
As easily as when Apollo's bird,
The falcon, flying from a lofty rock,
Follows a dove high up into a cloud
And, having caught it, claws its innards out
While bloody feathers float down to earth.

All this does not escape the watchful eye
Of him who sows the seeds of men and gods,
As he sits high on the top of Olympus.
He rouses Tarchon the Tyrrhene to go
Where the battle is fiercest, driving him
To anger with cruel goads. So, among the slaughter
And among the wavering troops, Tarchon rides on,
Encouraging his squadrons, calling out

A word here, a word there, each hears his name
And beaten men are summoned back to battle.
'What are you afraid of? You're a shameless lot,
Always lazy, you Tyrrhenes, now this cowardice
Has taken hold of you. A woman scatters you
Like a lot of sheep and in the wrong direction!
What do we have swords for? What are these spears
Doing in our right hands? You are quick enough
To get to Venus in nocturnal battles
Or be there when the curved whistle sounds
For Bacchic dances. Think about feasts
With cups on loaded tables (these are the things
You really care about) while you await
The seer who will announce the good omen
And the fat sacrifice is waiting for you
Deep in the groves.' With that he spurred his horse
Into the thick of the fight, he faced death
Willingly enough himself: like the wind
He charged straight at Venulus and snatched him,
Enemy as he was, from the back of his horse
And hugged him to his breast with his right arm,
Applied the spurs and so carried him off.
A shout rose to the heavens and all the Latins
Turned their eyes to the spectacle. Tarchon then
Flew over the flat ground carrying before him
Both the man and the arms, and broke off
The iron tip of his spear, then felt about
For exposed parts on which he could inflict
A deadly wound: his enemy, still struggling,
Kept his hand from his throat, with all his strength
Trying to keep this violence at a distance.
And as when a tawny eagle, soaring upwards,
Carries a captured serpent, tangling its feet
And gripping the snake with its claws, the wounded creature
Writhes and turns its coils and all its scales
Rise erect and hisses come from its mouth
As it raises its head; the eagle meanwhile
Attacks its victim with its crooked beak
And beats the air with its wings: just so Tarchon
Bears off his prey from the Tiburtian lines
With a triumphant swoop; both his example

And his success are followed by the Tyrrhenes
As they attack. Then Arruns, whom the fates
Have claimed already, circles around Camilla,
Swift though she is, and with dexterity
Anticipates her movements, poising his javelin
And trying to place himself at an advantage.
Wherever the virgin in her fury rushes
Among the ranks, Arruns approaches her
And silently keeps close on her tracks:
Where she has had a victory and withdraws,
The young man stealthily pulls his horse's head round;
He tries first one approach and then another,
Covering the whole circuit from every side
And all the while in his relentless hand
The inevitable spear quivers in readiness.
   It happened that Chloreus, dedicated
To Cybele, whose priest he once was,
Came into sight, far off but conspicuous
In Phrygian armour which flashed as he rode
Spurring his foaming horse which was protected
By leather covered with bronze scales like feathers,
And with a clasp of gold. Chloreus himself
Was brightly dressed in a strange reddish purple;
Gortynian arrows flew from his Lycian bow
Which gleamed at his shoulder decked with gold;
Golden too was the helmet the seer wore;
His saffron cloak with rustling linen folds
Was fastened in a knot with a golden clasp;
His tunic and barbarian hose were decorated
By gold embroidery. The virgin who
Perhaps hoped to hang up Trojan arms
Upon a temple gate or saw herself
Dressed up in golden trophies, went in pursuit
As recklessly as if she had been out hunting
And tore through the intervening ranks
With all the fury of a woman set
On spoil and plunder: when, at last,
Seizing a moment when he was not in view,
Arruns let fly his spear with this prayer:
'Greatest of gods, Apollo, whom we worship
Before all others, guardian of Soracte

The holy mountain; feeding your blazing flames
With heaps of pines we, as your votaries,
In our devotion pass through the fire,
Walking bare-footed on the glowing embers;
Grant, father, that this shame be taken from us
And from our arms, Omnipotent. As for me,
I seek no spoils, no trophies from the virgin:
I look to other deeds to make me famous;
If only this intolerable plague
Fall by a wound I give her, I will go
Back to my native city without honour.'
   Phoebus heard and, although he gave no sign,
Granted the prayer in part, but for the rest
He scattered it among the flying winds:
That he who made the prayer should see Camilla
Fall in a sudden death and by his hand,
That much he would admit: but that the killer
Should be seen back in his proud country, that
He would not grant, that plea was borne away
By squalls to lose itself in the south wind.
As the spear Arruns threw whizzed through the air
The Volscians all immediately thought of the queen
And turned their eyes on her, but she herself
Was quite oblivious to the stir in the air
And of the sound of the spear as it passed through the sky
Till, carried to its destination, it stuck
Under her naked breast and, driven deep,
Drank up her virgin blood. Then, anxiously,
Her comrades flocked round to support their mistress
As she was falling. Arruns, more moved than any,
Part with joy, part with fear, made his escape,
Trusting his weapons no further, and afraid
To face those of the virgin. And as a wolf
When he has killed a shepherd or great bullock
Does not wait for the avenging weapons
Which must follow but, without hesitation,
Makes off into the mountains, avoiding paths,
Knowing he has been reckless, tail between legs,
And tries to get to the forest: just so Arruns,
Troubled by what he has done, steals away
From observation, flight is enough for him now,

And tries to lose himself among the fighting.
Camilla, who is dying, tugs at the spear
But the iron point is fixed between her ribs,
The wound is deep. She is limp through lack of blood,
Her eyes begin to close in the chill of death
And the once rosy colour leaves her cheeks.
As she expires she says some words to Acca,
A girl of her own age in whom she trusts
Above all others, and who is her confidante:
'So far, Acca my sister, I have managed;
This bitter wound has now finished me
And all around grows black. Make your escape
And bear my last commissions straight to Turnus:
Let him take over now and save the city.
And now, good-bye.' The reins fell from her grasp
As she was speaking, she slid helplessly
Down to earth. She was cold; little by little
She freed herself entirely from her body,
Her neck relaxed as she lay down her head,
A prisoner to death, yielding her arms.
Her spirit with a groan fled bitterly
To the Shades below. At once an immense shout
Went up and struck the golden stars: Camilla
Was dead, the fight grew fiercer, all the Trojans,
The Tyrrhene nobles, with Evander's squadrons
Concentrated their forces and rushed forward.
   But Opis, as Diana's sentinel,
Had long been seated on a mountain-top
From which she watched the battle unafraid.
When, amidst all the shouts of fighting men,
She saw far off Camilla done to death,
She groaned and from the bottom of her heart
Spoke these words: 'Alas, virgin, you have paid
Too great a price for your attempt to challenge
The Teucrians in battle. All for nothing
Have you served Diana in the wilds
And worn her sacred quiver on your shoulder.
Yet your queen has not left you comfortless
Even in the throes of death, nor will this death
Be without reputation among men,
Nor will they say that you died unavenged.

Whoever it was who violated your body
By wounding you, will pay for it with his life.'
At the foot of the mountain stood a mound,
The massive tomb of king Dercennius,
Shaded by a dark ilex; the lovely goddess
Took a rapid leap and stood on top of it
And thence she saw at once where Arruns was.
As she caught sight of him, pleased with himself
And puffed with vanity, she said: 'Why go
So far out of your way? You should be here:
Come here and perish, take your due reward
For the death of Camilla. Even you
Are to die by the weapons of Diana.'
With that the Thracian drew a winged arrow
From her gilded quiver and then bent her bow
To its full extent, so that the tips of it
Met and she, with her hands level, touched
The iron point with the left, and with the right
Holding the string of her bow, she touched her breast.
At the same moment Arruns heard the whistle
Of the flying arrow, with a twang in the air
And the point pierced his body. Him his comrades
Paid no attention to but left him dying,
Moaning with his last breath, up on the plain
Among the unknown dust; Opis flew off,
Borne through the air up to the heights of Olympus.
    Meanwhile, to Turnus waiting in the woods
Acca brings bitter news of all this tumult,
His mind is full of it: the Volscian lines
Destroyed, Camilla dead, the enemy
Beside themselves and carrying all before them
Victoriously, fear reaching even the town.
He, in a rage (the merciless divinity
Of Jove himself demands no less) deserts
His ambush in the hills and leaves the forest
To its own wildness. Hardly out of sight
Was he, hardly down on the level, when
The great Aeneas entered the open pass,
Crossed the ridge and emerged from the dark wood.
So both were soon moving towards the walls,
At speed, with all their forces, and little distance

Between the armies; at the same moment
That Aeneas from afar had his first view
Of the plains smoking with dust and saw before him
The columns of Laurentians, Turnus recognised
The relentless Aeneas in arms, heard the tramp of feet
And the breathing of the horses. They would at once
Have come to grips and tried their luck in battle
Had Phoebus not brought his horses down
Tired to the rosy seas towards Iberia
And, as day slipped away, brought in the night.
They camped before the town and built defences.

# BOOK XII

# BOOK XII

When Turnus saw the Latins crushed and broken
By their reverses, all staring at him,
Demanding he should be as good as his word,
He blazed up more, his anger was implacable
As were his pride and courage. He was like a lion
In Punic country who, wounded to the heart
By hunters, only then begins to show
What fight he has in him, and joyfully
Tosses his mane over his muscular neck
Then, with no sign of fear, snaps off the weapon
The rascal has planted in him, and roars
From a mouth dripping with blood; so Turnus was,
Alight with growing violence. Recklessly
He spoke to the king: 'It certainly is not Turnus
Who is hanging back; there is no need for them,
Those cowards that Aeneas has as followers
To take back what they said and wriggle out
Of the engagement; I will fight him now.
So, father, let the holy rites begin
And announce the terms. Either my own right hand
Shall, while the Latins sit and watch this Dardan
On the run from Asia, send him down to Tartarus
And so refute the charge of cowardice
They bring against us all – so, with my sword;
Or, if I fail, then let him have us, vanquished,
And let him take Lavinia as his bride.'
  Latinus was unmoved and answered quietly:
'Young man, you show outstanding courage, but
The more you show your mettle, the more necessary
It is for me to think what would be best
And to weigh doubtfully all that might happen.
You have a kingdom from your father Daunus
And many towns your own hand has taken;

Latinus too has gold and is open-handed.
There are in Latium and in Laurentine country
Other unmarried girls not of low birth.
Let me then tell you what is in my mind
Although it is not easy for me to say it:
I will conceal nothing, you for your part
Take to heart what I say: it was not for me
– So all the gods and all men declared –
To match my child with any of her old wooers.
My love of you prevailed so far, so far
The claims of kin and my own wife's tears
That I made light of all my obligations:
I stole the promised bride from her betrothed
And took up arms in an unrighteous cause.
What ill fortunes have followed me since then,
What wars, you can see, Turnus, for yourself,
For you have been the first to bear the brunt.
Twice beaten in great battles we could hardly,
Even in the city, see hope for Italy;
The Tiber more than once warmed with our blood
And the vast plains are still white with our bones.
Why am I so driven from pillar to post?
What mad thoughts make me change my mind? For if
With Turnus dead, I would accept these allies,
Why should I not instead end our contention
While he is safe and sound? What would your kinsmen
The Rutulians say, or the rest of Italy
If – and may fortune will it otherwise –
I sent you to your death when you were asking
To marry my daughter? Think how fortunes shift
In war; have pity on your aged father
Already sorrowing because he is parted from you
In distant Ardea, his home and yours.'
     The violence of Turnus is not lessened
– Far from it – by these words; indeed, it mounts,
It is as if the medicine makes him sick.
When he could speak again, he started thus:
'I beg you, sir, have no concern for me,
But let me make the bargain, death or honour.
My spears have points and I can send them flying
And they draw blood as well as anyone's.

His goddess-mother won't be there with a cloud
To hide him this time when he runs away
And it is no good wrapping up in shadows.'
    But the queen, whom this new turn of events
Dismayed, was weeping. As if she foresaw
Her own death, she embraced the intemperate youth
She meant to have as son-in-law: 'Turnus,'
She said, 'If these my tears mean anything
Or if you feel any trace of respect
For me, Amata, you who are our one hope,
The comfort of my miserable old age,
On whom rest all the glory and the sovereignty
Of Latium, and the future of our house,
One thing I beg of you: avoid the Trojans.
Whatever dangers there may be for you
In such a conflict, Turnus, are mine too:
For I will not outlive the hateful day
When I, a captive, see Aeneas here
And have to take him for a son-in-law.'
Lavinia heard her mother's voice, and tears
Ran down her burning cheeks on which blushes
Flamed up and spread all over her glowing face.
It was as when someone stains Indian ivory
With crimson dye, or when a bunch of lilies
Reddens because a rose is set among them.
The girl showed just such colours on her face.
Turnus fixed his eyes on her, love confused him.
He was the hotter for war, and had few words
When he addressed Amata: 'Do not, mother,
For heaven's sake send me out to a battle
Testing as this one must be, with your tears,
They are ill-omened; it is not for Turnus
To put off death if that is what fate intends.
Idmon, go now and give the Phrygian king
This message which he will not want to have:
Tomorrow, when the crimson dawn rolls out
And the sky reddens, he is not to send
His Teucrians out to fight against Rutulians;
Teucrians can rest and the Rutulians too;
We two will settle this with our own blood:
Whoever wins shall have Lavinia.'

That said, he rapidly went into the palace
And called for horses: he was glad indeed
When he saw them there snorting before his eyes;
They were the same that Orithyia herself
Gave to do honour to Pilumnus, whiter
Than snow they were and faster than the wind.
The charioteers stood by them eagerly,
Patting their great chests resoundingly
With hollowed hands, and combing out their manes.
Turnus himself threw over his shoulders
His corselet stiff with gold and palest bronze;
He fixes on the sword he is to use,
His shield and the red plumes of his helmet;
The sword is the one the smoky Vulcan
Had forged especially for his father Daunus
And tempered sizzling in the Styx. He then
Violently snatched up his powerful spear
Which leaned against a column in the hall
– Spoil of Auruncan Actor – and he shook it
So that it quivered, and as he did so shouted:
'Now, my spear, you have never failed me yet,
Now is the time! Great Actor carried you,
Now Turnus has you in his hand. Enable me
To bring this half-man's body to the ground,
Pierce his corselet, that I may rip it off
With this strong hand, and foul in the dust
Those Phrygian locks, arranged with curling irons,
And swamped with scent.' He is possessed by furies,
It is as if his whole face gave off sparks;
Fire flashes from his eager eyes: as a bull
Anxious to go into battle, utters
Terrifying bellows and, willing his anger
Into his horns, charges the trunks of trees
And throws his head in the air to toss the winds,
Stamping the sand before the fight begins.
   Meanwhile Aeneas, cruelly armed already
With those arms which were his mother's gift,
Whetted his appetite for war, his anger
Roused, glad at the challenge and the terms
Which had been offered to conclude the war.
He re-assured his comrades and he comforted

Iülus who was grieved, telling them everything
That the fates had in store. Then he gave orders
For clear replies to go to King Latinus
Declaring his conditions for the peace.

   The dawn of the next day had hardly scattered
Its light upon the mountain-tops; the sun
Had hardly brought his horses up from the sea
Breathing out brilliance from their expanded nostrils:
Rutulians and Teucrians were making preparations,
Pacing out distances on the flat ground
Below the great city walls where the fight was to be,
Setting the hearths and the grassy altars
For the gods both parties worshipped.
Some, decked in ritual aprons, with their brows
Bound in verbena, brought spring-water and fire.
The legions of Ausonia moved out,
Pouring through the city gates in close formation.
From the other side came all the Trojan army
In quick time, and all the Tyrrhenes too
With a variety of arms, in battle order
As if they were indeed to fight that day,
The captains, splendid in their gold and purple
Darting among the thousands of their troops:
Mnestheus of the house of Assaracus,
The valiant Asilas, and then Messapus
The tamer of horses and the son of Neptune.
At a given signal both parties retired
To their own ground; they stuck their spears in the earth
And set their shields against them The mothers then
And all the crowd of the unarmed, streamed out,
With old men who no longer had their strength;
They took possession of the towers and roof-tops
While others stood above the lofty gates.

   But Juno, from the top of that small hill
Known as the Alban now, though in those days
It had no name, no honour and no glory,
Was watching, looking out over the plain,
The twin arrays of Laurentine and Trojan
And the city of Latinus. It was thus
That she addressed herself to Turnus's sister,
A goddess speaking without hesitation

To the goddess who presided over pools
And sounding rivers: for the king of heaven,
Jupiter himself, had consecrated her
To that high honour for the innocence
He had taken from her: 'Nymph, splendour of rivers,
Most pleasing to my mind, to you alone
Of all the Latin virgins who have graced
The insatiable bed of the magnanimous Jove
Have I so given preference that a place
In heaven itself was not too much for you:
Juturna, lest you should reproach me now,
Learn from me of the grief that must be yours.
While Fortune seemed to bear with it, the Fates
Allowed Latium to have her sovereignty
And I protected Turnus and the city;
But now I see the young man in a struggle
To which his destinies must be unequal;
His last day and a hostile power draw near.
I cannot turn my eyes towards this battle
Nor towards the pact which it must consummate.
If you dare anything which yet may favour
Your brother, do it; it is proper that you should.
Perhaps there is a better time ahead.'

  Juno had scarcely finished, when Juturna
Burst into tears and three or four times
She struck her hand against her noble breast.
'This is no time for tears,' Saturnian Juno
Spoke again: 'Hurry, if there is any way
Of doing it, rescue your brother from death,
Or start the battle but abort the treaty.
Be daring, I tell you.' With this exhortation
She left Juturna to her indecision,
Troubled in mind by these heavy blows.

  Meanwhile the kings – Latinus in great pomp
In a chariot with four horses, with his temples
Blazingly circled by twelve golden rays
To indicate his solar ancestry;
Turnus with two white horses, in his hand
Waving two spears with broad points of iron;
From the other side, our ancestor Aeneas,
The origin of all our Roman stock,

With burnished starry shield and god-like weapons,
Ascanius next to him, Rome's other hope –
They issued from their camps: meanwhile a priest
In spotless robe has brought a young pig
Sired by a bristling boar and, yet unshorn,
A two-year sheep: these animals he sets
Beside the flaming altars. The two kings,
Turning their eyes towards the rising sun,
Sprinkled the salty meal and, with their swords,
Marked the heads of the victims and, from goblets,
Upon the altars poured libations. Then,
His sword still drawn, the devout Aeneas prayed:
'Be witness now to me who pray to you,
Sun, and this earth for which I have been able
To carry out such labours, and you, Father
Omnipotent – and you, Saturnia
His consort, now be kindlier, O goddess,
Now I pray; and you, renowned Mavors
Under whose power, as under a father's hand
The fortunes of war turn; springs and rivers
I call on too, and all that may be worshipped
In high heaven, and all the influences
In the blue seas: if by chance victory
Should fall to Turnus the Ausonian
It is our compact that we who are vanquished
Retire to Evander's city; Iülus
Shall leave these fields and never afterwards
Shall any of the followers of Aeneas
Take arms again to fight against this kingdom.
But if it is on me that victory smiles
– As so the case may rather be, I think,
And may the gods rather confirm this outcome! –
I shall not then expect Italians
To take their orders from the Teucrians,
Nor do I seek to make this realm my own:
But let the two nations, both unconquered,
Together and on equal terms contract
A league between them which shall last for ever.
The gods and their appurtenances be mine:
The arms shall be Latinus's affair,
My father-in-law's; and as my father-in-law

He shall have all his due authority.
The Teucrians shall build me a new city
To which Lavinia shall give her name.'
  So spoke Aeneas first; Latinus followed,
Looking up at the sky, his right hand
Stretched upwards to the stars: 'I swear, Aeneas,
By this same earth and sea, by these same stars,
By sun and moon, and by the two-faced Janus,
By the infernal powers and the domain
Of the implacable Dis: may the great Father
Who guards our treaties with his thunderbolt
Hear what I say. My hand upon the altar,
I declare by these fires and deities
Now set between us, no passage of time
Shall break this peace for the Italians,
This pact shall stand whatever may befall;
No force shall ever turn my will aside,
No, not if it should cast the dry land
Into the sea, confusing waves and floods
And melt the heavens in Tartarus:
As this sceptre' (with that he indicated
The sceptre in his hand) 'shall never more
Put forth new twigs or leaves or offer shade,
Now that it lacks a mother, being cut off
From the stock below, and shorn of all its growth;
Once a great branch, it has now been enclosed
By the artificer's skill in seemly bronze,
To be borne in the hand of Latin senators.'
  But the Rutulians thought the fight unequal;
It had long seemed so to them, this way and that
Their minds swayed in confusion; the more now
As they see how ill-matched the armies are.
Advancing quietly with downcast eyes
And standing as a suppliant at the altar,
Turnus adds to the trouble; there he is
With wasted cheeks, his youthful form pallid.
His sister Juturna saw how things stood,
The talk spreading, the crowd in many minds;
Immediately she went among the army,
Appearing in the shape of Camers, who
Came from a race of great ancestors;

His father bore a famous name for courage
And he himself was valiant in arms.
Into the middle of the army she went,
Knowing what she should do, and started rumours,
This and that, then she spoke more at large:
'Rutulians, oh! and are you not ashamed
To throw away one life for such as we are?
You see before you all the Trojans: there are
All the Arcadians too, with the Etruscans,
Prophetic bands of those hostile to Turnus
Why, if only every other man of us were here
We should not find an enemy apiece.
Fame will raise Turnus to the gods, whose altars
He stands before, and dedicates himself,
And he will live upon the lips of men:
But we, when we have let our country go,
Shall find ourselves forced to obey proud masters
Yet now we dawdle here and are indifferent.'
    Such words as these made the young men hot-headed;
Now more and more a murmur makes its way
Through the ranks like a snake; the Laurentines
Were changed by it, they and the Latins too.
Those who had hoped only to rest from battle
And find some safety for their own affairs
Want now to take up arms, their prayer is
The treaty should be called off, they pity
Turnus and find the part allotted to him
Is less than fair. To these considerations
Juturna adds a weightier; she produces
A sign high in the heavens, than which nothing
Could more affect the minds of the Italians,
It is a cheating portent. Through the red sky
The tawny bird of Jove flew in pursuit
Of waterfowl in noisy disarray,
A winged troop, when suddenly he swooped
Down to the water and rapaciously
Seized a fine swan, lifting it in his talons.
Then the Italians were all attention
As all the birds wheeled clamorously, they marvelled;
The sky was dark with wings and in a cloud
They flew to mob their enemy in the air;

The eagle, such was the weight of the assault,
Gave way, defeated, and so dropped its prey
Into the river and escaped into clouds.
    Then indeed the Rutulians saluted
The omen with a shout, spreading their hands out
To indicate their readiness to fight.
Tolumnius the augur was the first to speak:
'This is what I was waiting for,' he said,
'This is what I was praying for. I accept.
The hand of the gods is in it; I will lead you,
Take up your swords, you who have fared so ill,
Whom a rapacious alien terrifies
With the ravages of war along your coasts
As if you were a flock of strengthless birds.
He too will flee, and out across the deep
Will spread retreating sails. Now altogether,
Close your ranks, now is the time for battle,
Your king is being snatched away, defend him!'
    Having said this, running forward he hurled
His spear straight at the enemy; the shaft
Gave out a piercing whistle as it cut
A sure course through the air. At the same moment
A great shout went up from the ranked spectators,
All in confusion now, boiling with fury.
The spear flew on to where it chanced its path
Was blocked by the handsome figures of nine brothers,
All born of one faithful Tuscan wife
To the Arcadian Gylippus: one
Was struck, the spear pierced him through the middle,
Near where the buckle of his belt tightened
Against his belly; he was a fine lad
In gleaming armour, the spear went through his ribs
And stretched him out upon the yellow sand.
His brothers then, a spirited company,
Were set alight by grief: some drew their swords,
Some gripped their spears, all rushed blindly forwards.
The columns of Laurentians ran to meet them
While from the other side there came a flood
Of Trojans, Agyllines and, with painted armour,
Arcadians, a single thought in their minds,
That only arms could now decide the matter.

They stripped the altars of the burning brands
And the whole sky was darkened by their spears
Which fell like iron rain. The sacred bowls
And flames are carried away, Latinus himself
Makes off, carrying his insulted gods,
The pact not honoured. The rest bring out their chariots
Or jump into their saddles and at once
Are on the spot with their swords at the ready.
    Messapus, eager that the truce be broken,
Turns his horse threateningly towards Aulestes,
A Tyrrhene king wearing his insignia:
The king starts back, his head and shoulders reel
Back on the altars behind. Hot after him
Messapus follows, his spear in his hand,
High on his horse, and strikes him from above
In spite of all his pleas – a heavy blow
With an enormous weapon – then he says:
'That's it, for him, and he's a better victim
To give to the great gods!' Then the Italians
Crowd round and strip his body while it is warm.
Corynaeus snatches a charred brand from the altar
And, crossing Ebysus's path as he comes up
To aim a blow, pushes flames in his face
And sets his massive beard alight; well-singed,
It gives a smell of charring. Following this
He seizes with his other hand the forelock
Of his bewildered enemy, then jerking
His knee forces his body to the ground
And whips a rigid sword into his side.
Podalirius, pursuing the shepherd Alsus
As he charges with the front line of attackers
Through a shower of darts, towers over him
With his naked sword, but Alsus, swinging his axe,
Faces him and splits him brow to chin
So that the blood is pouring over his armour.
An iron sleep, a merciless repose
Fall on his eyes, they close into endless night.
    Aeneas, conscious of the gods, stretched out
His right hand unarmed and stood bare-headed,
Calling out to his men: 'Where are you off to?
What is the meaning of this sudden quarrel?

Control your anger! We have made a truce
And all the terms are settled: I alone
Have the right to do battle, so allow me.
Forget your fears: I will make good the treaty
With my own hand; for by these sacred rites
Turnus must fall to me.' But as he spoke,
Before he had even finished, see, an arrow,
A whizzing arrow flew in his direction,
Sent by what hand, or through what confusion,
Remains uncertain, as, too, who it was,
Whether chance or a god, which brought this honour
To the Rutulians: it was a secret glory,
No-one could boast that he had wounded Aeneas.
    When Turnus saw Aeneas drawing back
Out of the ranks, his captains in confusion,
A sudden hope burned in him: he called for horses
And in a flash he jumped into his chariot
And gathered up the reins. As he swept on,
Many and many were the strong bodies of men
He gave to Death; many a man sent flying
Half-dead, and ranks were crushed under his wheels;
He seized spears as he went and sent them after
Those in retreat before him. He is like Mavors
Beside the waters of the icy Hebrus,
Bloody and banging on his shield, beating up war,
As he lets his horses go, and on the wide plain
They fly before the south wind and the west wind
And farthest Thrace whimpers under their hoof-beats,
While all around him gabble faces of Fear,
Anger and Trickery, who attend the god:
Just so Turnus eagerly lashes his horse
Smoking with sweat as he rides through the battle,
Trampling upon enemies pitiably slain:
The swift hooves scatter blood like dew
And turn up gore with sand. Already Death
Has had the gift of Sthenelus, Thamyrus,
Pholus – the two latter killed hand-to-hand,
The first speared from a distance; from a distance too
Glaucus and Lades, both sons of Imbrasus,
Boys whom Imbrasus himself had brought up
In Lycia and equipped with matching weapons

To fight either on foot or on horseback
On animals which could outstrip the wind.
   In another part of the field Eumedes
Rides into the thick of the battle; famous in war,
He is the son of old Dolon and he bears
His grandfather's name; in heart and hand he is
His father over again, who once demanded
As a reward for spying out the Greek camp
The chariot of Peleus's son: but for his daring
The son of Peleus gave him something else
And he no longer wanted Achilles' horses.
When Turnus, from a distance, saw he was there
On the open plain, he sent his light spear after him
Through the intervening space; pulled up his horses
Then jumped out of his chariot and came down
Upon a falling man already dying
And, with his foot upon his neck, wrenched
The sword from his hand and deep in his throat
Coloured the glittering blade with the man's blood,
Adding a comment: 'So there, Trojan, you have
The ground you wanted when you went to war;
Lie there, you have the measure of Hesperia.
That is the prize for those who dare to taste
My sword: and so it is they found their city.'
Then throwing his spear once again he sent
Asbytes to keep him company,
Then Chloreus and Sybaris, with Dares,
Thersilochus, Thymoetes – this last thrown
Over the head of his bucking horse.
And as the breath of the Edonian north
Roars on the deep Aegean and compels
The waves to shore, and as the wind sweeps down
The clouds chase through the sky: so Turnus is;
Wherever he cuts a path the line gives way
And the ranks turn and run; his impetus
Carries him on, his crest shakes in the breeze
That meets his chariot. It was too much for Phegeus,
This furious progress, and he threw himself
Against the chariot and with his right hand
He wrenched aside the heads of the maddened horses.
While he was dragged on, hanging to the yoke,

The spear-head found his unprotected side
And broke the double corselet, where it stuck,
Giving the body a light lick of a wound.
Phegeus, his shield in place, turned on his enemy
And tried to help himself with his drawn sword.
But a wheel sent him headlong as it whirled
Swiftly forward, and threw him on the ground.
Turnus then followed up and with his sword
Between the bottom rim of the helmet
And the top of the breast-plate, took his head off
And left the trunk lying upon the sand.
  While, on the field, Turnus brings death to many,
Mnestheus and the reliable Achates,
Ascanius with them, bring Aeneas to camp,
Bleeding, and resting every other step
On his long spear. He is in a rage, and tries
To pull the arrow with the broken shaft
Out of his side, and calls upon his friends
To deal with it the quickest way they can;
Cut the wound with a broad-sword and extract
The arrow-head from its hiding-place deep in
And send him back to where the fighting is.
Then Iapyx, the son of Iasus, came,
A man whom Phoebus loved before the others
And to whom, when he himself was suffering
The pains of love, once gladly offered his arts,
His own gifts – his augury, his lyre,
His own swift arrows. Iapyx, to defer
The death of his sick father, made his choice:
He would know the virtues of herbs, the way of healing
And practise the quiet arts which bring no glory.
Complaining bitterly, Aeneas stood
Leaning on his great spear among a crowd
Of men-at-arms, with the grieving Iülus,
While he himself could not be moved by tears.
The old man threw his cloak back from his shoulders
And like a true physician set to work
Making a great show with his skilful hands
And Phoebus's potent herbs – all to no purpose.
He tried in vain to pull the arrow out,
Taking the iron head of it in his forceps.

He had no luck, nor did his master Apollo
Assist in any way, and on the field
The cruelties and horrors are increasing,
Calamity comes closer. In the sky
Hangs a great cloud of dust, the cavalry
Approach, and in the middle of the camp
There falls a rain of spears. To high heaven
Rise the foreboding shouts of fighting men
As they fall under the hard hand of war.

    Then Venus, feeling her son's pain as her own,
With a mother's care gathered from Cretan Ida
Dittany stalks fullgrown with leaves and flowers
With purple petals: the plant is not unknown
To wild goats who seek it when an arrow
Pierces their flanks. She brought it down, her face
Veiled in a thick mist, and then steeped it
In a bright cauldron of water from a stream
For its secret virtues, adding a sprinkling of juices,
Health-giving ambrosia, scented panacea.
With this water the aged Iapyx
Dressed the wounds, not knowing what he did,
When suddenly all the pain left the body,
All the blood in that deep wound ceased to flow.
Then as he took his hand away, the arrow
Came out without his help, and all the strength
Welled up anew as it had been before.
'Quick, bring him arms and armour! Why stand there?'
With that call Iapyx became the first
To stir them up against the enemy.
'This does not come by human means,' he said,
'Nor any master's art, Aeneas, nor
Is it my hand that saves you. Someone greater
– A god – does this, and sends you back again
To works still greater.' Aeneas, eager to fight,
Had sheathed his legs in their golden armour,
First one and then the other and, impatient
Of all delay, flourished his spear already.
Once his shield had been fitted at his side,
His corselet on his back, kissing Ascanius
As best he might in his helmet, he addressed him:
'Learn from me, boy, what courage and hard work are,

From others, better fortune. Now my right hand
Will cover you in battle and will lead you
Where the rewards are great. Mind you remember,
When you are grown up as you soon will be,
What sort of people you come from; try to be like
Your father Aeneas and your uncle Hector.'
   These words delivered, his huge figure went
Out at the gate, brandishing the great spear;
With him Antheus and Mnestheus
Raced out, in close column a whole crowd
From the deserted camp, as in a stream.
The whole plain is a confusion of blind dust
And the earth shakes under the tread of feet.
Standing upon the rampart opposite
Turnus observed them coming; the Ausonians
Saw them and through the marrow of their bones
Ran a cold shudder; first, before all the Latins,
Juturna heard them, recognised the sound
And fled away in terror. Over the field
Aeneas swept on advancing his dark line.
As, when the sky breaks open and a storm
Moves in to land from far out at sea,
The peasant's heart is filled with foreboding,
He trembles, poor wretch: trees will come down, he knows,
Crops will be ruined, everything will be flattened:
Before the rain the winds fly and their voices
Are heard along the shore: just so the Trojan
Leads and drives on his line against their enemies,
They are packed round him in close-pounded columns.
Thymbraeus strikes the unwieldy Osiris
His sword does it, Mnestheus fells Arcetius,
Achates Epulo and Gyas Ufens;
Tolumnius the augur falls, who was
The first to throw his spear against the enemy.
A shout rises to heaven, the Rutulians,
Routed in their turn, show their backs and fly,
Away over the fields in a cloud of dust.
Aeneas does not deign to cut them down,
Death is not for them, or those he encounters
On foot or on horseback, or who come to attack him;

It is Turnus alone he tries to track down
Through the clouds of dust, it is him alone he challenges.
   The fear of this so strikes Juturna's mind,
Brave though she is, she jolts the charioteer
Metiscus right out of Turnus's chariot
As he wields the reins, and leaves him on the ground
Far from his guide-pole; she herself takes his place
And guides the rippling leather with her own hands,
Assumes control in the guise of Metiscus,
Voice, body and armour. Like a black swallow
Swooping through the great house of some rich nobleman,
Dipping her wings through the lofty halls
To pick up scraps of food for her noisy young,
Twittering now in an empty courtyard, now
In the moist air over a pool, Juturna flies
Through the midst of the enemy, carried on by the horses
And scours the whole field rapidly in her chariot,
Now here, now there, exhibiting her brother
In triumph but not letting him come to grips
With anyone, she sweeps away with him.
Aeneas no less diligently seeks
To follow the twisted circles of her tracks,
Looking for his man, and through the broken ranks
Calls him at the top of his voice. But whenever
He caught sight of him or tried to catch
The flying feet of the horses, at once Juturna
Wheeled the chariot away from him. What should he do?
He tosses uselessly upon the tide;
Now one course comes to mind and now another.
Then Messapus, light of foot and carrying
Ready in his left hand a pair of spears
Tipped with iron, poised one of them, took aim
And sent it straight at him. Aeneas stood still,
Fell on his knee and got behind his shield;
But none the less the swift spear carried off
The top of his helmet and the topmost plumes.
Then indeed he was angry; forced by treachery,
When he saw horses and chariot far away,
Calling on Jove to witness the altars profaned
By the breaking of the pact, he plunged at last
Into the midst of the enemy; terrible

And carrying all before him, he began
A cruel slaughter of whatever came his way
And gave rein to all his pent-up anger.
　　So many bitter things, so many deaths,
All those great captains gone! What god can tell
The story of it, or record in song
How now Turnus, and now the Trojan hero
Impels them over the entire plain?
Was it your pleasure, Jupiter, that two nations
Who were to live in endless peace thereafter
Should come together with such force? Aeneas
With the Rutulian Sucro first – and this
Was what first brought the Trojans to a halt;
He caught him in the side and his cruel sword
Went through the ribs and deep into the chest
– The speediest of ends. It did not take long.
Turnus threw from their horses Amycus
And his brother Diores and, himself on foot,
Struck one with his long spear as he advanced,
The other with his sword, cut off their heads
And hung them on his chariot, dripping blood
And so carried them off. Aeneas killed
Talos and Tanais and brave Cethegus,
Three in the one encounter, and sad Onites
Of Theban stock; his mother was Peridia:
Turnus killed the two brothers sent from Lycia
Which is Apollo's land and, from Arcadia
Menoetes who in his youth had hated war
Though it did him no good; he was a fisherman
On the Lerna and the neighbouring fishing streams
And his poor home was there, his father
Was no great lord, but one of those who sow
Land not their own. Turnus and Aeneas
Were like fires started at the opposite end
Of a dry forest, among crackling laurel,
Or like two foaming rivers rushing down
From lofty mountains, roaring as they go,
Racing to sea and each in its tracks
Leaving a ruin behind: with just such fury
The two captains rush through the thick of the fighting;
Within each of them a sea of anger,

Now, now, their hearts are bursting, no
Thought of defeat touches them, they rush
With all their strength to where the blows are thickest.
   Murranus, who recalls the ancient names
Of ancestors and of their fathers' fathers,
A whole line from the royal house of Latium,
Is knocked out of his chariot by a stone;
A huge piece of rock Aeneas whirls
In his direction, throws him to the ground,
Under the yoke, entangled in the reins,
The wheels go over him, the swift hoofs clatter,
The horses who have no thought of their master
Trample him underfoot. And Turnus meanwhile,
As Hyllus rushes at him furiously,
Catches him with a dart through his gold headband;
It goes through the helmet to the brain
And there it stops. Nor did your right hand,
Cretheus, you the bravest of all the Greeks,
Save you from Turnus; nor did all his gods
Protect Cupencus, once Aeneas came,
Although his brazen shield was interposed
The weapon found its way into his heart.
The Laurentine plains saw you too, Aeolus,
Go down to earth and lie there on your back:
You whom the Argive armies could not worst
Nor even Achilles by whom Priam's realms
Were overturned, you fall here at last
And here you cross the boundaries of death;
Your noble home stood at the foot of Ida,
Lyrnesus was your home, but your tomb is here
In Laurentine soil. The whole Latin army
And all the Dardanians were transformed:
Mnestheus and the courageous Serestus,
Messapus, tamer of horses, brave Asilas,
The Tuscan battalion and Evander's men,
The Arcadian squadron: one and all made efforts
Up to the very limits of their strength;
None had a moment's respite, all were struggling
Man to man in one immense conflict.
   The lovely mother of Aeneas then
Put him in mind to go up to the walls,

Turning his men against the town itself
To shake the Latins with a sudden disaster.
As he was tracking Turnus through the battle
He cast his eyes round this way and that
And caught sight of the city still immune
From that great war, and in a harmless quiet.
At once the image of more desperate fighting
Presents itself: he calls Mnestheus,
Sergestus and brave Serestus, his captains,
Plants himself on an eminence where the rest
Of the Trojan army hurry up to listen,
Crowding together but not letting go
Of shields or spears. Then, standing in the midst of them,
He says: 'Do at once what I tell you; Jupiter
Is on our side; let no man hesitate
Because this is a sudden change of plan.
This very day – unless they will agree
To submit and take orders from their conquerors –
I will destroy the city and Latinus's
Kingdom, which have brought about the war
And level the roof-tops smoking to the ground.
Am I to wait until it suits Turnus
To try his hand in battle against me
And, once defeated, to meet me again?
This, countrymen, is what is here in question
In this iniquitous war. So, quickly now,
Bring fire-brands, we already have a treaty,
Flames will enforce it.' When he had finished speaking
Everyone was of a mind to try the remedy;
They formed a wedge and pushed towards the town.
All at once ladders and fires appeared.
Some charge the gates and kill the first they come to,
Others hurl weapons till the sky is darkened.
Aeneas is among the first, beneath
The walls he stretches out his hand;
In a loud voice he accuses Latinus:
He calls the gods to witness that he is forced
Again to have recourse to battle, forced
A second time to treat Italians as enemies;
This is the second treaty to be broken;
Among the fearful citizens there is discord:

Some give orders to open up the city
And throw the gates wide to the Dardanians,
Dragging the king himself on to the ramparts;
Others fetch weapons and rush to defend the walls.
It is as when a shepherd has tracked bees
Into some nook in the pummice and has filled it
With acrid smoke, while its inhabitants,
Fearful at these events, crawl hurriedly
Through the wax paths of their camp, and buzzing
Noisily grow ever more furious;
The stinking blackness curls round about their dwellings;
Deep in the rocks a hidden murmur sounds
And the smoke issues on the empty air.
    A fresh misfortune then befell the Latins,
Weary as they were, and shook the whole city
To its foundations with a wave of grief.
The queen who from the roof of her palace
Saw the approach of the enemy, right to the walls,
And flames flicking to the roof-tops, unopposed;
Rutulian forces nowhere to be seen
And none of Turnus's troops: unhappy woman,
She thinks that in the fury of the fighting
The young man has been killed: a sudden grief
Turns her mind upside down, she cries out
That it is she is the cause of all these ills,
The guilt is on her head; out of her wits,
Full of wild reckless talk, her death is coming,
She tears her purple robes with her own hand
And from a high beam she ties a noose
For a dishonoured death. The Latin women,
Poor wretches, hear of it; first Lavinia,
Her hand tearing the blossoms of her hair,
The roses of her cheeks, and then a crowd
All round her, are distracted; the great halls
Ring with their lamentations. Through the whole town
The melancholy story spreads, and with it
Dejection. With his garments rent, Latinus
Walks to and fro, thunderstruck at the fate
Which has befallen his wife, and at the ruin
Which has come to his city; as he goes,
Defiling his white hair with dust and ashes.

   Meanwhile in a far corner of the field
Turnus pursues a small band of stragglers;
He is less full of fight than he was
And less and less delighted with the triumph
His horses bring him. Then from the town a breeze
Brings him the sound of shouting and blind terror;
He strains his ears as the confused noise strikes them:
A murmur which cannot mean anything good.
'I am in trouble! What can it be, this grief
Which shakes the city walls? What is this cry
Which comes to me from so far away?' He speaks
And as he does so pulls at the reins,
Coming to a frenzied halt. Then his sister
Who, still in the shape of the charioteer
Metiscus, had guided the horses and the car,
Faced him and addressed him in these words:
'This way, Turnus, let's go after the Trojans,
Following wherever we may have a victory:
Others can guard the houses well enough.
Aeneas is attacking the Italians;
That is his battle: let us go for the Teucrians
And send them where they belong. In numbers killed,
In honour too, you will do as well as he!'
Turnus replied:
'Sister – for I have known you all along
Since with your tricks you first upset the treaty
And threw yourself into this war – it is useless
To pretend you are not the goddess. But who was it
Sent you down from Olympus to play such a part?
Was it so you should see your wretched brother
Die a cruel death? For what am I to do?
Is there a chance I should find safety now?
Before my own eyes I have seen Murranus
– Than whom no dearer now remains to me –
Calling out to me loudly as he died,
A strong man finished by a stronger wound.
The luckless Ufens fell, rather than see
Disgrace befall me: the Teucrians are possessed
Of him, body and armour. Shall I endure
Their houses razed to the ground – it was all I needed –
And not throw Drances' words back in his teeth?

Shall I show my back and give this land the spectacle
Of Turnus running away? Is death so terrible?
Be kind to me, you spirits of the dead,
For those above have turned away their eyes.
I will come down to you a stainless soul,
Clear of the cowardice you hate, nor ever
Unworthy of my valiant ancestors.'
   No sooner were the words out of his mouth
Than, through the middle of his enemies
Carried on a foaming horse, Saces comes galloping;
He is wounded in the face by an arrow
And appeals to Turnus by name: 'Turnus, in you
Is our last hope; have pity on your people!
The thunder of Aeneas's arms threatens
To overthrow the topmost citadels
Of the Italians and bring all to ruin;
Already fire-brands fly upon the roof-tops.
The Latins turn their faces towards you,
They look to you; while King Latinus himself
Hesitates as to whom he should call his sons
And which alliance he should now incline to.
Besides all that the queen, who trusted you,
Has killed herself and in a state of terror
Fled from the light of day. Before the gates
Messapus and the valiant Atinas
Alone prevent a rout. Around them stand
On either side, close-packed battalions
With drawn swords bristling like a field of corn
While you drive round here on deserted grass-lands.'
Turnus, shocked and bewildered by all this,
Stood staring and in silence; in his heart
Rises a tide of shame and grief and madness,
Love stung by fury, consciousness of courage.
Then, as the shadows clear and once again
Light dawns upon his mind, he turns towards the walls,
His eyes ablaze and, standing in his chariot,
Looks back with vehemence at the great city.
   But see now, a whirlwind of flame was rising
Coil after coil to the sky, between the landings
Of a tower it had fastened on – a tower which Turnus

Himself had built and fitted with wheels and high-thrown
    gangways.
'Now, sister, see, the fates will have their way;
Hinder me no more, but let me follow
Where the god and my hard fortune call me.
Without question, I must fight Aeneas,
And without question – bitter as it is –
I must submit to death; nor will you, sister,
Any more see your brother put to shame;
It is madness, yes, but first let me be mad.'
He spoke and quickly jumped from his chariot
And rushed across the field between his enemies,
Between their spears, and left his sister sorrowing;
With rapid stride he broke through the lines.
He was like a rock from the top of a mountain
When, torn out by the wind, either because
A whirling storm has washed it out, or else
With the passage of years time has loosened it,
It rushes headlong down the mountain-side,
Bouncing over the ground, and carries with it
Head-over-heels trees and cattle and men;
So Turnus rushed, scattering the ranks before him,
Up to the walls of the city, where the earth
Is deep in blood, the air whistles with spears.
He made a sign with his hand and called out:
'Now let them be, you Rutulians,
And, Latins, keep your darts to yourselves:
Whatever fortune may be here, is mine:
Better that one should suffer, I for you,
Make good the treaty and settle by the sword.'
They all drew back and left him room enough.
    Our ancestor Aeneas, having heard
The name of Turnus, abandons the walls at once,
Abandons the lofty towers, he does not hesitate
But breaks off all the tasks he has in hand;
Exultant and happy, he thunders on his shield;
He might be Athos, he might be Eryx, or
Apennine, father of mountains himself, when he
Roars through his quivering oaks and in his joy
Raises his head with its snowy top to the winds.
Now indeed, each more keenly than the others,

Rutulians, Trojans, all the Italians,
Turn their eyes on him: those who held the walls,
Those who below beat them with battering rams,
All took their armour from their weary shoulders.
Latinus himself watches with stupefaction
These two great heroes, born in such different places,
Meeting to settle the issue with their swords.
And they, as soon as a place has been cleared for them,
Run rapidly forward, first throwing their spears,
And start the battle, clattering their brazen shields.
The earth groans; they deal blow after blow
In quick time; their courage takes all the chances.
They are like bulls in the vast stretch of woodland
In Sila, or on the summit of Taburnus,
Who charge at one another in deadly battle
While the men who tend the herds drop back in terror
And all the beasts stand by in silent fear,
The heifers doubtful who will be king of the wood
Whom all the herds must follow; violently
The two bulls come together, each wounds the other;
Their horns are interlocked and neck and shoulders
Are bathed in streams of blood; the whole wood
Re-echoes with their bellowing; so it is
Trojan Aeneas and the Daunian hero
Clash shield to shield, and with the noise of it
The heavens are filled. Jupiter himself is holding
The scales in even balance, then sets on them
The diverse fates of the two contestants,
Deciding whom the struggle will condemn
And which scale sink under the weight of death.
    Now Turnus dashes forward, thinking it safe,
Rises to his full height with his sword raised
And strikes: the Trojans shout, the anxious Latins
Shout too, and both the armies are on tip-toe;
But the perfidious sword breaks and deserts
Its raging master half-way through his blow,
Only flight can help him. Swifter than the east wind
He flies, with a glance at the unfamiliar hilt
In his defenceless hand. The story is
That when in his headlong haste he leapt
Behind his horses yoked for the first fighting

He left his father's sword behind him, so
Anxious was he and seized that of Metiscus,
His charioteer: and while the Trojan stragglers
Showed their backs, it served; but when it came
Afterwards to the arms Vulcan had made,
The arms of a god, the mortal blade flew to bits
As the blow fell, and gave way like ice;
The fragments glittered in the yellow sand.
So Turnus flew like a madman over the plain,
Now this way and now that, weaving his way
Uncertainly round and round: for on all sides
A crowding ring of Teucrians hedged him in,
Here there was marshland, there, the lofty walls.
    Close behind, though his knees are half-numb
From the arrow-wound which still hinders his pace,
Aeneas followed step for step, pressing
Hard on his worried enemy: it is
As when a hunting dog has found a stag
Caught in a river or cut off by the line
Of red feathers, and runs at him barking,
But the stag, frightened by the snares and by
The high banks of the river tries to escape
In a thousand directions at once, the Umbrian hound
Clings to him eagerly, with gaping mouth,
Now holding him or on the point of holding him
And snapping at him, closing his jaws on nothing.
Then a great cry goes up, the banks and pools
All around answer, in the sky above
There is a noise like thunder. So Turnus,
As he flies, accuses the Rutulians,
Calling to each by name and demanding
His usual sword. In the face of this Aeneas
Threatens death and destruction to any man
Who dares come near, they are trembling, he
Terrifies them more, saying he will raze the town,
And wounded as he is he presses on.
Five times they follow round in a circle
And five times deviously retrace their steps:
It is no trifling sporting prize they seek;
What they contend for is the blood of Turnus.

It happened that a bitter wild olive
Had stood here, a tree that was sacred to Faunus,
Revered of old by sailors who, escaping
From the waves used to fasten gifts on it
For the god of Laurentum and hang up
Their votive garments; but the Teucrians,
Disregarding all this, had cut it down
So that the ground was clear for the contest.
Here stood Aeneas's spear, it was to this
His throw had borne it, there it was fixed
In the tough root. The Dardan leaned forward
And stretched his hand to try to pull the point out
So that he could follow with his spear
The enemy he could not catch on foot.
Then indeed Turnus was mad with fear:
'Faunus, have pity, I beg you; gracious earth,
Hold the point fast, if ever I was diligent
In doing you the honours which the Trojans
Have so profaned with war.' This was his prayer
And he did not invoke the gods in vain,
For though Aeneas paused and struggled long
The stump was stubborn and no strength of his
Could open up the bite of that hard wood.
The Daunian goddess, once again assuming
The figure of Metiscus, ran forward
And gave her brother back his own sword.
But Venus was indignant that the nymph
Presumed so far and was allowed so much;
Approaching, she pulled the spear from the deep root.
Both heroes were exultant, with fresh arms
And refreshed courage, one trusting his sword,
The other tall and threatening with his spear,
Both breathless as they faced each other in battle.
    Meanwhile the king of great Olympus spoke,
Addressing Juno, as from a golden cloud
She looked down on the scene: 'What will the end be,
Wife? What after all is left? You know
And you yourself confess it, that Aeneas
Is patron of this land and that heaven claims him,
The Fates indeed must raise him to the stars.
What device have you still? What do you hope for

As you lie there among the icy clouds?
Was it well that a god should be dishonoured
By a mortal wound? Or indeed that the sword
(For without you what could Juturna do?)
Taken from Turnus should be given back to him
To increase the strength of men already vanquished?
Give up at last now, yield to my entreaties,
Neither stay silent, eaten up by grief,
Nor let me hear those bitter cares of yours
Once more on your sweet lips. The end has come.
Over land and sea you could harry the Trojans,
You could start a war which never should have been,
Wreck a family and bring mourning to a wedding:
More than that I forbid you.' So Jupiter;
The goddess who was Saturn's child replied
With downcast looks: 'Because I knew indeed,
Great Jupiter, that such was your will,
I have reluctantly abandoned Turnus
And these lands: nor would you see me here
Alone upon my aery throne and bearing
Whatever might befall, for good or ill,
But, in a circle of flame, I should be there
Right by the line of battle, dragging the Teucrians
Into murderous fighting. As for Juturna,
I did say she could help her unfortunate brother,
That I confess, and sanctioned acts of daring
To save his life; but not recourse to weapons
Or that she should draw a bow on his behalf;
I swear this by the inexorable fountain-head
Of Styx, the only name feared by the gods.
Now I withdraw and leave these fights in loathing.
This one thing not forbidden by the fates
I ask of you for Latium and the glory
Of your own race: when with this happy union
– And so be it – they now confirm the peace,
When they are one in laws as in their treaties
Do not give orders for the native Latins
To change their ancient name, nor turn Trojans,
To be known as Teucrians nor to change their speech
Nor dress in strange fashion. Let Latium be
And through the centuries let there be Alban kings.

Let there be a Roman stock, Italian courage
Giving it strength. Troy has indeed fallen;
Let her fall and with her the Trojan name.'
  The author of men and of all that is
Smiled: 'You are a true sister of Jove,
The second child of Saturn: so great the waves
Of anger which swell up within your heart:
I grant your wish, I give myself up
Defeated and content. The Ausonians
Shall keep their ancestral speech and customs
And with them, keep their name; the Teucrians,
Mingled with them in body only, shall sink.
I will add Trojan rites to the Latin
And make all Latins with a single language.
From these, and tempered with Ausonian blood,
Shall come a race which you shall see surpass
Men, and surpass the gods in their devotion,
No race shall do you honour as they will.'
Juno assented and in her delight
Completely changed her mind, and so it was
She went from heaven and left her cloud behind.
  This done, the Father ponders in his heart
Another scheme, and makes his preparations
To drive Juturna from her brother's side.
Men say there are twin horrors called the Furies
Untimely Night bore at a single birth
With Tartarean Megaera, both alike
Coiling like serpents and the wings she gave them
Filled with the winds. These two wait by Jove's throne
Or at the threshold of the dread king's palace,
Sharpening the fears of trembling mortals when
The king of the gods would deal out ghastly death
And sickness, or when he punishes towns with war.
One of these Jupiter sent swiftly from heaven
And bade her be an omen to Juturna:
She flew and came to earth in a whirlwind.
She was like an arrow flying from a bowstring
Through a cloud, armed with poison, sent on its way
By Parthian or Sidonian, a weapon
For which there is no cure; it hisses secretly
Through the swift shadows: for the child of Night

So sped and made for the earth. And when she saw
The Ilian army and the troops of Turnus,
Suddenly she shrank to assume the shape
Of that small bird which sometimes in the night
Perches on tombs or upon lonely roof-tops
And sings late and importunate in the darkness;
So changed, the fell creature flew to and fro
Before the face of Turnus, hooting and, with her wings
Beating against his shield. A sudden numbness
Weakened his limbs, from fear, the horror of it
Made his hair stand on end and his voice stuck.

    But as from far away she recognised
The Furies' whistling wings, in her unhappiness
His sister Juturna let her hair go loose
And tore at it, dug her nails into her face
And hit herself on the chest: 'Turnus,' she said,
'How can your sister help you now? Or what
Remains to me for all my hardiness?
By what art can I drag out your existence?
Can I oppose such a portent? No, for me
The battle is over. Do not frighten me,
Birds of ill-omen: I recognise your wing-beat,
The sound means death, and I will pay attention
To what the great spirit of Jove requires.
Is this the return he makes for my virginity?
Why did he give me everlasting life?
Could I not die as others do? Now surely
I could end all this anguish, and accompany
My brother among the shades! What, I immortal!
Can anything in life be sweet to me
Without you here? What earth be deep enough
To yawn and swallow me who am a goddess
Into the underworld?' And with these words
And many a moan, she wrapped about her head
Her watery mantle, plunging into the river.

    Aeneas shook his spear thick as a tree
And, moving forward into battle, rage
In his heart, cried: 'Turnus, what stops you now?
You still shrink from me? This is not a race;
Now we must have it out hand to hand
With deadly weapons. Take what shape you will,

Show what your courage or your wiles amount to;
Get yourself wings and follow the course of the stars
Or shut yourself in the bowels of the earth.'
The other shook his head: 'It is not your words,
Fiery though they may be, fierce though you are,
Which cause me terror but it is the gods
And Jupiter who is my enemy.'
He said no more but, spying near at hand
An ancient, giant stone which chanced to lie there,
A boundary marker set to stop disputes;
A dozen chosen men of such physique
As the earth now produces could but barely
Lift it upon their shoulders; but that hero
Picked it up in his agitated grasp
And threw it in the direction of the enemy,
Stretching himself up as he ran forward.
But as he runs he does not know himself
– Not in his pace, not as he lifts his hands up
Or as he sets the great stone on its way:
His knees give, his blood is frozen cold.
The stone itself, whirling through empty air
Does not go the whole distance or reach its mark.
And as at night in dreams, when languid rest
Closes our eyes, we seem to want to advance
On a course dear to our hearts, yet all our efforts
Somehow fail; we cannot speak, our body
Lacks its accustomed energy, no sound
Or word comes out: so it is now with Turnus.
However hard he tries to make his way,
The fearsome goddess will not give him passage.
Then in his heart he feels only distraction;
He stares at the Rutulians and the town,
Faltering in fear and trembling as the spear
Threatens him; he sees no way out, no way
Of pressing on against the enemy,
His chariot gone his sister, his charioteer.
  But as he hesitates Aeneas flourishes
His fatal spear, watching for the right moment,
Then lets it fly with all his weight behind it,
The full distance. Never was such a roar
From stones ejected from a siege-engine

Against a wall, never were there such crashes
From a bursting thunderbolt. The spear flies on
Like a dark whirlwind carrying destruction
And goes right through the edge of the corselet
And the outer circle of the sevenfold shield:
Then with a hiss it passes through the thigh.
At the blow the gigantic Turnus sank,
His knee bent down to the earth. All the Rutulians
Sprang up and groaned, while round about the hills
Roared again and from all the wooded slopes
The echo sounded back. Turnus, subdued
And suppliant now, looked up and stretched his hand out,
Making his plea: 'I have deserved it,' he says.
'Make the most of your luck. If any thought
Of an unhappy parent touches you
– And you had such a father in Anchises –
I beg you, pity the old age of Daunus
And give me back to him and to my people
Or, if you'd rather, give them my dead body.
You are the winner; the Ausonians
Have seen me beaten, stretching out my hands;
The bride, Lavinia, is yours: your hatred
Could rest content with that.' Aeneas paused,
Standing with rolling eyes, fierce in his armour
And more and more the words affected him,
Softening his purpose until suddenly,
High on Turnus's shoulder he caught sight of
The ill-starred sword-belt, flashing with the studs
He knew so well, for this was the equipment
Young Pallas had been wearing when Turnus struck him
And left him on the ground, finished – and now
There it was on those shoulders as a sign
That here was an enemy. Aeneas's eyes
Drank in the sight of these relics, reminders
Of a bitter pain, then, blazing with fury
And terrible in his anger, he called out:
'You who since then have worn the spoils of one
So dear to me, look to escape me now?
Pallas it is gives you this stroke, and Pallas
Who makes the sacrifice justice demands,

Your criminal blood.' With that, white-hot,
He buried his sword full in the breast before him.
Turnus's limbs grew slack and with a groan
A life not fit to live fled to the shades.

# CORRIGENDA

p. 4: 'Diomed': *Diomede* (cf. pp. 32, 209).

p. 14: 'There were the Atrides': 'Atrides' is singular: read *Atridae* or *sons of Atreus*.

p. 15: 'Pergamus': *Pergama* (cf. pp. 20, 36, 45, 60, 69, 97, 99, 147, 162, 267, 308).

p. 15: 'Her one breast sticking out': *Her right breast* (there was a version of the Amazon myth that said they had only one breast; but according to this version they burnt off the right breast and left the chest there bare to free up the arrow arm).

p. 22: 'Sichaeus': *Sychaeus*.

p. 35: Neoptolemus/The sons of Peleus': *the son*.

p. 49: 'Iülus': *Iulus* (cf. pp. 106, 130, 131, 157, 182, 194, 243, 245, 251, 255, 283, 301, 337, 339).

p. 60: 'Thymban': *Thymbran*.

p. 61: 'Pergamus': *Pergamum*.

p. 63: 'Iasus': *Iasius*.

p. 86: 'Iarbus': *Iarbas*.

p. 89: 'Cytherian': *Cytherean*.

p. 97: 'Grynian': *Grynean*.

p. 109: 'Prosperpine': *Proserpina* (cf. pp. 153, 158).

p. 132: 'The lads who take part are now known as Troys': the Latin here is very weird, but best probably to read *are now known as 'Troy'*, with quotation marks likewise around 'the Trojan troop' in the next line.

p. 145: 'The Cecrops' children': *Then*.

p. 165: Pirothoüs': *Pirithoüs*.

p. 172: 'See how the Decii': *See now*.

**p. 172:** 'Drusii': *Drusi.*

**p. 173:** 'kill the Aeacid': *overthrow* (Aemilius Paullus did not actually kill Perseus, although he did die after some years in captivity).

**p. 210:** 'Pallantium': *Pallanteum.*

**p. 221:** 'Nereus's daughter, the wife of Tithonus,/Could move you by her tears': *Nereus's daughter and the wife of Tithonus/Could move you by their tears* (Nereus's daughter (Thetis) and the wife of Tithonus (Aurora) are two separate characters).

**p. 222:** 'one of the Aeoliae': *one of the Aeolians.*

**p. 222–3:** 'Cyclops' (singular): *Cyclopes.*

**p. 224:** 'Greatest of Teucrian captains': *'Greatest of Teucrian captains.*

**p. 228:** 'There is a vast grove near an icy stream,/The Caere': *There is a vast grove near the icy stream/Of Caere.*

**p. 231:** 'Anthony': *Antony.*

**p. 235:** 'Pilumnus, his father': *his ancestor.*

**p. 235:** 'Corynthus': *Corythus* (cf. p. 289).

**p. 244:** 'But you, who are more than my own age': *who are more my own age.*

**p. 256:** 'Led by the Charioteer': *pluuialibus Haedis* literally is 'at the time of the rainy [constellation of the] Kids'.

**p. 274:** 'Dindymus': *Dindymum.*

**p. 287:** 'Laurentium': *Laurentum.*

**p. 290:** 'Gave him a wound he could not see coming': *give.*

**p. 308:** 'Caledon': *Calydon.*

**p. 321:** 'Hippolyta': *Hippolyte.*

**p. 345:** 'And as the breath of the Edonian north': *north wind.*

**p. 346:** 'Then Iapyx, the son of Iasus': *Iasius.*

**p. 361:** 'By Parthian or Sidonian': *Parthian or Cydonian.*

# NOTES

Like all ancient poets, Virgil revelled in the rich variety of the beautiful and resonant names of mythology and history, so that the poem is full of titles, patronymics and synonyms: along with 'Trojan', for example, we find 'Dardanian', 'Pelasgian', 'Teucrian'. If a name is not annotated here readers should consult the Glossary. Many of the references explain themselves as the story goes along: there is no need, for example, to explain Virgil's initial description of the Carthaginians as 'Tyrian colonists' (p. 1), since Venus herself soon tells us the tale of the migration from Tyre (p. 11). Finally, as in all sweeping historical narratives, there is a cast of thousands and a host of locales: many of these people and places are mentioned only once, and not all of them are important enough to find a place in the Notes or Glossary.

## BOOK I

**p. 1 Lavinian shores:** Aeneas' eventual foundation in Latium was called Lavinium after his second wife, Lavinia.

**p. 1 his own gods:** founding a city is a religious act in the ancient world. In Virgil's day the chief executives of the Roman state still sacrificed to the Trojan gods in Lavinium at the beginning of their term of office.

**p. 1 Alban fathers:** Alba Longa, founded by Aeneas' first son, Ascanius/ Iulus, is the home for the family for over three hundred years, providing the continuity between Aeneas and his descendant Romulus, founder of Rome itself.

**p. 1 Libya:** in the ancient world, the whole of North Africa.

**p. 2 the judgment of Paris:** a beauty competition which was the cause of the Trojan war, when the Trojan prince Paris spurned Hera and Athena (Juno and Minerva) in favour of Aphrodite (Venus), who offered him Helen as bride.

**p. 7 Scylla, Cyclops:** as we read in Book III, Aeneas and his men have glimpsed these Homeric monsters in the course of their travels.

**p. 8 Antenor:** along with Aeneas, the other Trojan hero whom tradition asserted had escaped from Troy; here he is said to have also arrived in Italy, and founded Padua.

**p. 8 I will speak:** prophecies from Jupiter guaranteeing eventual Roman victory appear to have featured in Virgil's (now lost) Roman epic predecessors, Naevius and Ennius. Here the prophecy skips over almost all the action of the poem, taking us down to the current day and the apotheosis of Aeneas' descendants.

**p. 9 reigned for three years:** Aeneas will be dead three years after the poem ends.

**p. 9 Ascanius, who is now called Iulus:** the descent of the family of Julius Caesar from the son of Aeneas was an old story before Virgil's birth.

**p. 9 Juno herself ... Will be of better counsel:** Juno will start to favour the Romans, according to this chronology, some time between the foundation of Rome and the conquest of Greece – Virgil appears to be following the canonical, Ennian, version, whereby Juno was fully reconciled to the Romans only during their second war against Carthage (218–202 BC).

**p. 9 And so the time will come:** Jupiter prophesies that the Romans, the offspring of the Trojan royal house ('the house of Assaracus') will conquer Greece, capturing the Homeric homes of Achilles (Phthia), Agamemnon (Mycenae) and Diomede (Argos).

**p. 9 a Trojan Caesar:** almost certainly both Julius Caesar and his adopted son, Augustus.

**p. 9 Quirinus:** the divine title of Romulus.

**p. 10 the son of Maia:** Mercury.

**p. 10 Harpalyce:** an obscure reference; she is unknown before Virgil.

**p. 11 Agenor:** an ancestor of the Phoenicians in Tyre (hence 'Punic' and 'Tyrian' here).

**p. 12 new Carthage:** 'Carthage' means 'new city' in Phoenician.

**p. 12 the Hide:** the similarity between the Phoenician word for the citadel of Carthage ('Bosra') and the Greek word for an oxhide ('byrsa') led to this story.

**p. 12 My race was born there:** see DARDANUS on p. 390.

**p. 13 Paphos:** a town in Cyprus, dear to Aphrodite/Venus, where she came ashore after her miraculous birth from the sea.

**p. 14 the Atridae:** the sons of Atreus, Agamemnon and Menelaus.

**p. 15 the son of Tydeus:** Diomede, who killed Rhesus at Troy before his horses could graze or drink and make Troy invincible.

**p. 15 The body of Hector:** a version of Book XXIV of Homer's *Iliad*, where Priam meets Achilles to ransom Hector's body.

**p. 15 like Diana:** the simile (originally from Homer) places Diana near her favoured shrines in Sparta (by the river Eurotas) or her birthplace Delos (the site of Mt Cynthus).

**p. 18 Saturn's own country:** see Book VIII (p. 219) for the story of how Saturn hid in Latium after his overthrow by Jupiter.

**p. 21 Cythera, Idalium:** the island Cythera and the town of Idalium on Cyprus were famous cult-sites of Venus/Aphrodite.

**p. 22 Acidalian:** an epithet of Venus, a learned reference, now obscure.

**p. 23 Iopas:** the mysterious song of the Carthaginian bard recalls the bardic performances Odysseus hears at the court of the Phaeacians during his wanderings in the *Odyssey* (Book VIII).

## BOOK II

**p. 27 a Myrmidon/ Or a Dolopian:** the contingents of Achilles and Neoptolemus respectively.

**p. 27 a horse:** the famous Trojan horse is not referred to in Homer's *Iliad*, but Odysseus hears the Phaeacian bard sing of it in the *Odyssey*: Virgil's hero tells the story himself.

**p. 28 Capys:** in Book X (p. 270) we learn that this man will be the founder of the Italian city of Capua.

**p. 29 Palamedes:** the rivalry between Palamedes and Odysseus was a famous topic for numerous (now lost) tragedies and epics (as Virgil acknowledges by saying 'It is public knowledge', p. 30).

**p. 30 the Ithacan:** Ulysses, king of Ithaca.

**p. 30 the oracle of Phoebus:** Apollo's oracle at Delphi dates from long after the Trojan war – this is one of Virgil's many deliberate anachronisms.

**p. 30 A bloody sacrifice:** a reference to the sacrifice at Aulis of Agamemnon's daughter Iphigenia, at the very beginning of the Greek expedition to Troy.

**p. 32 the Palladium:** a Trojan talisman, sacred to Pallas, on which the safety of the city depended. Sinon gives the usual Greek story of its theft by Diomede and Ulysses; Roman versions said that the Palladium somehow ended up in the temple of Vesta in Rome, along with the other holy objects brought from Troy by Aeneas.

**p. 33 But if the horse should penetrate the city:** in a way Sinon's lying prophecy comes true, since Asia, in the form of the Romans (offspring of the Asian Trojans), does 'live/ To see its soldiers under Pelops' walls', when Rome conquers the Greeks, descendants of Pelops (grandfather of Agamemnon and Menelaus).

**p. 33 Larissan:** Larissa is the main city of Thessaly, the area of Greece where Achilles grew up.

**p. 35 The son of Peleus:** strictly Achilles is the son of Peleus, and Achilles' son Neoptolemus is the grandson; but Virgil here wishes to make Neoptolemus into another Achilles.

**p. 35 At the chariot's tail:** as described in Homer's *Iliad*, Book XXII.

**p. 37 the straits of Sigeum:** the mouth of the Hellespont.

**p. 37 The last day:** the fulfilment of Homeric prophecies uttered by Agamemnon and Hector, 'there will be a day when Troy will be destroyed' – that day has come.

**p. 40 Cassandra ... dragged from Minerva's shrine:** Juno has already alluded (p. 2) to the penalty that Ajax and the other Greeks will pay for angering Minerva by this gross sacrilege – the rape of Cassandra is traditionally the moment at which divine favour turns against the Greeks.

**p. 47 the Scaean gate:** famous from Homer's *Iliad* as the main gate of the city of Troy.

**p. 47 I have survived the capture of Troy once:** Troy had been sacked once before, by Hercules, after he had been defrauded by the then king, Laomedon.

**p. 48 Since the time when the Father of gods and men/Breathed on me:** after sleeping with Venus to beget Aeneas, Anchises boasted of his luck and was punished with a crippling bolt from Jupiter.

**p. 49 a prodigy appeared:** Roman religion paid much attention to such extraordinary events, seeing them as signs from the gods. Prodigies were sent by the gods either with or without human request: the fire on Ascanius' head is an example of the latter category, the shooting star an example of the former.

**p. 52 Then you will come to the Hesperian land:** it is striking that

Aeneas receives the first prophecy of his fate, including his remarriage, from the ghost of his wife.

## BOOK III

**p. 58 Gradivus:** see MARS on p. 394.

**p. 58 Getic:** Thracian.

**p. 59 a sacred and most pleasing island:** Delos, birthplace of Apollo ('the Archer'), and a focus of his cult.

**p. 61 Mother Cybele:** Anchises mentions briefly the chief symbols of the Great Mother's cult and iconography.

**p. 61 Cnossus:** chief city of Crete.

**p. 61 Idomeneus:** one of the leading Greek heroes in the Trojan War. His exile from his Cretan home is an early example of the disasters that befell the Greeks after the war.

**p. 62 Sirius:** the Dog-Star, which rises at the hottest time of summer.

**p. 62 Penates:** the household gods of Aeneas and Troy, which become the public Penates of Lavinium and Rome.

**p. 63 Corythus:** the name of the father of Dardanus and Iasius, and of his city (usually identified with Cortona).

**p. 66 the Actian shores:** Aeneas is unknowingly celebrating games at the very spot where his descendant Augustus will later win the Battle of Actium against Antony and Cleopatra, and institute regular Actian games.

**p. 67 Helenus:** Virgil inherited from earlier tradition the general story of how Helenus, a noted prophet and a son of Priam, married Andromache after the death of Neoptolemus/Pyrrhus, to whom she had been given as booty after the sack of Troy; it is his invention to bring Andromache into the Aeneas-story, so as to show a contrast between those Trojan survivors who live on in the past and those who move on into the future.

**p. 68 Priam's virgin daughter:** Polyxena was sacrificed on Achilles' tomb after the sack of Troy to appease his ghost.

**p. 69 Clarian laurel:** Clarus was another oracular shrine of Apollo, to whom the laurel was sacred.

**p. 71 Here the Locri:** in these lines Helenus advises Aeneas to avoid Magna Graecia, the area of Southern Italy inhabited by Greeks.

**p. 71 In this your children's children should follow you:** a particularly clear case of how Virgil shows Aeneas first exemplifying typically Roman forms of behaviour (in this instance, sacrificing with the head covered, and not with the head bare, as did the Greeks).

**p. 71 the narrows of Pelorus:** the Straits of Messina, where ancient scholars located the traditional mythological monsters of Scylla and Charybdis.

**p. 72 the cape/Of Pachynus:** the southern point of the triangle of Sicily, which Aeneas is advised to circumnavigate rather than risk Scylla and Charybdis.

**p. 76 the Cyclops' coast:** Odysseus' encounter with the Cyclops is one of the most famous episodes of the *Odyssey*, and this is the closest Virgil brings the two heroes, who only miss each other by three months.

**p. 77 Enceladus:** a giant who fought against Jupiter and was imprisoned under a huge mountain (usually not Aetna).

**p. 77 the strange figure of an unknown man:** as these words show, Virgil invented the story of Achaemenides, in order to bring his hero into the same orbit as Homer's.

### BOOK IV

**p. 90 as when Apollo:** this simile connects to the simile on p. 15, where Dido is compared to Apollo's twin sister, Diana.

**p. 91 they are spending all the winter long/In idle pleasure:** one of the places where the parallelism between Aeneas/Dido and Antony/Cleopatra is most clear.

**p. 95 And so addresses him:** the following exchange of speeches is very tragic in style, evoking in particular the exchange of speeches between Jason and Medea in Euripides' *Medea*.

**p. 97 Grynian Apollo ... Lycian oracles:** references to yet more shrines of Apollo, at Gryneum and Patara.

**p. 97 Caucasus ... Hyrcanian:** remote and savage areas in the northeast of the known world.

**p. 101 As when Pentheus:** the similes in these lines compare Dido to two famous tragic characters, Pentheus (from Euripides' *Bacchae*) and Orestes (from Aeschylus' *Eumenides* and Euripides' *Orestes*); the comparisons highlight the way in which the epic at this point is becoming 'The Tragedy of Dido'.

**p. 104 Laomedon:** see above note for p. 47, for the proverbial deceitfulness of the Trojan king, Laomedon.

p. 106 **Then you, O Tyrians:** the following curse becomes the cause of the Carthaginian Wars, as Virgil establishes tight bonds between his new Roman epic and the first Roman epics, of Naevius and Ennius, which had had the Carthaginian Wars as a central concern.

## BOOK V

p. 115 **I will arrange contests:** funeral games (often gladiatorial) were an important part of Roman life, and a set-piece of epic since the funeral games for Patroclus in Book XXIII of Homer's *Iliad*.

p. 116 **A slippery serpent:** in Roman funerary art serpents regularly represent the spirit of the dead.

p. 117 **Entered for the first contest are four ships:** in Homer the first event is a chariot-race, but Virgil realistically allows for the fact that Aeneas' expedition has very few horses, let alone chariots, while at the same time giving himself the opportunity for innovation.

p. 117 **The line from which the house of Memmius comes:** the theme of continuity between past and present, constant throughout the poem, is particularly strong at this point.

p. 125 **Dares:** this invented figure, with his earlier victory over a relative of 'Bebrycian Amycus', reminds the reader of Apollonius' *Argonautica*, which describes Polydeuces' defeat of Amycus in a boxing match. The brutality of Virgil's contest is contemporary; it is interesting, however, that Virgil does not include a gladiatorial combat in his games, although Homer has one in *Iliad* XXIII (between Diomede and Telamonian Ajax).

p. 130 **A portent:** a mysterious reference, which probably refers both to the future greatness of Acestes' city, Segesta, and to the famous comet of 44 BC; this comet appeared during games to Venus held in honour of the recently dead Julius Caesar by his adopted son, and was interpreted by Caesar's partisans as the path of his soul ascending to heaven.

p. 132 **great Rome in turn/Took over and preserved the ancient practice:** Julius Caesar revived the aristocratic equestrian 'Game of Troy', and its regular performance was keenly overseen by Augustus.

p. 132 **The lads who take part are now known as Troys:** this is a strange piece of Latin, but a better translation would be *are now known as Troy*.

p. 136 **Acesta:** Acestes gives his name to the new foundation, which the Greeks called Egesta, and the Romans Segesta.

**p. 140 I saved Aeneas:** though on the Greek side in the *Iliad*, Poseidon did once intervene on the other side, to save Aeneas from Achilles (Book XX).

**p. 140 with one man lost at sea ... who will give his life for many:** the persistent sacrifice theme of Roman tradition emerges here, as the joint success of the expedition requires the sacrifice of Palinurus.

**p. 141 The Sirens' rocks:** the Sirens of mythology had been a desperate threat to the Argonauts and Odysseus with their bewitching songs; as Aeneas comes even closer to the historical portion of his journey, the Sirens are now mere rocks.

### BOOK VI

**p. 145 Euboean coast/Of Cumae:** Cumae was colonised by people from the Euboean city of Chalcis.

**p. 145 Trivia:** 'Goddess of the Three Ways', i.e., Hecate, the underworld manifestation of Apollo's sister, Diana.

**p. 145 the death of Androgeos:** it was the death at Athens of Minos' son, Androgeos, that led to the annual payment to the Minotaur.

**p. 146 a huge cavern:** in 1932 the original of the Sibyl's cave was discovered, a 6th century BC tunnel, set in the flank of the hill running parallel to the ancient shoreline; Virgil exaggerates its extent, but it remains a very remarkable monument.

**p. 147 For you then, Phoebus, and for Trivia:** Aeneas prophesies Augustus' construction of a temple for Apollo and Diana (dedicated 28 BC), and his transfer there of the Sibylline oracles.

**p. 149 Orpheus etc.:** a list of heroes and demi-gods who had successfully gone to the Underworld and returned.

**p. 150 a golden bough:** perhaps the most discussed mystery in the poem, with innumerable proposed solutions.

**p. 151 Aeolid:** i.e., son of Aeolus.

**p. 153 the Eumenides' mother and her great sister:** Night and Earth ('Eumenides'='Furies').

**p. 155 many beasts shaped out of kind:** all of these monsters are composites or multiples of one kind or another, tokens of the flux or chaos that it is the mission of Aeneas and his descendants to reduce to order.

**p. 156 Then Palinurus came by:** like Misenus at the beginning of the book, Palinurus provides an explanation of a contemporary geographical feature's name, the headland still called Capo di Palinuro just by Velia on the Lucanian coast, southeast of the Bay of Naples.

p. 160 **The fields of mourning:** Odysseus had met the ghosts of many famous women in his visit to Hades in *Odyssey* XI; here Virgil locates renowned heroines of Greek mythology, celebrated in tragedy and in Alexandrian poetry; amongst them now is his new heroine, Dido, destined to be even more famous.

p. 161 **Here Tydeus met him:** Tydeus, father of Aeneas' old foe Diomede, is the first of three of the Seven against Thebes whom he now meets; they are followed by a group of dead from Aeneas' side in the Trojan War.

p. 165 **the Lapithae:** this Thessalian tribe included two famous sinners, Ixion (punished for attempting to rape Juno) and Pirithoüs (punished for attempting to steal Prosepina from the Underworld). Another Lapith, Phlegyas, the father of Ixion, is mentioned further down this page; he was punished for burning down Apollo's temple after the god raped his daughter, Coronis.

p. 166 **The Thracian priest:** Orpheus, the archetypal musician.

p. 170 **Come now and I will tell you what glory:** the account of reincarnation makes possible a review of Roman history, in the future from Aeneas' perspective. The 'Parade of Heroes', as it is usually called, is packed with references to many historical figures, obscure to a modern audience, but as well known to Virgil's audience as Drake or Nelson. Anchises first points out the kings of Alba Longa, direct descendants of Aeneas, from whom springs Romulus, founder of Rome; we next see the second Romulus, Augustus, following in the family line. The parade then reverts to chronology, with the kings of Rome after Romulus, and Brutus marking the beginning of the Republic: the catalogue of Republican heroes that follows has no clear overall chronological pattern. Space forbids annotating or glossing many of these individuals.

p. 171 **Nomentum:** the first in a list of Latin towns that were once of some note, but had more or less vanished by Virgil's day.

p. 171 **The Maeotian land:** the area around the Sea of Azov.

p. 172 **But who is that . . .?:** Numa Pompilius, the second king of Rome. He is followed by the third king, Tullus Hostilius, the fourth, Ancus Marcius: reference follows to the Tarquins, the fifth and seventh.

**p. 172 the avenging Brutus:** Brutus avenged the rape of Lucretia by the son of the last king, expelled the royal family and founded the Republic; one of his first acts as consul was to execute his own sons for plotting to restore the monarchy. Shortly afterwards Anchises points to another Roman commander who was famous for executing his son, 'Torquatus, cruel with the axe' (same page).

**p. 172 Decii:** this family was famous for self-sacrifice on the battle-field.

**p. 172 Camillus:** Camillus saved Rome after it was sacked by the Gauls in 390 BC.

**p. 172 But those you see together in gleaming armour:** Julius Caesar and Pompey, linked by Pompey's marriage to Caesar's daughter, represented here at the moment (49 BC) when Caesar left his province in Gaul to invade Italy and precipitate the Civil War that led to the end of the Republic.

**p. 173 a spirit who will triumph over Corinth:** L. Mummius, who sacked Corinth in 146 BC; he is followed by 'That other', L. Aemilius Paullus, who defeated Perseus, King of Macedonia and reputed descendant of Achilles ('the Aeacid'), at Pydna in 168 BC. These men are so famous they do not need to be named, just as one might refer to 'the famous man who defeated the French Emperor at Waterloo' without fear of incomprehension. These are followed by more summary references, which cluster around the Carthaginian Wars in particular.

**p. 173 kill the Aeacid:** Aemilius Paullus didn't actually kill Perseus, although he did die after some years in captivity: *overthrow* would make more sense here.

**p. 173 Fabii:** Anchises refers especially to Q. Fabius Maximus ('the greatest'): his delaying tactics against Hannibal in the Second Punic War gave rise to the nickname 'Cunctator', literally 'Delayer'; the name was originally an insult ('Slowcoach', 'Dillydallyer'), but ultimately a compliment ('waiting for the moment').

**p. 173 Marcellus:** a great hero in the war against Hannibal, the captor of Syracuse, and one of only three men in Roman tradition to win 'the choicest spoils' by killing an enemy commander in hand-to-hand combat ('for the third time'). A descendant of his was the first husband of Augustus' sister, Octavia, and the child of this marriage, Marcellus, was to be the heir of the Emperor, who had no male issue: the premature death of Marcellus at the age of 19 in 23 BC is commemorated in Anchises' closing words ('The fates will show this young man to the world/But give him no existence after that'). The vision of Roman history ends with a genuine anticipation of the unknown future before Virgil's audience: if Marcellus will not follow Augustus, who or what will?

**p. 174 Sleep has two gates:** another mysterious and much-discussed passage – why does Aeneas return to the world above by the Gate of Ivory, the source of false dreams?

## BOOK VII

**p. 188 From Inachus:** Inachus is the patron deity of Argos, Juno's favourite Greek city. She is on her way from Argos to Carthage ('Pachynus in Sicily' is halfway).

**p. 189 Mars had strength/To ruin the great race of the Lapiths:** the destructive fight between Lapiths and Centaurs is only here attributed to Mars' instigation.

**p. 189 Calydon:** Diana sent a monstrous boar to terrorise the people of Calydon in punishment for being overlooked in sacrifice by their king.

**p. 189 Your dowry, girl:** Juno's rhetoric is made more sinister by the fact that she is traditionally the goddess of marriage.

**p. 189 To dream of firebrands:** when pregnant with Paris, Hecuba dreamt of giving birth to a firebrand.

**p. 191 Evoe Bacchus:** the cry of the Bacchante when inspired by the god.

**p. 192 Danaë and her Acrisian colonists:** Acrisius, king of Argus, the father of Danaë, put her and her baby son Perseus in a chest, in response to an oracle saying that her son would one day kill him. The usual version had the chest drift to the islands of Seriphus, but Virgil follows the version that said Danaë drifted to Latium.

**p. 198 There was a custom in Hesperian Latium:** the gates of Janus' temple were opened during times of war and closed during times of peace, and Augustus three times ceremoniously closed them; their opening by Juno symbolises the end of the peaceful past in Latium.

**p. 200 Helicon:** the homes of the Muses, who are the goddesses addressed here as Virgil approaches the catalogue of Italian troops. Homer had summoned the aid of the Muses in similar language at the beginning of his catalogue of Greeks in *Iliad* II. The catalogue is a stock element of epic; Virgil has another one in Book X, of the Etruscan allies who accompany Aeneas. He draws on existing traditional accounts and adds much of his own invention.

**p. 202 the Allia/The river with the name of ill omen:** it was at the river Allia that the invading Gauls routed the defending Roman army as they approached Rome in 390 BC.

## BOOK VIII

**p. 210 a huge sow with a litter ... of thirty piglets:** the traditional foundation omen in the Aeneas legend, either of Alba Longa or Lavinium; Virgil brings in the thirty piglets as a link to the notion that Alba Longa will be founded by Ascanius after thirty years of his rule (p. 9).

**p. 210 Comrades of King Evander:** Virgil inherited the tradition that the site of Rome had been once inhabited by Greeks from Arcadia under Evander. He capitalises on this opportunity in order to send his hero to the site of future Rome, ostensibly to seek the cavalry reinforcements he needs for fighting on the Latin plain, but fundamentally to bring him into physical contact with the city, its monuments and associations.

**p. 212 those which now ... but in Evander's day:** the antithesis between past and present, signalled as soon as the site of Rome is seen, is powerfully felt throughout the book: can contemporary Rome, in all its splendour and might, preserve the admirable moral values associated with the antique life of the first inhabitants of the site?

**p. 212 It happened that day:** the day is 12 August, feast-day of Hercules at the great altar in the Forum Boarium. Aeneas' arrival is linked with the liberating victory of Hercules over Cacus, and also with the victory of Augustus over Antony and Cleopatra, for Augustus entered the city the day after Hercules' feast-day to begin the celebration of his triple triumph (29 BC).

**p. 213 So both our families come of the same blood:** such recoveries of shared ancestry were the stock in trade of ancient diplomats.

**p. 215 a shaggy lion's skin:** another link between Aeneas and Hercules, who wore the untanned skin of a lion.

**p. 217 Potitius first ... And the Pinarian family:** these families had control of the cult of Hercules at the altar in the Forum Boarium until 312 BC, when it was taken over by the state. Augustus arranged for a man with the significant name of Potitus to be one of the consuls in the year he celebrated his triple triumph (29 BC).

**p. 218 the Salii:** the 'Jumping' or 'Dancing' priests, the Salii had their status boosted by Augustus, whose name was introduced into their hymn by the Senate in honour of his victory at Actium.

**p. 218 So they sang:** the list of Hercules' victories is traditional, as is the theme of his civilising triumphs over creatures of chaos, but the praise of Hercules acquires new significance in this context, since the grotesque monsters of myth are to be replaced by adversaries of a more historical and lifelike nature (Turnus, Mezentius, Antony).

**p. 219 Then all of them ... Walked back to the city:** the route takes them from Rome's pastoral origins (Lupercal, asylum), via the Republican centres of the Capitol and Forum, to the Palatine, where the new Romulus, Augustus, now lives.

**p. 220 the Lupercal:** Evander's explanation for the name of this cave is a Greek one, from 'Lycaean Pan' – 'wolf' is *lupus* in Latin and *lykos* in Greek, so that 'Wolf-cave' is explained as coming from 'Wolfish' Pan. Many such etymologies cluster here: 'Argiletum' is explained as 'Argus-death' (*letum* is Latin for 'death'); the cows 'moo' in the Roman forum because the gate from the forum to the Palatine was called *Mugonia*, which sounded to a Roman like 'Moo-gate'.

**p. 220 the Tarpeian rock,/Now golden:** the temple of Jupiter on the Capitoline hill, named here as 'the Tarpeian rock', was the grandest and most conspicuous monument in the city.

**p. 221 the house/Of a poor man, it was Evander's palace:** Virgil places in the same location on the Palatine hill the house of Evander, of Romulus (333 years later), and of Augustus (over 700 years later still).

**p. 221 Nereus's daughter, the wife of Tithonus:** Nereus' daughter (Thetis) and the wife of Tithonus (Aurora) are two separate characters, the mothers, respectively, of Achilles and Memnon: *Nereus' daughter and the wife of Tithonus*. Virgil explicitly invites the reader to compare his narrative with that of its models in Homeric and Cyclic epic.

**p. 222 one of the Aeoliae:** the adjective doesn't seem to be used like this – *one of the Aeolians* is possibly better.

**p. 224 The Lydian people:** the Etruscans were commonly thought to have been migrants from Lydia.

**p. 229 a shield of inexplicable texture:** based on the Homeric shield made for Achilles by Hephaestus in *Iliad* XVIII, Aeneas' shield is covered in important events from Roman history. It has many incidents from the period of the Seven Kings, then the salvation of the city from three great threats: the Gallic invasion of 390 BC; the conspiracy of Catiline in 63 BC; and – climactically – Antony and Cleopatra, with the Battle of Actium (31 BC) and Augustus' triple triumph (29 BC).

**p. 229 The she-wolf with the twin boys:** Romulus and Remus were exposed by their grandfather, but saved and suckled by a she-wolf in the Lupercal at the foot of the Palatine hill.

**p. 229 the Sabine women:** the first Romans were all men, and Romulus organised the 'Rape of the Sabine women' to provide wives for his band of outlaws and outcasts: the women prevented war between their new husbands and King Tatius, leader of the Sabines from Cures.

**p. 229 Tearing Mettus apart:** Mettus, king of Alba Longa, tricked the Roman king Tullus Hostilius when they were supposed to be allies against Veii and Fidenae, and was brutally punished. After his death Alba Longa was destroyed and its inhabitants transferred to Rome.

**p. 230 Porsenna:** Lars Porsenna of Clusium, who attempted to restore the last king of Rome, Tarquin, after his expulsion: the resultant siege of Rome includes the stories of Horatius Cocles defending the bridge and Cloelia escaping from being an Etruscan hostage.

**p. 230 At the top Manlius:** the Gauls captured all of the city apart from the Capitol, and Manlius was in charge of the Capitoline garrision when the Gauls attempted a surprise night attack, detected only by the hissing of Juno's sacred geese.

**p. 230 Salii:** see note on p. 218 (the 'headgear' and heavenly 'shields' actually belong to them). The Luperci are another guild of priests, and this portion of the shield also includes an image of female religious piety ('Chaste matrons . . .').

**p. 230 Catiline:** according to Cicero, the consul of the year, Catiline plotted the overthrow of the constitution (63 BC); he was denounced by Cicero and left the city, dying at the head of a rebel army in the next year. Cato vigorously supported Cicero, demanding the death-penalty for Catiline's co-conspirators; after Julius Caesar's victory over Senatorial forces in North Africa during the Civil War, he committed suicide rather than surrender (46 BC).

**p. 231 all Leucate alight:** Leucate is the southern extremity of the island of Leucas, some thirty miles south of Actium; Virgil appears to associate it with Actium.

p. 232 **the snowy threshold/Of shining Phoebus:** the magnificent temple of Apollo on the Palatine, adjacent to Augustus' house, and part of his residential complex; it was dedicated the year after the triumph (28 BC).

p. 232 **Nomadic people:** in the following lines Virgil gives a more optimistic than accurate picture of the limits of Roman power, with people and places from the extreme boundaries of the known world all submitting to the Empire.

## BOOK IX

p. 237 **He attacked, calling on his cheering men/For fire:** in his attack on the ships and, later in the book, on the camp, Turnus is acting the part of Hector, whose greatest moment of success in the *Iliad* comes when he attacks the Greek camp and sets fire to their fleet.

p. 240 **Palladium:** see note for p. 32.

p. 241 **Nisus was captain of the gate:** the night-raid out of the besieged camp is modelled on an episode in the *Iliad*, where Odysseus and Diomede steal the horses of Rhesus and kill the Trojan spy, Dolon (Book X). Virgil's version is very different in its sentimentality and sensationalism, and in its emphasis on the love between the two protagonists and on their youthful and ultimately fatal rashness.

p. 254 **Numanus Remulus:** his speech reflects many of the unconventional 'Orientalist' prejudices of the Romans, and highlights the complexities of the poem's theme of Eastern influence upon Western culture; it also shows the difficulties of Augustan attempts to preserve antique Roman values in a modern, cosmopolitan urban culture.

p. 258 **the Euboic shore of Baiae:** Baiae, settled by Euboeans, was a fashionable seaside resort in the Bay of Naples; Prochyta (modern Procida) and Inarime (modern Ischia) are small islands off the nearby coast.

p. 259 **A new Achilles:** a vital theme in the war-books is the success or failure of the characters' imitation of their Homeric prototypes. Here Turnus is Achillean in his prowess, but his ultimate failure is signalled by the fact that he is following in the final footsteps of Achilles, who was killed when he pursued the Trojans right inside the walls (in the post-Homeric poem, *Aethiopis*).

## BOOK X

**p. 265 the palace of supreme Olympus:** Homer has a number of divine councils in the *Iliad*, and two in the *Odyssey*; Virgil amalgamates them into one set-piece episode, in which the main divine antagonists of the poem collide in debate.

**p. 265 There will be time enough for fighting later:** this appears to be a prophecy not simply of Hannibal's invasion of Italy at the beginning of the Second Punic War, but of the support Juno gave the Carthaginians during that war. Virgil is alluding to the Ennian tradition, which dated Juno's final reconciliation to the Roman cause during the Hannibalic war.

**p. 266 Nor have I seen . . . the last of my own wounds:** an allusion to *Iliad* V, where Aphrodite is wounded by Diomede. Throughout this speech, Venus obsessively views the action of the poem as nothing but a re-run of the events of Homer's Trojan War; her version is inadequate both poetically (since Virgil is not simply repeating Homer), and historically (since the new foundation in Italy will be something completely novel in human history, not simply another Troy).

**p. 268 You smuggle Aeneas:** another reference to *Iliad* V, where Aphrodite and Apollo rescue Aeneas from Diomede; Juno will herself soon be forced to rescue Turnus from Aeneas by the same device (pp. 286–7).

**p. 269 I will remain impartial:** readers must judge for themselves how impartial Jupiter is as they read the ensuing narrative.

**p. 269 his Stygian brother:** Dis.

**p. 269 the Dardan boy:** Ascanius.

**p. 270 Orician:** from Oricus, a port on the Illyrian coast in modern Albania.

**p. 271 Now goddesses, open your Helicon:** a second catalogue, this time of Trojan allies. Homer has a catalogue of Trojan allies in *Iliad* II, to follow his (much longer) catalogue of Greeks. Practically all of the chieftains mentioned here are nonentities who play no part in the subsequent narrative (Abas is soon killed later in this book, and Aulestes is unmentioned until he is killed by Messapus early in Book XII). The one exception is the third one mentioned, Asilas. He is a master of what the Romans of Virgil's time called 'the Etruscan lore', specialised forms of divination; with the one exception of this arcane religious knowledge, Etruscan culture has vanished, swallowed up in the Roman commonwealth. The catalogue thus illustrates one of the poem's main themes, the continual amalgamation of diverse groups into a ceaselessly evolving Roman identity.

**p. 272 Mantua:** Virgil's home-town, here celebrated as an early prototype of successful ethnic blending. The city is said to be named after a prophetess, Manto, whose name recalls the Greek word for prophet (*mantis*).

**p. 280 Turnus's sister:** the first mention of Juturna (though she is not named yet), who will play such an important role in the plot of Book XII.

**p. 282 the unspeakable crime:** a famous incident from Greek mythology, the murder by the daughters of Danaus of their cousin-bridegrooms on their wedding-night (only one of the fifty girls relented).

**p. 282 sacrifices to the dead Pallas:** Aeneas' rage recalls that of Achilles, who sacrifices twelve young Trojan captives on Patroclus' funeral pyre in *Iliad* XXIII.

**p. 284 Like Aegaeon:** the extremity of Aeneas' passion is remarkably characterised when he is compared to a giant who fought against Jupiter.

**p. 291 Huge as Orion:** Aeneas' great adversary in this Book is in his turn compared to a monstrous giant, the huge Orion, who gave his name to the constellation.

**p. 296 quite consciously:** one of the many touches which give a gladiatorial and professional atmosphere to Mezentius' final moments.

### BOOK XI

**p. 307 All of us ... Have suffered unspeakable penalties:** see note above for p. 40 for the sack of Troy as the moment when the gods' favour turns against the Greeks. Diomede refers to the storm Minerva sent against the home-coming Greeks off the Euboean promontory of Caphareus, and to the disasters of the main Greek commanders, including Menelaus' journey to Egypt ('the pillars of Proteus'), Neoptolemus' death, Idomeneus' migration from Crete, the shipwreck and settlement in Africa of the Locrians (the people of Ajax son of Oileus), the killing of Agamemnon by his wife Clytemnestra.

**p. 308 violated/The right hand of Venus with a wound:** see note for p. 266.

**p. 309 Aetolian forces:** the people of Diomede.

**p. 317 Latona's daughter:** Diana (Latona is the Latin for Leto).

**p. 320 Aconteus/Is thrown off:** stirrups were invented after the ancient world, so that ancient cavalry engagements result in a lot of combatants falling off their mounts.

**p. 321 they resemble/The Thracian Amazons:** Virgil mentions the two most famous Amazons of mythology, Hippolyte, killed by Hercules for her girdle, and Penthesilea, killed by Achilles at Troy.

### BOOK XII

**p. 338 the goddess who presided over pools:** there was an ancient 'Pool of Juturna' by the temple of Vesta in the Roman Forum, and Virgil first associates this deity with Turnus and the Aeneas legend.

**p. 344 Sent by what hand ... Remains uncertain:** Juno's words later (p. 360) imply that Juturna was responsible.

**p. 345 the son of old Dolon:** Dolon is the Trojan spy killed by Odysseus and Diomede in *Iliad* X.

**p. 349 It is Turnus alone he tries to track down:** at this stage Aeneas is still doing his best to keep to the terms of the truce.

**p. 357 In Sila, or on the summit of Taburnus:** mountains of southern and central Italy give specificity to the simile's action.

**p. 357 Jupiter himself is holding/The scales:** as he had in the corresponding scene in *Iliad* XXII, at the duel of Achilles and Hector.

**p. 359 Meanwhile the king of great Olympus spoke:** the final conversation between Jupiter and Juno resolves many of the issues of the plot, allowing for the definitive end of Troy and opening the way for Juno's full embracing of the future Romans as her own people; whether she is fully reconciled at this stage depends largely upon how we read the apparent references to her future involvement in the Hannibalic war at the beginning of Book X.

**p. 361 By Parthian or Cydonian:** the Parthians and Cretans were famous archers.

**p. 364 with a hiss it passes through the thigh:** in *Iliad* XXII Achilles' spear wounds Hector fatally in the neck, although allowing him to speak; it is crucial that Turnus' wound is not mortal, opening up the dilemmas of Aeneas' response to Turnus' plea, and of the reader's response to Aeneas' choice.

# GLOSSARY OF NAMES AND EPITHETS

ACCA, companion of Camilla, who in Book XI receives her last commands and brings Turnus the news of her death.

ACESTES, half-Trojan, half-Sicilian hero, ruler of Segesta in Northwest Sicily, near Mt Eryx, an important cult-centre of Venus.

ACHAEAN, Greek.

ACHAEMENIDES, companion of Ulysses, whom Aeneas rescues from the Cyclops Polyphemus at the end of Book III.

ACHATES, constant companion of Aeneas.

ACHERON, a river of the Underworld; the Underworld in general.

ACHILLES, son of Peleus and the sea-goddess Thetis, mightiest and most terrible of the Greek heroes at Troy, killer of many Trojans, in particular of Aeneas' relative Hector.

ACOETES, an Arcadian, sometime armour-bearer of Evander, companion to Pallas.

ACTIUM, a promontory in the Gulf of Ambracia in Western Greece, which gave its name to the sea-battle in which Augustus and Agrippa defeated Antony and Cleopatra (2 September, 31 BC).

AEACID, a descendant of Aeacus, a member of the royal family of Achilles.

AEOLUS, king of the winds, his kingdom was situated in the Lipari (or 'Aeolian') islands off the northeast coast of Sicily.

AGAMEMNON, brother of Menelaus, and leader of the Greek expedition against Troy.

AGRIPPA, M. Vipsanius Agrippa (64/3–12 BC), right-hand man of Augustus, in command of the left wing at Actium.

AGYLLA, Caere, modern Cerveteri, Etruscan city once ruled by Mezentius.

AJAX, son of Oileus, a Greek hero who incurs the anger of Minerva for raping her priestess, Cassandra, at the sack of Troy.

ALETES, elderly Trojan commander, who participates in the conference before the night raid of Nisus and Euryalus.

ALLECTO, 'Relentless One', a Fury, who is summoned by Juno in Book VII to sow the seeds of war between Trojans and Latins.

ALOEUS, father of the giants Otus and Ephialtes, enemies of Jupiter.

AMATA, wife of Latinus, mother of Lavinia; favouring Turnus' suit of her daughter, she is driven mad by Allecto and commits suicide as Turnus faces defeat.

AMAZONS, warrior-maidens who live independently of men.

AMPHITRYON, see HERCULES.

ANCHISES, the father of Aeneas by Venus, rescued by Aeneas from the sack of Troy; dies near Segesta in Northwest Sicily.

ANDROGEOS, Greek warrior killed during the sack of Troy.

ANDROMACHE, wife of Hector, and mother of their son, Astyanax, who was killed by the Greeks after the sack of Troy; she is subsequently married to Neoptolemus and then Helenus.

ANNA, sister of Dido.

ANTENOR, a Trojan hero in Homer, whom later tradition said escaped from the sack of Troy: Virgil makes him the founder of Padua.

APOLLO, Augustus' favourite god, the Greek and Roman god of healing, music, prophecy and archery; also 'Delian', 'Phoebus'.

ARDEA, town in Latium, home of Turnus.

ARGIVE, Greek.

ARRUNS, Etruscan, priest of Apollo at Soracte, who kills Camilla and is in turn killed by Opis.

ASCANIUS, son of Aeneas and Creusa. His alternative name, Ilus ('Trojan'), changed to Iulus, was claimed as the origin of the name of the family of Julius Caesar. He is in command in Book IX while Aeneas is away at Pallanteum, but is too young to play an active part in the war.

ASSARACUS, member of the Trojan royal house, brother of Ganymede and grandfather of Anchises.

ATLAS, North African mountain, pillar of the sky; as a mythological character, the grandfather of Dardanus.

AUFIDUS, the main river of Apulia, flowing into the Adriatic.

AURORA, Dawn, wife of Tithonus, mother of Memnon.

AURUNCAN, Campanian.

AUSONIA, Italy.

AVENTINUS, Italian ally of Turnus, born on the Aventine hill at the site of Rome, son of Hercules and Rhea.

AVERNUS, a volcanic crater lake near Naples, whose sulphuric nature led to its association with the Underworld.

BACCHANTE, a devotee of Bacchus.

BACCHUS, the Greek Dionysus, god of wine.

BELLONA, Italian goddess of war.

CACUS, 'Bad Man', son of Vulcan, a monster who lives in a cave under the Aventine hill at Pallanteum; he is killed by Hercules after stealing some of the cattle he was bringing home from Geryon.

CAECULUS, the founder of Praeneste, who leads a contingent of rustics to fight for Turnus.

CAENEUS, the woman Caenis, granted invulnerable masculinity as a recompense for losing her virginity to Neptune.

CAIETA, modern Gaeta, a town on the coast between Cumae and Ostia, named after Aeneas' nurse, who died there.

CALCHAS, the seer of the Greek army at Troy.

CALLIOPE, a Muse, invoked by Virgil as he begins the narrative of Turnus' prowess in the attack on the Trojan camp in Book IX.

CALYBE, priestess of Juno at Ardea, whom Allecto impersonates to deceive Turnus in Book VII.

CAMILLA, daughter of Metabus, Amazon-like ally of Turnus, leader of the contingent of Volsci, killed by Arruns at the end of Book XI.

CARMENTIS, mother of Evander, a prophetic nymph, who gave her name to the Carmental gate.

CARTHAGE, a colony of the Phoenician city Tyre, Rome's greatest Mediterranean enemy, antagonist in the three bitter 'Punic' wars of 264–41, 218–202, and 149–46 BC.

CASSANDRA, a daughter of Priam, famous in the post-Homeric tradition as a prophetess doomed never to be believed, raped by Ajax, son of Oileus, from the altar of Minerva during the sack of Troy.

CATILLUS and CORAS, twin brothers, allies of Turnus, leaders of the contingent from Tibur.

CECROPS, first king of Athens, hence 'Cecrops' children' = 'Athenians'.

CELAENO, chief of the HARPIES.

CERBERUS, three-headed guard-dog of the Underworld, once stolen by Hercules as one of his twelve labours.

CERES, the Greek Demeter, goddess of cereal crops and agricultural fertility in general.

CHARON, the ferryman of the Underworld, who transports shades of the dead across the Styx.

CHARYBDIS, a gigantic whirlpool that threatens shipping in the Straits of Messina between Sicily and Italy.

CHIMAERA, a composite monster (snake, lion, she-goat), killed by Bellerophon.

CIRCE, one of the principal threats to Odysseus in the *Odyssey*, an enchantress who turns men into swine; Aeneas passes by her island at the beginning of Book VII.

CLAUSUS, a Sabine hero, the eponymous ancestor of the family of the Claudii.

CLOANTHUS, Trojan, commander of the *Scylla* in the ship-race in Book V.

COCYTUS, 'Wailing', a river of the Underworld.

COROEBUS, a Trojan ally, in love with Cassandra, killed attempting to rescue her during the sack of Troy.

CORYTHUS, see DARDANUS.

CREUSA, Aeneas' first wife, mother of Ascanius/Iulus, who dies during the sack of Troy.

CUMAE, a small town near the Bay of Naples, home of the Sibyl and site of a temple of Apollo.

CUPID, son of Venus, a god of love.

CURETES, a Cretan cult-group of youths, associated by the Roman poets with the worship of the Great Mother.

CYBELE, see GREAT MOTHER.

CYCLADES, a group of islands in the Aegean Sea centring on Delos.

CYCLOPES, a race of one-eyed giants, employed as the workers of Vulcan; see POLYPHEMUS.

CYLLENIAN, see MERCURY.

CYMODOCEA, a sea-nymph, transformed from one of Aeneas' ships, who helps his passage back to the camp in Book X.

CYTHEREAN, see VENUS.

DAEDALUS, archetypal craftsman, designer of the Cretan labyrinth, father of Icarus; his story is told at the beginning of Book VI.

DANAAN, Greek.

DARDANUS, son of Corythus, the founder of the Trojan race (hence 'Dardan' = 'Trojan'), whom Virgil says originally came from Corythus in Italy.

DARES, Trojan, beaten in the boxing match of Book V by the Sicilian Entellus.

DEIPHOBUS, son of Priam and Hecuba, who married Helen after the death of Paris, and is killed and mutilated by Menelaus at the sack of Troy with Helen's connivance.

DELOS, the centre of the Cyclades in the Aegean, the birthplace of Artemis and her twin Apollo (hence 'Delian' = 'Apollo'); also 'Ortygia'.

DIANA, the Greek Artemis, twin sister of Apollo, virgin goddess of hunting; also 'Latona's daughter', 'Latonian', 'Trivia'.

DIDO, the mythical founder of Carthage, famous before Virgil but almost certainly not earlier linked in a love affair with Aeneas; also 'Elissa'.

DINDYMUM, mountain on the Cyzicus peninsula in Northwest Asia Minor, sacred to the Great Mother.

DIOMEDE, Greek hero at Troy, who fought and defeated Aeneas in combat there, and wounded the hand of his mother Venus, now settled in exile at Arpi, in Southeast Italy; also 'the son of Tydeus'.

DIS, king of the Underworld; also 'Orcus', 'Pluto'.

DOLOPIAN, Greek.

DRANCES, an Italian, enemy of Turnus, skilled in rhetoric and political intrigue.

EDONIAN, Thracian.

ELISSA, see DIDO.

ELYSIUM, the abode of the blessed in the Underworld.

ENTELLUS, Sicilian, victor over Dares in the boxing match in Book V.

ERATO, a Muse, invoked by Virgil at the beginning of Book VII.

EREBUS, the Underworld.

ERIDANUS, a mysterious river, identified by Virgil with the Po.

ERIPHYLE, wife of the prophet Amphiaraus, responsible for his death, and killed in revenge by her son Alcmaeon.

ERULUS, threefold man-monster slain by Evander in his youth.

ERYX, son of Venus and the Argonaut Butes, half-brother of Aeneas; the mountain and town of Eryx in Sicily, cult-site of Venus, are named after him.

EURYALUS, beloved of Nisus, assisted by him to victory in the foot-race in Book V and killed together with him in the night raid in Book IX.

EVADNE, wife of Capaneus, one of the Seven against Thebes; she committed suttee on his funeral pyre.

EVANDER, a refugee from Arcadia, son of Carmentis, father of Pallas (i), founder of Pallanteum on the site of Rome; host of Aeneas in Book VIII.

FAUNUS, the Greek Pan, a rustic deity, father of Latinus.

FURIES, Underworld deities responsible for instigating madness and punishing sin.

GARAMANTIANS, an African people.

GERYON, a monster with three heads or bodies, killed by Hercules for his cattle.

GNOSIAN, Cretan.

GORGON, a snake-haired female monster, associated with the Furies, the sight of whom turned the viewer into stone. Decapitated by Perseus, her head was claimed by Minerva for her breastplate.

GREAT MOTHER, a Phrygian earth-mother goddess, situated by Virgil on Mt Ida, and regarded as the mother of all the gods; also 'Berecyntian', 'Cybele'.

GYAS, Trojan, commander of the *Chimaera* in the ship-race in Book V.

HALAESUS, a Greek who fights on Turnus' side against Aeneas, and is killed by Pallas in Book X.

HAMMON, see JUPITER.

HARPIES, 'Snatchers' in Greek, winged female monsters who had once victimised Phineus until he was rescued by Jason and the Argonauts; they attack the Trojans after they leave Crete.

HECATE, the chthonic manifestation of the goddess Diana, associated with magic.

HECTOR, victim of Achilles, greatest Trojan hero in Homer's poetry, a relative of Aeneas, and a model for him to outdo by being victorious rather than defeated.

HECUBA, wife of Priam and mother of a host of famous men and women.

HELEN, wife of Menelaus, who ran away with Paris to Troy, thus setting the Trojan War in motion.

HELENUS, son of Priam, a noted prophet, who marries Hector's widow Andromache, and prophesies to Aeneas in Book III.

HERCULES, mightiest of the Greek heroes, son of Alcmena and Jupiter, but often referred to as the son of Amphitryon, Alcmena's mortal husband. A one-time sacker of Troy, who nonetheless becomes a prototype for Aeneas, as one who goes down to the Underworld and back, who performs mighty deeds of violence to civilise the world, and who is rewarded with apotheosis at the end of his labours; also 'Tirynthian'.

HESPERIA, 'the western land', Italy.

HIPPOLYTUS, son of Theseus and step-son of Phaedra; Virgil's version of his fate, involving his translation to Italy, is told at the end of Book VII.

HYDRA, many-headed water-snake, killed by Hercules, now in Tartarus.

IAPYX, son of Iasius, a Trojan healer, taught by Apollo, who attempts to cure Aeneas' arrow-wound in Book XII.

IARBAS, African king, son of Jupiter, spurned as a suitor by Dido.

IBERIA, Spain.

IDA, a mountain close to Troy, home of the Great Mother; also a mountain in Crete, likewise dear to the Great Mother.

IDALIAN, see VENUS.

ILIA, 'Trojan woman', the mother of Romulus and Remus by the god Mars.

ILIONEUS, prominent Trojan in Aeneas' force, who leads the embassy to Latinus in Book VII.

ILIUM, Troy; hence 'Ilian' = 'Trojan'.

INACHUS, ancestral king of Argos; hence 'Inachan' = 'Argive', 'Greek'.

IO, daughter of Inachus, king of Argos, raped by Jupiter and transformed into a heifer, guarded by hundred-eyed Argus.

IOPAS, bard at the Carthaginian court.

IRIS, the messenger of Hera/Juno in the post-Homeric tradition.

IULUS, see ASCANIUS.

JANUS, two-headed god of doorways, an ancestor of Latinus.

JUNO, goddess of marriage, wife and sister of Jupiter, daughter of Saturn (hence 'Saturnia'), the chief enemy of the Trojans (as the Greek goddess Hera) and friend of Carthage (as the Carthaginian goddess Tanit).

JUPITER, the Greek Zeus and African Hammon, husband and brother of Juno, son of Saturn, and the supreme god of the Roman state.

JUTURNA, sister of Turnus, given immortality by Jupiter after being raped by him; at Juno's instigation she assists Turnus throughout Book XII.

LAOCOON, Trojan priest of Neptune, killed by the gods for warning the Trojans against accepting the wooden horse.

LAODAMIA, after one night of marriage, her husband Protesilaus left her to become the first man to die at Troy.

LAOMEDON, proverbially treacherous king of Troy, father of Priam; he cheated Hercules out of his agreed payment for building the walls of the city and saw the city sacked as a result.

LARES, singular LAR, household gods, especially those brought from Troy to Italy by Aeneas.

LATINUS, eponymous hero of the Latini, king of Latium, son of Faunus, husband of Amata and father of Lavinia.

LATIUM, the coastal plain in central Western Italy inhabited by the Latini (speakers of Latin).

LAURENTINE, of the people of King Latinus in Latium.

LAUSUS, son of Mezentius, killed by Aeneas in Book X while protecting his wounded father.

LAVINIA, daughter of Latinus and Amata, second wife of Aeneas, mother of Silvius.

LENAEAN, Bacchic.

LETHE, 'Oblivion', 'Forgetfulness', a river of the Underworld.

MAEONIA, an area of Lydia, origin of the Etruscans; hence 'Maeonian' = 'Etruscan'.

MARS, the Greek Ares, the god of war, father of Romulus and Remus; resident in Thrace; also 'Gradivus', 'Mavors'.

MAVORS, see MARS.

MEMNON, the son of Dawn, king of the Ethiopians, an ally of the Trojans during the Trojan War, killed by Achilles.

MENELAUS, brother of Agamemnon, husband of Helen; the Greeks went to Troy to recover his bride from Paris.

MERCURY, the Greek Hermes, the messenger of Jupiter; also 'Cyllenian', 'son of Maia'.

MESSAPUS, one of the most important heroes on the Latin side, a son of Neptune, leader of the contingent of the Falisci, the people on the west bank of the Tiber north of Rome.

METABUS, father of Camilla.

METISCUS, Turnus' charioteer, displaced and impersonated by Juturna in Book XII.

MEZENTIUS, father of Lausus, king of Agylla (Caere) in Etruria, expelled by his people after years of brutal tyranny, takes refuge with Turnus and is a principal ally of his against Aeneas. He and his son are both killed by Aeneas in Book X.

MINERVA, the Greek Athena, daughter of Jupiter and traditional enemy of Troy; also 'Pallas', 'Tritonian'.

MINOS, king of Crete, husband of Pasiphaë, father of Androgeos, after his death a judge in the Underworld.

MISENUS, Aeneas' trumpeter, who dies at the beginning of Book VI and is met by Aeneas in the Underworld.

MNESTHEUS, Trojan hero, commander of the *Sea Dragon* in the ship-race in Book V, and prominent in the war in Italy, being left in joint command of the camp in Book IX during Aeneas' absence.

MUSAEUS, a musician, regularly associated with Orpheus.

MYCENAE, in Homer the citadel of Agamemnon, often used to refer to Greece in general.

MYRMIDONS, the troops of Achilles (and Greeks in general).

NAUTES, Trojan soothsayer who advises Aeneas after the attempted burning of the fleet in Book V.

NEOPTOLEMUS, son of Achilles, who kills Priam during the sack of Troy; also 'Pyrrhus'.

NEPTUNE, the Greek Poseidon, god of the sea and traditional enemy of Troy.

NEREUS, a sea-god; hence 'Nereids', his daughters, nymphs of the sea.

NISUS, lover of Euryalus, helps him win the foot-race in Book V and dies with him in the night raid in Book IX.

NUMICIUS, small river in Latium in which Aeneas drowned.

NUMIDIANS, a major North African people, bordering on Carthage, famous for their horsemanship.

OEBALUS, ally of Turnus, leader of the contingent from Southern Campania.

OENOTRIAN, Italian.

OPIS, a nymph of Diana's, who came from Thrace to Delos; in Book XI, on Diana's orders, she avenges the death of Camilla by shooting Arruns.

ORCUS, see DIS.

ORESTES, son of Agamemnon, who is hounded by the Furies after killing his mother Clytemnestra in revenge for her murder of Agamemnon; he kills Neoptolemus/Pyrrhus for taking his bride Hermione, the daughter of Menelaus and Helen.

ORITHYIA, wife of the North Wind, Boreas.

ORONTES, ally of Aeneas, drowned in the storm in Book I.

ORTYGIA, see DELOS.

OSTIA, the port of Rome, and the site of Aeneas' camp when he arrives in Latium.

PALAMEDES, Greek hero who tricked Odysseus into serving in the Trojan War and who was in turn framed by Odysseus as a traitor and executed.

PALINURUS, Aeneas' helmsman, whom he meets in the Underworld.

PALLAS (i), son of Evander, King of Pallanteum, principal ally of Aeneas; his death at the hands of Turnus in Book X is the principal event in the plot of the war-narrative.

PALLAS (ii), see MINERVA.

PANDARUS and BITIAS, mighty Trojan warriors, sons of Alcanor, who open the camp to the enemy in Book IX; both are killed by Turnus.

PANTHUS, Trojan priest of Apollo, killed during the sack.

PARIS, Trojan prince, son of Priam and Hecuba, who stole Helen to start the Trojan War.

PARRHASIAN, Arcadian.

PASIPHAË, wife of Minos, mother (by a bull) of the Minotaur, half-man, half-bull.

PELASGIAN, Greek.

PENATES, household gods of Troy, brought by Aeneas to Italy and housed in the temple of Vesta.

PENTHESILEA, queen of the Amazons, an ally of the Trojans during the Trojan War, killed by Achilles.

PERGAMA, the citadel of Troy.

PHAEDRA, daughter of Minos, wife of Theseus, victim of an illicit passion for her stepson, Hippolytus.

PHAETHON, a Homeric epithet of the Sun; also the name of a son of the Sun, killed by Jupiter's thunderbolt when he caused havoc by failing to control his father's chariot.

PHLEGETHON, 'Burning', a river of the Underworld.

PHOEBUS, see APOLLO.

PHRYGIAN, Trojan.

PICUS, a Latin king turned into a woodpecker by Circe, son of Saturn, father of Faunus and grandfather of Latinus.

PILUMNUS, an Italian god of agriculture, great-great-grandfather of Turnus.

PLUTO, see DIS.

POLITES, a son of Priam, killed by Neoptolemus before Priam's eyes during the sack.

POLYDORUS, a son of Priam, sent to refuge with the king of Thrace during the Trojan War; he was murdered by the king for the gold he brought with him.

POLYPHEMUS, one of the Cyclopes, a one-eyed monster blinded by Ulysses, whom Aeneas encounters at the end of his wanderings in Book III.

PORTUNUS, god of harbours.

PRAENESTE, important Latin town, founded by Caeculus.

PRIAM, the last king of Troy, killed by Achilles' son Neoptolemus during the sack.

PROCRIS, mistakenly killed by her husband Cephalus.

PROSERPINA, the Greek Persephone, queen of the Underworld, bride of Dis.

PUNIC, Phoenician/Carthaginian.

PYRRHUS, see NEOPTOLEMUS.

RHADAMANTHUS, brother of Minos, like him a judge in the Underworld.

RHESUS, an ally of the Trojans in Homer, killed by Ulysses and Diomede.

RHOETEAN, Trojan.

ROMULUS AND REMUS, twin sons of Mars and Ilia; Romulus killed his brother when they quarrelled at the moment of founding Rome.

RUMOUR, daughter of Earth, sister of the giants, who spreads abroad gossip and hearsay, in particular, versions of what Aeneas and Dido are doing after their 'marriage' in Book IV.

RUTULIAN, the people of Turnus, located around Ardea.

SALMONEUS, king of Salmone in Elis, killed by a thunderbolt from Jupiter in punishment for mimicking Jupiter's command of thunder and lightning.

SARPEDON, son of Zeus, one of the greatest heroes on the Trojan side in the *Iliad*, killed by Achilles' friend Patroclus in Book XVI.

SATURN, the Greek Cronus, father of the Olympian gods; after his overthrow by Jupiter he sought refuge in Latium, where his rule is remembered as a Golden Age.

SCYLLA, a sea-monster who terrorises the Straits of Messina between Sicily and Italy.

SERGESTUS, Trojan, commander of the *Centaur* in the ship-race in Book V, and left in joint command of the camp in Book IX during Aeneas' absence.

SIBYL, a prophetess, esp. the Sibyl of Cumae, Deiphobe, inspired by Apollo, who is Aeneas' guide through the Underworld in Book VI.

SICANIAN, (i) Sicilian; (ii) an obscure people living in antique Latium.

SIDONIAN, Phoenician/Carthaginian.

SIGEUM, a promontory on the Trojan plain; hence 'Troy'.

SIMOIS, with Scamander/Xanthus one of the two rivers running through the Trojan plain.

SINON, Greek whose rhetoric deceives the Trojans into accepting the wooden horse.

STYX, 'Hateful', a river of the Underworld; hence 'Stygian'.

SYCHAEUS, husband of Dido, murdered by her brother Pygmalion.

SYRTES, feared stretches of coastal shallows between Carthage and modern Libya.

TARCHON, leader of Aeneas' Etruscan allies, most prominent of the Etruscan warriors.

TARTARUS, the place of the damned in the Underworld.

TEUCER, (i) the ultimate ancestor of the Trojan race (hence 'Teucrian' = 'Trojan'); (ii) a Greek hero at Troy, who was exiled on his return home and founded a new Salamis on the island of Cyprus.

TIBER, the river on whose banks Rome is built, the boundary between Latium and Etruria.

TIBUR, important Latin city, home of Catillus and Coras.

TISIPHONE, 'Avenger of murder', one of the Furies.

TITANS, sons of Sky and Earth, the generation of gods before the Olympians, vanquished by Zeus/Jupiter in cosmic struggle.

TITYOS, giant who is punished in Tartarus for attempting to rape Leto, mother of Apollo and Diana.

TOLUMNIUS, an augur in Turnus' army, who throws the first spear to violate the truce at the beginning of Book XII, and is killed in the subsequent fighting.

TRINACRIAN, Sicilian.

TRITON, a sea-god.

TRITONIAN, see MINERVA.

TROILUS, a son of Priam, killed by Achilles; his death was one of the fated signs of Troy's doom.

TROY, the focus of Greek heroic epic, whose fall is commemorated in Homer's poetry, and the supposed origin of the Romans' ancestors according to tradition long before Virgil; also 'Dardania', 'Ilium', 'Pergama'.

TURNUS, son of Daunus of Ardea and the sea-deity Venilia, a Latin prince, suitor of Lavinia, and principal antagonist of Aeneas in the war in Latium.

TYRRHENIAN, Etruscan.

UFENS, ally of Turnus, leader of the contingent of Aequi, killed in battle in Book XII.

ULYSSES, the Greek Odysseus, hero of Homer's *Odyssey*, memorable for his cunning and treachery.

UMBRO, ally of Turnus, leader of the contingent of Marsi, a medicine-man and snake-charmer.

VENILIA, a sea-deity, mother of Turnus.

VENULUS, Latin, sent on an embassy to Diomede to try to persuade him to join the war against Aeneas.

VENUS, the Greek Aphrodite, goddess of love; as the mother of Aeneas an ally of Troy and the ancestress of the Roman people as a whole; also 'Cytherean', 'daughter of Dione', 'Idalian'.

VESTA, the Greek Hestia, the goddess of the hearth, associated by Virgil with the household gods brought by Aeneas from Troy to Latium.

VIRBIUS, ally of Turnus, son of Hippolytus/Virbius.

VOLCENS, Rutulian cavalry commander, who captures and kills Euryalus and is himself killed by Nisus in Book IX.

VOLSCIANS, an Italian people, allied to Turnus.

VULCAN, the Greek Hephaestus, husband of Venus, god of fire and the master-smith of the gods; also 'lord of Lemnos'.

XANTHUS, see SIMOIS.

# SUGGESTIONS FOR FURTHER READING

The best further reading is Homer's *Iliad* and *Odyssey*, followed by Virgil's earlier poetry, the *Eclogues* and *Georgics*. There are useful introductions to Homer and Virgil by Jasper Griffin in the Oxford University Press *Past Master* Series. The most accessible and helpful general introduction to the *Aeneid* is W. A. Camps, *An Introduction to Virgil's 'Aeneid'* (Oxford, 1969); there are also general introductions by R. D. Williams (Allen and Unwin, 1987) and K. W. Gransden (Cambridge, 1990), and a brilliant literary interpretation by W. R. Johnson, *Darkness Visible: A Study of Vergil's Aeneid* (University of California, 1976).

For the historical background, one must still begin with Ronald Syme's *The Roman Revolution* (Oxford, 1939), dated in many respects and unsympathetic to the position of literature in the period, but an enduring masterpiece; a very clear and up-to-date account of the Augustan period is available in A. Wallace-Hadrill, *Augustan Rome* (Bristol Classical Press, 1993). Hermann Broch's novel, *The Death of Virgil*, takes as its starting point the famous story of Virgil's dying wish that the *Aeneid* be burnt; the novel is not only an unforgettable evocation of Virgil's last days but also a superb piece of literary criticism and literary history.

The story of what the *Aeneid* has meant to Europeans since its publication is a very large one, practically co-extensive with the history of post-Augustan European literature. A good place to start is Dante's *Divine Comedy*. Scholarly studies include C. A. Martindale (ed.), *Virgil and his Influence* (Bristol, 1984), and T. Ziolkowski, *Virgil and the Moderns* (Princeton, 1993).

The professional scholarly literature on the *Aeneid* is very large and often extremely technical and detailed; only a small selection is offered here. Fortunately there is now an English translation of Richard Heinze's classic of Virgilian scholarship, *Virgil's Epic Technique* (Bristol Classical Press, 1993; originally published in German in 1903); another important German book is also available in English, Viktor Pöschl's *The Art of Vergil: Image and Symbol in the Aeneid* (University of Michigan, 1962); and some major essays of Gian Biagio Conte have been translated from Italian in *The Rhetoric of Imitation* (Cornell University, 1986).

Some influential studies in English include: B. Otis, *Virgil: A Study in Civilized Poetry* (Oxford, 1964); M. C. J. Putnam, *The Poetry of the Aeneid* (Harvard, 1965); G. W. Williams, *Techniques and Ideas in the Aeneid* (Yale, 1983); P. R. Hardie, *Virgil's Aeneid: Cosmos and Imperium* (Oxford, 1986); R. O. A. M. Lyne, *Further Voices in Vergil's Aeneid* (Oxford, 1987); F. Cairns, *Virgil's Augustan Epic* (Cambridge, 1990).

Articles are less accessible, but there are collections of articles in volumes edited by Steele Commager, *Virgil: A Collection of Critical Views* (Prentice-hall, 1966), and by S. J. Harrison, *Oxford Readings in Virgil's Aeneid* (Oxford, 1990).